FROM

Rube to Robinson

SABR'S BEST ARTICLES ON BLACK BASEBALL

EDITED BY John Graf

ASSOCIATE EDITORS: Duke Goldman & Larry Lester

Society for American Baseball Research, Inc.
Phoenix, AZ

From Rube to Robinson

ISBN 978-1-970159-40-0 ebook

ISBN 978-1-970159-41-7 paperback

LCCN 2020913532 (Library of Congress Call Number)

Cover design/Interior design: Rachael Sullivan

Photo Credits:

Cover Image: James E. Brunson, III.

Harry Buckner, Dick Redding: Todd Peterson

Sol White: National Baseball Hall of Fame and Library, Cooperstown, NY

Walter Ball: St. Paul Pioneer Press

Minneapolis Central High School baseball team: Courtesy Minneaoplis Public Library

World's All Nations Team, EACO Flour Team: Steven R. Hoffbeck and Peter Gorton

Oscar Charleston (both): National Baseball Hall of Fame and Library, Cooperstown, NY

Greenlee Field: NoirTech Research, Inc.

Terrell images of Jackie Robinson: National Baseball Hall of Fame and Library, Cooperstown, NY

Rufus Jackson/Seward Posey: NoirTech Research, Inc.

Birmingham Black Barons: Memphis Public Library

Negro League baseball magnates: National Baseball Hall of Fame and Library, Cooperstown, NY

(Photo courtesy of James E. Brunson, III.

CONTENTS

Integration and Black Baseball Socio-Economics

Closer

INTRODUCTION

John Graf

It almost goes without saying, that were it not for the Negro Leagues, modern professional baseball would be in a much different place.

A modest case in point: Years after his retirement, former major leaguer Jerry Kenney was asked by a sportswriter in his boyhood proving ground of Beloit, Wisconsin, "What if your pro baseball career had happened, say 15 or 20 years later, after free agency and endorsement deals turned the sport into a mega-dollar business?" Kenney, who patrolled the infield and outfield for the New York Yankees and Cleveland Indians from 1967 until 1973, replied: "I think more about what it would have been like if it had been 15 or 20 years earlier, before Jackie Robinson came along. I wouldn't have had a career."[1]

Certainly, had it not been for Robinson's breaking White baseball's color line in 1946 in the International League with Montreal and the following season with the National League Brooklyn Dodgers, Kenney's career, and those of countless others, would have been very different indeed. And just as certainly, had it not been for his predecessors in the Negro Leagues, Robinson's own career trajectory would not have been the same. And had it not been for Andrew "Rube" Foster, the founder of the Negro National League, those predecessors would have found their circumstances quite different as well.

In his book *The Heritage*, journalist Howard Bryant illustrates a capsule history of Black baseball through a conversation he had with famed manager Dusty Baker, a one-time protégé of Henry Aaron's during the mid-1960s: "...I told him I could take him through the history of Black baseball, from 2017 back to 1920, the first days of the Negro Leagues, in just four handshakes, starting with his:

> Dusty shook hands with Henry Aaron.
> Henry shook hands with Jackie Robinson.
> Jackie shook hands with Satchel Paige.
> Satchel shook hands with Rube Foster.[2]

With apologies to Mr. Bryant, two more handshakes will take us all the way back to the beginning of Black professional baseball:

> Rube Foster shook hands with Sol White.
> Sol White shook hands with Bud Fowler.

With those handshakes in mind, this volume, *From Rube to Robinson*, aims to bring together the best Negro League baseball scholarship that the Society for American Baseball Research (SABR) has ever produced, culled from its journals, Biography Project, and award-winning essays. The book begins with a nineteenth-century "Old Testament" prelude before delving into the launch of "the Ship" that was the Negro National League (NNL).

Todd Peterson's "May the Best Man Win: The Black Ball Championships 1866–1923" inventories claims to baseball supremacy that preceded the Colored World Series competition that began in 1924. It touches on the teams, the player personnel, and other personalities in a skillful balance. A Sol White reference at the end of the article to the adage "may the best man [and now, reflecting changing times, woman] win" informs Peterson's title. White's appeal to fair play and equality was an early suggestion that, as Peterson has championed, the Negro Leagues were and are deserving of being called major leagues.[3]

The late Jerry Malloy, whose name graces SABR's annual Negro League Conference, covers an early attempt at forming a Black baseball circuit in "The Pittsburgh Keystones and the 1887 Colored League." Malloy points out that the short-lived league managed to garner the acceptance of the National Agreement of 1883 between the National League and the American Association, something no other Black organization was able to do.[4]

Jay Hurd profiles the great Sol White, a Hall of Fame player, manager, and executive who also made his mark writing about Black baseball and its challenges in a variety of venues. He penned the epochal *Sol White's History of Colored Base Ball* in 1907.[5]

Originally in SABR's 1994 volume *The Negro Leagues Book*, Larry Lester's updated "Rube Foster" describes the multi-faceted career of the legendary pitcher, manager, team owner, and guiding force behind the 1920 formation of the Negro National League. Foster's teams outran and outwitted the opposition while the league provided an organizational infrastructure that strengthened Black baseball as a sporting and community institution.[6]

In "John Donaldson and Black Baseball in Minnesota," Steven R. Hoffbeck and Peter Gorton tell the story of the legendary southpaw who amassed over 5,000 strikeouts and 400 wins during his long career and was part of the NNL's 1920 inaugural season with the Kansas City Monarchs.[7]

Certainly deserving of headliner status is Oscar Charleston, considered by many to be the greatest Negro Leagues player ever, and deemed by author Bill James to be the fourth-best player of all time behind only Babe Ruth, Honus Wagner, and Willie Mays.[8] Jeremy Beer, whose *Oscar Charleston: The Life and Legend of Baseball's Greatest Forgotten Player* was chosen as SABR's 2020 Seymour Medal winner (which honors the best book of baseball history or biography published in the previous calendar year), examines and rebuts the common contention that Charleston was a villainous one-man wrecking crew in need of anger management in "Hothead: How the Oscar Charleston Myth Began."[9]

Two seminal Negro Leagues researchers, Dick Clark—who sadly passed away in 2014—and John Holway, provide a detailed snapshot of the 1921 NNL season that helps locate the campaign in larger context. A sidebar from the original 1985 article detailing SABR's Negro Leagues Committee's efforts to compile a statistical history has been added as a bonus.[10]

Harking back to Phil Lowry's classic SABR publication *Green Cathedrals*, which compiled data on big league ballparks including Negro Leagues venues, are two articles that originally appeared in *Black Ball: A Negro Leagues Journal*.[11] Both pieces were McFarland-SABR Baseball Research Award winners.

James Overmyer's "Black Baseball at Yankee Stadium" describes the tenant/landlord relationship of Negro Leagues teams with the New York Yankees during the 1930s and 40s. Overmyer subtitled his piece "The House that Ruth Built and Satchel Furnished (with Fans)," and utilized the financial records of the Yankees to make his case regarding the money-making prowess of Black baseball in the US's most-populated city.[12]

Geri Driscoll Strecker's "The Rise and Fall of Greenlee Field" is a cradle-to-grave biography of the Pittsburgh Crawfords' stadium, covering—among other things—its location, ownership structure, architect, zoning process, brick façade and other park characteristics. The on-the-field performance of the Craws is touched upon and (spoiler alert) the story comes full circle as she describes the bulldozing of the site to make way for a public housing project.[13]

The final section of the book covers integration and the socio-economics of Black baseball. Leading off is Larry Lester's masterful "Can You Read, Judge Landis?" which takes its name from a headline urging baseball's high commissioner to assert his powers to end baseball's color line. Lester refutes the contention that Judge Kenesaw Mountain Landis was blameless for the persistence of baseball's segregation by focusing on the tireless efforts of the African American press and social activists who challenged baseball to make good on its promise of equal opportunity.[14]

Baseball's official historian John Thorn and the late Jules Tygiel weigh in with "Jackie Robinson's Signing: The Real, Untold Story," which considers integration from a unique perspective. The color line that had been drawn in the 1880s was broken in the 1940s, but rather differently than previously thought.[15]

Japheth Knopp's "Negro League Baseball, Black Community, and the Socio-Economic Impact of Integration" explores Kansas City as a case study in the effects of integration, asking: "...whether the manner in which desegregation occurred did in fact provide for increased economic and political freedoms for African Americans, and what social, fiscal, and communal assets may have been lost in the exchange."[16]

Brian Carroll's "Early Twentieth-Century Heroes: Coverage of Negro League Baseball in the *Pittsburgh Courier* and the *Chicago Defender*" studies the partnership of the African American press, local business communities, and baseball men such as Rube Foster to form the Negro National League and the later Eastern Colored League. Carroll cites newspaper coverage that considers ball club owners as community heroes until the 1930s, when the profiles of individual players were raised to star status from an inferior position. As Carroll describes, while some players were at times vilified as greedy by owners and reporters alike, other players such as Satchel Paige emerged who radiated excellence on the field and personality both on and off the diamond.[17]

Duke Goldman's in-depth and meticulously referenced "The Business Meetings of Negro League Baseball (NLB)," segues from baseball diamonds and uniforms to executive digs and business attire. The article concerns NLB's winter and in-season meetings from the formation of a second Negro National League in 1933 through the last gasp of the Negro American League in 1962. Accounts of club and player transactions, bickering administrative factions, interleague squabbles, strained relationships between Black and White owners and promoters, and controversies over the "clowning" antics of some teams can be found here.[18]

Fittingly, the collection closes with longtime Black ball player and manager (and former SABR member) Gentleman Dave Malarcher's poignant ode to Oscar Charleston, which first appeared in the 1978 *Baseball Research Journal*.[19]

The articles in *From Rube to Robinson* collectively assert that Black baseball's history belongs directly alongside that of White or segregated baseball. Furthermore, the development of Black baseball as an institution was a part of the larger struggle for racial justice. The challenges of life on and off the field of a professional baseball player were experienced by Black players in ways unique to a population denied the promise of full emancipation. When White baseball shut down the promise of equal opportunity with the "gentlemen's agreements" of the 1880s, it guaranteed that the lot of the Black ballplayer would be bound up with the attempt of the larger Black population trying to overcome the legacy of slavery.

Can there be any doubt this establishes the 100-year anniversary of the formation of the Negro National League in 1920, the first Black baseball organization to survive a full season, as a monumental development in both the history of baseball and the history of the United States as a whole? In commemoration of that anniversary, we present a collection of some of SABR's "greatest hits."

Notes

1 Jim Franz. "From Beloit to the Bronx," *Beloit Daily News*, Stateline Legends series, 1995. 8-11.

2 Howard Bryant, *The Heritage: Black Athletes, A Divided America, and the Politics of Patriotism* (Boston: Beacon Press. 2018), 239-240.

3 Todd Peterson, "May the Best Man Win: The Black Ball Championships, 1866–1923" in the *Baseball Research Journal*, Spring 2013, 7-24; Peterson, *The Negro Leagues Were Major Leagues*, (Jefferson, North Carolina: McFarland, 2019).

4 Jerry Malloy, "The Pittsburgh Keystones and the 1887 Colored League" June 1995, *Baseball in Pittsburgh*, edited by Paul Adomites and Dennis DeValeria.

5 Jay Hurd, "Sol White," SABR's BioProject, 2011, https://sabr.org/bioproj/person/2f9d1227

6 Larry Lester, "Andrew (Rube) Foster," in *The Negro Leagues Book*, Dick Clark and Larry Lester, eds. (Cleveland: SABR, 1994), 40-41.

7 Steven R. Hoffbeck and Peter Gorton, "John Donaldson and Black Baseball in Minnesota," *The National Pastime*, 2012, 117-122.

8 Bill James. *The New Bill James Historical Baseball Abstract* (New York: The Free Press, 2001).

9 Jeremy Beer, "Hothead: How the Oscar Charleston Myth Began," *Baseball Research Journal*, Spring 2017, 5-15; Beer, *Oscar Charleston: The Life and Legend of Baseball's Greatest Forgotten Player* (Lincoln, Nebraska and London: University of Nebraska Press, 2019).

10 Dick Clark and John B. Holway (1985),"Charleston No. 1 Star of 1921 Negro League," *Baseball Research Journal*, 1985, 63-70.

11 Philip J. Lowry, *Green Cathedrals: The Ultimate Celebration of All Major League Ballparks* (Fifth Edition: Phoenix: SABR, 2020).

12 James Overmyer, "Black Baseball at Yankee Stadium," *Black Ball: A Negro Leagues Journal*, Vol. 7, 2014, 5-31.

13 Geri Driscoll Strecker, "The Rise and Fall of Greenlee Field: Biography of a Ballpark," *Black Ball: A Negro Leagues Journal*, Vol. 2, No.2, Fall 2009, 37-67.

14 Larry Lester, "Can You Read, Judge Landis?" *Black Ball: A Negro Leagues Journal*, Vol. 1, No. 2, Fall 2008, 57-82.

15 John Thorn and Jules Tygiel, "Jackie Robinson's Signing: The Real, Untold Story" in *The National Pastime #10*, 1989, 1990, 7-12.

16 Japheth Knopp, "Negro League Baseball, Black Community, and The Socio-Economic Impact of Integration," *Baseball Research Journal*, Spring 2016, 66-74.

17 Brian Carroll, "Early Twentieth-Century Heroes: Coverage of Negro League Baseball in the *Pittsburgh Courier* and the *Chicago Defender*" *Journalism History*, Vol. 32, No. 1, Spring 2006, 34-42.

18 Duke Goldman "The Business Meetings of Negro League Baseball," in *The Winter Meetings: Baseball's Business, Vol. 2, 1958-2016*, Steve Weingarden and Bill Nowlin, eds., Marshall Adesman and Len Levin, associate eds., (Phoenix: SABR, 2017), 390-458.

19 Dave Malarcher, "Oscar Charleston," *Baseball Research Journal*, 1978, https://sabr.org/research/oscar-charleston

A NOTE ON THE USE OF LANGUAGE AND PERIOD TERMINOLOGY

Larry Lester

The words "Colored" or "Negro" or "organized" are employed throughout *From Rube to Robinson* as terms prevalent in common usage when the events described in this manuscript took place. Far from intending to make a political statement, some of our writers were hoping to recreate the spirit, attitude, and sentiment by using language that is no longer deemed appropriate.

In the mid-1920s, the eminent W.E.B. DuBois launched a letter-writing campaign to media outlets suggesting that the word "negro" be capitalized, as he found "the use of a small letter for the name of 12 million Americans and 200 million human beings a personal insult." *The New York Times* adopted DuBois' recommendation, as stated on their March 7, 1930, editorial page: "In our Style Book, Negro is now added to the list of words to be capitalized. It is not merely a typographical change; it is an act in recognition of racial respect for those who have been generations in the 'lower case.'"

As we evolve socially and in scripture, I capitalize the words "Black" and "White" because I use them synonymously with other terms that are *always* capitalized, African American and European American. For years, publications like *Ebony* and *Essence* have always proudly capitalized the B, with many books and publications following suit this year.

In September 2019, President John Allen of the Brookings Institution announced in its style guide the organization would capitalize Black when used to reference census-defined Black or African American people, along with further revisions to a handful of other important racial and ethnic terms.

While there is no standard rule on whether references to race should capitalized, many writers rely on the *Associated Press Stylebook* that calls for capitalization of Black and White. Let's note, starting with the 2000 Census, all racial and ethnic categories are capitalized—including White. It is now also officially SABR style to capitalize Black and White when referring to people in all SABR publications.

Let's also note the term "organized" is problematic as it has become a dog whistle to imply that Negro League baseball was unorganized. This coded language taps into and reinforces stereotypes. The implication that the Black leagues were unorganized is unfounded. Black teams played under the same *Official Baseball Rules*, in the same stadiums, and ordered their uniforms, equipment, bats and baseballs from the same suppliers as the major league teams. The players had contracts, statistics were kept, and a schedule was printed in the newspapers. The infrastructures of the Black leagues and the White leagues were identical.

The adjective "organized" is a term based on the assumption that baseball historians possess subjectivity of what qualities define "organized." Consequently, it is considered a judgmental term whose meaning is dependent on the user's perspective, and thus best avoided. As we celebrate the Centennial of the Negro National League's founding, let us be mindful of the words of National Baseball Hall of Fame first baseman, Walter "Buck" Leonard, "We were not unorganized, we were just unrecognized!"

The *From Rube to Robinson* anthology represents articles written during different periods of our literary evolution. With all due respect to the Eastern Colored League, the National Association for the Advancement of Colored People, and the United Negro College Fund, our editors have taken some liberties in bringing this finished product in alignment with contemporary usage.

Early Black Ball–
The Old Testament

MAY THE BEST MAN WIN: THE BLACK BALL CHAMPIONSHIPS 1866–1923

Todd Peterson

This article was published in the Baseball Research Journal, *Spring 2013.*

During a playoff game in October 1905, Leland Giants pitcher Walter Ball rushed onto the diamond at Chicago's West Side Park and threw a punch "with all the force of his arm," at Fred "Pop" Roberts's face. The Chicago Union Giants second baseman wound up with a large lump over his eye and had to leave the contest, while Ball—who was not even playing that Sunday—broke his own hand. Only the interference of umpire George McGurn prevented the other players from "making a general battle royal." The Union Giants went on to win, 5–2, but the antagonism between the two squads precluded them from finishing the series.[1]

The brawl between once-and-future teammates Ball and Roberts illustrates the intensity Black teams brought to playoff encounters. In 1899 the *Chicago Tribune* speculated that a proposed championship series between the Chicago Unions and Chicago Columbia Giants would be so "fiercely fought" that it would not be surprising "if razors did not take the place of bats before the game was finished." During the penultimate contest of the 1913 New York Lincoln Giants and Chicago American Giants "world series," shortstop John Henry "Pop" Lloyd was spiked so badly by a sliding Jess Barbour that an artery in his leg was severed and the future Hall-of-Famer was rushed to Chicago's Provident Hospital.

African Americans were prohibited from participation in the major leagues (and their precursor the National Association) from 1871 to 1946 (not counting limited opportunities in 1879 and 1884), longer than they have been allowed to participate. For most of that time, top-flight segregated Black baseball teams operated independently without the sanction of an official league. Despite the lack of a league structure, these clubs battled annually for regional and national supremacy.

Far from being a haphazard operation, the anointing of an African American champion was a serious undertaking which, although a more elastic process than its major league counterpart, nevertheless rarely failed to identify the best team. Longtime blackball player and historian Sol White noted in 1906 that such championship contests "occur yearly in colored base ball, East and West, and go far to keep up the interest among colored patrons of the National game."[2]

These playoff games generally drew large crowds and generated a lot of money—legitimate and otherwise. Way back in 1877 a *New Orleans Times* reporter taking in a local Black playoff noted, "besides championship honors the clubs always contend for the possession of a money stake," and that "promiscuous betting runs riot among their adherents when a game is on." The result was a "desperately exciting game of baseball," as the host of enthusiastic fans howled "themselves hoarse" and a "perfect pandemonium marked the progress of the game whenever one nine passed its rival's score."[3]

1866-1871: THE EARLY YEARS

Shortly after the Civil War, several quality African American baseball teams emerged in urban areas with large Black populations such as Washington D.C., Philadelphia, and New York. Much like their White counterparts, the Black squads grew out of the social clubs of the day, and soon began vying with each other for preeminence. In October 1866 the Bachelor Base Ball Club of Albany, New York journeyed to Philadelphia and handily beat the hometown Pythian and Excelsior nines in match games before large crowds.[4]

The following year saw an explosion in intercity activity as the Bachelors and multiple outfits from Washington, Philadelphia, and Brooklyn competed for top honors. In

(Photo courtesy of the author)

Harry Buckner's RBI triple clinched the 1901 title for the Columbia Giants

October the Brooklyn Unique and Philadelphia Excelsior drew a huge crowd to the Satellite grounds in Williamsburg, New York, to witness their tilt for "the colored championship of the United States." The contest was a "remarkably lively" one, with both captains threatening to pull their clubs off the field several times after umpiring decisions went against them. The Excelsiors were clinging to a 42–37 lead in the seventh inning when it became too dark to see the ball and the game was called in their favor. As the *New York Herald* reported, "The Philadelphians and their friends re-formed in procession and, with the drums and fifes, marched back to the ferry and crossed to this city, highly delighted with their victory."[5]

When the dust settled a few weeks later, the Philadelphia Pythian and Brooklyn Monitor had established the most valid title claims, although the two squads did not meet on the diamond. However, after demolishing the Washington Alert and Mutual clubs in the nation's capital that summer, the Pythian were presented "a rich and massive silver ball and a beautiful rosewood bat," by that city's Ladies Croquet Club. The Pythian ultimately settled the question in October 1868 by downing the Monitor, 27–9, at Columbia Park in Philadelphia.[6]

Although the Pythian remained the team to beat, the epicenter of Eastern blackball briefly shifted to upstate New York, where a number of clubs had picked up the Albany Bachelors mantle. In September 1869 the best of them, the Fearless of Utica, swept a home-and-home set from the remarkably-nicknamed Heavy Hitters of Canajoharie, before challenging, "any colored club that chooses to dispute their claim to the championship."[7] A year later the Mutual of Washington, led by Charles Douglass, son of the great orator Frederick Douglass, undertook a tour of western New York and demolished seven local outfits by an aggregate score of 345–78. The District nine landed in Utica in late August to take on the Fearless for the "championship of the United States." The two squads played five innings in a "mean" drizzle until the game was called with the Mutual holding an 18–10 advantage. The Washingtonians declared that the contest was halted by agreement of both parties, but the Utica lads "denied having made such arrangement" and claimed a 9–0 forfeit, boasting they were willing to play "until the bases pulled anchor and floated off."[8] Way out west (the Ohio River served as the demarcation point between Eastern and western Black clubs), the Chicago Blue Stockings, "dusky athletes who are employed as waiters in the various hotels and restaurants," captured the "colored

championship of Illinois," during the summer of 1870 by taking two out of three games from the uniquely-named Rockford Pink Stockings. The new champs' reign was short-lived, as another Windy City squad, the Uniques, poached their slugging catcher "Big" George Brown off their roster the following spring and crushed the Blue Stockings, 39–5.[9] In September of 1871, the Uniques undertook the first continental blackball tour, traveling east to play squads in Pittsburgh, Baltimore, Washington D.C., and Troy, New York. The trip climaxed in Philadelphia where the "champion of the west" Uniques split a pair of contests with the "champion of the east" Pythian, before huge crowds on the grounds of the National Association's Athletics. The series garnered nationwide newspaper coverage as "the fielding of the Unique was very good, as was the batting of the Pythian," in two well-played games. There would be no rematch. The Unique returned home just in time for the Great Chicago Fire on October 8 which brought a halt to all local baseball activity for a while. The Pythians dissolved after the brutal assassination of their shortstop and captain Octavius Catto during an October 10 election riot.[10]

1875-1885: THE BEGINNINGS OF COMMERCIALISM

The genteel amateurism of the early post-Civil War era gradually gave way to a new breed of elite Black players and teams that played predominantly for money. With the growing commercialism, however, came increased competition and controversy. The first three games of the 1875 western showdown between the revitalized Chicago Uniques and the upstart St. Louis Blue Stockings were marred by biased umpiring, walkouts, stalling, and an unfortunate attempt by Chicago backstop Ben Dyson to throw the series for $25.[11]

Needing a win to stay alive in the series, the Uniques were leading, 17–14, in the bottom of the ninth inning of the fourth contest at Chicago's White Stockings Park when umpire William Thacker called the game because of "darkness, crowd, and disputes among players." Although the St. Louis club had two men on base with none out at the time, the arbiter declared the contest in favor of the Uniques, and "all bets on the grounds were paid." A few hours later, after learning some of his friends lost money owing to his decision, Thacker reversed himself and awarded a 9–0 forfeit to the Blue Stockings. This came as small consolation to the Blues' William Pitts and William Mitchell, who were severely injured when the St. Louis squad's omnibus was stoned by the angry mob that invaded the field.[12]

The Blue Stockings got a small measure of revenge the following June when they swept the Uniques in St. Louis. After the second contest, the squads retired to Rueben Armstrong's bar, where "the feeling was of partisan character," and "a row finally occurred." During the ensuing melee, Benjamin Beatty of the Chicago squad fired a pistol at the saloon keeper, resulting in his arrest and no more Uniques/Blue Stockings games.[13]

By the early 1880s, American hotels were regularly employing Black baseball clubs to entertain their guests. In September 1882, one such outfit representing the West End Hotel of Long Branch, New Jersey, dropped a 10–8 decision to the Philadelphia Orions before 500 spectators at New York's Polo Grounds for the "colored championship." The West Ends rebounded a year later by crushing the Crescents of Princeton, New Jersey, 20–2, in a "grand colored championship match" at the Polo Grounds.[14]

In September 1885, Philadelphia's Keystone Athletic squad, representing the Argyle Hotel of Babylon, New York, took the Orions "into camp by a score of 6-to-4," before signing three of their number, including pitcher Shep Trusty. With the subsequent backing of Trenton capitalist Walter Cook, the "Babylon boys" became the Cuban Giants, stocking their roster with the best Black players in the country, chief among them Clarence Williams, Bill Whyte, and twirler George Stovey. The Giants completed the 1886 season "with a grand record made against National League and leading college teams," while establishing their blackball dominance that August by crushing the fledgling New York Gorhams, 25–4, and the more established Brooklyn Alpine, 24–0.[15]

1886-1887: THE FIRST LEAGUES

The success of the Cuban Giants and the plethora of top-flight African American teams throughout the country led to the formation of the first intercity Black leagues. In March 1886 the Southern League of Colored Base Ballists was formed by Jacksonville, Florida, politician and newspaperman John Menard. Consisting of teams from Alabama, Florida, Georgia, Louisiana, South Carolina, and Tennessee, the rather loose federation operated from June until August. The *Memphis Appeal-Avalanche* anointed their hometown Eclipse, led by pitcher William Renfroe, champions, although they dropped season series to both the New Orleans Unions and the Louisville Falls City.[16]

Less successful was the National Colored Base Ball League, which collapsed after a couple of weeks in May 1887. The Cuban Giants opted not to join the six-team circuit, but won 12 out of 14 games against the Philadelphia Pythians, New York Gorhams, Boston Resolutes, Louisville Falls City, and Pittsburgh Keystones, while outscoring the league squads, 159–48.[17]

1888-1892: RIVALRIES ESTABLISHED

In August 1888, a tournament "for the colored championship of the world," was held between the top four Black clubs in the east. Playing before huge crowds in New York City and Hoboken, New Jersey, the Cuban Giants easily won all five-games they played, capturing the silver ball donated by their owner John M. Bright. Sol White's Pittsburgh Keystones were the surprise of the event, also winning five-games, with their two defeats coming at the hands of the Giants. The New York Gorhams finished a disappointing third, while one reporter opined that the winless Norfolk Red Stockings "should never leave Virginia to play ball."[18]

Not present at the tourney, but very anxious for a crack at the Giants, were the New Orleans Pinchbacks, the Southwest's premier Black club. Originally known as the W.L. Cohens, the Louisiana nine dropped an 1886 championship playoff to the New Orleans Unions before changing their name in honor of politician P.B.S. Pinchback, the first Black governor of a US state. The club also swiped three of the Unions' best players, including pitching phenom George Hopkins, who had struck out ten or more batters in each game that season. In August the Pinchbacks traveled to Illinois, along with "five car-loads of gentlemen" supporters to meet a strong semipro club called the Chicago Unions.[19]

Over 1,500 fans gleefully watched the Unions edge the Pinchbacks, 4–1, in the opener at South Side Park. Joe Campbell struck out 14 batters for the victors, while Hopkins fanned 17 in defeat. The next afternoon, 1,800 cranks turned out to witness an even better game, which the Southerners won, 6–5, on the strength of 20 strikeouts by Hopkins and a two-run ninth-inning home run by their second baseman A. Defauchard. The Pinchbacks took the rubber match, 14–7, a couple of days later as Hopkins whiffed 14 more, giving him 51 punchouts in three games.[20]

The Pinchbacks, who conversed in "English and French and always swear at the umpire in French," continued on to St. Louis where they swept a three-game set from the West End club. A strengthened West End squad journeyed to the Crescent City in late October and stunned the Pinchbacks, 4–3, at the New Orleans Ball Park despite 13 more strikeouts by George Hopkins. A persistent rain delayed the second contest between the two clubs for a week, and after it ended in a 3–3 tie the Missouri outfit decided to stick around a few more days to play it off. The West Ends jumped out to a 7–0 lead after 2 1/2 innings, but the Pinchbacks rallied and tied it with two runs in the bottom of the ninth, before W.J. Turner triumphantly crossed the plate with the winning run in the tenth inning as "the crowd went wild."[21]

George Hopkins moved north in 1890 to join the Chicago Unions, and Walter Cohen's Pinchbacks never got their chance to play the Cuban Giants. According to Sol White, the Cubes' only remaining "full-fledged" rival was the New York Gorhams, although they had a difficult time proving it on the diamond. From August 1886 through 1890, Ambrose Davis's Manhattan-based club played the Giants over 25 times, but managed only four wins and two ties.[22]

The only force able to stop the Cuban Giants was their owner John Bright, whose extreme frugality motivated 11 of his players, including superstar pitcher George Stovey, to jump in 1890 to J. Monroe Kreiter's York, Pennsylvania, franchise in the Eastern Interstate League, where they were renamed the Colored Monarchs. The prodigal players briefly returned to the Giants' fold in 1891, but in mid-May many of them defected again, this time to Davis's Gorhams who were operating out of Harrisburg, Pennsylvania, for the season. The Big Gorhams, as they were popularly known, claimed a 100–4 record, and crushed the Giants five straight times by an aggregate score of 77–22 to finally lay claim to the "colored championship."[23]

The Gorhams reorganized in the spring of 1892 under the management of one William Primrose, but John M. Bright blocked the team from playing games on Long Island and most of their key players, including future Hall-of-Fame infielder Frank Grant, rejoined the Giants. In late September the "Cubes" met the Gorhams, representing the Champlain Hotel of Bluff Point, New York, one final time, demolishing them, 18–1, before a huge crowd of 2,500 on the Long Island grounds.[24]

By the summer of 1893, boom had given way to bust, for the nation's economy as well as on the diamond, and Bright's Cuban Giants were the only professional Black team left operating east of the Mississippi. In October 1894 the Giants ventured to Chicago to take on the Unions, now the premier team of the west. The Giants found the "amateur" Unions "somewhat easy" and swept a two-game set, including a 14–7 shellacking in the opener at South Side Park.[25]

1894-1898: CHALLENGERS TO THE CUBAN GIANTS

As the century ran out, two new professional African American clubs rose to challenge the Cuban Giants and Unions. In the fall of 1894 blackball pioneer Bud Fowler and young slugger Grant Johnson organized the Page Fence Giants in Adrian, Michigan. Financed by a woven wire company and a bicycle manufacturer, Fowler's novices barnstormed throughout the Midwest in 1895 racking up a record of 118–36–2, while serving notice to the Unions by clubbing them three times by a combined score of 66–21.[26]

John Bright's penurious ways led most of his 1895 Cuban Giants to abandon the team en masse the following March and form a new club under the co-op plan (wherein a team's expenses were deducted from the gate receipts, and the balance split evenly among the players), christened the Cuban X-Giants. Bookkeeper Edward B. Lamar was recruited to keep track of the financial side of the operation as well as to spar with Bright in the press. Lamar challenged the Cuban Giants to a winner-take-all-the-receipts series on several occasions throughout the season, but Bright ignored the defi's, other than to note that the X-Giants were, "getting most terribly defeated everywhere... thereby injuring the Genuine Cuban Giants' great reputation."[27]

Undaunted, the Cuban X-Giants traveled to Michigan in September to battle the Page Fence Giants for a $1,000 stake and the "colored championship of the United States." Playing before appreciative crowds in Ohio, Michigan, and Indiana, the young Page Fence squad outscored "the famous sluggers of the East," 172–137, en route to an 11–8 series win. For their efforts the Michigan lads received "beautiful medals from their manager" and, perhaps more importantly, "extra compensation." E.B. Lamar claimed that six of the X-Giants had played hurt, but took some solace in the $1,000 purse his club earned after convincingly sweeping a two-game set with the Chicago Unions before heading back to the Big Apple.[28]

(Photo courtesy of the author)

Dick Redding was one of the former Lincoln Giants who joined the Lincoln Stars in 1914.

In 1897 the Cuban Giants and Lamar's X-Giants finally met in an Eastern championship series played in New Jersey and Connecticut over the course of an October week. Prior to the playoff, it was unkindly suggested that "both teams will be searched before they enter the grounds to guard against a flourish of razors during the exciting moments of the battle." The Sunday opener at Weehawken, New Jersey was a hard-fought, back-and-forth affair that the X-Giants managed to tie with two runs in the final frame, before the game was called because of darkness. Lamar's squad went on to win the title by walloping Bright's bunch, 28–5, in the next two games before dropping the meaningless Sabbath tilt at Weehawken before a crowd of over 3,000 people.[29]

After another year of squabbling over players and guarantees, the two squads met again on three successive Sundays in October 1898. The X-Giants copped a wild and wooly first contest in Hoboken, New Jersey, with James Robinson leading the way with three hits including a double and a home run. "The Black Rusie" also came on in relief and pitched three scoreless innings to close out the 9–7 win. When the teams returned to Hoboken a week later, "the arguments between the players were more lively," and "hostilities threatened to break out" on several occasions. The hard luck "Genuine" Cuban Giants out-hit and out-fielded their rivals but fell, 7–6, after their two-run ninth-inning rally was snuffed out by a great stop and throw by the X-Giants second baseman Ross Garrison. Lamar's charges also won an anticlimactic third match, 17–10, at Newark. That was enough for John Bright. The two clubs never played for the championship again.[30]

1899-1902: EAST MEETS WEST

The East-West barnstorming playoffs lasted for a few more years, however. A couple of weeks before the X-Giants final tussle with Bright's Cuban Giants, Lamar's squad schooled the Chicago Unions by winning six out of nine games played in Illinois, Wisconsin, and Indiana. The X-Giants returned to the Midwest in June 1899 and their "superior hitting" helped them down the Unions 11 games to seven before several "enormous" crowds.[31]

The Unions and Page Fence Giants generally avoided each other, getting together for only a game or two each year. In 1899 the Michigan team relocated to the Windy City and became the Chicago Columbia Giants. Acquiescing to public demand, the two squads agreed to meet in a winner-take-all-receipts, best-of-five series in September. Playing before crowds in excess of 9,000, the Columbia's big southpaw George Wilson out-dueled fellow lefty Bert Jones in the two first matches, 1–0 and 4–2. In the third game, shortstop Grant "Home Run" Johnson mashed a grand slam off Jones, the object of a bidding war between the clubs that spring, to launch the Giants to a 6–0 victory and net them "a big bunch of money."[32]

The Cuban X-Giants ventured west again in June 1900 and the Unions finally defeated their old nemesis, thrashing Lamar's club 12 games to five. The three-week series culminated with a "brilliant" 6–3 victory in Chicago, as Bert Jones scattered five hits and scored two runs to aid his own cause. According to Sol White, "the western teams won as they pleased this year." The Columbia Giants walloped John Bright's Cuban Giants in another June showdown that began and finished in Chicago. Columbia's George "Rat" Johnson clouted a walk-off home run in the bottom of the ninth inning of the denouement to give George Wilson an "exciting" 10–9 win.[33]

The Unions and Columbia Giants renewed their conflict that October, splitting a pair of games and tying another, leaving the "colored championship of the world" "undecided." In July 1901 the Unions' traveling secretary, Frank Leland, effectively stole most of the team from owner William Peters and formed a new squad called the Chicago Union Giants. Leland's outfit and the Columbia Giants faced off that fall at South Side Park to settle "the colored championship." The Columbias won a pair of games to nab the title, with Will Horn scattering six hits and Harry Buckner crushing a run-scoring triple in the 3–2 climax.[34]

Unable to find suitable grounds in Chicago, the Columbia Giants relocated to Big Rapids, Michigan, during the 1902 season, and hooked up with the Union Giants one last time to settle scores. Leland's squad took two out of the first three games at Chicago's South Side Park, behind its 23-year-old Texas wunderkind twirler Andrew Foster, who fanned 10 batters while vanquishing the Columbias, 7–3, in the opener. Foster had left the Union Giants by the time the clubs met up again in Big Rapids in late August. The Chicago nine captured one game, but the Michigan squad's own 19-year-old wonder boy pitcher, Johnny Davis, won two decisions in as many days to deadlock the season series.[35]

1903-1906:THE PHILADELPHIA GIANTS TAKE ON THE CUBAN X-GIANTS

In 1903, Davis and many other former Columbia Giants joined an emerging Iowa concern called the Algona Brownies. The Hawkeye club beat Leland's Union Giants 10 games to five for the western title. The series culminated in Des Moines in August and a bench-clearing, bat-swinging, donnybrook broke out during the penultimate contest after Union Giants catcher Andrew Campbell slammed into his opposite number, George "Rat" Johnson, at home plate. The rival backstops exchanged punches, touching off a melee that ended only after several policemen stormed the field.

Johnson had the last laugh as Algona won, 2–0, to capture the crown.[36]

Several other Chicago ballplayers, including Harry Buckner and Bill Monroe, headed east in 1903 to play for a rising powerhouse named the Philadelphia Giants. Sol White, along with sportswriters H. Walter Schlichter and Harry Smith, had organized the Pennsylvania squad the previous summer, recruiting several former Cuban X-Giants along the way. Lamar's squad initially rebuffed offers to play White's new charges, but after "two years of squabbling, challenges, and counter challenges" the clubs agreed to meet in a best-of-nine championship series in the fall of 1903.[37]

The playoff, contested over two weeks in Brooklyn, Pennsylvania, and New Jersey, was "fought with the bitterest feeling," with the X-Giants prevailing by winning five of the first seven games. Andrew Foster, who had joined Lamar's unit in June, dominated the event, winning all four of his starts, fanning 21 batters while allowing only six runs. Foster also banged out six hits, including a double and triple, while X-Giants first baseman Robert Jordan led all batters with a .560 average.[38]

Proving the eternal blackball adage, "If you can't beat them, steal them," Sol White enticed Foster (now called Rube) to join the Philadelphia Giants the next season for $90 a month, and he again proved to be the difference-maker in another fall playoff between the rival clubs. White's squad captured two out of three bitterly fought games before enormous crowds at Atlantic City's Inlet Park. The burly Texan won the first and last contests, striking out 18 batters in the initial go-around, and giving up but two hits in the finale. Foster also batted .400, tempering some of the damage caused by X-Giants second baseman John "Pat" Patterson who hit two home runs in the series and stole five bases.[39]

A dispute over Cuban pitcher José Muñoz precluded the X-Giants and Philadelphia Giants from playing each other in 1905. The following year both squads joined the International League of Independent Professional Baseball Clubs, an interracial Eastern semipro circuit. After splitting their first two contests, the teams met in a Labor Day doubleheader at Philadelphia's Columbia Park to resolve the league championship. More than 12,000 fans, the largest blackball crowd ever, looked on as starters Rube Foster and Harry Buckner were each reached for ten safeties. The Phillies got to Buckner "when bingos meant runs" however, while Foster twice retired the X-Giants with the bases full to nab the essential 3–2 victory, earning the beautiful silver cup donated by circuit president William Freihofer. Philadelphia also won the second game 4–1. This was the end of the line for Edward Lamar's nine. The following April it was announced that "the Cuban X-Giants have retired from the field."[40]

While the Philadelphia Giants reigned supreme in the east, the western blackball title still ran through the Windy City. To avoid confusion with William Peters' Chicago Unions, Frank Leland rechristened his squad the Leland Giants in February 1905. To add to the confusion, Peters appropriated the Chicago Union Giants moniker for his club. The two teams met at Auburn Park on four consecutive Sundays in October 1905 to decide matters, with Johnny Davis pitching the Lelands to an 8–2 triumph in the opener. The Union Giants held late leads in the next two contests, but the Lelands rallied to tie them both before darkness fell. George Wilson and George "Rat" Johnson returned from Renville, Minnesota, to lead the Unions over their rivals 5–2 in game four, with Walter Ball's assault of Fred Roberts putting an end to the series. Auburn Park was again the locale the following October when Leland's squad twice shut out the Union Giants by identical 5–0 scores, effectively finishing them as a top-flight unit.[41]

In the fall of 1906 Walter Schlichter and promoter Nat Strong organized the National Association of Colored Baseball Clubs of the United States and Cuba, a rather informal organization consisting of the Philadelphia Giants, Brooklyn Royal Giants, Cuban Giants, and Abel Linares's Cuban Stars. The member clubs agreed to play a minimum of five-games against each other in various Eastern locales, including Philadelphia, Harlem, and Atlantic City. The title came down to a late September confrontation at Brooklyn's Washington Park. The Philadelphia Giants, with Hall-of Famers Pete Hill and John Henry Lloyd, edged the Royal Giants, 4–2, as Dan McClellan scattered six hits to nail down the club's fourth consecutive championship.[42]

1907-1909: LELAND GIANTS REIGN

Upset with Walter Schlichter's cost-cutting measures, Rube Foster jumped to Chicago in 1907 to join the Leland Giants, bringing along seven other top Eastern players. In

June 1908 Foster put up a $2,500 purse of his own money and offered to take the Lelands to Philadelphia to play Schlichter's club for either a percentage or winner-take-all. Instead the Phillies traveled to the Windy City in late July for a showdown series. The Chicago squad won three out of the first four contests before Philly twirler Harvey Martin, instructed by Sol White to "just spit on the ball and let it go," downed the Lelands on two consecutive days to even matters, and the locals declined to play off the tie. Quakers shortstop John Henry Lloyd "was a whale at fielding and batting," during the six games, collecting 11 hits (five off of Foster) and scoring 10 runs.[43]

In July 1909 the Leland Giants journeyed 400 miles northwest to play the St. Paul Gophers, a crack unit comprising several former Chicago players as well as infielder Felix Wallace, former Birmingham Giants third baseman "Candy" Jim Taylor, and his pitching sibling, "Steel Arm" Johnny. The Gophers took three out of five thrilling games played at St. Paul's tiny Downtown Park, with John Taylor out-dueling Giants lefty Charles "Pat" Dougherty, 3–2, in the finale. Sore loser Rube Foster, who had missed the series with a leg injury, later snarled that "no man who ever saw the Gophers play would think of classing them as world's colored champions."[44]

1910-1911: EASTERN CHAMPIONSHIPS, WESTERN CHAMPIONSHIPS

Frank Leland responded to the defeat by signing five Gophers, including Wallace and the Taylor brothers, to his new squad, the Chicago Giants, during the offseason. Foster and Leland parted ways in September 1909, with Rube curiously retaining the Leland Giants designation and his old boss keeping most of the roster. Foster held on to Pat Dougherty and Pete Hill, and signed several Eastern stars for his squad, including John Henry Lloyd. The big Texan claimed to have the "best colored team in the world," but for whatever reason his wrecking crew didn't face a really top-flight contender in 1910. Frank Leland took his Chicago Giants back to the Twin Cities in July however, where they easily won four out of five-games from the Gophers to nab the "world's colored championship." "Cyclone" Joe Williams, a 24-year-old flame thrower from Texas, fanned 18 batters in winning two contests, while Felix Wallace cracked a couple of homers against his old mates.[45]

The Eastern blackball scene was also fragmenting. The Philadelphia Giants disbanded in July 1911 shortly after their 21-year-old hurler "Cannonball" Dick Redding and his battery-mate Louis Santop joined the Lincoln Giants, a new Harlem-based squad assembled by Sol White. The Lincolns, owned by promoter brothers Jess and Eddie McMahon, helped mitigate the collapse of Nat Strong's league when John Connor's Royal Giants met the non-sanctioned club in a playoff. Eastern honors, however, came down to a three-game set, each contested for a $1,000 purse, between the Lincoln Giants and the Cuban Stars. Hall-of-Famer José Mendéz started all three games for the Cubans and won twice, fanning 21 batters as the Islanders copped the series two games to one. Over 20,000 fans turned out to witness the first two contests at the American League Park in New York.[46]

The 1911 western title was decided in July, when Rube Foster's newly-minted Chicago American Giants downed Frank Leland's heavily favored Chicago Giants six games to two. Playing before record-breaking crowds at Schorling Park, the American Giants rotation of Bill Lindsay, Pat Dougherty, and Frank Wickware outpitched "Cyclone" Joe Williams, Walter Ball, and "Big" Bill Gatewood to annex the series, while their teammate Pete Hill punched out 14 hits, including three doubles and a homer. The loss cost Leland a $500 side bet with Foster and triggered his club's decline, with most of his top players seeking employment elsewhere the following season.[47]

1912-1919: THE "INDEPENDENT" CHAMPIONSHIPS

During the ensuing decade, the leading Eastern Black club would often venture west in late summer, usually to play the American Giants for the "Independent" championship of the United States. Although their title claims were rather presumptuous, the Brooklyn Royal Giants invaded Chicago in 1912 but met with little success, being swept in six games by Foster's men. The Royals returned to the Windy City in 1914 under the management of Nat Strong, who had wrested control of the squad from John Connor, but despite the presence of emerging ace William "Dizzy" Dismukes, Brooklyn lost all seven games with the American Giants.[48]

Sol White wrote in 1906 that "when teams travel to a far section of the country to meet for a championship struggle, there is always given to the visitors a most hearty welcome." Things had changed by July 1913, when Rube Foster brought his American Giants to New York. After splitting four contests with the Royal Giants, Foster trotted out Frank Wickware to pitch the opener against the Lincoln Giants at Olympic Field. Problematically, the "Red Ant" had accepted $100 to start for the Lincolns only a few days before, and the managers of the two clubs argued for over an hour as to Wickware's eligibility before the match was called off. In the four games the clubs did play, Joe Williams pitched the Lincolns to two victories; the clubs battered each other to an 11–11 tie; and the American Giants staged a furious ninth-inning rally to pull out the fourth contest 6–5. The teams were to play a fifth time, but Foster protested the Lincoln's substitution of Royal Giants Frank Earle for the ailing Jude Gans and the game was cancelled, disappointing another large gathering.[49]

Enormous crowds also turned out at Schorling Park when the teams reconvened in Chicago a week later. Foster imported "Steel Arm" Johnny Taylor to start one contest and his Hall-of-Fame brother Ben to play first base, but to no avail as the Lincolns captured six of ten games to decisively win the championship. Joe Williams was the key to the scrap, winning five times while tossing nearly 65 innings for the pitching-depleted Easterners. John Henry Lloyd batted .319 for the New York squad before being injured, and the ageless wonder Grant "Home Run" Johnson chipped in with a .316 mark. As usual, Pete Hill led the Chicago cause with a .333 average, but he did not register an extra base hit. Even notorious sore loser Foster allowed that the Lincolns' "great playing and wonderful defense was never surpassed, if equaled on any diamond," although he also blamed the Chicago fans for not rooting vociferously enough for his squad.[50]

In late August it was reported that several Lincoln Giants hadn't been paid their full salaries in weeks because of financial reverses the McMahons had incurred from their boxing promotions. After running afoul of Nat Strong, the brothers lost control of their club to New York hustler Charley Harvey. Undeterred, the pair formed a new squad called the Lincoln Stars in the spring of 1914, and eventually signed up several members of their old cast including John Lloyd, Dick Redding, and center fielder Spottswood Poles. The two Lincoln outfits would not play each other, but the McMahon team went to Chicago in the summer of 1915, splitting a classic 10-game set with the American Giants before Foster's club edged them four games to three in a 1916 rematch.[51]

The season of 1915 also found the American Giants in a bitter regional imbroglio with the Indianapolis ABCs. The Hoosier club, under the management of cagey South Carolinian Charles Isham Taylor, featured a devastating lineup that included C.I.'s brother Ben, shortstop Elwood "Bingo" DeMoss, and 18-year-old center fielder Oscar Charleston. Foster's club took three out of five June games from the talented Indianapolis squad at Schorling Park, with soft tossing "Dizzy" Dismukes garnering the two ABC wins. A month later at Indianapolis's Federal League Park, the "Taylorites" beat the Giants four straight times to eliminate Chicago from "the colored championship of America," but not before Foster pulled his team from the field in the first contest, complaining of poor playing conditions. Pete Hill was allegedly struck on the nose by a police officer. C.I. Taylor and Chicago second baseman Harry Bauchman got into a shoving match, and another local cop threatened to "blow Rube's brains out." A motivated Pete Hill slammed four home runs in the final two matches, while an incensed Rube Foster declared that C.I. Taylor was "down and dirty," an "ingrate," and a "stool pigeon," after which the ABCs manager threatened a libel suit.[52]

Foster and Taylor met in Indianapolis in July 1916 to bury the hatchet and schedule another round of games beginning in late August. Any thought that the clubs' behavior might improve was quickly dispelled in the opener in Chicago when the ABCs Bingo DeMoss took a swing at umpire Harry Goeckel after being called out on a close play at home. C.I. Taylor was tossed out of game two for arguing with the arbiter and the American Giants proceeded to take three out of the first four contests, before the finale ended in a 3–3 tie.[53]

The series resumed in Indianapolis in late October. The Giants copped the first game, 5–3, before "Dizzy" Dismukes pitched the ABCs to three victories and the Indianapolis squad won another contest by forfeit when Rube Foster pulled his club off the field after being ejected for refusing to remove a fielder's mitt while coaching at first base. The championship belonged to Taylor's nine again, although Foster groused that as twelve games had been originally agreed to, it was "impossible" for either side to claim victory.[54]

Unable to beat the ABCs, Rube swiped one of their best players, Bingo DeMoss, and signed Eastern ace "Cannonball" Dick Redding for good measure. Between June and early September 1917, the American Giants and Taylor's outfit faced off 25 times, with Foster's revitalized club taking 19 out of those contests. Dick Redding won eight out of his nine decisions against the Hoosier squad, and put the exclamation mark on the Giants' championship on August 19 by dominating the ABCs, 4–2, before 7,000 unhappy fans at Indianapolis's Washington Park.[55]

The American Giants' next regional challenge came in 1919 from the Detroit Stars, a newly-formed club featuring several Foster cast-offs including player-manager Pete Hill. The clubs began their series in June, and the Giants, propelled by the devastating Hall-of-Fame outfield tandem of Oscar Charleston and Cristóbal Torriente, captured five of the first six contests. The talented Stars, featuring blackball greats John Donaldson, José Mendéz, "Candy" Jim Taylor, and emerging slugger Edgar Wesley, rebounded to win the next five-games, outscoring the Giants, 50–27, before Chicago ace Dick Whitworth stopped the carnage and evened things up with a 9–1 victory.[56]

Due to the terrible Chicago race riots that summer, the Giants were forced to contest most of the playoff in the Motor City. The clubs settled matters during a weekend in early August. Ironman twirler Andrew "Stringbean" Williams allowed but two safeties, out-dueling the great Donaldson as Chicago took the opener, 2–1. Veteran Giants third baseman Bill Francis doubled and tripled the next day as the "Fosters" wrapped up another title with a 5–3 triumph.[57]

1912-1919: THE BROOKLYN ROYAL GIANTS AND LINCOLN GIANTS COMPETE IN THE EAST

While the American Giants dominated the west, the Brooklyn Royal Giants and Lincoln Giants battled for Eastern supremacy. From 1912 through 1919 the two squads clashed in doubleheaders about every other Sunday and almost always on Memorial Day, Independence Day, and Labor Day. At stake was the Eastern crown which was captured by the Lincolns in 1912, 1913, 1914, and 1917. The Royal Giants finally broke through and annexed the title in 1916, while in 1918 each squad won nine games against each other and ran out of season before playing off their tie.[58]

For several seasons, fireballers Joe Williams and Dick Redding gave the Lincolns a devastating 1–2 punch, before the "Cannonball" departed for other pastures. From 1911 through 1916 (save 1915 when the Royal Giants were on hiatus) Redding posted a 17–7–1 record versus the lads from Brooklyn and on two occasions he started and won both ends of a doubleheader against them. "Cyclone" Joe was victorious in 24 out of 35 decisions against the Royal Giants between 1912 and 1920, including six shutouts.[59]

The two aces "held grievances against each other for some time," however, and Redding matriculated to the Lincoln Stars and the American Giants before hooking up with the Royal Giants in the spring of 1918. Pitching against each other for the first time, Redding posted three straight decisions over Williams before being called up by the US Army. The "Cannonball" briefly returned to Brooklyn the next season, and the Cyclone edged him, 1–0, in the series opener, tossing a no-hitter while fanning 12 batters, before the "biggest gathering" in Olympic Field history.[60]

In the spring of 1919, former Brooklyn owner John W. Connor retooled a middling Atlantic City nine called the Bacharach Giants by raiding his old club for Dick Redding, John Henry Lloyd, and catcher Ernest Gatewood, leaving the Royal Giants lineup "practically shot to pieces." A similarly depleted Lincoln squad waxed the Brooklyn squad in nine of their 12 meetings that summer, led by Joe Williams, "without whom there would be no team."[61]

Neither the Lincolns nor Brooklyn would play Connor's renegades, but he discovered a suitable foil from the Philadelphia suburb of Darby. Over the course of the preceding decade, postal employee Ed Bolden had transformed the Hilldale Athletic Club boy team into a powerhouse professional outfit, featuring such up and comers as outfielder George Johnson and spit-balling ace Phil Cockrell. Hilldale won three out of the first five-games with the Atlantic City nine in early June, before their veteran center fielder Spottswood Poles jumped to the Bacharachs. When the two squads played again in late August before 15,000 frenzied fans in Atlantic City, Hilldale catcher Yank Deas "said something to Poles in whispered tones," instigating a fight between the two that escalated into a bench-clearing brawl that was finally stopped by the Atlantic City police.

The Darbyites pulled out a 1–0, 10-inning victory, but the Bacharachs, due in no small part to 11 base hits by Poles, proceeded to win the next five-games to capture the Eastern crown.[62]

1920-1923: THE NEGRO NATIONAL LEAGUE AND EASTERN CHAMPIONSHIPS

Both the Detroit Stars and Chicago American Giants ventured east in the summer of 1919 to play Hilldale and the Bacharachs, with the four clubs splitting a handful of games. The emergence of so many financially viable professional teams led to the organization of the Midwestern-based Negro National League in February 1920. Not surprisingly, Foster's American Giants, led by Cristóbal Torriente, southpaw twirler Dave Brown, and third baseman Dave Malarcher proved to be the association's dominant force, capturing the first three pennants.[63]

Rube Foster's entreaties to expand the NNL out east were rebuffed by the area moguls, although Connor's Bacharachs joined as an associate member. Various antipathies among club owners left the 1920 Eastern title chase in a muddled state. The Bacharach Giants refused to play the Royal Giants or Hilldale because of their "league agreement," although player raids and lawsuits between the squads probably also played a part. Conversely, the *New York Age* doubted the Lincoln Giants could call themselves champions "and have anyone except their owners recognize their claim unless they play every team in the field to oppose them."[64]

In June Lincoln captain Joe Williams approached John Connor about "crossing bats" and the clubs scheduled two midsummer doubleheaders at Brooklyn's Ebbets Field. Dick Redding pitched his club to three victories, including a pair of shutouts over Joe Williams as the Bacharachs claimed a share of the Eastern championship. A crowd of about 16,000 "clamorous fans" watched the initial clash, while threatening weather and a transit strike kept the crowd down to about 10,000 for the second double-dip.[65]

In August the Bacharachs headed west to take on the American Giants. The Bees captured the first match in Gary, Indiana, by a score of 11–4, but lost all three played at Schorling Park. The Atlantic City outfit's belligerent behavior was also called into question, with third baseman Oliver Marcell being censured "for making immoral movements with parts of his body that would resemble a hoochy-coochy dancer." In October the two clubs hooked up again and divided a string of games played throughout the Eastern seaboard, with Dick Redding downing the Westerners three times, twice by shutout. The series concluded with a Sunday doubleheader at Ebbets Field. A ninth-inning triple by Chicago pinch-hitter George "Tubby" Dixon off Redding gave the American Giants a 2–0 win in the opener, and they grabbed the five-frame finale, 1–0, as well.[66]

Under the leadership of John Henry Lloyd, the Brooklyn Royal Giants underwent a revival in 1920 and by season's end were also proclaiming themselves "Colored World Champions." In the first half of the season, the Royals copped three out of five-games from their old rivals, the Lincoln Giants, with two of their wins coming on ninth-inning rallies. From June through mid-October the Brooklyn squad battled Hilldale in another "championship series." Brooklyn won six games against four defeats and two ties, as John Lloyd collected 14 hits in the series, including a three-run game-winning homer, and turned "many base hits into outs by his flashing fielding." Lloyd left Brooklyn the following year to manage the Columbus Buckeyes and by the end of the decade the Royal Giants had degenerated into "a mediocre bunch without an outstanding player."[67]

Hilldale became an NNL associate member in 1921 and resumed its rivalry with the Bacharach Giants. The two split 18 decisions from June through October, with the Darbyites barely outscoring their rivals, 96–92. Connor and Bolden scheduled a doubleheader at New York's Dyckman Oval on October 30 to break the tie. Phil Cockrell scattered five hits while Otto Briggs, Louis Santop, and Chaney White all homered in Hilldale's 7–2 triumph. The Quaker nine was leading, 2–1, in the second contest when it was called because of darkness and the title was theirs.[68]

Foster's Giants were also prowling the East that October, playing both contenders. In a series that lasted over three weeks, the American Giants bested the Bacharachs by a single game. Dave Brown shaded Dick Redding, 5–4, in the decider, aided by Dave Malarcher's sixth-inning home run. Chicago also took two out of the first three contests against Hilldale, as left fielder Jimmy Lyons ran wild on the bases, stealing home twice. After a hard fought 5–5 tie, Bolden's ace Phil Cockrell downed the Giants for the second time, clubbing three hits on his own behalf including a homer, in a 15–5 rout that evened the series. Former American

Giants twirler Dick Whitworth shut down his old mates on three hits in the last game. His new teammates reached curveballer Bill Holland for 11 safeties, and Hilldale wrested "championship honors" with a 7–1 triumph. The predictably ungracious Rube Foster moaned about the ditch-lined outfield at Hilldale Park and that the Darby club refused to abide by the "playing rules."[69]

John Henry Lloyd displaced Dick Lundy as manager-shortstop of the New York version of the Bacharach Giants the following season. From Memorial Day through the Fourth of July, the Bees and Hilldale played five doubleheaders before crowds averaging in excess of 10,000 fans, to decide the Eastern crown. John Connor's club captured six of 10 games in a heavy-hitting series, although Bolden's outfit outscored them, 67–61. John Lloyd registered a trio of three-hit games for the Gotham crew, while George Johnson laced over 15 base hits for Hilldale, and mashed four home runs in the Memorial Day twin bill in Darby.[70]

The Bacharachs had opened the season by beating the American Giants three out of five times in Chicago and they returned in August to renew their struggle with the NNL leaders. The clubs halved the first four games at Schorling Park, with catcher Julio Rojo twice driving home the game-winning run in the Bacharachs final at bat and the American Giants bunting their way to a 7–2 triumph in the fourth match despite managing only four base hits.[71]

Both owners desperately wanted to win the finale, which turned out to be "one of the greatest games played anywhere," replete with "brilliant fielding, eight fast double plays, and catches after long runs." Bacharach twirler Harold Treadwell fanned 12 and scattered eight hits while blanking the American Giants for 19 innings. But his teammates could do nothing with Chicago starter Ed "Huck" Rile or Dave Brown, who came on in relief in the fifth. The jug-eared lefty allowed only six singles for the next 15 frames, and struck out 12 batters, including a bases-loaded punchout of George Shively in the top of the 18th inning. In the bottom of the 20th, Cristóbal Torriente drew a walk off Treadwell, was sacrificed to second, and scored the game's only run on a single by Dave Malarcher, beating weak-armed right fielder Ramiro Ramirez's throw home by five feet.[72]

Three days later, Hilldale followed the Bacharachs into Chicago for another five-game set. Spitballer Phil Cockrell did Treadwell and Brown one better, tossing a no-hitter while walking only three batters during the Easterners' 5–0 triumph. The American Giants won the next two contests before Cockrell, who "throws a mean, mean baseball," flummoxed Chicago 5–3 on four hits. It was déjà vu all over again in the bottom of the 12th inning of the deciding game, when Giants first baseman Leroy Grant drew a walk and later beat a throw home by Hilldale's Hall-of-Fame shortstop Judy Johnson to give the Fosterites a 7–6 win.[73]

In 1923 both Hilldale and the Bacharachs severed their association with the NNL and threw in with Nat Strong to form the Eastern Colored League (ECL). During the next two years, the ECL raided the western circuit for several players, including Hall-of-Famers Oscar Charleston, Raleigh "Biz" Mackey, and Ben Taylor, thus rendering any regular or postseason activity between the two organizations extremely unpalatable.[74]

In early September 1924, NNL czar Rube Foster and the ECL owners hammered out their differences in "one of the most peaceful meetings in the history of organized Colored baseball," and agreed to stage a best-of-nine-game "world's series" in October. After nearly 60 years the blackball championship had seemingly hit the big time.[75]

There should be little dispute that the majority of the blackball playoffs were contested by squads of big-league caliber. Previous research has revealed that the African American teams beat major leaguers in head-to-head competition nearly 60 percent of the time and defeated minor-league outfits at about the same clip the American and National League clubs did.[76]

While no one is asking the New York Yankees to give back any of the titles they won during the segregated era, it seems obvious that more recognition needs to be given to the Black champions and their achievements. In the fall of 1905, Philadelphia Giants owner Walter "Slick" Schlichter challenged the winner of the upcoming World Series to determine, "who can play base ball best—the White or the Black American." Schlichter's defy was ignored by the Philadelphia Athletics and New York Giants, prompting Sol White to postulate:

> Of course, there is a possibility of the colored man winning and that would be distasteful to many followers of the White team, but true sport recognizes

no color nor clan and it should always be, may the best man win.[77]

Notes

1 *Chicago Inter Ocean* (Illinois), October 23, 1905; *Chicago Record Herald* (Illinois), October 23, 1905.

2 Sol White, *History of Colored Base Ball, Compiled With Other Documents on the Early Black Game 1886–1936*, Compiled and introduced by Jerry Malloy (Lincoln, Nebraska and London: University of Nebraska Press, 1996), 35.

3 *New Orleans Times* (Louisiana), September 4, 1877.

4 *Albany Evening Journal* (New York), September 27, October 5, 1866; *Syracuse Daily Standard* (New York), October 4, 1866.

5 *New York Herald* (New York), October 4, 1867.

6 *National Republican* (District of Columbia), September 2, 1867; Anthony DiFiore, "Advancing African American Baseball: The Philadelphia Pythians and Interracial Competition in 1869," *Black Ball* 1, no. 1 (Spring 2008): 60.

7 *Utica Daily Observer* (New York), September 10, 21, 1869.

8 *Buffalo Evening Courier and Republic* (New York), August 22, 26, 1870; *Utica Daily Observer* (New York), August 22, 24, 1870; *New York Clipper* (New York), September 3, 1870; Lawrence D. Hogan, *Shades of Glory: The Negro Leagues and the Story of African-American Baseball* (Washington DC: National Geographic, 2006), 11–12.

9 *Chicago Tribune* (Illinois), August 24, 1870; Michael E. Lomax, *Black Baseball Entrepreneurs* (Syracuse, New York: Syracuse University Press, 2003), 28; James E. Brunson III, *The Early Image of Black Baseball* (Jefferson, North Carolina: McFarland and Company, 2009), 38; *Chicago Times* (Illinois), May 31, 1871.

10 *Chicago Tribune* (Illinois), September 19, 1871; *Philadelphia Inquirer* (Pennsylvania), September 18, 20, October 11, 12, 1871; *New York Tribune* (New York), September 18, 1871; *Milwaukee Sentinel* (Wisconsin) September 21, 1871; Brunson, 43.

11 *Chicago Tribune* (Illinois), September 8, 1875; Brunson, 42, 61.

12 *St. Louis Republican* (Missouri), September 9, 1875; Brunson, 67; *St. Louis Daily Globe* (Missouri), October 15, 1875; *Chicago Inter Ocean* (Illinois), October 14, 15, 1875.

13 *St. Louis Daily Globe* (Missouri), June 14, 16, 1876.

14 Brunson, 112; *New York Globe* (New York), July 28, August 18, 1883; *New York Herald* (New York), September 13, 1882, September 7, 8, 1883.

15 White, 8, 10, 12; *Trenton True American* (New Jersey), August 14, 1886; *Trenton Evening Times* (New Jersey), August 25, 1886.

16 Bill Plott, "The Southern League Of Colored Base Ballists," *Baseball Research Journal*, Volume 3 (1974) ; Thomas Aiello, "A Case For The Negro Southern League," *13th Annual Jerry Malloy Conference Booklet*, 2010; *New Orleans Times Picayune* (Louisiana), June 7, 17, 18, 20, 21, 22, July 31, August 2, 1886; *New York Freeman* (New York) August 14, 1886.

17 *New York Clipper* (New York), February 11, 1887; *Sporting Life* (Philadelphia, Pennsylvania), June 1, 1887; *Trenton Evening Times* (New Jersey), November 3, 1887.

18 White, 16; *New York Age* (New York), August 25, September 1, 1888; *New York Sun* (New York), August 20, 21, 23, 24, 25, 26, 27, 28, 1888; *New York Herald* (New York), August 23, 1888.

19 *St. Louis Republic* (Missouri), August 28, 1888; *New Orleans Times Picayune* (Louisiana), October 25, November 15, 1886; *Chicago Tribune* (Illinois), August 19, 22, 1888.

20 *Chicago Tribune* (Illinois), August 22, 25, 1888; *Chicago Inter Ocean* (Illinois), August 22, 23, 24, 26, 1888; *St. Louis Republic* (Missouri), August 26, 1888.

21 *St. Louis Republic* (Missouri), August 26, 27, 29, 1888; *New Orleans Times Picayune* (Louisiana), August 29, October 29, November 1, 2, 1888.

22 *St. Louis Republic* (Missouri), August 28, 1888; *Chicago Inter Ocean* (Illinois), August 26, 1888; White,14; *Cleveland Gazette* (Ohio), March 22, 1892; *New York Herald Tribune* (New York), September 9, 1887, September 19, 1888; *New York Sun* (New York), July 16, 1888; *Philadelphia Inquirer* (Pennsylvania), August 2, 3, 1889.

23 White, 16, 18, 20, 150, 151; *New York Sun* (New York), May 20, 21, 1891; *Philadelphia Inquirer* (Pennsylvania), April 20, June 26, 1891; *New York Herald* (New York), May 18, 19, July 14, 27, October 5, 12, 1891; *Harrisburg Patriot* (Pennsylvania), June 12, 13, 15, 1891; *Lebanon Daily News* (Pennsylvania), June 16, 17, 1891.

24 White, 24; *Harrisburg Patriot* (Pennsylvania), September 21, 1891; *New York Herald* (New York), March 16, September 26, 1892; *Cleveland Gazette* (Ohio), March 22, 1892; *Pittsburgh Courier* (Pennsylvania), March 12, 1927.

25 White, 24, 37; *Chicago Tribune* (Illinois), September 14, 1891, October 6, 1894; *Chicago Inter Ocean* (Illinois), October 23, 1893; *New York Sun* (New York), October 7, 1894.

26 White, 24, 37; *Chicago Tribune* (Illinois), September 14, 1891, October 6, 1894; *Chicago Inter Ocean* (Illinois), October 23, 1893; *New York Sun* (New York), October 7, 1894.

27 Lomax, 145–146; *New York Sun* (New York), August 15, 1896; *Washington Times* (District of Columbia), May 23, 1896.

28 White, 37; *Lima Times Democrat* (Ohio), September 12, 1896 *Sporting Life* (Philadelphia, Pennsylvania), October 31, November 14, 1896; *Adrian Daily Telegram* (Michigan), September 26, October 3, 1896; Lomax, 152.

29 *Jersey City News* (New Jersey), October 6, 1897; *New York Sun* (New York), October 4, 5, 1897; *Jersey City Journal* (New Jersey), October 11, 1897.

30 *Sporting Life* (Philadelphia, Pennsylvania), March 26, April 16, November 5, 1898; *Jersey City Journal* (New Jersey), October 3, 10, 1898.

31 *Sporting Life* (Philadelphia, Pennsylvania), November 5, 1898; *Janesville Daily Gazette* (Wisconsin), July 3, 1899; White, 37–38.

32 Lomax, 159–160, 166; White, 38; *Illinois Record* (Springfield, Illinois), March 18, 1899; *Chicago Tribune* (Illinois), April 8, September 3, 4, 18, 25, 1899.

33 White, 38, 40; *Janesville Daily Gazette* (Wisconsin), June 12, 1900; *Oak Park Times* (Illinois), August 10, 1900; *Chicago Tribune* (Illinois), June 25, July 2, 1900.

34 *Chicago Tribune* (Illinois), October 8, 14, 1900, September 29, 1901; *Jackson Citizen Patriot* (Michigan), October 17, 1900; *Chicago Inter Ocean* (Illinois), October 14, 1901; Lomax, 171; Frank Leland, *Frank Leland's Baseball Club*, (Chicago: Fraternal Printing Co., 1910), 5, 7.

35 *Chicago Tribune* (Illinois), July 28, August 4, 1902; Robert Peterson, *Only The Ball Was White* (New York and Oxford: Oxford University Press, 1992), 104; *Big Rapids Pioneer* (Michigan), July 23, August 20, 21, 1902.

36 White, 40; *Des Moines Register and Leader* (Iowa), August 10, 1903; *Upper Des Moines Republican* (Iowa), August 12, 1903; *Maxwell Tribune* (Iowa), August 13, 1903.

37 White, 31, 40.

38 White, 40, 42; *Philadelphia Inquirer* (Pennsylvania), June 28, September 13, 18, 1903; *Camden Post Telegram* (New Jersey), September 14, 16, 26,1903; *Trenton Evening Times* (New Jersey), September 15, 1903.

39 White, 44, 46, 146; *Philadelphia Inquirer* (Pennsylvania), September 2, 3, 4, 1904.

40 Phil S. Dixon, *Phil Dixon's American Baseball Chronicles, Great Teams: The 1905 Philadelphia Giants Volume Three* (Charleston, South Carolina, 2006),

55; White, 33; *Philadelphia Inquirer* (Pennsylvania), May 8, September 4, 1906, April 14, 1907. (Self-published: Charleston, SC, 2006) Xlibris.

41 *Chicago Tribune* (Illinois), February 26, October 2, 9, 1905, October 22, 1906; *Chicago Inter Ocean* (Illinois), October 16, 23, 1905, October 15, 1906; White, 46.

42 *Trenton Evening Times* (New Jersey), October 29, 1906, October 14, 1907; *New York Press* (New York), September 22, 1907.

43 *Chicago Defender* (Illinois), February 20, 1915; Leland, 6; *Indianapolis Freeman* (Indiana), June 27, 1908; October 2, 1909, March 5, 1910; *Chicago Tribune*, 1908 July 28, 29, 30, August 3, 7, 8, 1908; Sol White, *New York Age* (New York), January 10, 1931

44 St. *Paul Pioneer Press* (Minnesota), July 27, 28, 29, 30, 31, 1909; *Indianapolis Freeman* (Indiana), November 13, 1909.

45 *Indianapolis Freeman* (Indiana), October 2, November 13, 1909; *St. Paul Pioneer Press* (Minnesota), July 25, 26, 27, 28, 29.

46 *New York Age* (New York), August 3, 10, 24, September 7, 21, 1911; *The New York Times* (New York), August 20, 1911; *Brooklyn Eagle* (New York), September 5, 1911.

47 *Indianapolis Freeman* (Indiana), July 8, 1911; *Chicago Tribune* (Illinois), June 29, July 3, 4, 5, 6, 30, 31, 1911; *Chicago Examiner* (Illinois), July 7, 1911.

48 *Poughkeepsie Daily Eagle* (New York), March 30, 1916; *Indianapolis Freeman* (Indiana), June 1, 1912; *Brooklyn Eagle* (New York), March 4, 1913; *Chicago Defender* (Illinois), September 12, 1914.

49 White, 35; *New York Age* (New York), July 17, 24, 1913; *Chicago Defender* (Illinois), July 26, 1913.

50 *Chicago Tribune* (Illinois), July 28, 29, 30, 31, August 1, 10, 13, 14, 1913, *Indianapolis Freeman* (Indiana), August 16, December 20, 1913.

51 *New York Age* (New York), August 21, 1913; April 9, 1914; *Brooklyn Daily Star* (New York), August 21, 1914.

52 *Chicago Tribune* (Illinois), June 21, 22, 24, 1915; *Chicago Examiner* (Illinois), June 23, 25, 1915; *Chicago Defender* (Illinois), July 24, 31, 1915; *Indianapolis Freeman* (Indiana), July 24, 31, August 14, 1915.

53 *Indianapolis Freeman* (Indiana), July 15, 1916; *Chicago Defender* (Illinois), September 2, 9, 1916; *Chicago Tribune* (Illinois), August 28, 29, 30, 31, September 1, 1916.

54 *Chicago Defender* (Illinois), October 28, November 4, 18, 1916; *Indianapolis Freeman* (Indiana), October 28, November 4, 1916; Paul Debono, *The Indianapolis ABCs* (Jefferson, North Carolina: McFarland and Company, 1997), 69.

55 *Chicago Defender* (Illinois), January 27, March 17, June 23, July 28, August 11, 25, September 8, 1917; *Chicago Tribune* (Illinois), June 11, 12, 13, 20, July 16, 17, 18, 20, August 5, 6, 7, 10, 11, 1917; *Detroit Free Press* (Michigan), August 4, 1917; *Chicago Examiner* (Illinois), August 9, 1917; Debono, 190.

56 *Chicago Defender* (Illinois), April 5, 1919; *Chicago Tribune* (Illinois), June 16, 18, 19, 20, 1919; *Detroit Free Press* (Michigan), July 27, 28, 29, 30, 31, August 1, 3, 4, 1919.

57 *Detroit Free Press* (Michigan), August 10, 11, 1919.

58 *New York Press* (New York), September 3, 12, 1912, August 18, 1913; *Philadelphia Inquirer* (Pennsylvania), September 27, 1914; *New York Age* (New York), October 12, 1916, October 4, 1917; *Chicago Defender* (Illinois), October 19, 1918.

59 *New York Age* (New York), September 28, 1911, June 26, 1913, July 6, 1918, May 10, July 5, 1919; *Brooklyn Eagle* (New York), September 11, 1916, June 6, 1920; *New York Sun* (New York), June 25, 1917.

60 *Chicago Defender* (Illinois), May 18, 1918; *New York Sun* (New York), June 3, 1918, May 5, 1919; *New York Age* (New York), May 10, 1919.

61 *New York Age* (New York) May 10, May 24, 1919; *Chicago Defender* (Illinois), May 24, June 7, 1919; *New York Evening Telegram* (New York), May 2, 1920; *Philadelphia Inquirer* (Pennsylvania), June 9, 1919.

62 Neil Lanctot, *Fair Dealing and Clean Playing: The Hilldale Club and the Development of Black Professional Baseball 1910–1932* (Syracuse, New York: Syracuse University Press, 2007), 51–52; Philadelphia Inquirer (Pennsylvania), June 6, 9, 10, 11, August 27, 28, September 9, 1919; *Chicago Defender* (Illinois), June 14, August 30, September 20, 1919.

63 *Philadelphia Inquirer* (Pennsylvania), July 17, 19, August 22, 1919; *Bridgeton Evening News* (New Jersey), July 19, 1919; *Detroit Free Press* (Michigan), August 4, 5, 6, 7, 8, 1919; *Chicago Defender* (Illinois), August 30, 1919; Peterson, 83–84, 259; John Holway, *The Complete Book Of Baseball's Negro Leagues: The Other Half Of Baseball History*, edited by Lloyd Johnson and Rachel Borst (Fern Park, Florida: Hastings House Publishers, 2001), 139.

64 *Chicago Defender* (Illinois), May 8, 1920; *Philadelphia Tribune* (Pennsylvania), June 12, September 18, 1920; *New York Age* (New York), May 22, 1920.

65 *New York Age* (New York), June 19, July 17, September 4, October 23, 1920; *Brooklyn Eagle* (New York), July 12, August 30, 1920.

66 *Chicago Defender* (Illinois), August 14, October 16, 1920; *New York Evening Telegram* (New York), October 10, 1920; *Brooklyn Eagle* (New York), October 11, 18, 1920.

67 *Washington Bee* (District of Columbia), October 2, 1920; *New York Sun* (New York), May 3, 1920; *Brooklyn Eagle* (New York), June 6, 1920; *Philadelphia Inquirer* (Pennsylvania), June 11, September 16, October 15, 16, 1920; *Philadelphia Tribune* (Pennsylvania), June 19, August 7, 14, September 25, October 9, 1920; Rollo Wilson, *Pittsburgh Courier* (Pennsylvania), September 15, 1928.

68 *Chicago Defender* (Illinois), December 11, 1920; *New York Evening Telegram* (New York), October 26, 1921; *Philadelphia Tribune* (Pennsylvania), November 5, 12, 1921.

69 *Defender* (Illinois), October 1, 8, 22, 1921; *Chicago Tribune* (Illinois), October 24, 1921; *Philadelphia Inquirer* (Pennsylvania), October 5, 10, 1921; *Philadelphia Tribune* (Pennsylvania), October 15, 22, 1921.

70 *Chicago Defender* (Illinois), March 18, June 24, 1922; *Philadelphia Inquirer* (Pennsylvania), May 31, June 5, July 3, 5, 1922.

71 *Chicago Defender* (Illinois), August 12, 19, 1922.

72 *Chicago Defender* (Illinois), August 26, 1922.

73 *Chicago Defender* (Illinois), August 26, September 2, 1922.

74 *New York Age* (New York), December 16, 1922; Lanctot, 93, 97–98;Debono, 95–96.

75 Frank Young, *Chicago Defender* (Illinois), September 13, 1924; Holway, 192–194; Larry Lester, *Baseball's First Colored World Series* (Jefferson, North Carolina: McFarland and Company, Inc. Publishers, 2006), 110, 116, 126, 134.

76. Mark Armour, "The Effects of Integration, 1947–1986," *Baseball Research Journal*, No. 36 (2007), 54; Holway, 471; Scott Simkus, "The World Was Flat: The Realities and Road Map For Major League Classification (Part One)," *Outsider Baseball Bulletin*, no. 96 (April 4, 2012), 3–4.

77 White, 49, 51.

THE PITTSBURGH KEYSTONES AND THE 1887 COLORED LEAGUE

Jerry Malloy

(A note of thanks for research compiled by Raymond J. Nemec, Vern Luse, L. Robert Davids, and Robert W. Peterson. —J.M.)

This article was published in the SABR 25 Convention Journal, *1995.*

Although Philadelphia was the most prominent center of early African American baseball, the 1887 Pittsburgh Keystones produced the leadership for the era's most successful (or least unsuccessful) Black baseball league, the League of Colored Base Ball Clubs.

Commonly referred to as the "Colored League" or the "National Colored League," it barely managed to get off the ground and crashed prematurely, providing a paltry precursor to the Negro National League which Rube Foster would found 33 years later, in 1920. Yet the ill-starred circuit's contribution to the history of Black baseball, and Pittsburgh's role in it, is worth noting. For, not only did the Colored League launch several notable careers, most significantly that of the Keystones' Sol White, it also accomplished something that even the formidable Foster could barely even hope to dream: it was accepted, if not exactly embraced, by the exalted polity of the National Agreement.

On the Same Footing as Whites

> The prospect of organizing this League meets with the hearty approval of every person as something that should have been done long ago, so that our people could have been on the same footing as Whites so far as baseball is concerned.
>
> —Walter S. Brown, *Sporting Life*, October 27, 1886

The Colored League was not the first known attempt to form a circuit of professional Black teams. That distinction belongs to the Southern League of Colored Base Ballists of 1886, the subject of an article by Bill Plott in the *Baseball Research Journal* of 1974. Unfortunately, the historical record of this ambiguous enterprise remains etched in vapor. Individual statistics, team standings, and even league membership have eluded substantial recovery as local press coverage was scattered and scant. Such was not the case with the Black league of the following year. In October 1886, *Sporting Life* reported the intention of Walter S. Brown, owner of the Pittsburgh Keystones, to create a Colored League for 1887. Brown was a news agent at Pittsburgh's Central Hotel, as well as the Smoky City's correspondent for the *Cleveland Gazette*, a prominent African American weekly newspaper.

Brown signaled his intention to muscle up the local team by enlarging its name to the Big Keystone Base Ball Club. He also cast his net beyond the Black neighborhoods of Pittsburgh, eventually signing two Ohioans: Sol White, a slugging infielder from Bellaire, and catcher-outfielder Weldy Walker of Steubenville, younger brother of Fleet Walker. Both Walkers had played for Toledo in 1884, when it was a member of the major league American Association, though Weldy's role was minor compared to Fleet's.

The upstart league received its first setback when the Cuban Giants, unwilling to sacrifice Sunday bookings in Brooklyn, New York, declined Brown's invitation to join. Based in Trenton, New Jersey, the Cuban Giants had just completed their inaugural season as the first team of salaried African American ball players and already were established as the nation's most glamorous Black team, a distinction it would retain throughout the 1880s. Indeed, Sol White, Black baseball's first historian, wrote 20 years later that it had been the success of the Cuban Giants that "led some people to think that colored base ball, patterned after the National League...would draw the same number of people."

Undeterred by the Giants' decision, Brown convened a December 9 meeting of delegates from Baltimore, Boston, Louisville, Philadelphia, Pittsburgh, and Washington DC at Eureka Hall on Pittsburgh's Arthur Street. Agents from Chicago failed to attend, but those from Cleveland and Cincinnati did. While neither city entered the League, Cincinnati was represented by Bud Fowler, the pioneering star Black ballplayer and aspiring entrepreneur, who took time off from his winter job as a barber to investigate the Colored League's possibilities. The delegates elected Brown president, adopted the rules of major league baseball, and agreed to reconvene four months later in Baltimore where Brown would become league secretary.

In the meantime, league officials busied themselves with matters large and small. They spurned an offer from the Spalding Company to furnish a championship pennant in exchange for use of its baseballs. Instead they adopted the Reach ball, also used by the American Association, in return for providing awards (by various accounts, gold medals or trophies) for leaders in batting average and fielding percentage.

On March 14 and 15, 1887, delegates met at the Douglass Institute, a distinguished Black social and cultural center in Baltimore. They acknowledged the experimental nature of the season by scheduling many open dates to allow for (hopefully) profitable exhibition games. Player salaries were to range from $10 to $75 per month; each club was to hire a local umpire; visiting teams were guaranteed $50 plus half the gate receipts ("the revenue from the grand stands not included"), and were to receive $25 from the home team in case of rainout.

Just as future major league owners (especially in Pittsburgh and Washington, DC) would rent their stadiums to Negro League teams, two members of the Colored League, the Keystones and Lord Baltimores, arranged to play in major league parks: at Pittsburgh's National League grounds, Recreation Park, and at Oriole Park, home of the American Association's Baltimore team. The Falls City club of Louisville was said to be the only Black team in the nation that owned its own grounds, "a handsome park at 16th Street and Magnolia Avenue." However, construction f the park was not completed in time for the season opener on May 6.

In reporting that the players would average about $50 per month in salary, the *Cleveland Gazette* darkly asked, "Will they get their money?" But optimism reigned among the league's creators, who were "enthusiastic and say the success of the new organization is assured," wrote the *Gazette*. In a hearty spirit of self-congratulation, the delegates, in full evening attire, repaired to a lavish reception and banquet at the Douglass Institute, generously hosted by the Lord Baltimores.

> Why Do They Need Protection?
>
> "The several minor (league) organizations that will form a combination against the League and American Association (includes)...the Colored League..."
>
> —*The Sporting News (TSN)*, January 15, 1887

One source of this optimism was that the fledgling circuit had become party to the National Agreement, placing it within the orbit of what we now call professional baseball. On January 15, 1887, *TSN* published a roster or players signed by teams aligned with the National Agreement, including eight Colored League franchises: the Baltimore Lord Baltimores, Boston Resolutes, Cincinnati Browns, Louisville Falls City, New York Gorhams, Philadelphia Pythians, Pittsburgh Keystones, and Washington, D.C. Capital Citys. Neither Cincinnati nor Washington ever took the field, but the Capital Citys' proposed roster included Sol White and Frank C. Leland, both of whom would shape African American baseball's destiny through the first decade of the next century. With the dawning of the new year, the new league was within the domain of professional baseball.

The Colored League joined an alliance of various minor leagues which was formed to combat the theft of players by the two major leagues. *Sporting Life* derided the Colored League's admission into baseball's official family as preposterous. "WHY DO THEY NEED PROTECTION?" they bellowed on April 13th:

> The League will attempt to secure the protection of the National Agreement. This can only be done with the consent of all the National Agreement clubs in whose territory the colored clubs are lo-

> cated. This consent should be obtainable, as these clubs can in no sense be considered rivals to the White clubs, nor are they likely to hurt the latter in the least financially. Still, the League can get along without protection. The value of the latter to the White clubs lies in that it guarantees a club undisturbed possession of its players. There is not likely to be much of a scramble for colored players... owing to the high standard of play required and to the popular prejudice against any considerable mixture of races.

In reality, the Colored League's desire to gain entry into White baseball was far from fatuous. Rather, it was a pragmatic response to bitter experience. S.K. Govern, one of the Philadelphia Pythians' backers, had managed the Cuban Giants in 1886 (and would do so again in 1887). He undoubtedly reminded his colleagues that George Stovey, the masterful Black pitcher, had been stolen from the Cuban Giants by the Eastern League's Jersey City team only six months prior, in mid-season. Without the protection of the National Agreement, the Cuban Giants were powerless to retain Stovey.

In addition, during the 1886 season, the Cuban Giant Arthur Thomas rejected an offer to sign with Philadelphia of the American Association, and Stovey nearly signed with the New York National League team. Even with the supposed protection of the National Agreement, there is evidence that White minor leagues were tampering with Colored League players as early as February 1887. Also, in 1887 African Americans played on twelve minor league teams, seven of them for five clubs in the prestigious International League alone.

Not until 1889 did the mighty Cuban Giants join White baseball, representing Trenton in the Middle States League. But the entire Colored League of 1887 could proclaim membership before a game had been played.

The 13-Game Season

> The National Colored League opened its championship season at Recreation Park, Pittsburgh, on May 6, in a game between the Gorhams of New York and the Keystones of Pittsburgh. Previous to the game there was a grand street parade and a brass band concert. The game was well-contested and quite exciting. About twelve hundred people were present. The score was: Gorhams 11, Keystones 8.
>
> —*New York Freeman*, May 14, 1887

In February, *Sporting Life* predicted that it would be "highly improbable" that the Colored League would survive a single season, and they were emphatically correct. Appropriately, Pittsburgh, home of the league's flagship franchise, was the site of the alpha and omega of its brief season. Thirteen days after the festive opener, the Keystones lost to the visiting Lord Baltimores, 6-2, in the last of the unlucky league's 13 games.

Before the Colored League was a week old, the Boston Resolutes were stranded in Louisville, reported *TSN*, and "at last accounts...were working their way home doing little turns in barbershops and waiting on table (sic) in hotels." The marooned Resolutes undoubtedly took small comfort in claiming the championship by winning their sole contest. By May 27, the Gorhams, Pythians, and Lord Baltimores were reported as "the only teams able to keep up," and one day later Walter Brown "reluctantly and sadly admitted that the Colored League was no more as an organization." The Colored League's final standings were as follows:

Wins Against	Bos	Phi	NY	Pit	Bal	Lou	W-L	Pct.
Boston	-	0	0	0	0	1	1-0	1.000
Philadelphia	0	-	1	1	2	0	4-1	.800
New York	0	0	-	1	0	1	2-2	.500
Pittsburgh	0	1	0	-	2	0	3-4	.428
Baltimore	0	0	0	2	-	0	2-4	.333
Louisville	0	0	1	0	0	-	1-2	.333

Sol White attributed the league's quick demise to insufficient financial backing. Yet he had words of praise for the effort:

> The short time of its existence served to bring out the fact that colored ball players of ability were numerous. The teams, with the exception of the Keystones, of Pittsburgh, and the Gorhams, of New York, were composed mostly of home talent, so they were not necessarily compelled to disband. With reputations as clubs from the defunct Colored League, they proved to be very good drawing cards

in different sections of the country. The Keystones and Gorhams, especially, distinguished themselves by later defeating the Cuban Giants.

AFTERMATH

The Colored League was the last hurrah in African American baseball for the Pythians, though new owners attempted a reorganization. The Pythians were namesakes, rather than direct descendants, of the famed Philadelphia team whose application for membership in the National Association of Base Ball Players was rejected (in writing) in 1867, and was the first recorded Black club to play a White team, two years later.

Black baseball's first backers were gentlemen's social clubs, such as the Pythians, but its future was in robust professionalism, with the Cuban Giants leading the way. Among aspirants to their throne, the New York Gorhams gave the Cuban Giants their first stiff challenge. The Gorhams were run by player-manager Ambrose Davis, "the first colored man in the East to venture into professional baseball..." according to Sol White, who added that Davis "proved to be of great assistance to the game by his competitiveness in producing teams to combat the great Cuban Giants."

When the Colored League collapsed, Davis launched a tenacious campaign to supplant the Cuban Giants, culminating in 1891, when he signed most of their best players, and renamed his team the Big Gorhams. Sol White judged them the best team in nineteenth-century Black baseball. Along the way, Davis doggedly continued to sign good players, even knowing that the best, such as Bob, Oscar, and Andy Jackson (the latter two brothers), and Sol White, would be gobbled up by the Cuban Giants. Other prominent Cuban Giants who had played in the Colored League were Arthur Thomas, William A. Selden, and William Malone.

The flagship team of the league, Brown's Pittsburgh Keystones, did not fare quite as well. They made one last run in 1888, when they finished second to the Cuban Giants—but ahead of Ambrose Davis's Gorhams—at a late-season tournament in Newburgh, New York. Davis retaliated by signing the Keystones' best player, Sol White. Thereafter, the Keystones may have carried on as a local semipro team. Sol White played briefly with the Keystones during a half-hearted attempt at a revival in 1892 but he quickly moved on.

As for Walter S. Brown, he was last seen in September 1888, sorting mail as a railroad postal clerk between Pittsburgh and New York City.

SOL WHITE

Jay Hurd

This article was written for SABR's Baseball Biography Project*, 2011.*

Racial discrimination did not miraculously disappear in 1863 with the Emancipation Proclamation, nor did it cease with the Civil War's end in 1865. However, even as race relations remain a topic, the process for dealing with race faced an evolution. Speaking to this evolution, Jerry Malloy, in his 1995 Introduction to *Sol White's History of Colored Base Ball* (originally published in 1907), states that:

> Sol White was a member of a tragic generation of African Americans, born within a few years of the Civil War. He and his contemporaries reached adulthood at a time, in the mid-1880s, when the brutal protocols of racial discrimination that soon would follow seemed by no means inevitable.[1]

Solomon White—also known as King Solomon White, or Sol White—was born in Bellaire, Ohio on June 12, 1868, three years and two months after Lee met Grant in Appomattox Court House. One of baseball's early historians, White was born in a northern state very near West Virginia, a state which had been accepted into the Union in 1863, only five years before his birth, and where much of his early career in baseball would occur.

Very little is known of Sol White's early years—his parents/family, his education, his social life– according to sources including Jerry Malloy, Negro League historian. However, it is known that while in his teens, he began, in 1883, what would become a 40-year career in professional baseball. In a newspaper piece in the *Pittsburgh Courier* of March 12, 1927, Floyd J. Calvin states that:

> Bellaire, Ohio, where Sol was born, had three White teams, the Lillies, the Browns, and the Globes. As a boy Sol hung around the Globes and then came the time when the Globes had an engagement with the Marietta team. One of the Globe players got his finger smashed, and since they all knew Sol, the captain pushed him into the game.[2]

The captain of the Marietta team was Ban Johnson, who would later become president of the American League. Calvin adds, "Sol takes pride in having played against Ban when he was an obscure captain of a hick town club."[3]

Sol White's professional career began in 1886 after three years with the barnstorming Bellaire Globes. In 1886, Sol played with the integrated Wheeling (West Virginia) Green Stockings of the Ohio State League. While with the Green Stockings he played third base and hit .370 in 52 games. At this time, his presence on a White team, in a predominantly White league, was not problematic. Indeed, African American ballplayers – John W. "Bud" Fowler, George Stovey, Frank Grant, Jack Frye, and Robert Higgins—played regularly in barnstorming and professional leagues, includ-

(Courtesy National Baseball Hall of Fame and Library, Cooperstown, NY)

Sol White

ing the minor leagues of otherwise-segregated pro baseball. By 1887, however, anti-Black sentiment fomented by White players led to opposition to integrated teams. Change was clearly in the offing. Sol left Wheeling, in 1887, to play with the Pittsburgh (Pennsylvania) Keystones. After a mere 13 games, he left the Keystones as that team and a newly-formed League of Colored Base Ball Players (or National Colored Base Ball League) folded. He continued to play baseball, however, when he returned to Wheeling.

In 1888 Sol returned to the Keystones—at this time not a professional team—who were playing in a four-team tournament with the Gorhams (New York), the Red Sox (Norfolk, Virginia), and the Cuban Giants (Trenton, New Jersey). The Keystones played well, losing only to the powerful Cuban Giants. The other teams, surprised by the Keystones' success, did note the presence of one man "other than home talent [i.e., professional caliber]." That man was Sol White.[4]

Having established himself as a talented ballplayer, Sol spent the 1889 season with the Gorhams of New York City. Despite the New York City component of the team's name, the Gorhams represented Easton, Pennsylvania, in the Middle States League.[5] The Gorhams did not fare well that season, and left the league before the championship would be won by the Cuban Giants of Trenton, New Jersey. In 1890, feeding what would become a regular occurrence, not without legal and personal battles, players left the Cuban Giants. The players fled the miserly ways of John M. Bright to glean the generosity of J. Monroe Kreiter of York, Pennsylvania. Bright maintained a Cuban Giants team, but Sol White joined the Monarchs of York.

By 1891, amidst additional controversy, owner Ambrose Davis renamed his Gorhams the Big Gorhams. Players, including Sol White, again leapt at an opportunity for more money and became members of Davis's new team. The team was successful, but, as did other African American teams, struggled financially. White found it necessary to play, in 1892, for the Pittsburgh Keystones and for a team formed at the Hotel Champlain, Bluff Point, New York (while with the Hotel team he also waited on tables). In 1893 and 1894 he played for J.M. Bright's "revived Cuban Giants, the only Black professional team in the country in either season."[6]

Although primarily an infielder, at 5'9", 170 pounds, he could play nearly any position. He clearly exhibited a high caliber—major league level—of play.

Although Adrian "Cap" Anson would be afforded much credit for forcing "Negroes out of organized baseball"[7], it was evident "that a majority of White baseball players in 1887, both Northerners and Southerners, opposed integration in the game."[8] White players now regularly refused to play with African Americans. By the turn of the century, segregation in baseball became the norm. Sol did play in the White minor leagues, on African American teams, and would soon join others in the not-uncommon movement from one all-Black team to another. During his five years in White baseball, he never hit lower than .324. In 159 minor league games he hit .356, scored 174 runs, and stole 54 bases.[9]

In spite of the many obstacles Sol continued to play into 1895 when he played 10 games for a team in the integrated Western Tri-State League, in Fort Wayne, Indiana. In that same year, he joined the Page Fence Giants of Adrian, Michigan. This team, funded by the Page Woven Wire Fence Company, did not have a home field and travelled by private rail coach. Experiences with this team would continue to feed Sol information to be recorded later in his life, when Sol White the baseball historian would emerge. Sol remained with the Page Fence Giants for one season, batting a healthy .404. In 1896, White joined the Cuban X-Giants, who would be defeated by the Page Fence Giants.

In 1896, Sol enrolled in Wilberforce University in Xenia, Ohio, as a theology major.[10] Wilberforce University, founded in 1856, was named after an English abolitionist and supported by the African Methodist Episcopal Church. Jerry Malloy states that:

> He received high grades in a curriculum that included reading, grammar, arithmetic, physiology, history, elocution, spelling, and U.S. history. Meanwhile, he developed the innate interest in history that ultimately made him the Livy [ancient Roman historian] of African American baseball.[11]

While at Wilberforce, White began to form friendships and partnerships which would guide him into positions of management and ownership of African American baseball teams. Preparation for his role as historian of African American baseball was nearly complete.

In 1897, Sol returned to the Cuban X-Giants where he remained for three seasons. By 1899, the X-Giants held enough talent to defeat the Chicago Columbia Giants—formerly the Page Fence Giants—nine out of 14 games. After the 1899 season, manager John Patterson of the Chicago Columbia Giants, aware of White's talent, signed him for the 1900 season. Although White noted that the Columbia Giants were "the finest and best equipped colored team that was ever in the business",[12] he remained with the team for only one season. After another brief stint with the Cuban X-Giants in 1901, Sol stepped into a partnership with H. Walter Schlichter and Harry Smith—White sportswriters from Philadelphia—to form the Philadelphia Giants. White served as player-manager the Philadelphia club until 1909.

From 1902 to 1907, White and his Philadelphia Giants were quite successful due, in large part, to a pitcher named Rube Foster. In 1907, however, Rube Foster left the team to become a member of the Leland Giants of Chicago. Foster would soon compete for talent, assuming control of Frank Leland's Giants, and thus begin his movement toward the founding of the Negro National League in 1920.

White saw his Philadelphia Giants win numerous regular-season games, as well as Black championships. Additionally, his Giants posted many wins over White teams, such as those in the New England League. He even issued challenges to National and American League champions—notably a 1906 challenge to the winner of the World Series between the Chicago Cubs and the Chicago White Sox (a challenge unanswered). However, it was while with the Philadelphia Giants that White published his *Sol White's Official Base Ball Guide*, copyrighted in 1907 by Sol and H. Walter Schlichter, sportswriter and sports editor of the White newspaper, the *Philadelphia Item*, and White's Philadelphia Giants partner.[13] This is the work which helps to define Sol White, the ball player, the historian, and the man.

White's playing career would not end until 1911. His final active roles in baseball included: managing of the Boston Giants in 1912; serving as secretary for a Columbus team of the Negro National League in 1920; managing the Fear's Giants of Cleveland (a Black minor league team) in 1922; managing the Cleveland Browns of the Negro National League in 1924; and coaching for the Newark Stars of the Eastern Colored League in 1926.

Sol White played baseball with talent and drive; he supported and valued his fellow players. White took great pride in his play, and in the African American teams. He also played for the money, although salaries for him and his fellow ball players were substantially lower than salaries for White major leaguers (he noted that "the average major leaguer made $2,000.00 in 1906, while the average Black netted only $466.00").[14]

History shows that Sol White, with Rube Foster, and others, "had held Black baseball together throughout 60 years of apartheid, making [Jackie] Robinson's debut possible",[15] Sol White's many contributions to baseball became more evident by the 1920s. In 1922, when he briefly managed a Black minor league team, the Giants of Cleveland, catcher William "Big C" Johnson, whose experience included a stint on a U.S. Army baseball team which fielded, among others, Wilber "Bullet" Rogan, said that Sol White is "the best educated man I ever played with. Sol wanted what they never were able to get—a reporter to keep records. They never had enough money to hire a man like that."[16]

John Holway refers to Sol White as "an infielder who would go on to become the most influential figure in the first decades of Negro baseball."[17] Today, referred to as a Renaissance Man, Sol White is remembered for his great contributions to the recording of baseball history. White stated that:

> Baseball is a legitimate profession. It should be taken seriously by the colored player. An honest effort of his great ability will open the avenue in the near future wherein he may walk hand in hand with the opposite race in the greatest of all American games—baseball.[18]

When no longer directly involved with the game, White maintained baseball connections through writing columns for the *New York Amsterdam News* and the *New York Age*. It is apparent that Sol hoped to update, even on an annual basis, his *Base Ball Guide*. He did maintain correspondence with H. Walter Schlichter, and in a letter of 1936, Schlichter suggests:

> Why not see the editor of your colored paper and try to sell him a history of colored baseball which

> you could write either as a single article or as a series. Except for recent years you have all the data in the book and I would be glad to furnish the cuts and pictures. It looks to me to be worth trying.[19]

Sadly, the resources were not available for him to continue publishing his *Guide*.

White died, penniless[20], at the age of 87 on August 26, 1955. *The American National Biography* states that he died in Harlem, New York City where he lived for a number of years, although the National Baseball Hall of Fame and Museum notes that he died in Central Islip, New York. Sol White is buried in Frederick Douglass Cemetery in the Oakwood neighborhood of Staten Island, New York.[21] In 2012, the Negro Leagues Baseball Grave Marker Project, whose mission is to identify the final resting place of Negro League Baseball players and mark the graves of those found unmarked, delivered the granite marker for King Solomon "Sol" White.[22]

Sol was elected to the National Baseball Hall of Fame, via a special Negro Leagues Committee, in 2006. His plaque in the Hall identifies him as an "outstanding player and manager" of the "Pre-Negro Leagues, 1887–1912" and the "Negro Leagues, 1920–1926." The plaque also recognizes "*Sol White's Official Base Ball Guide* of early Black baseball teams, players, and playing conditions."

Perhaps it is his *Base Ball Guide* which best exemplifies Sol White the man. In it he writes candidly and "as accurately as possible"[23] to describe the makeup and history of African American teams. In dedicating his work "To the players and managers of the past and present and the patrons of colored base ball"[24] Sol demonstrates his real admiration for the game. He also reveals a desire to recognize baseball's past, acknowledge its present, and step into its future. Sol lived to see Jackie Robinson play with the Brooklyn Dodgers in 1947. As Frank Ceresi and Carol McMains note in their May 2006 *Baseball Almanac* article "Renaissance Man: Sol White":

> What quiet pride Sol [White] must have felt when, as an old man living alone in Harlem, he saw Jackie Robinson break down the blight on the game we now, quite antiseptically, refer to simply as the 'color barrier.'

Sol White was known to be an intelligent and insightful man, using his mental acuity as well as his physical ability. For this he was respected by fellow players, owners, managers, promoters, rooters, and newspaper men. It is also for this that Sol White is respected and admired today.

Notes

1 Sol White, *Sol White's History of Colored Base Ball: With Other Documents on the Early Black game, 1886–1936*, compiled and introduced by Jerry Malloy (Lincoln: University of Nebraska Press, 1995), li-lii.

2 Floyd J. Calvin. "Sol White". *Pittsburgh Courier*, March 12, 1927. White, 143.

3 Floyd J. Calvin. "Sol White". *Pittsburgh Courier*, March 12, 1927. White, 144.

4 White, xxiv.

5 White, xxvi.

6 White, xxxi.

7 Robert Peterson, *Only the Ball Was White: A History of Legendary Black Players and All Black Professional Teams before Black Men Played in the Major Leagues* (Englewood Cliffs, NJ: Prentice Hall, 1970), 30.

8 Peterson, 30.

9 White, xxv.

10 David Bernstein. "Solomon White," *American National Biography* (New York: Oxford University Press), v.23, 239.

11 White, xlvii.

12 White, 28.

13 White, xlviii.

14 David Pietrusza, Matthew Silverman, and Michael Gershman, eds. *Baseball: The Biographical Encyclopedia.* (New York: Total/SPORTS ILLUSTRATED, 2000), 1221.

15 John B. Holway, *Blackball Stars: Negro League Pioneers.* (Westport, CT: Meckler Books, 1988), 7.

16 Holway, 7.

17 John Holway, *The Complete Book of Baseball's Negro Leagues: The Other Half of Baseball History.* (Fern Park, FL: Hastings House Publishers, 2001), 21.

18 Pietrusza, 1221.

19 White, 157-158.

20 John Thorn, http://ourgame.mlblogs.com/2012/12/28/sol-white-recalls-baseballs-greatest-days/.

21 John Thorn, http://ourgame.mlblogs.com/2012/12/28/sol-white-recalls-baseballs-greatest-days/.

22 Larry Lester, editor, *The Courier*: A Publication of SABR's Negro Leagues Committee (SABR, September 2012), 5.

23 White, preface, 3.

24 White, preface, 3.

ANDREW (RUBE) FOSTER: GEM OF A MAN

Larry Lester

Updated version from The Negro Leagues Book *by SABR, 1994.*

Andrew Bishop Foster

Bat/Throw: Right/Right—5'9", 235 lbs.

Born: Wednesday, 17 September 1879, La Grange, TX[1]

Died: Tuesday, 9 December 1930, Kankakee, IL

Cemetery: Lincoln Cemetery, Section 6, Latitude: N 41° 40' 15.7", Longitude W 87° 42' 04.9", Blue Island, IL

HALLS OF FAME

- 1981 NATIONAL BASEBALL HALL OF FAME
- 1998 TEXAS SPORTS HALL OF FAME
- 2004 TEXAS BASEBALL HALL OF FAME

Folks who knew Rube called him a pitcher, a cheater, a ticket taker, a popcorn maker, a show maker, a showstopper, a money maker and, of course, a game breaker. He could do it all. The ultimate baseball attraction in one package—this was Rube Foster.

Reared in Texas by a preaching father and a gospel-singing mother, Foster disobeyed his parents to pursue a career between the white foul lines. He had the God-given ability to organize and promote teams, but much credit goes to Frank Leland, a product of Fisk University, who tutored a young Rube to immortal stardom.

Young Rube's vision began in 1897 with the Austin (Texas) Reds of Tillotson College (now Huston-Tillotson University). The following year, he joined the semipro Yellowjackets in nearby Waco. Here, he developed a nasty screwball thrown from his unique submarine delivery. Entering the new century Foster signs with Frank Leland's Chicago Union Giants for $40 a month and 15 cents a day for meal money.

In 1903, Foster headed East to play for the Cuban X-Giants. That fall, he posted four victories in a seven-game series against the Philadelphia Giants for the so-called "Colored Championship of the World." After joining Lamar's Cuban X-Giants, Andrew Foster's reputation as a fine pitcher expanded with a victory over the Major Leagues' top southpaw ace Rube Waddell in 1903, while leading the league with 34 complete games that season. Nat Strong, manager of the Murray Hills, a midtown Manhattan semipro team, recruited Waddell to pitch against Lamar's Cuban X-Giants on blue Sunday. The classic duel at Olympia Field between Foster and Waddell saw the X-Giants excel, 6-3 with both pitchers going the distance. A tired rubber-armed Waddell, listed in the *New York Sun* (August 3, page 6) as "Wilson" in the line score gave up 11 hits, and Foster yielded seven hits. Both pitchers worked without their regular catchers: Waddell with O'Neil, and Foster with Big Bill Smith, normally an outfielder for the X-Giants.

The wandering Foster switched over to the Philly team the next season, 1904, and re-encountered his old teammates for bragging rights to the "colored" title. Foster accounted for both victories in the best-of-three series. He struck out 18 batters in one game, beating then-current major league record of 15 set by Fred Glade of the St. Louis Browns.

In 1907, he returned to Chicago and joined the Leland Giants, leading them to a 110-10 won-lost record, including 48 straight wins. In 1909, the Giants entered the tough integrated city league. In Foster's first eleven starts, he won eleven games, with four shutouts. Such a dominating force that season, after one commanding victory an *Indianapolis*

Freeman newspaper's headlines simply stated: "FOSTER PITCHED, THAT'S ALL" with no box score listed.

By 1910, the Leland Giants were the chatter of every clubhouse. They christened a ballpark in an all-White neighborhood near 69th and Halsted, as the Leland Giants Base Ball Park. Foster now serving as player-manager, amassed in his opinion the greatest team of all time. Featuring such stars as John Henry "Pop" Lloyd, the notorious streak hitter Pete Hill, Grant "Home Run" Johnson, catcher extraordinaire Bruce Petway and great pitchers like Frank Wickware and Pat Dougherty, the Leland team won 123 of 129 games. This team compelled John McGraw of N.Y. Giants fame to announce, "*If I had a bucket of whitewash that wouldn't wash off, you wouldn't have five players left tomorrow.*"

The following season, Foster formed a partnership with John Schorling, a White businessman. Together they purchased Old Roman's, a ballpark at 39th and Wentworth, from White Sox owner Charlie Comiskey. The park became home of Black baseball's finest team, the Chicago American Giants. Foster billed his team as "THE GREATEST AGGREGATION OF COLORED BASEBALL PLAYERS IN THE WORLD." The Giants normally played semipro teams for a guarantee of $60, rain or shine, with fifty percent of the gross receipts guaranteed if their ace Rube Foster would pitch.

Although an outstanding pitcher, a dependable team owner and a brilliant manager, perhaps Rube Foster's most impressive fulfillment came with the creation of the Negro National League of Colored Base Ball Professionals, better known as the Negro National League (NNL). It consisted of eight ships of hope to battle the sea of racism. The league's motto was "*We Are the Ship, All Else the Sea.*" Going against the tide of segregation, Rube's voyage would become an obsession. Foster, the genetic Eve of Black baseball, birthed a confederacy of clubs that embraced a permanent existence of quality baseball. It became the first league of color to survive a full season. For years, Captain Rube struggled without a life preserver in his attempts to keep his boat afloat.

From his throne in Chicago, Foster ran the NNL as a noble emperor. He realized the need for balanced competition, as he moved players from team to team, even sending his American Giant star Oscar Charleston to the Indianapolis ABCs. He often lent money to failing franchises to help meet their payroll and advanced monies to his own players. With unparalleled influence, Foster was the undisputed kingpin of Black baseball in the Midwest.

With brains and influence, Rolodex Rube seemed invincible. In 1926, the czar-like dictator, with the booming baritone voice, succumbed to mental illness and was institutionalized in Kankakee, Illinois. One of baseball's greatest minds was suddenly torn from the game. Four years later, the son of Sarah Watts and Rev. Andrew Foster, Sr., was buried in Lincoln Cemetery near Chicago.

Foster, with his dedicated, high-minded approach to baseball, was the force behind all subsequent major Negro Leagues. In November of 1930, renowned sportswriter Frank "Fay" Young, for *Abbott's Monthly*, testified on behalf of the late legend, "*One of the most brilliant figures that the great national sport has ever produced. Rube knew every technicality of the game, how to play it, and how to make his men play it. A true master of the game.*"

Foster redefined the art of baserunning, hit-and-run techniques, and the do-or-die sacrifice play. He used creative ways to "stretch" a hit, to "steal" a run and eventually "swipe" a victory. In 1981, justice was served as Foster was found guilty of larceny and sentenced to a life term, without parole, into Cooperstown's Baseball Hall of Fame.

Overall, his life history was a real page-turner. Rube was a phenomenal pitcher, a magnificent manager, a powerful organizer and even greater humanitarian. He had the face of a koala bear, the heart of laborer John Henry, the smile of Billy Dee Williams, the essence of Malcolm X, the vision of Dr. Martin Luther King, the oratorical skills of James Earl Jones with the creative genius of Ray Charles. Rube Foster was the most robust blend of baseball expertise ever assembled.

Notes

1 The 1880 Census shows the Foster family living on the McKinny plantation in Winchester, Fayette County, Texas. An eight-month old Andrew Bishop is listed with his father, mother, one brother and two sisters. Land deed records suggest the Foster family lived as cotton sharecroppers for widower J.L.T. McKinny and his son Edgar on the southeastern side of Winchester, about 18 miles northwest of La Grange. The 1900 Census (the 1890 Census was mostly destroyed by fire in 1921) shows the family living in Calvert, Texas, the most commonly cited birthplace for Andrew Bishop Foster.

Nearing Launch of "The Ship"

JOHN DONALDSON AND BLACK BASEBALL IN MINNESOTA

Steven R. Hoffbeck and Peter Gorton

This article was published in The National Pastime, *2012.*

"The problem of the twentieth century is the problem of the color line."—W.E.B. DuBois.[1]

For sixty years, professional baseball was as segregated as the Deep South. From 1887—when the unspoken national agreement prohibited African Americans from major league baseball—to 1947, when Jackie Robinson broke the color line, Black ballplayers were shut out of the highest levels of the White game.[2] How could Black players, in Minnesota and in other states, respond to being banned from baseball? Well, they could have just given up and accepted segregation as grim reality. Or, young Black men could resolve to integrate the sport, town by town, city by city, one baseball diamond at a time. That's what happened in Minnesota.

Renowned author Sinclair Lewis, a native Minnesotan, once said: "To understand America, it is merely necessary to understand Minnesota."[3] Let's look at the state's story.

In 1858, Minnesota joined the United States and its constitution declared that there would be no slavery in the state.[4] In 1868, Minnesota extended voting rights to African Americans.

The Minnesota Constitutional Rights Law of 1899 prohibited discrimination in hotels, theaters and restaurants, and other public places, but such a law did not apply to professional baseball. Still, the Black population of Minnesota yearned for full social equality because they faced a haphazard maze of discrimination against their best efforts, a denial of rights and opportunities, of narrow-mindedness at best and unreasoning hatred at worst.

Minnesota's Black ballplayers, therefore, worked to dismantle baseball's color line themselves.

In the 1890s, pitcher Walter Ball integrated the St. Paul city public-school baseball teams and youth teams. In 1897, Ball and the Young Cyclones ballclub won the St. Paul City Amateur Championship—he was the lone Black player on an otherwise all-White team.[5]

After the turn of the century, Minnesota towns began to import some Black players for their formerly all-White teams. In 1900 the small-town Waseca ballclub secured Black pitchers George Wilson and Billy Holland—two men who had played for the best Chicago-area African American teams of the late 1890s. Waseca's EACO Flour team brought the first Black ballplayers to the ball-diamonds of southern Minnesota, and they won the state semiprofessional championship.[6]

In 1902, Walter Ball became the first Black player on St. Cloud's formerly White semipro ballclub. Similarly, Billy Williams, also from St. Paul, integrated his high school team and other area teams.[7]

Minnesota's own Bobby Marshall gained entry onto the Minneapolis Central High School baseball team in the late 1890s and then broke the color line on the University of Minnesota's baseball squad in 1904.[8]

Black businessman Phil "Daddy" Reid established Minnesota's first all-Black professional ball club, the St. Paul Colored Gophers, in 1907, gathering top talent from Chicago and elsewhere. Home-grown Bobby Marshall became the "star slugger" on the Colored Gophers team in 1909, when the Colored Gophers claimed the championship of Black baseball by defeating Rube Foster's Chicago Leland Giants three games to two. The Colored Gophers barnstormed throughout the Upper Midwest for five years, 1907–1911, bringing a fast and colorful brand of Black baseball to towns that had never before seen an African American ballplayer on their local diamonds.[9]

(Courtesy St. Paul Pioneer Press/Author's Collection)

Walter Ball (1880–1946), one of St. Paul's best amateur pitchers in 1898, became a premier hurler among Minnesota semiprofessionals by 1902. In 1903 Ball moved to Chicago where he became one of the greatest pitchers in Black baseball through 1921.

The decade from 1910 to 1919 brought a new wave of Black barnstorming teams to Minnesota from other locales. Premiere among these was the All Nations ballclub, a multi-racial team founded in 1912 by James Leslie (J.L.) Wilkinson (1878–1964). Wilkinson was a genius in marketing and publicity, as well as a true baseball man. Although Wilkinson was White, he believed that baseball fans in Minnesota and throughout the Midwest would pay to see the very best and enthusiastically embrace the skills of a truly professional touring team brought in from the top ranks of Black baseball and a world that was learning to play America's game.

The All Nations team in 1913 looked like the face of modern baseball with players coming from all over the world. It was composed of "men from all nations, including Chinese, Japanese, Cubans, Indians, Hawaiians…and the Great John Donaldson, the best colored pitcher in the United States today, also the famous [José] Mendéz, the Cuban."[10] The All Nations squad competed against anyone who would play them—White semipro teams, regional all-star teams, and professional all-Black teams.

The key player on the team, John Donaldson (1891–1970), received top billing through 1918 and would spend many years barnstorming through Minnesota. Known as a power pitcher, Donaldson was lauded as "the "greatest colored pitcher" of the decade.[11] Newspapers printed a quotation from New York Giants manager John McGraw: "If I could change the color of his skin I would give twenty thousand dollars for Donaldson and pennants would come easy."[12] When Donaldson fanned 29 batters in a 16-inning game, the *St. Paul Pioneer Press* judged the contest to have been "one of the best games ever played in the state."[13]

José Mendéz (1887–1928), dubbed Cuba's "Black Diamond," was the team's second top star. He beat the Philadelphia Athletics in 1910, struck out Ty Cobb on three swinging strikes, and was labeled the "Black Mathewson" after subduing Christy Mathewson and the New York Giants in 1911 by throwing four innings of scoreless relief.[14]

Donaldson, Mendéz, and the All Nations brought interracial baseball to a host of Minnesota's cities, from International Falls in the north to Sleepy Eye and Blue Earth in the south. What began as a novelty ballclub quickly became a great team, and by 1916, the All Nations vied for supremacy among the best professional teams in America outside of major and minor league ball.[15]

In 1920, Rube Foster, supported by others, organized the eight-team Negro National League. John Donaldson, who had pitched so many times in Minnesota, rejoined José Mendéz as a ballplayer on Wilkinson's new Kansas City Monarchs team.

Minnesota had several all-Black teams in the 1920s, including the Askin and Marine Colored Red Sox and the Uptown Sanitary ballclub, but the state was not awarded a Negro League franchise. Racial attitudes seemed to harden in the Twenties as southern Blacks migrated north, Minnesotans began to fear Reds and foreigners, and the Ku Klux Klan stirred up hate in the "Jazz Age." Donaldson again toured Minnesota in 1922–1923 because K.C. Monarchs owner Wilkinson needed barnstorming cash to prop up his franchise.

In the mid-1920s, as Rube Foster's mental health deteriorated and disharmony between the Eastern Colored League and the Negro National League brought turmoil to Black baseball, John Donaldson jumped from the Monarchs back to Minnesota. By this time he had pitched almost everywhere in the nation, including a number of occasions on the national stage. He had battled Rube Foster's Chicago American Giants in 1916, and in 1918, Donaldson went head-to-head against the great Smokey Joe Williams of the New York Lincoln Giants.[16]

No longer a young man, John Donaldson accepted an offer to play semiprofessional ball in Minnesota for the 1924 season, when he was 32 years old. He joined the Bertha Fishermen, a ballclub based in the small central Minnesota town of Bertha. Money was the chief reason—he was offered $325 per month, more than Negro Leaguers were making at the time. What's more, Donaldson's wife, Eleanor, was from the Twin Cities, and the couple could visit family members easily.[17] In any case, when Donaldson led the squad to the Minnesota State Semiprofessional Championship in his first season, he brought instant statewide recognition to his new club.

Nineteen-twenty-seven was a momentous year. The major league season was spectacular: Babe Ruth, the mag-

(Author's Collection)

World's All Nations, 1912, barnstorming club sponsored by the Hopkins Brothers sporting goods company of Des Moines, Iowa. John Donaldson, pitcher (front, third from right), was known as "The World's Greatest Colored Pitcher" throughout his 30-plus years on the mound. After his playing career Donaldson was hired as the first Black scout in the major leagues.

(Courtesy Minneapolis Public Library/Author's Collection)

Bobby Marshall (second row, left) integrated the 1900 Minneapolis Central High School baseball team and then broke the color line on the University of Minnesota nine. Marshall (1880–1958) played first base for the St. Paul Colored Gophers and other teams, and the multi-sport star became the first Black player in the National Football League (1920).

nificent slugging Bambino, set a home-run record with 60 circuit clouts. The New York Yankees, led by their "Murderer's Row" of superstars— Earle Combs, Mark Koenig, Babe Ruth, Lou Gehrig, Bob Meusel, and Tony Lazzeri—earned recognition as one of the greatest first six hitters in a lineup of all time.[18]

It was also the year that a Minnesotan, Charles Lindbergh Jr., made world headlines when he successfully crossed the Atlantic in a solo flight. Lindbergh's hometown was Little Falls, a thriving community located along the Mississippi River, smack-dab in the central part of Minnesota, Accordingly, Little Falls gave its favorite son a true hero's welcome-home event on August 25, 1927. The Lindbergh Homecoming Committee arranged for a morning parade, a noon baseball game between the House of David barnstorming ballclub and Bertha, an afternoon motorcade, and an evening banquet.[19] Lindbergh was scheduled to arrive at 2:00 that afternoon, so the parade and baseball game were warm-up activities for the estimated crowd of fifty-thousand adoring Lindbergh fans.

The House of David ballclub amazed spectators with its dazzling skills. The bewhiskered ballplayers of this spiritual sect from Benton Harbor, Michigan, never knew a razor or scissors for beard or hair, but they knew baseball, having practiced their skills religiously. They had been touring the countryside since the 1910s and had a dominant reputation, although none of the men were Goliaths or Samsons in power.[20]

The Bertha Fishermen ballclub featured a Black battery of pitcher John Donaldson and catcher Sylvester "Hooks" Foreman. Foreman had been a mainstay with the Kansas City Monarchs and had a long-standing connection with

Donaldson. The pitcher had faced the House of David previously, and his Bertha team had beaten the longhaired team by a score of 2–0.

Game day featured the morning parade through the streets of Little Falls, with bands playing, kids smiling, and dignitaries waving. Six thousand fans packed the grandstands and bleachers, while thousands more watched from behind wire fencing that surrounded the ballpark.[21]

At high noon the mayor of Little Falls, Austin Grimes, threw out the ceremonial first pitch and then handed the ball to Donaldson. The pitcher proceeded to throw two shutout innings, allowing no hits, and then switched to center field because he had thrown too many innings in his previous start.

Wisely, the management of Bertha's ballclub had arranged for the mysterious Lefty Wilson as a "ringer" to lend assistance to Donaldson. The two knew each other well, having been opponents in Negro League games several years earlier.

Lefty Wilson was not his real name. He was a fugitive from justice, hiding in the hinterlands of Minnesota's semipro ball and his real name was Dave Brown. Under his real name he had become famous as one of the best left-handed pitchers in the Negro League and a key player on Rube Foster's Chicago American Giants from 1920 to 1922.

In 1923 Brown jumped ship, signing with the New York Lincoln Giants of the upstart Eastern Colored League. On May 1, 1925, Brown won a ballgame in New York, allowing just one run. After the game, however, policemen came to arrest Brown and two of his teammates for their involvement in a street brawl outside a nightclub in which one of the brawlers ended up dead. Brown fled from the ballpark that night and escaped from the city and a national manhunt.[22]

(Author's Collection)

The EACO Flour team in Waseca, Minnesota, brought the first Black pitchers to the area in 1900 and won the state semipro championship.

The authorities never found Brown. He had seemingly disappeared, slipping away into the deepest rural areas of southwestern Minnesota. There, amidst cornfields and cow pastures, Brown became "Lefty" Wilson, performing in ignominy in towns like Pipestone and Ivanhoe and Wanda. Donaldson, no doubt, assisted Bertha in securing Wilson from the Wanda team to pitch in the Lindbergh homecoming game.

In the game itself Wilson allowed only two hits to the House of David barnstormers, combining with Donaldson in a 1–0 shutout. Donaldson scored the game's only run.[23]

As for Charles Lindbergh, he basked in the adulation of his fellow Minnesotans. The aviation hero landed the "Spirit of St. Louis" monoplane outside of town at about 2 p.m., and the townspeople paraded him through his old hometown.

Aviator Lindbergh had arrived after the ballgame had ended, and this perfectly symbolized a segregated America. Donaldson and Lefty Wilson were on the wrong side of the color line, toiling on the mound in relative obscurity. The international hero never saw them, and they likely caught little more than a glimpse of Lindbergh from afar. While the White Lindbergh was naturally feted for his historic flight, he clearly had opportunities unavailable to Black Americans. For Black men like Donaldson and Lefty Wilson, they could experience fame, but no matter how well they performed, their recognition would always be restricted by the limited nationwide interest in Black baseball.

After Lindbergh's celebrated homecoming, Wilson pitched in Minnesota for several more years and then moved away, falling off the map and the historical record. Donaldson continued as he always had, pitching wherever he got the largest paycheck, a growing necessity as the twenties melted into the 1930s and the Great Depression.

The Negro Leagues crumpled into disarray after 1929 as the Depression clipped spending power, and the players scattered to cities where they could hope to earn a meager living playing ball. Barnstorming baseball teams continued to traverse Minnesota and the rest of the country, earning dimes and nickels for the players. The *Chicago Defender* claimed that the Black ballplayers who played for Minnesota teams in the later 1920s and into the 1930s earned the highest pay of any African American baseball stars in the nation. Donaldson stayed in the game, gathering former Negro League players in 1932 for his own team in Fairmont, Minnesota, calling it the Donaldson's All-Stars.[24]

Minnesota finally got a Negro League team in 1942—the Minneapolis-St. Paul Gophers—although baseball historians don't even bother to call it a franchise. The league they joined, the Negro Major Baseball League of America, was a flimsy patchwork that existed merely to provide opponents for the Cincinnati Clowns, which had been denied entry into the Negro American League.

After the Second World War, in 1946, Jackie Robinson broke the minor league color line in Montreal; a year later, under the tutelage of Branch Rickey, he broke the major league color barrier. Donaldson had retired from baseball in 1943 at age 52. With the integration of the sport, Donaldson finally joined major league ball in one of few capacities then open, becoming the first Black major league scout for the Chicago White Sox.[25]

Donaldson had begun his career in Missouri in 1908 and pitched just about everywhere over the next 35 years. Despite the many stops, Donaldson had a stellar reputation in knowledgeable baseball circles. Former Negro League ballplayers selected him as their first-team left-handed pitcher in the definitive 1952 *Pittsburgh Courier* newspaper poll. Modern research over the past decade has only enhanced that reputation. Intense combing of North American newspapers, both in newly-digitized and old microfilm versions, has shown that John Donaldson earned 413 wins in his career, the most by any left-handed pitcher in Black baseball history. Documented strikeout totals for Donaldson are equally impressive as he accumulated 5,091 in his lifetime—again, the most strikeouts for an African American left-handed pitcher in all of baseball history.[26] We consider John Donaldson the best left-handed barnstorming pitcher in Black baseball history.

It might be argued that the Black ballplayers from 1887 to 1947 sought to rectify social injustice by developing their individual talent, so that they would be a credit to the "Negro race." This was the accomplishment of the "talented tenth" of Black Americans, as called forth by early civil rights leader W.E.B. DuBois—to rise and pull others up with them "to their vantage ground." While the talent level was wildly uneven and the organization often chaotic, there can be little doubt that blackball hosted some of the finest individuals to ever play baseball.[27]

In 2006, Major League Baseball sought to correct some of the errors of the past when a select list of Negro League and pre-Negro League players, managers, and owners gained posthumous entry into the National Baseball Hall of Fame. Included in this group were two who had barnstormed through Minnesota: J.L. Wilkinson, the White owner of the All Nations (1912–1918) and the Kansas City Monarchs, who guided the Monarchs to become among the most successful franchises in Black baseball history, and José Mendéz, whose early career in Cuba and his accomplishments with the Monarchs, including leading the team to three consecutive Negro League pennants (1923–25) as player-manager, gave him a reputation as a premier Black pitcher of his generation.[28] Regrettably, John Donaldson was bypassed despite the support of non-voting Fay Vincent, the former baseball commissioner and chairman of the special election committee, who believed Donaldson would make the final list. Vincent had become well-versed regarding Donaldson's reputation and statistics.[29]

The contributions of Black ballplayers in Minnesota are better known now because SABR researchers have worked together to document and preserve the history of Black baseball in the state since the 1970s. What is significant about this story is that Black baseball players in Minnesota, such as John Donaldson, José Mendéz, Bobby Marshall, and Walter Ball, as a microcosm of baseball in America, played the national game in order to integrate baseball, and they succeeded, ultimately, in breaking the color line—one diamond at a time, team by team, town by town.

Notes

1 "Worlds of Color," *Foreign Affairs* 20, (April, 1925): 423, in Herbert Aptheker, *Writings by W.E.B. DuBois in Periodicals Edited by Others* (Millwood, NY: Kraus-Thomson Organization Limited, 1982), Vol. 2, 1910–1934, 241.

2 The color line was not fully entrenched in minor league baseball until 1895.

3 Sinclair Lewis, *The Minnesota Stories of Sinclair Lewis* (St. Paul: Borealis Books, 2005), 15.

4 "150 Years of Human Rights in Minnesota," Minnesota Department of Human Rights, http://www.humanrights.state.mn.us/education/video/sesq.html, accessed on August 26, 2011.

5 *St. Paul Pioneer Press*, August 12, 1897, 7; Jim Karn, "Drawing the Color Line on Walter Ball, 1890–1908," in *Swinging for the Fences: Black Baseball in Minnesota* (St. Paul: Minnesota Historical Society Press, 2005), 34–36.

6 Jim Karn, "Drawing the Color Line on Walter Ball, 1890–1908," in *Swinging for the Fences: Black Baseball in Minnesota* (St. Paul: Minnesota Historical Society Press, 2005), 44–45.

7 Todd Peterson, *Early Black Baseball In Minnesota* (Jefferson, NC: McFarland & Company, 2010), 10–13.

8 "Opening of the Baseball Season," *Minneapolis Tribune*, April 7, 1900, 9; "Baseball at Varsity," *Minneapolis Tribune*, April 3, 1904, 30; Steven R. Hoffbeck, "Bobby Marshall: Pioneering African-American Athlete," *Minnesota History* (Winter 2004–2005), 159, 163.

9 Steven R. Hoffbeck, "Bobby Marshall, the Legendary First Baseman," in *Swinging for the Fences: Black Baseball in Minnesota* (St. Paul: Minnesota Historical Society Press, 2005), 62–73.

10 Advertisement for All Nations in *Blue Earth [MN] Post*, September 2, 1913, 4.

11 Advertisement in *LeMars* [IA] *Globe Post*, May 22, 1913, n.p.; ad in *Rock County* [Luverne, MN] *Herald*, May 23, 1913, 11, col. 4.

12 "Marshall After Championship," *Marshall News Messenger*, August 1, 1913, 1.

13 "Play a 16-Inning Game," *St. Paul Pioneer Press*, August 25, 1913, 7.

14 "Cuban Nine Defeats Athletics," *New York Times*, December 14, 1910, 14; "Joy In Cuba When Cobb Strikes Out," *New York Times*, December 18, 1910, C6; "Bliss in Cuba," *Washington Post*, December 23, 1910, 11.

15 *Minneapolis Tribune*, July 29, 1914, p. 12; *Blue Earth Post*, September 2, 1913, 4; *Sleepy Eye Herald Dispatch*, August 8, 1913, 4.

16 "All Nations Tackle the American Giants," *Chicago Defender*, September 23, 1916, 25: "World's Champions Break Even, *Chicago Defender*, October 7, 1916, 7; "Donaldson Again Bows," *Chicago Defender*, July 13, 1918, 9.

17 Peter Gorton, "John Donaldson, a Great Mound Artist," in *Swinging for the Fences: Black Baseball in Minnesota*, 2005.

18 "New York Yankees," BaseballLibrary.com, http://www.baseballlibrary.com/teams/team.php?team=new_york_yankees, accessed on August 25, 2011.

19 "Colonel Lindbergh Home Thursday," *Little Falls Herald*, August 19, 1927, 1.

20 "Bertha To Play House of David Team This Noon," *Little Falls Daily Transcript*, August 25, 1927, 5; "Ball Team Keeps Beard Monopoly," *New York Times*, May 24, 1934, 25.

21 "Bertha Wins, 1–0, From House of David Team," *Little Falls Daily Transcript*, August 26, 1927, 5.

22 "Local Baseball Players Alleged to be Mixed in Shooting of Benj. Adair," *New York Age*, May 2, 1925, 1.

23 "Bertha Wins, 1–0, From House of David Team," *Little Falls Daily Transcript*, August 26, 1927, 5.

24 Highest pay extrapolated from "Webster McDonald Will Quit Baseball In 1936," *Chicago Defender*, April 20, 1935, p. 17; from 1928 to 1932, McDonald was "the highest paid Race player in the country" when he played for the Little Falls, MN, White team.

25 "Chi Sox Sign Donaldson As Talent Scout," *Chicago Defender*, July 9, 1949, 16; "Majors In New Search For Negro Ball Players," *Chicago Defender*, July 9, 1949, 1.

26 John Donaldson statistics from http://johndonaldson.bravehost.com, accessed on October, 2020; Spahn and Johnson stats, Baseball Library.com, and BaseballReference.com.

27 Tim Marchman, "Squeeze Play," *Wall Street Journal*, March 11, 2011, A13; W.E.B. Du Bois, "The Talented Tenth," from *The Negro Problem: A Series of Articles by Representative Negroes of To-day* (New York, 1903), http://www.yale.edu/glc/archive/1148.htm, accessed on August 30, 2011.

28 "J. Leslie Wilkinson," Hall of Fame plaque, National Baseball Hall of Fame, http://www.mlb.com/mlb/photogallery/hof_2006/year_2006/month_07/day_27/c..., accessed on August 25, 2006; "José Mendéz," Hall of Fame plaque, http://baseball-hall.org/hof/Mendéz-José, accessed on August 29, 2011.

29 Murray Chass, "A Special Election for Rediscovered Players," *New York Times*, February 26, 2006, 8, 12.

HOTHEAD: HOW THE OSCAR CHARLESTON MYTH BEGAN

Jeremy Beer

This article was published in the Baseball Research Journal, *Spring 2017.*

April 11, 2015, marked the centenary of Oscar Charleston's debut in American professional Black baseball. The event passed without fanfare. Even though Charleston was inducted into the Hall of Fame in 1976, many of today's devoted baseball fans do not recognize his name, and when Charleston is thought of at all, it is often as a talented but temperamental hothead. There are many reasons for Charleston's neglect, including his early death and lack of descendants. One of the unfortunate consequences of this neglect has been the persistence of a false image of Charleston as a dangerous loose cannon, bordering on psychopathic. Charleston began to gain this reputation because of an event that occurred at the end of his rookie season. The story of how that happened is usually highly condensed and often mangled. It deserves to be told in full.

Ranked in 2001 by Bill James as the fourth-greatest player of all time, Charleston may have been the most respected man in Black baseball in the years before Jackie Robinson signed with the Brooklyn Dodgers.[1] As James pointed out, Charleston is "regarded by many knowledgeable people as the greatest baseball player who ever lived."[2] One of those people was a longtime Cardinals scout named Bennie Borgmann. Soon after former Negro Leagues catcher Quincy Trouppe started scouting for the Cardinals in 1953, Borgmann told him, "Quincy, in my opinion, the greatest ball player I've ever seen was Oscar Charleston. When I say this, I'm not overlooking Ruth, Cobb, Gehrig, and all of them."[3]

Buck O'Neil claimed that Charleston was even better than Willie Mays, whom O'Neil regarded as the greatest major leaguer he had ever seen. O'Neil described Oscar as "like Ty Cobb, Babe Ruth, and Tris Speaker rolled into one."[4] In a poll of 24 Negro League historians conducted around the turn of the millennium, Charleston received more votes for greatest player in Negro Leagues history than anyone else.[5] While the data are incomplete, Gary Ashwill's sabermetrically-oriented Seamheads.com currently estimates that Charleston compiled more Win Shares than any other player in Black baseball history.[6] Charleston even played a role in the game's integration. He was one of the first Black scouts for a major league team when Branch Rickey began using him to evaluate Negro League players for the Dodgers. The Dodgers only signed future Hall of Fame catcher Roy Campanella because of Charleston's advice.[7] In the face of this, Charleston's obscurity seems highly unjustified.

Mark Ribowsky, among others, has given us the image of Charleston as a barely human berserker. "With his scowl and brawling tendencies, Charleston was a baleful man, and he enjoyed watching people gulp when he got mad," wrote Ribowsky in his not entirely reliable history of the Negro Leagues.[8] Charleston was an "autocrat," he claimed, a man with a "thuggish reputation" who was "barbaric on the basepaths."[9] He was "a great big snarling bear of a man with glaring eyes and a temper that periodically drove him beyond the edge of sanity." Oscar may have "compiled a long record of achievement on the field," but he also had "a police record almost as long."[10]

Those who have dug into the sources know that such a portrait is wildly distorted. No contemporary sportswriter or anyone who knew Charleston personally ever called him a thug, and Charleston emphatically did not have a substantial police record. While he was happy to join fights in progress, he infrequently started them. And although as a young man, especially, he had a quick temper, he was not, to use Ribowsky's adjective, "barbaric."

Then, too, context matters. In both Black baseball and the majors, violence was vastly more common during the first decades of the twentieth century than it is today. Ballplayers almost routinely got into fights with opposing ballplayers, with their own teammates, with coaches and managers, with umpires, and with fans. As Charles Leerhsen demonstrates at length in his new, judicious biography of Ty Cobb, it was a time in which fighting and violence were integral to the game—and, arguably, American society as a whole. "The drama critic George Jean Nathan, an avid baseball fan, counted 355 physical assaults on umpires by players and fans during the 1909 season alone."[11]

Oscar Charleston, in fact, was characteristically self-disciplined and reasonably good-humored, not to mention significantly more intellectual than most of his ballplayer peers, Black or White. Numerous extant photos show him smiling. Accounts do not dispute that Charleston was exceptionally tough, and we know he had a passion for boxing.[12] But John Schulian, who spoke to a number of ex-teammates and relations for his splendid *Sports Illustrated* essay on Charleston, told me that "you get the feeling...that here is this rough ballplayer who would fight anybody, crash into anything, take out fielders, but was a real puppy dog."[13] Rodney Redman, whose father knew Charleston well, and who himself was close to Charleston's brother Shedrick, said that he never heard anything negative about Oscar: "My father only said good things about him." Mamie Johnson, who played for Oscar on the 1954 Indianapolis Clowns, said, "What I would say is that he was a beautiful person." Did she enjoy playing for him? "Oh yes, he was great." James Robinson, who played for Oscar on the 1952 Philadelphia Stars, remembers him as "mild" and "friendly." Clifford Layton, another member of the 1954 Clowns, recalls Charleston as "a very intelligent man" whose "personality was beautiful."[14]

In short, Charleston was certainly not a dark-souled, frightful hooligan. So how has this image taken hold?

EARLY LIFE AND ARMY BASEBALL OVERSEAS

Oscar McKinley Charleston was born in Indianapolis on October 14, 1896. Tom and Mary Charleston, along with three sons, had likely arrived earlier that year, migrating to Indiana by way of Nashville.[15] The Charlestons moved frequently—living in at least 10 different homes while Oscar was a child, mostly on the north side of the vibrant, African American Indiana Avenue neighborhood—and they were a

(National Baseball Hall of Fame and Library, Cooperstown, NY)

Charleston is shown here in the uniform of the Santa Clara Leopardos, circa 1923. The 1923-24 Leopardos, for whom Charleston played, were considered the best Cuban team in history—a team so dominant that halfway through the season the league simply declared them champions and then reorganized.

spirited lot.[16] Mary was once hauled into court for greeting a deputy with an ax. Brothers Roy, Berl, and Casper each had multiple run-ins with the law.[17] Roy eventually channeled his thymos well enough to become a locally prominent boxer.[18]

Oscar finished the eighth grade at Indianapolis Public School No. 23, but he did not attend high school, where he would have been prohibited from playing on school athletic teams in any case.[19] After finishing school, he likely went to work to supplement the family income. He also reputedly spent time as a batboy for the ABCs, whose home park was located within just a few blocks of the peripatetic Charlestons' Indiana Avenue homes.[20]

Alas, you can't be a batboy forever, and the work then available to a Black teenager in Indianapolis could not have been particularly rewarding. The United States military offered an attractive alternative. So in early 1912, fewer than two years after he had completed his eighth-grade year, Oscar Charleston decided to join the Army. Giving his birthday as October 14, 1893 (rather than 1896), he enlisted on March 7, 1912. Oscar was accepted and assigned to the 24th Infantry, Company B. On April 5, he shipped out for the Philippines.

During his three years of service in the Philippines, Charleston's prowess on the diamond made him a star. There were "few more popular baseball players in the islands than Charleston," claimed the *Manila Times*, and "everybody knows that he is the boy to make good in any position."[21] The position at which Charleston made good was not center field, where he would later excel, but pitcher. In July 1914, after the completion of the 1913–14 professional Manila League season in which Charleston's all-Black 24th Infantry regiment had fielded a team, he was chosen by Manila's *Cablenews-American* newspaper to be its starter in an exhibition game against the rival *Manila Times*. Just seventeen at the time, Charleston hurled a one-hit shutout for this integrated all-star team, striking out 10 and walking two. He also hit a triple.[22] (The catcher for the *Manila Times* club that day was Charles Wilber Rogan, later known as "Bullet" or "Bullet Joe," and possibly the greatest two-way player of all-time.[23] Rogan was Charleston's usual receiver on the 24th's regimental squad, which obviously had a heck of a battery.)

We get a glimpse into this period of Charleston's life from a letter he saved in his personal scrapbook. Dated August 1, 1914, the letter was written by an acquaintance stationed at the headquarters of the Philippine Constabulary in Manila. The all-star game in Manila had prevented Charleston from keeping an appointment with the writer, who excuses him for his absence. After all, "All of us and 90% of the fans around Manila, believe that in addition to being the best pitcher in the Philippine Islands, you are also all around, the best ball player in this neck of the woods." The writer signs off by assuring Oscar that "Captain Loving and Mr. Waller join me in wishing you success in all your undertakings."[24]

Among other things, this letter indicates that at a young age Oscar was already taking delight in, and had a talent for attracting, thoughtful companions. The Captain Loving mentioned in this letter was Walter Howard Loving, leader of the constabulary band, which he had led at William Howard Taft's inaugural presidential parade in Washington, DC. In 1914, Loving was in the midst of a long and distinguished military career that would include serving as an undercover agent for the US government during World War I. Few Black Americans in the Philippines would have been more prominent than Loving. To have established a friendly acquaintance with him as a 17-year-old private must have been quite a thrill.[25]

Charleston's scrapbook and photo album make clear that throughout his life he maintained an interest in music and ideas, and that he tended to seek relationships with others who shared these interests and who were striving to rise socially. This very much includes his two wives, Hazel Grubbs and Jane Blalock Howard, who were highly intelligent and came from respectable, ambitious, pillars-of-the-community sorts of families. A rounded view of Charleston's life indicates, in other words, that he would have hated being regarded as a thug—a fact which makes his early troubles controlling his temper all the more poignant. Not until late in his life was Charleston able to consistently overcome this family legacy.[26]

BEGINNING WITH THE ABCS

After his discharge from the Army in March 1915, Charleston headed home to Indianapolis, where he presented himself to Indianapolis ABCs manager C.I. Taylor. (Taylor's full name was Charles Isham, but he was universally known by his initials.) Taylor had purchased a half interest in the ABCs in 1914 from Thomas Bowser, a White bail bondsman who had bought the team from Ran Butler in 1912. In the last years of Butler's ownership, the ABCs' talent and fan support had declined. The late Butler years saw the team playing mainly at home, presumably to save money, and using gimmicks like a 793-pound umpire known as Baby Jim to lure folks to games.[27] It took just one year for Taylor to begin to change the ABCs' fortunes dramatically.

Rube Foster is more commonly named as early Black baseball's most important institutional pioneer, but C.I. Taylor was nearly as formidable as Rube—and significantly less given to chest-thumping egotism than his rival. Like the rotund Foster, the thin C.I. was a southern minister's son. He was also an Army veteran and a graduate of Clark College in Atlanta. Aside from his consuming commitment to baseball, this background played out in predictable ways: C.I. believed in self-help, discipline, practice, conditioning, and strategy—"scientific" baseball, as it was called at the time. He detested rowdiness, drunkenness, and gambling, and surrounded himself with intelligent, well-mannered men. At least two of his players published poetry, many were recruited from Black colleges, and a number went on to successful managerial careers. C.I. was civically active, too, the sort of man who served on YMCA fundraising committees. His managerial efforts led to increased community support for the ABCs, more stadium improvements, and—gradually, haltingly—a more female- and family-friendly game environment.[28]

Of course, winning was also high on the list of things three of his brothers—Ben, Candy Jim, and Steel Arm Johnny, all of them college men like C.I.—were exceptional ballplayers themselves. They didn't always play for C.I.'s teams, but when they did, they were a tremendous help. When C.I. came to Indianapolis from West Baden, Indiana, where he had been leading a team called the West Baden Sprudels, he brought Ben, a first baseman, with him. From the Sprudels he also brought to Indy pitcher William "Dizzy" Dismukes (later to become Buck O'Neil's beloved mentor), outfielder George Shively (a resident of Bloomington, Indiana), and light-hitting shortstop Morty "Specs" Clark.

Thanks to C.I., by early in the 1915 season the ABCs had accumulated a good deal of talent. Taylor, Shively, Clark, third baseman Todd Allen, and catcher Russell Powell formed the position-player core. The starting pitching rotation was anchored by Dismukes and Louis "Dicta" Johnson, an accomplished spitballer (at the time a perfectly legal, if unhygienic, pitch). Former Sprudel second baseman Elwood "Bingo" DeMoss—according to Bill James, the best bunter in Negro League history—came on board in early May.[29]

Shortly after Oscar got back to Indianapolis in spring 1915, he presented himself to C.I. Taylor for a tryout.[30] Taylor knew he had something special on his hands. By April 9, he was telling the local papers that he had signed a "crack southpaw."[31] Two days later, at Northwestern Park, a couple of blocks from where his family now lived, Oscar's stateside career in professional Black baseball began.[32] Taking the mound against the semipro Indianapolis Reserves, he notched a shutout, giving up two hits in the first inning, but only one more the rest of the game. He also struck out nine, walked none, and pitched six perfect innings.[33]

Oscar's start seemed to augur a future as a mound ace, but the second game Charleston pitched in 1915 for this talented ABCs team complicated things. Against a team of White minor-league players calling themselves the All-Leaguers, he gave up six runs in the ABCs' loss. He also homered to right and was robbed of another hit when the left fielder snared a line drive. The 18-year-old Oscar's home run was "one of the longest drives seen at the local park" and the longest ever to right field, claimed the *Indianapolis Freeman*. Charleston had not been back in the States for a month, but he was already being hailed as "one of the most promising young pitchers seen at Northwestern Park. He pitches like a veteran, besides fielding his position and batting in great fashion. The fans should watch this youngster, he will be one of the best."[34]

The following Sunday, Taylor had Oscar in center field for a rematch with the All-Leaguers. The ABCs had been left with a hole in the outfield when Jimmie Lyons jumped to the St. Louis Giants, so to the outfield Oscar went.[35] He homered yet again in the ABCs' 14–3 victory.[36] Charleston's bat was far too valuable not to be in the lineup every day. Oscar would start on the mound four days later, but for the rest of the season he would serve only occasionally as a starting pitcher. No one complained. Oscar's fielding, baserunning, and his power, in that order, stood out much more than his pitching.

By June, when the *Indianapolis Freeman* ran photos of the speedy ABCs outfield of George Shively, Charleston, and midseason addition Jim Jeffries, the paper was claiming that "[t]his trio of outer gardeners looks to be the best in the game."[37] In the Black game, at least, that was probably not an exaggeration. Even when Charleston screwed up—as he did on June 24, when he misplayed an easy fly to center against the Chicago American Giants, allowing the winning run to score in the five-game series' rubber game—he was liable to redeem himself in short order. Thus, a few days after that costly error against the Giants, when the ABCs took on the Cuban Stars before a record crowd at Northwestern Park, he made what the *Star* called "two remarkable running one-handed catches," one of which led to a double play.[38]

Against the Indianapolis Merits, one of the city's strongest White semipro teams, "Charleston made a circus catch in deep center, pulling the ball down with one hand," helping to win what was billed as the city championship for the ABCs, 14–1.[39, 40] Given the short, thin mitts then in use, in 1915 the one-handed catch was comparatively rare, and one gets the impression from contemporary newspaper accounts that Charleston was one of its first impresarios. The press frequently reported that his fielding "featured," the era's adjective of choice. Sometimes it was "sensational," and once it was so good that fans were "startled." In August, the *Freeman* praised Charleston for playing center field "for all there is in it."[41] Oscar's range was most impressive to observers, but his arm was good, too. In games against top-tier opponents, he finished second on the team to George Shively with nine outfield assists.[42]

The 1915 ABCs liked to run—that was part of scientific baseball, as taught by Taylor and practiced in the big leagues with such flair by Cobb. Against the Fort Wayne Shamrocks, for example, the team stole nine bags.[43] Charleston was not the team's most prolific base stealer, but he held his own with speedy teammates like Shively and DeMoss. In 57 games, he stole 14 bases and legged out five triples, tied for tops on the team. For a while, later in the year, Taylor batted him leadoff.

Oscar's power came and went in this rookie season, fading down the stretch as the ABCs faced better pitching and as pitchers seeing Oscar for the second and third time made adjustments. But homering in three of your first six games leaves a lasting impression, especially when they are no-doubters, and especially when you are playing in the Deadball Era. (Against top competition, the mammoth Pete Hill's six home runs was highest among elite Black professional clubs in 1915.) Oscar was the "slugging soldier," the "heavy-hitting outfielder," even though he only hit one more homer the rest of the year.[44] At this point in his career, he was only a decent hitter. Overall, he batted .258 against top opponents in 1915. His teammates Shively and Ben Taylor hit significantly better. Oscar's best series came against the talented Cuban Stars in June, when he went 7-for-19 with a home run, a double, and three stolen bases and helped the ABCs win four out of five.

Charleston may not have been the ABCs' best player—not yet—but the well-rounded quality of his game led the *Freeman* to dub him, on one occasion, the "Benny Kauff of the semi-profs." Kauff manned center field for the Brooklyn Tip-Tops of the upstart Federal League. Brash and flashy, he was well known to locals, first, because he had played center field for the Federal League's pennant-winning Indianapolis Hoosiers in 1914, and second, because prior to Dizzy Dean he was probably the greatest trash-talker in baseball history. Kauff had no problem saying things like "I'll make them all forget that a guy named Ty Cobb ever pulled on a baseball shoe," and "I'll hit so many balls into the grandstand that the management will have to put screens up in front to protect the fans and save the money that lost balls would cost." To top it off, he dressed, in the words of Damon Runyon, like "Diamond Jim Brady reduced to a baseball salary size." With respect to their games the comparison of Charleston to Kauff was not totally inapt, but, unlike Benny, Oscar did not boast in the press—and he didn't have the funds to indulge in diamond tiepins and silk underwear.[45]

On the whole, in 1915 Charleston did as well as anyone might hope for an 18-year-old rookie. But there is one indication that there may have been trouble behind the scenes. For a period of at least three games in July, Oscar did not-play for the ABCs. No reason for his absence was given in the *Star* or in the *Freeman*, but when he returned to the team Elwood Knox of the *Freeman* referred to his being "back in the fold again."[46] Perhaps he had been injured. Perhaps the and C.I. had butted heads. Perhaps Oscar was having trouble controlling that troublesome family temper.

THE INDIANAPOLIS POST-SEASON BRAWL

On September 9, 1915, the ABCs played their last game of the year against a top-tier non-White team, winning, 4–2, against the Cuban Stars. They had gone 37–25–1 against the top clubs, and they had absolutely rolled through lesser competition, including contests with White teams like the Chicago Gunthers, the Indianapolis Merits, and the unforgettably-named Terre Haute Champagne Velvets.[47]

No matter who they had faced in 1915, Dizzy Dismukes and Dicta Johnson had been fantastic at the top of the ABCs rotation, with Dismukes throwing a no-hitter against the Chicago American Giants on May 9 and matching the New York Lincoln Stars' Dick "Cannonball" Redding pitch-for-pitch in a 1–1, 15-inning tie in which both pitchers went the distance. First baseman Ben Taylor had shown himself one of the best hitters not playing in White segregated baseball, and Shively and DeMoss had also had fine seasons. The ABCs had gone 9–3 against the Chicago American Giants,

13–9 against the Cuban Stars, and 4–4–1 against the Lincoln Stars, the three teams that were their top competition—in the argot of the time, the "fastest" teams out there.[48] No one doubted that the ABCs were a very good team. This is how things stood in late September 1915, as the ABCs prepared to undertake what was becoming an annual tradition of post-season games against White all-star teams at Indianapolis's Federal Park. Since the middle of the season the ABCs had been playing their Sunday home games at this new stadium, thanks to growing crowds that their usual home field of Northwestern Park simply could not accommodate. These all-star teams—the term was used loosely—consisted largely but not exclusively of Indianapolis natives returning home after their seasons in minor league ball had ended, as well as players from the high-minors Indianapolis Indians and other city teams.

The papers loved these games. The daily *Star* promoted them heavily, breathlessly reporting who and who would not play for the all-star teams, inserting editorial asides about the relative strength and hopes of the teams, printing trash talk, playing up the racial rivalry angle, and fairly openly taking the side of the White teams as the games went on. For the brawl that occurred on October 24, the White press shoulders at least a little of the blame.

The first games were scheduled for Sunday, September 26. "The colored champs"—the ABCs, that is—"had fairly easy sailing on their trip over the state" recently, admitted the *Star*; the ABCs had beat up on teams from Kokomo, Rochester, Columbus, and other Indiana burgs. But "Sunday it is thought they will meet with stronger opposition."[49] The White all-stars would include players from various leagues in and levels of the minors. The ABCs would be tested, predicted the *Star*. "The ABCs always take delight in polishing off any league teams, but they probably will be forced to step at their best today to turn the trick."[50] Eh, not really. The team of mostly low-minors "all-stars" that showed up on September 26 was no match for Taylor's club, which won the first game, 12–1, and the second, mercifully shortened after five innings by darkness, 7–0. Collectively, Dicta Johnson and Dismukes gave up seven hits on the day. Charleston went 2-for-8 with two stolen bases. The ABCs stole 11 bags in game one alone. "Manager Taylor of the ABCs has drilled so much base-running knowledge into his

(National Baseball Hall of Fame and Library, Cooperstown, NY)

Oscar Charleston poses with his second wife, Jane Grace Blalock of Harrisburg, Pennsylvania, whom he married in November 1922. The photo was probably taken in Cuba, where Oscar played winter ball, shortly thereafter.

colored champs that it is going to take an all-powerful outfit to grab a game from them," conceded the *Star*.[51]

The White players set out to put together such a club. Frank Metz, who played first base for the American Association's Indianapolis Indians, organized a new squad to take on the ABCs the following Sunday. The Indians' Joe Willis, who had had a brief major-league career with the Cardinals, would pitch, and several other Indians and players from the Louisville Colonels would join in. "It looks like the ABCs are due for a trouncing Sunday when they battle Frank Metz's All-Stars at Federal Park," chortled the *Star*.[52] The all-star outfield was "expected to show something in the way of distance slugging," and Smiling Joe Willis's left-handed pitching would "prove quite puzzling to the colored champs." Willis even called his shot: "[T]he big fellow says he'll win if given a few runs."[53] Metz's all-star team proved much better than the previous Sunday's, but still it could not beat the ABCs, the game ending in a 3–3 tie after 12 innings. Dismukes pitched seven innings of no-hit ball in relief of Dicta Johnson, and Charleston went 3-for-5 with a stolen base. Three thousand fans saw a "spicy game" full of "swell stops and neat catches," but no winner.[54]

By now the big-league season was over, and there was no more messing around. Indianapolis native son Donie "Ownie" Bush was coming back to town, and he would lead the all-stars the following Sunday against the ABCs, just as he had the previous year, when his all-stars had gone 2–2 against Taylor's club.[55] Bush,28, couldn't hit his way out of a paper bag, but he was fast, exceptionally disciplined at the plate (he had led the American League in walks five times already), and a slick fielder at shortstop. That combination of talents was good enough to place him third in the MVP voting of 1914. With him would not be Ty Cobb, who had better things to do, but three other Tigers teammates: outfielder Bobby Veach, who had led the AL in both doubles and RBIs that year; George "Hooks" Dauss, who had won 24 games with a 2.50 ERA and was also an Indianapolis native; and George Boehler, a reliever from nearby Lawrenceburg, Indiana. Also scheduled to play was the Yankees' Paddy Baumann, yet another Indianapolis man who as a utility player had just hit .292.[56] This new all-star team was a different beast. Bush's club beat the ABCs, 5–2, on October 10. Dauss and Boehler frustrated the ABC batters with curves, striking out 12. Oscar went 0-for-4.

The ABCs were a "disappointed lot."[57] Two games remained in the series, and these were the only contests all year in which they could show to others, and to themselves, how well they stacked up against major-league, or at least near-major-league, competition. Then, too, the racially tinged needling of the White papers had to rankle. As the *Star* wrote the next week, apropos of nothing at all, "The All-Stars expect, next Sunday, to teach Tom Bowser's men their ABCs."[58] Taylor had his club practicing all week. On Thursday, Bush announced that the Brooklyn Robins' Dutch Miller would be added as the All-Stars' catcher. C.I. responded by welcoming back Jimmie Lyons as his right fielder. Unfortunately, Dismukes had decided to head to Honolulu with Rube Foster's American Giants, so Dicta Johnson would start this time for the ABCs, while for the all-stars the White Sox's Reb Russell would fill in for Hooks Dauss, whose wife had taken ill. Russell had just posted a 2.59 ERA for the Sox, so this was not necessarily a downgrade.

Four thousand, five hundred fans showed up at Federal Park on the afternoon of Sunday, October 17. They watched Dicta Johnson throw a masterful game, giving up only four hits over 11 innings. The ABCs, sporting new uniforms for the occasion, finally won, 3–2, on Ben Taylor's walk-off (the term wasn't used then) base hit that scored Shively from second. It was far from a boring game. In fact, "until the deciding run was registered in the 11th the fans were kept in an uproar by sensational plays on both sides."[59] Oscar, who had turned 19 three days earlier, went 2-for-4 with a double off the Mississippian Reb Russell, who "would no doubt draw the color line in the future," chuckled the Black *Freeman*.[60]

The rubber game was set for the next Sunday, October 24. Excitement was high, and it built even more when it was reported first that Benny Kauff himself was headed to town to play for the all-stars, and next that Cannonball Redding, "the best colored hurler in the business," would pitch for the ABCs.[61] Redding wasn't just coming to Indianapolis from New York for one game. In early October, C.I. had announced that his club would undertake a Cuban tour immediately after the season's end. The ABCs were scheduled to leave right after this final game of the season, and Redding would accompany them. Reb Russell, allegedly angry over his defeat, would take the mound again for Bush's club. The day finally arrived. The all-star team wasn't at its best. Kauff had not made it, and neither Veach (who had only played the first game) nor Miller would play. Bush, Baumann, and Russell were the team's only true big-leaguers. Perhaps that only put the ABCs more on edge. Not only were they tired from the long season, but with the all-stars not even at full strength the ABCs *had* to win this game—especially with five thousand screaming fans in the stands.

The all-stars scored first, plating one in the top of the second. In the meantime, the ABCs were having trouble solving Russell. When the fifth inning began, it was 1–0 all-stars. Donie Bush made it to first. Then he took off on Redding. ABCs catcher Russell Powell threw to second, where Bingo DeMoss was covering. The throw beat Bush, but umpire Jimmy Scanlon, who was White, signaled safe.[62] That's when all hell broke loose.

Like Tris Speaker, to whom he would later be frequently compared, Charleston played a famously shallow center field, and when Bush started for second [base] he no doubt sprinted in to back up the play. After Scanlon's safe signal, he was already close to the action when he saw DeMoss lose it. DeMoss pushed Scanlon, then swung at him. Scanlon put up his fists, and the men began to grapple. A moment later, Oscar, still running at top speed, arrived and clocked Scanlon. His punch to the umpire's left cheek left him gashed, bloodied, and lying on the ground.[63]

Umpires were not immune to the violence that was common on the field in those days. Earlier that season at Northwestern Park, an umpire had allegedly hit Chicago American Giants outfielder Pete Hill over the head with a pistol—the mere fact of pistol-packing umpires gives one some idea of the temper of that era.[64] But still, for a Black man playing in a mixed-race game to slug a White umpire who was already engaged with another Black player was to cross any number of lines, and Charleston must have known that immediately. If he didn't, the enraged fans that began to stream onto the field probably clued him in. Players from both teams also began to converge on the action at second base. The police—twelve patrolmen and six detectives—were close behind. The scene was chaotic. Just who fought whom is unclear, but it seems that most of the combat now took place between fans—it was very nearly, said the next day's *Star*, a full-fledged "race riot." The police used their billy clubs freely to break up the fighting. Several drew revolvers, but did not use them. The players themselves, from both teams, tried to restore order. Finally, the police gained control of the situation and the fans returned to the stands.

Oscar, if the *Star*'s account can be credited, had slipped away. The *Star* claimed that "he kept on running" after decking Scanlon, and if that was true it was the last time he ever ran away from a fight. He may have been genuinely scared for his life. The Indianapolis of 1915 wasn't all that friendly to Blacks in the first place, and Blacks who assaulted White representatives of authority were not exactly assured of dispassionate justice.[65] "The police had considerable trouble finding" Oscar, reported the *Star*, but eventually they located him. He and Bingo were placed under arrest and carted off to jail. The game, amazingly, then continued, Scanlon still umpiring. The ABCs, perhaps pondering whether and how they would get out of the park unscathed, managed just one hit in the game and were defeated, 5–1.

C.I. Taylor was embarrassed, dismayed, furious. Not only did he deeply wish to make baseball a more reputable activity, his entire identity was centered on being a respected member of the Indianapolis community. He knew that this ugly incident in a White ballpark would be held against all of the African American residents of the city as proof of their ineradicable savagery, especially at a time when a fresh wave of Black migrants from the South was contributing to heightened racial tensions. But he had made arrangements to take this team to Cuba, and, probably realizing that the best thing to do was to get the club out of town as quickly as possible, he went forward with his plans. His co-owner Tom Bowser bailed Oscar and Bingo out of jail, and by evening the ABCs were embarked on their journey.

When the team's train stopped in Cincinnati, Taylor wired the *Star* with a statement. He made it clear where his sympathies lay. Not with his young players—and especially not with Oscar.

> That was a very unwarranted and cowardly act on the part of our center fielder. There can be no reason given that will justify it. Umpires Geisel and Scanlon are gentlemen. I am grateful to Bush and Bauman (sic) and all the players of the All-Stars for their earnest efforts to ward off trouble and their kind words to me after the incident. The colored people of Indianapolis deplore the incident as much as I do. I want to ask that the people do not condemn the A.B.C. baseball club nor my people for the ugly and unsportsmanlike conduct of two thoughtless hotheads. I can prove by the good colored people of Indianapolis that I stand for right living and clean sport. I have worked earnestly and untiringly for the past two years in an effort to build a monument for clean manly sport there and am sorely grieved at the untimely and uncalled for occurrence at Federal Park today. Again I ask that the people do not pass unjust judgment on my club or me.[66]

It must have been an awkward trip to Florida. Bingo DeMoss had started the fight, but it was Oscar who took all of the heat. His actions had escalated things terribly, but from his point of view, he had come to a teammate's aid.[67] Was that entirely wrong? It would remain true throughout his career: Oscar didn't usually start fights, but he loved to join them. And when he came to your aid, it was with fists flying. The man was simply not a natural peacemaker.

The next day, Oscar and Bingo were formally charged with assault and battery, and their case continued until November 30. A couple of days later they and the rest of the ABCs disembarked in Havana.

LETTERS FROM CUBA

By the time he reached Cuba, Oscar had cooled off. On November 1 he sent a statement to the *Freeman*. It is the first time we hear his voice in the historical record:

> Realizing my unclean act of October 24, 1915, I wish to express my opinion. The fact is that I could not overcome my temper as oftentimes ball players can not. Therefore I must say that I can not find words in my vocabulary that will express my regret pertaining to the incident committed by me, Oscar Charleston, on October 24th.
>
> Taking into consideration the circumstances of the incident I consider it highly unwise and that is a poor benevolence. I am aware of the fact that some one has said that they presume I am actuated by mania, but my mind teaches me to judge not, for fear you may be judged.
>
> Yours respectfully,
>
> Oscar Charleston[68]

Was the "some one" who had accused Oscar of "mania" C.I.? It isn't clear. In any case, the apology was good enough for the *Freeman*, which encouraged readers to accept it. The paper emphasized that Oscar had "become exceedingly sorry."

> An apology was due from Mr. Charleston, a fact which finally dawned on him. He has done the very graceful thing in acknowledging his error, and which leaves him no less a man. The bravest are the tenderest. Considerable harm has been done because of the happening, and which a string of apologies from here to Cuba could never altogether righten. However, he has helped some, and he has set himself right individually and with his team and race.[69]

C.I., on the other hand, remained angry, even after a few days in the Caribbean. He remained eager to deflect any blame from landing on his own head. Four days after Oscar wrote his apology, Taylor sent from Cuba another statement about the whole affair in which he partially excused DeMoss but continued to take Charleston to task.

> I am very grieved over the most unfortunate and degrading affair pulled off by DeMoss and Charleston. Umpire Scanlon was wholly blameless. His decision might have been questionable, but there is not one word that can be said justifying the perpetrators of that unfortunate and untimely happening. It was an awful climax of my last year's work.
>
> I feel that I should not be censured for the conduct of these two men. Neither should our club, for I do not believe that there is any man on the club outside those two who would have committed such an ungentlemanly and unsportsmanlike act. Every member has expressed to me his deepest regrets. And, too, I believe that if DeMoss had any idea that things would have turned out as they did he would not have raised a hand to push the umpire. Remember we are not trying to shadow him for his actions. He needs no defense—he was wrong. But knowing him as I do, I am fully convinced that his conduct was worse than his heart.
>
> As far as Charleston is concerned, he really doesn't know. He is a hot-headed youth of twenty years [actually nineteen; either C.I. was mistaken or Oscar had lied about his age] and is irresponsible, who is to be pitied rather than censured.[70]

It all added up to a bad time for Oscar in Cuba, a place Black teams had been visiting in the late autumn almost every year since 1900. Following the established tradition of the "American Series," the ABCs were installed at Havana's Almendares Park, where they played twenty games against three Cuban teams—Habana, Almendares, and San Francisco—between October 30 and December 2.

In subsequent years, Oscar would perform so well in Cuba that he would become a national legend. But with the brawl still fresh and his manager criticizing him in the press, in 1915 he could not get going. He batted .191, showing no power (he had only two extra-base hits in 77 plate appearances), and was caught stealing on half of his attempts. Taylor started him on the mound once and he was hammered, giving up 10 runs, eight earned.

Certainly the competitive and proud Oscar must have been in a sour mood, which couldn't have helped advance the cause of reconciliation with C.I. On November 25, midway through the ABCs' Cuban tour, Taylor announced that he had kicked Oscar off the team. He had "persisted in disobeying club rules."[71] The expulsion didn't last long: Oscar missed exactly one game. After the ABCs played their last game on the island on December 2, finishing their tour with a record of 8–12, Charleston returned to Indianapolis with the team.[72]

THE CONSEQUENCES

Charleston and Bingo had missed their November 30 trial date, of course—costing Bowser his $1,000 bond—and were promptly rearrested upon their return to Indianapolis. Their trial took place on December 7, Scanlon testifying for the prosecution. Judge Deery dealt with them leniently. Neither would have to serve any time. Oscar was fined ten dollars plus court costs, and Bingo five dollars plus costs.[73] The legal drama was at an end, but the ramifications of the brawl were still playing out. Several days before the trial, the police used the fight as an excuse to declare that no games between Black and White teams would henceforth be allowed in the city. "It occurs to me that it is time to call a halt in baseball playing between Whites and Blacks when two teams of mixed colors cannot play a game without trouble," announced a police captain. It was a good time to make such an announcement, since Blacks could be blamed for the decision. "I have talked to several witnesses, and there is no doubt but what the two colored players incited trouble."[74] The city's decision looked like a blow to the ABCs, who had played a couple dozen games against White teams in 1915. This step backwards was exactly what C.I. Taylor had feared.

A few years later, Donie Bush, enraged by a call, punched umpire Bill Dinneen "in the stomach and jaw" in a major league game. He wasn't even ejected—not until after the inning ended, anyway, when he threw a ball at Dinneen.[75] Bush and Charleston weren't so different from each other after all, or from the other rough-edged players of the Jazz Age. Both were intense, competitive, widely respected men. It's not too surprising to learn that, sometime after the ugly incident at Federal Park, these baseball lifers began to call each other friend.[76]

Perhaps because he was Black, Charleston's temper exacted a far higher reputational cost than did Bush's. As player, manager, and scout, Oscar Charleston would go on to compile one of the finest baseball résumés of any player of any race.[77] Yet more than a century later, the capsule narrative about him remains distorted by the ugliness that marred the end of his rookie season. That is how the myth began, and one of the reasons why the full truth about Charleston remains obscured.

Notes

1 Bill James, *The New Bill James Historical Abstract*, rev. ed. (New York: Free Press, 2001), 358. James defends this ranking at some length in the pages that follow.

2 James, *The New Bill James Historical Abstract*, 189.

3 Quincy Trouppe, *Twenty Years Too Soon: Prelude to Major-League Integrated Baseball*, rev. ed. (St. Louis, MO: Missouri Historical Society Press, 1995 [1977]), 118.

4 Buck O'Neil, *I Was Right on Time: My Journey from the Negro Leagues to the Majors* (New York: Simon & Schuster, 1996), 25.

5 William F. McNeil, *Cool Papas and Double Duties: The All-Time Greats of the Negro Leagues* (Jefferson, NC: McFarland, 2001), 192.

6 See http://www.seamheads.com/NegroLgs/player.php?ID=134&tab=2. First developed by Bill James, a win share is a comprehensive measure of player value that takes into account, at least theoretically, both offense (including baserunning) and defense.

7 See Peter Golenbock, *Bums: An Oral History of the Brooklyn Dodgers* (Mineola, NY: Dover, 2010 [1984]), 114; and Joe King, "Campanella Not Antique But Modernizer," *The Sporting News*, July 18, 1951, 3. My thanks to Neil Lanctot for leading me to these sources.

8 Mark Ribowsky, *A Complete History of the Negro Leagues, 1884 to 1955* (New York, NY: Birch Lane Press, 1995), 87.

9 Ribowsky, *A Complete History of the Negro Leagues*, 277.

10 Mark Ribowsky, *The Power and the Darkness: The Life of Josh Gibson in the Shadows of the Game* (New York: Simon & Schuster, 1996), 45–46.

11 Charles Leerhsen, *Ty Cobb: A Terrible Beauty* (New York: Simon & Schuster, 2015), 331. Leerhsen documents the violence characteristic of baseball during the Cobb era in numerous other places throughout this biography.

12 Charleston's personal scrapbook and photo album attest to this judgment. The scrapbook includes numerous boxing-related clippings, including a Cuban-newspaper story about Charleston going into the ring himself in Cuba. Oscar's brother Roy was a prominent and successful fighter in Indianapolis. The Charleston scrapbook and album are kept at the Negro Leagues Baseball Museum in Kansas City, Missouri. They were acquired by historian Larry Lester from Charleston's niece Anna Bradley, who seems to

have acquired them from Oscar's sister Katherine. Lester also acquired and donated to the museum Oscar's collection of Cuban cigarette baseball cards.

13 John Schulian, telephone interview, November 7, 2015. Schulian's article on Charleston is the best piece ever written about the man. It is collected in Schulian's *Sometimes They Even Shook Your Hand: Portraits of Champions Who Walked Among Us* (Lincoln, NE: University of Nebraska Press, 2011).

14 Rodney Redman, telephone interview, December 28, 2015; Mamie Johnson, telephone interview, August 12, 2015; James Robinson, telephone interview, December 28, 2015; Clifford Layton, telephone interview, August 21, 2015.

15 The Charlestons probably arrived in Indianapolis in 1896 (1) because the first year in which they are known to have lived in Indianapolis is October 1896, when the newspapers mentioned the birth of a new son, and (2) because in contrast to later editions, the Charlestons are not listed in any Indianapolis city directory prior to 1897, which implies they moved to the city in 1896 too late to be included in that year's directory. It is possible that the 1896 (or even earlier) directories missed them, of course, but given the frequency with which they were listed thereafter, it isn't all that likely.

16 City directories make it clear that the Charlestons lived in at least ten different places before Oscar enlisted in the Army in 1912. From Oscar's birth until he was four, the Charlestons lived in the Martindale neighborhood on Indianapolis's northwest side, and after that in the Indiana Avenue neighborhood, but no one address and no one street was home for very long.

17 For the story about Oscar's mother, Mary, see *Indianapolis News*, August 24, 1901, 6, and September 3, 1901, 9. Several newspaper accounts reveal that Oscar's brothers Roy and Berl had multiple run-ins with the law. See, e.g., for Roy, *Indianapolis News*, November 7, 1900, 8, and for Berl, *Indianapolis Journal*, January 9, 1903, 8. Oscar's brother Casper is listed as a ward of the Julia E. Work Training School in the small town of Plymouth, Indiana, in the 1910 United States census. The facility, known as Brightside, served as a home and training center for, among others, juvenile delinquents and "incorrigible" children sent there by the courts.

18 See, for example, "Ash Gets Shade in Ten-Round Contest," *Indianapolis Freeman*, December 16, 1911, 7; "In the Field of Sport," *Indianapolis Freeman*, June 29, 1912, 7; "The New Crown Garden," *Indianapolis Freeman*, July 13, 1912, 5; "In the Field of Sport," *Indianapolis Freeman*, November 16, 1912, 7; and "Boxing Contest at the Indiana Theater," *Indianapolis Freeman*, November 23, 1912, 6.

19 Oscar's sister Katherine said that Oscar's highest educational level was the eighth grade in the questionnaire she filled out for the National Baseball Hall of Fame in 1976. This questionnaire is also the source of the claim that Oscar attended P.S. No. 23.

20 That Oscar served as a batboy for the ABCs was stated in many articles written about him later in life. Since he was in all likelihood the source of this information, it is probably true, though I have not been able to confirm it.

21 The article from the *Manila Times* was published in the *Indianapolis Freeman* on January 1, 1916. The *Freeman* was an African American newspaper that covered the Negro leagues closely.

22 This information comes from Geri Driscoll Strecker's bio of Joséph Coffindaffer, available at http://sabr.org/bioproj/person/c6fd7724. The *Manila Times* provided extensive coverage of the buildup to this all-star game and of the 1913–14 Manila League season as a whole.

23 This the opinion of Larry Lester; in fact, he claims that given his prowess on the mound and at the plate, Rogan is the greatest player of all time, period. See William F. McNeil, *Cool Papas and Double Duties: The All-Time Greats of the Negro Leagues* (Jefferson, NC: McFarland, 2001), 183.

24 This letter is included in Charleston's personal scrapbook, which is kept at the Negro Leagues Baseball Museum.

25 For information on Loving, see, e.g., Robert Yoder, *In Performance: Walter Howard Loving and the Philippine Constabulary Band* (Manila: National Historic Commission of the Philippines, 2013).

26 Charleston was married to Hazel Grubbs, of Indianapolis, from 1917 to 1921. Her father, William, was a highly respected school principal, and her mother, Alberta, just as highly respected a music teacher. Oscar married Jane Blalock in 1922. Her father, Martin Luther Blalock, was a prominent A.M.E. minister in Harrisburg, Pennsylvania. By the time of Oscar's death in October 1954, Oscar and Jane had been separated for a number of years.

27 Paul Debono, *The Indianapolis ABCs: History of a Premier Team in the Negro Leagues* (Jefferson, NC: McFarland & Co.), 41. Although I have pieced together what follows from primary sources, Debono's book is a valuable source of material for and helpful guide to ABCs history.

28 The portrait of Taylor here is drawn based on information taken from numerous contemporary newspaper articles, but see also Debono, *The Indianapolis ABCs*, 30–71, inter alia.

29 James, *The New Bill James Historical Abstract*, 176.

30 Dizzy Dismukes, "Dismukes Names His 9 Best Outfielders," *Pittsburgh Courier*, March 8, 1930, 14. This article is also included in Charleston's personal scrapbook.

31 "A.B.C.s and Reserves Play at Northwestern," *Indianapolis Star*, April 9, 1915, 10.

32 1812 Mill. The house—and most of the street—is gone today, as is every other of the ten or more in which Charleston lived as a youth, as far as I can tell.

33 "A.B.C.s Shut Out the Reserves by 7–0 Score," *Indianapolis Star*, April 12, 1915, 10.

34 "A.B.C.'s Lose to the All Leaguers before Large Crowd—Pitcher Charleston Looks to Be a Wonder," *Indianapolis Freeman*, April 24, 1915, 5.

35 Lyons was known, like numbers of obviously good outfielders in the Negro leagues, as the "Black Ty Cobb," a designation often wrongly implied to have been more or less exclusively used for Charleston.

36 "Colored Boys Slug Ball, Beating All-Stars, 14 to 3," *Indianapolis Star*, April 26, 1915, 8.

37 "The Fast and Hard Hitting Out Field of the A.B.C. Ball Team," *Indianapolis Freeman*, June 19, 1915, 4.

38 "Cuban Stars Defeat the A.B.C.s in Flashy Game," *Indianapolis Star*, June 28, 1915, 8.

39 "Merits Have Been Hitting Ball Hard; Play A.B.C.s Sunday," *Indianapolis Star*, June 4, 1915, 10.

40 "A.B.C.'s in Form and Merits Have No Chance," *Indianapolis Freeman*, June 12, 1915, 4.

41 "Notes of the A.B.C.'s and Lincoln Stars," *Indianapolis Freeman*, August 21, 1915, 4.42.

42 These statistics and all others, unless otherwise noted, are taken from Gary Ashwill's invaluable Seamheads.com, with data input from Larry Lester and Wayne Stivers, which provides the best currently available Negro Leagues stats (they are more reliable than those found at baseball-reference.com). Seamheads counts only games against top-flight competition. For our purposes here, that means solely games against major Black professional teams.

43 "A.B.C.s Win at Fort Wayne," *Indianapolis Star*, September 15, 1915, 8.

44 "A.B.C.'s Trim Gunthers," *Indianapolis Freeman*, July 17, 1915, 4; "Notes of the A.B.C.'s," *Indianapolis Freeman*, July 17, 1915, 4.

45 This information on Kauff is taken from David Jones's excellent SABR BioProject article on Kauff. See http://sabr.org/bioproj/person/4a224847.

46 "Notes of the A.B.C.'s," *Indianapolis Freeman*, July 17, 1915, 4.

47 By my count. For what it's worth, Taylor reported an overall 71-26-3 record going into the game on October 24 against Donie Bush's All-Stars. Since they played a few games before Oscar arrived, and I am probably missing a few games, Taylor's claim is probably not too

inflated. Champagne Velvet was the name of a pilsner made by the team's sponsor, the Terre Haute Brewing Company. The brand, allegedly quite popular in Indiana during the first half of the twentieth century, has been recently revived by Bloomington's Upland Brewing Company.

48 Seamheads gives a triple slash line of .293/.385/.437 for Ben Taylor, .298/.385/.382 for Shively, and .214/.365/.274 for DeMoss. Those lines translate to OPS+s of 172, 156, and 106, respectively. Although these are the best stats we have, keep in mind that they should be taken with a grain of salt, as box scores are sometimes incomplete or contradictory, and some are missing entirely. Charleston's OPS+ in 1915 was 125.

49 "Stars Play A.B.C.s," *Indianapolis Star*, September 21, 1915, 11.

50 "A.B.C.s and Stars Play Double-Header," *Indianapolis Star*, September 26, 1915, 21.

51 "A.B.C.s Too Fast for Minor Leaguers," *Indianapolis Star*, September 27, 1915, 9.

52 "Chance for All-Stars," *Indianapolis Star*, October 1, 1915, 13.

53 "Southpaw in Shape," *Indianapolis Star*, October 2, 1915, 13. Both quotes at the end of this paragraph come from this source.

54 "Stars and A.B.C.s in a Drawn Battle," *Indianapolis Star*, October 4, 1915, 8.

55 See Scott Simkus, "ABCs vs. Donie Bush All-Stars, 1914," published on the Agate Type website on December 5, 2006.

56 All of the statistics in this paragraph taken from Baseball-Reference.com.

57 "Work for All-Stars," *Indianapolis Star*, October 12, 1915, 13.

58 "Williford at Indiana," *Indianapolis Star*, October 13, 1915, 10.

59 "Russell Beaten in Mound Duel," *Indianapolis Star*, October 18, 1915, 10.

60 "A.B.C.'s Beat All-Stars," *Indianapolis Freeman*, October 23, 1915, 7.

61 "Crandall to Be in All-Stars' Lineup," *Indianapolis Star*, October 24, 1915, 18. The statistics at Seamheads.com show that Redding had compiled a 1.06 ERA over 119 innings in 1915. No one had such numbers at hand at the time, of course.

62 Bush claimed that DeMoss missed the tag. The *Chicago Defender*, in its game report, states squarely that "Scanlon called what should have been an out safe." October 30, 1915, 7.

63 My account of this game is taken from the following articles: "Last Game Taken by the All-Stars," *Indianapolis Star*, October 25, 1915, 14; "Race Riot Is Balked by Police," *Indianapolis Star*, October 25, 1915, 1; "All-Stars Take Last Game," *Indianapolis Freeman*, October 30, 1915, 7; "Fight Ends A.B.C. Game," *Chicago Defender*, October 30, 1915, 7.

64 "American Giants in Fierce Riot at Hoosier City," *Chicago Defender*, July 24, 1915, 7. (The title of the article was sensationalist; there had been an on-field fight, but no riot.) It is also worth noting here that in 1916, DeMoss almost touched off another riot when he punched a White umpire in the face after being called out at home in a game against the Chicago American Giants. Charleston played in that game but was no part of the trouble. Why DeMoss has escaped being portrayed as a troublemaker is unclear. Perhaps it is the friendly-sounding nickname?

65 After all, in 1915 we are not that distant from the 1920s, when an estimated 27 to 40 percent of native-born White men in Indianapolis were official members of the Ku Klux Klan. See *The Encyclopedia of Indianapolis* (Bloomington, IN: Indiana University Press, 1994), 879.

66 The text of Taylor's wire was published in "In the Field of Sport," *Indianapolis Freeman*, October 30, 1915, 7.

67 Indeed, this was the *Chicago Defender*'s view of the matter: "Charleston came to DeMoss' aid," it reported. October 30, 1915, 7.

68 "Charleston's Unclean Act—He Is Very Sorry," *Indianapolis Freeman*, November 13, 1915, 7.

69 "Mr. Charleston," *Indianapolis Freeman*, November 13, 1915, 4.

70 "Manager Taylor Regrets A.B.C. Trouble," *Chicago Defender*, November 6, 1915, 7.

71 "Charleston Dropped by the A.B.C. Club," *Indianapolis Star*, November 26, 1915, 8.

72 For statistics and information about the A.B.C.s trip to Cuba, see Seamheads.com, from which these statistics are taken, and Severo Nieto, *Early U.S. Blackball Teams in Cuba: Box Scores, Rosters and Statistics from the Files of Cuba's Foremost Baseball Researcher* (Jefferson, NC: McFarland, 2008). Note that Nieto's statistics differ slightly from those on Seamheads.

73 "Baseball Verdict Withheld," *Indianapolis Star*, December 8, 1915, 2; *Indianapolis Star*, December 9, 1915, 13.

74 "Baseball Color Line Is Drawn by Police as Result of Fight," *Indianapolis Star*, December 5, 1915, 11.

75 Leerhsen, *Ty Cobb*, 328.

76 So said Indianapolis Indians business manager Ted Sullivan in 1954: "We were all great friends—Charleston, Donie, and I...." Quoted in "The Pres Box," *Indianapolis Recorder*, June 5, 1954, 11.

77 William McNeil's veterans ranked Charleston as the best manager in the leagues' history. Charleston was named the greatest player in Negro league history in his poll of historians. See his *Cool Papas and Double Duties*, 172 and 192, respectively.

CHARLESTON NO. 1 STAR OF 1921 NEGRO LEAGUE

Dick Clark and John B. Holway

This article appeared in the Baseball Research Journal, *1985.*

Oscar Charleston was known as "the Black Ty Cobb." Both men sprayed line drives to all fields and played a savage running game on the bases. But Charleston hit with power, which Cobb did not, and on the field he ran circles around the more famous Georgian. He was considered in a class with Tris Speaker in center field.

By common agreement among Black old-timers, Charleston was the greatest all-around player in the annals of the Negro Leagues. His modern counterpart would be Willie Mays, who played with a similar panache.

In 1921, Charleston had a year that not even Cobb, the Georgia Peach, could match. Oscar hit .434 in 60 games against the top Black teams and led the Negro National League (NNL) in batting, home runs, triples, and stolen bases.

These figures are the result of hundreds of hours of research by dedicated SABR members and others who pored over miles of microfilm of both Black and White newspapers in seven cities. It is part of an ongoing project to compile the most complete statistics possible for the Negro National League for the 1920–1929 period. Future projects will seek to cover the Eastern Colored League for the same decade, then move on to the Negro League data for the 1930s and 1940s. We feel confident that we have found every box score that still exists for the year 1921, although unfortunately many were apparently not published and presumably will never be found.

As compiled by project editor Dick Clark, here are the highlights of that year:

It was the second season of the new league, which was founded in the winter of 1919-20 by Rube Foster of the Chicago American Giants, J.L. Wilkinson of the Kansas City Monarchs, and owners of other midwestern Black clubs. Foster's American Giants won the first pennant in 1920 with ease.

As the clubs took spring training for the new season, one key sale was announced. The Indianapolis ABCs (named for the American Brewing Company, which owned them) sold their star outfielder, Charleston, to the St. Louis Giants. Charleston started fast for his new club, smashing two home runs and four singles in one game against the Chicago Giants (not the American Giants).

His feat was almost matched in the same game by Giants' rookie John Beckwith, who hit a home run, triple, and two singles in five at-bats. Beckwith, a moody man but a formidable slugger, would go on to become one of the four or five top home-run hitters of Negro League history. His name would be mentioned along with those of Josh Gibson, Mule Suttles, Turkey Stearnes, and Willard Brown.

Nine days after his duel with Charleston, Beckwith arrived in Cincinnati's Redland Field for a game against the Cuban Stars. Beck smashed a drive over the left-field wall just a few feet from the large clock. It was the first ball ever hit over the new barrier. Fans showered the promising youngster with coins and dollar bills as he crossed home plate.

St. Louis hitters terrorized the league that year largely because of the strange dimensions of the club's home field, which was built beside the trolley car barn. The barn cut across left field, leaving a short fence at the foul line. The fence quickly dropped back to a deep center field. Righthanded hitters had a great time aiming at the barn. Although Charleston was a lefty, he hit to all fields, and there is no way of knowing how much the short left-field fence helped him.

Foster's American Giants moved to the head of the league again, using Rube's unusual style of bunt-and-run offense combined with the finest pitching in the league. They finished last in league batting, with only one legitimate slugger, the Cuban Cristóbal Torriente, who hit .330 that year and is usually included on most authorities' all-time all-Black team along with Charleston. Bingo DeMoss, perhaps the best Black second baseman ever; Dave Malarcher, Jimmy Lyons, and Jelly Gardner represented the Rube Foster style, getting on base any way they could, bunting, hitting, and running, and waiting for Torriente to knock them in. Lyons was a veteran of Rube's earlier Chicago Leland Giants. He had served in the U.S. Army in France in World War I, playing against Ty Cobb's brother. In July Lyons fell 25 feet down an elevator shaft, but he was back on the field four days later. The accident didn't affect his hitting; he ended up batting .388 for the year.

Besides their speed, the American Giants were first in pitching effectiveness. Tom Williams had a record of 10-5. Dave Brown, the ex-convict whom some consider the best Black lefty of all time, compiled a 10-3 record. One of his victories was a one-hitter against the hard-hitting Monarchs. (Brown would later kill a man in a barroom, fight, flee to the West, then reappear as Lefty Wilson in Southwestern Minnesota.)

Foster, one of the shrewdest men ever to direct a baseball team, gave signals from the bench with his meerschaum pipe and used his team's speed and pitching to outplay the hard-hitting clubs. Yet oddly, in spite of their reputation, the American Giants stole few bases if the box scores are to be believed. Chicago relied on speed, but apparently Foster capitalized on it by taking the extra base on batted balls.

For example, in a game against Indianapolis in June the Giants were down, 18-0, so Foster threw away all the books. He ordered his "rabbits" to lay down 11 bunts, including six squeeze plays in a row. Torriente blasted a grand slam and catcher George Dixon hit another as the Giants scored nine runs in the eighth and nine more in the ninth to gain an 18-18 tie!

League teams played six games a week Saturday through Wednesday, including Sunday and holiday doubleheaders, from May through August. Some clubs played more games than others. The Chicago Giants, the weakest club in the league, played only 38 league contests, according to our count (which differs somewhat from the officially published standings), and spent most of their time barnstorming against White semipro teams. By contrast, the Kansas City Monarchs played 77 league games.

As the July heat descended on the Midwest, the American Giants clung to a slim lead over the hard-hitting Monarchs. Kansas City was led by pitcher Bullet Joe Rogan, the little ex-soldier who had been discovered by Casey Stengel while playing on a Black infantry team in Arizona two years earlier. Little Joe was already more than 30 years old but still one of the all-time stars of blackball history. Most Monarch veterans who saw him insist he was a better pitcher than Satchel Paige, the man who succeeded him as ace of the Monarch staff. Rogan posted a 14-7 record in 1921 and completed all 20 games he started.

Rogan was also a great hitter, though his average that year was only .266. He showed his power in one game, blasting a home run, triple and double in four at-bats against the Cubans.

There was only one no-hitter that summer. It was turned in by Big Bill Gatewood of third-place St. Louis. Six years later Bill would manage the Birmingham Black Barons when a skinny rookie named Satchel Paige joined the club. Satch credited Gatewood with teaching him the "hesitation pitch," which became one of Paige's best-known trademarks.

Another St. Louis hurler that year, Bill "Plunk" Drake, always claimed that Satch had learned the "hesitation pitch" from him. Drake had a magnificent season in 1921. St. Louis finished with 40 victories, and Drake was credited with 18 of them to lead the league. That is equal to at least 30 wins in the major leagues' present 162-game schedule.

The Detroit Stars finished fourth, led by outfielder-manager Pete Hill and catcher Bruce Petway. Hill was a veteran of the great Philadelphia Giants team of 1906, which also boasted Foster, Charlie "Chief Tokahoma" Grant, who had tried to join John McGraw's Baltimore Orioles in 1902 as an Indian, and young John Henry Lloyd. The Giants challenged the winner of the 1906 Cubs-White Sox World Series to a series to determine the championship of the United States. The challenge was never accepted.

Though few persons are still living who personally saw Hill play and none who saw him in his prime, many who did see him put him on their all-time all-Black outfield alongside Charleston and Torriente. In 1921, Hill could still hit; his .373 average was one of the best in the league.

Petway was considered one of the two best Black catchers of all time by those who saw him play. In November 1910, he faced Cobb in Havana and threw Ty out on attempted steals three straight times. On the third try, Ty saw that the throw had him beat and merely turned and ran back into the dugout. Petway, usually a banjo hitter, also out-hit Ty, .412 to .369, and Cobb stomped off the field vowing never to play against Blacks again

Unfortunately, injuries to Hill and to slugging first baseman Edgar Wesley hurt the Detroiters and they failed to mount a challenge for the pennant.

The ABCs, who had sold their top player, Charleston, finished fifth, although they had a great future star in catcher Raleigh "Biz" Mackey, up from Texas. The switch-hitting Mackey hit .289 that year and his seven home runs were third highest in the league. He would develop eventually into the man considered—at least by all who didn't see Petway—as the best catcher in Black baseball annals. Later Josh Gibson outhit him, but Black vets would have put Josh in the outfield in order to have Mackey behind the plate. After Mackey moved to Philadelphia, he was often compared to Mickey Cochrane.

In 1938, Mackey took a youngster named Roy Campanella and taught him all of his secrets. Later, Charleston urged Branch Rickey to sign Campy to a Brooklyn Dodger contract. The ABC first baseman was Ben Taylor, and again a generational debate rages as to whether he or his latter-day pupil, Buck Leonard, was the finest Black first baseman of all time. Taylor's 1921 batting average, .415, was third best in the league.

On August 21, Indianapolis pitching ace Harry Kenyon hooked up in a 17-inning duel with José LeBlanc of the Cubans. Both went the distance and Kenyon won, 6-5.

The Cubans finished sixth in the league. As usual they had some fine players but were handicapped by a weak bench. Most Black clubs carried 16 men; the Cubans had only 14. Pitchers got no relief and indeed often played the outfield between starts. LeBlanc started and finished all 18 games for which records could be found and ended with a 13-7 mark. Outfielder Bernardo Baró hit .347. Several years later he teamed with Martin Dihigo and Pablo Mesa to form one of the greatest defensive outfields of all time.

In 1921, Baró played next to Ramon Herrera, who hit .218. Four years later, Herrera would be playing in the American League with the Boston Red Sox, where he batted .385 in 10 games.

Another veteran of the 1906 Giants, John Henry "Pop" Lloyd, had been installed by Foster as manager of the Columbus Buckeyes. Next to the Chicago Giants, the Buckeyes were the weakest team in the league, but Lloyd, then 35 years old, had a great season. He went four-for-four in one game against the Cubans and ended up hitting .337. He also finished third in stolen bases behind youngsters Charleston and Torriente.

The last-place Chicago Giants had only one noteworthy performer, Beckwith. The next year both the Giants and the Buckeyes dropped out of the league.

Several clubs played non-league series against the best Black clubs in the still-unorganized East, teams such as the Philadelphia Hilldales and the Bacharach Giants of Atlantic City

These exhibition games are a bonanza for historians because the only records that are available for the great stars in the East, such as shortstop Dick Lundy, third baseman Oliver Marcell, and pitcher Cannonball Dick Redding, are for games played against the Western teams. Lundy hit .484 in 17 contests. Marcelle hit .303 in 28 games and Redding had a won-lost record of 7-9.

The Eastern teams would form their own league in 1923, raiding Foster's circuit of many of its stars, including Charleston, Dave Brown, Mackey, and Lloyd.

Meanwhile, a Black minor league, the Negro Southern League, played its first season in 1921. The Montgomery Gray Sox won the pennant, led by willowy Norman "Turkey" Stearnes, who soon moved up to the Detroit Stars and became one of the great sluggers of Black history.

As the NNL season headed down the stretch early in September, the American Giants still clung to a half-game lead over the Monarchs with six games left between the two leaders. They split the six contests, and Foster's men went on to win the championship again.

Rube took his team east by private Pullman to the scene of his great exploits with the X-Giants almost 20 years earlier. Against the Hilldales and future Hall of Famer Judy Johnson, Lyons singled, stole second, third, and home. In all, the American Giants stole nine bases, Torriente slugged a homer, and Chicago won the game, 5-2. Tom Shibe, the owner of the park, shook his head. "Now Mr. Foster," he marveled, "how do you make them move so on the bases?"

Chicago lost the next three games, then played the Bacharachs and split eight decisions with them.

Meanwhile, Charleston and the St. Louis Giants were playing the Cardinals, who won the first game in Sportsman's Park, 5-4, in 11 innings. The next day Oscar hit a home run to help beat Jesse Haines, 6-2. The Cards won the last three games.

Next Charleston traveled to Indianapolis to play a White all-star squad. He went two-for-four against Brooklyn's Jess Petty, including a ninth-inning home run that tied the game as the St. Louis Giants went on to win, 8-3. In six games against White major league pitching that fall, Charleston got nine hits in 27 at-bats with two home runs to climax a great season.

A STATISTICAL LABOR OF LOVE

(Editor's note: Clark and Holway were writing in 1985. To get an idea how far the compilation of Black baseball statistics has come in the meantime, see Seamheads.com and its Negro Leagues Database, which as of January 2020 included a full report on the major Negro Leagues from 1920 to 1948, with other years' research ongoing.)

The Negro League research project is an on-going labor of love that began around 1975 and has involved many fans, both in and out of SABR (Society for American Baseball Research), who have given of their time, money, and energy.

Batting and pitching statistics occasionally were printed in the Black press, but on inspection they turned out to be suspect. As a result, the SABR Negro Leagues Committee plans to recompile the data for every season, both those with and without published stats.

Negro League research carries problems not faced by other researchers. The records are scattered among many newspapers, both Black and White. Rarely did papers name winning and losing pitchers; these have had to be supplied by researchers using their best guesstimates. Some papers ran box scores without at-bats; these had to be estimated. Others did not include extra-base hits; when possible, these data were obtained from the game accounts. Sometimes all that is available is a line score, and, of course, for some games not even this was shown. Still, enough box scores have been found to begin to build a portrait in numbers of the great men of the Black leagues.

Despite its frustrations, the project carries rewards perhaps not found in other research. This is the last frontier of baseball exploration, a virgin continent of history and heroes as rich as that of the better-known and already well-traveled land of White baseball history.

Among those who have contributed to the project are Terry Baxter, John Bourg and family, C. Baylor Butler, Dick Clark, Harry Conwell, Dick Cramer, Deborah Crawford, Paul Doherty, Garrett Finney, Troy Greene, Richard Hall, John B. Holway, John Holway Jr., Merl Kleinknecht, Jerry Malloy, Joe McGillen, Bill Plott, Susan Scheller, Mike Stahl, and Charles Zarelli.

Black "Green Cathedrals"

BLACK BASEBALL AT YANKEE STADIUM: THE HOUSE THAT RUTH BUILT AND SATCHEL FURNISHED (WITH FANS)

James Overmyer

This article appeared originally in Black Ball: A Negro Leagues Journal*, 2014.*

The long relationship between Negro League baseball and Yankee Stadium that provided the Black leagues with both income and prestige began in 1930 when a millionaire lent his prized major league ballpark to a man who ran a union dedicated to bringing other rich men to heel.

The generous millionaire was Jacob Ruppert, Jr., president of a brewery hobbled by Prohibition, but also owner of the New York Yankees, then dominating the American League as winners of six pennants and three World Series in the 1920s. The team's Yankee Stadium, only in its eighth season and seating 62,000, was a gem among the revolutionary modern steel and concrete ballparks built since the turn of the century. Despite its enormous capacity the Yankees were able to keep it full, thanks primarily to their main attraction, star slugger Babe Ruth. The Babe homered on opening day in 1923, and sportswriter Fred Lieb labeled the park "The House That Ruth Built."[1]

The recipient of Ruppert's "loan" of his fabled ballpark was the Brotherhood of Sleeping Car Porters, a five-year-old union seeking to represent the African American men who staffed the Pullman sleeping cars on the passenger trains that provided most of the intercity transportation of the day. The porters' union had no other ties to baseball—this was just one of several major entertainment-related fundraisers to provide operating cash. And Ruppert, despite this gracious offer, had no other known connections with the Brotherhood.

But the tradition of Black baseball at the Stadium begun through Ruppert's beneficence would continue for nearly 20 years, interrupted only in the depths of the Great Depression. From the Porters' games on July 5 through the end of the 1948 season, when Negro League ball began to fail, a total of 225 games with at least one Black team involved were played, showcasing the best teams and players and putting money in the pockets of both the Negro Leagues and the Yankees organization.

With construction loans from White-owned banks scarce for African American enterprises, few Negro League teams could afford to build their own parks. Instead they usually rented grounds, often from a team in White organized baseball. Some of the most successful of these arrangements were enduring. The Homestead Grays rented the Washington Senators' Griffith Stadium for 10 years until the team went of business in 1948, the Newark Eagles used the Yankees' minor league Ruppert Stadium (named after Jacob Ruppert) for 13 seasons through that same year, and the Kansas City Monarchs played in that city's American Association minor league park (first called Muehlebach Field, although it later had other names) from 1937 until 1961. And the Negro Leagues' annual star attraction, the East-West All-Star Game, was played annually at Comiskey Park in Chicago beginning in 1933.[2]

But the Negro Leagues' long-term relationship with Yankee Stadium was broader in scope. The Stadium served as a home venue not for just one Black team, but as a showcase for all of Black big-league baseball, especially the Eastern teams in the second Negro National League, which began play in 1933. Twenty-one different Negro League teams, or squads considered to have been of equivalent ability in the years when there was no Black major league on the East coast, took the field at the Stadium in addition to several formal or ad hoc Black all-star teams. It is unlikely that any organized baseball park was the site of a more varied menu of Black ball.

Jacob Ruppert was descended from German brewers and had taken over running the Jacob Ruppert Brewing Company from his father late in the nineteenth century. Under Jacob, Jr.'s control the Manhattan Brewery was making more than a million barrels of beer when the Eighteenth Amendment to the U.S. Constitution and the accompanying Volstead Act legislation went into effect in 1920. Many breweries closed but Ruppert stayed in business, making legally allowable weak beer (with only 0.5 percent alcohol content) while riding out the nation's relatively brief dry experience.

A lifelong bachelor and man about town, Ruppert had extensive real estate holdings, including an apartment in Manhattan and an estate north of the city in the town of Garrison. He was captivated by show animals and owned racehorses and prize-winning St. Bernard dogs. But his favorite extracurricular activity was his ball team. Ruppert had tried to buy a big-league club since the turn of the twentieth century, losing out on the New York Giants and turning down a chance to buy the Chicago Cubs, because "I wasn't interested in anything so far from Broadway." In 1915 he bought a half share in the Yankees, who had never won a pennant since being founded in 1903 and became sole owner before the 1923 season. Ruppert was posthumously inducted into the National Baseball Hall of Fame in 2013, joining nine other figures from the Yankees' powerful teams of the '20s. At one time the National Guard aide de camp to New York's governor, he liked to be called "colonel."[3]

A. Philip Randolph, president of the Brotherhood of Sleeping Car Porters, had a nickname, too. A devout and outspoken pacifist during World War I, someone in Woodrow Wilson's administration had called him "the most dangerous Negro in America."[4] Neither Randolph nor his union looked threatening in 1930, though. The Brotherhood had been trying for five unsuccessful years to organize the African American porters on the famous Pullman sleeping cars and would have five more years of hard work before it reached a labor agreement with the company. The firm's founder, George Pullman, had a vision in the years following the Civil War of making his cars rolling hotels, with as many amenities as possible. His concept included a staff of employees who would ride the cars along with the passengers and provide them with hotel-like service. As Pullman saw it in the mid-nineteenth century, those service employees should be Negroes.

As a day-to-day businessman Pullman kept a tight hold on his dollars. He was utterly opposed to having any of his employees unionized, and his porters were no exception. He died in 1897, but his attitudes were faithfully adhered to by his corporate successors. Efforts had been made to organize the porters, but progress, such as it was, was limited. Unionization attempts in the company's headquarters city of Chicago died out, but Pullman porters were based all over the country and a group of veterans in New York City founded the Brotherhood. They hired Randolph as their president in 1925 even though he had never been a porter, nor ridden in a Pullman sleeping car. Up to then Randolph, an erudite native of Jacksonville, Florida, had an unprepossessing record as a union organizer who was never able to get a union on its feet, a Socialist political candidate who never won an election, and the publisher of a Negro monthly, "The Messenger," that was chronically struggling to be profitable. But he thrilled 500 porters crowded into a Harlem Elks hall in August with a vision of what a strong union could do for them, and the Brotherhood became more than a dream.[5]

Now Yankee Stadium would be the site of a fundraising doubleheader for the union over the 1930 Fourth of July weekend, pitting two top-ranked Negro teams against each other. The likely explanation for this strange matchup of Colonel Ruppert and the Brotherhood involves the distinctive nature of New York City politics at the time. In addition to his business and pleasure pursuits Ruppert had served four terms in Congress (from 1898 to 1907), backed by the city's Tammany machine. New York's political hierarchy was pretty simple in those days. The Tammany Society controlled the Democratic Party from its Manhattan headquarters known as Tammany Hall, and the Democrats usually controlled the city. Tammany's leadership, increasingly dominated by immigrants, especially the Irish, won the votes of the city's newcomers by explicitly catering to their needs for work, relief in hard times, and recognition in their new home. The tradeoff was more of a bargain between the politicians and the populace than an explicit campaign of social progress (the trade was a better existence for the voters in exchange for power and the spoils that went with it for the politicians). But Tammany's outreach was inclusive among potential Democratic voters, and New York's African Americans were included, too.

Brotherhood secretary-treasurer Roy Lancaster, one of the union's founders who had hired Randolph, was a political creature who belonged to Tammany Hall's Black wing. Lancaster was a longtime porter who Pullman officials had considered the most intelligent employee representative at a 1924 conference that resulted in a wage increase. Nonetheless, the company fired him in 1925 when his unionizing efforts became too enthusiastic. Lancaster then came to be regarded during this founding period as perhaps the second most important union leader after Randolph.[6]

It is not a stretch of the imagination to picture Lancaster working his way through the Tammany hierarchy to get the colonel to partner up for July 5. In fact, he later told a fellow Brotherhood official, C. L. Dellums of California, that was just what he had done: "I remember Roy telling me his [Ruppert's] name and that he couldn't be reached. No Negro seemed to have a chance to get anything put on in that park—for free, particularly. But Roy had enough connections to get that park." It appears he got an assist from Harlem Alderman Fred B. Moore, who, although a newly re-elected Republican, wrote a note of introduction to Ruppert for Lancaster, allowing the union man to get his foot in the door. So reported the Harlem Black weekly the *New York Age*, and although Moore was its publisher and there is the possibility his paper embellished his role, there is probably truth to the claim.[7]

There was also another relationship that may have contributed to the Stadium's loan, or at least made it more possible for the Yankees to actually consider. Prior to major league baseball rule 3.17, which bans non-team personnel from dugouts during games, celebrities were regularly seen sitting on the benches and chatting with the uniformed personnel. Black sportswriter Al Monroe, listing some of these instances in 1933, claimed that Negro League star John Henry Lloyd and Babe Ruth were friends, and when Lloyd "has an off day you'll always find the big Race man seated in the Ruthian dugout."[8]

The success of the fundraiser was significantly aided by the selection of the teams. The Lincoln Giants, one of the best-known Black ball clubs in New York, were the home team and the Baltimore Black Sox the visitors. The teams had been charter members of the Eastern Colored League and then the American Negro League, the two Negro Leagues on the East Coast until they went out of business just prior to the Great Depression.

Each team had an eventual member of the National Baseball Hall of Fame at first base. Lloyd, the Babe's friend, was also field manager for the Lincolns and Jud Wilson played first for the Sox. The Giants' outfield of Fats Jenkins in left, Clint Thomas in center, and Chino Smith in right was all-star caliber. The Black Sox infield that included Dick Lundy at shortstop and Frank Warfield at second base in addition to Wilson was mostly the same. Appropriately, the teams split the doubleheader. The Lincolns pounded Sox pitching in the first game for a 13-4 win. The Giants' Smith, Lloyd, and third baseman Orville Riggins each had three hits. Smith's were two homers and a triple. Baltimore left fielder Rap Dixon ripped two home runs in the second game, driving in all but one of the Sox runs while right-hander Lamon Yokely pitched a complete game for a 5-3 win.

The Brotherhood also staged a small track meet for the fans' further diversion. Sol Furth, a New York University track star, won the 100-yard dash, but a star Black runner, Phil Edwards, also from NYU and also a medal winner for Canada in the 1928 Olympics, lost the half mile to Fred Lorz, Jr., who had been spotted a 10-yard lead as a handicap. The best-known entrant, at least to New Yorkers, had no running medals to his name. Bill "Bojangles" Robinson, the actor and tap dancer of Broadway and movie fame, given a 25-yard head start, ran the rest of a 100-yard dash backwards and beat some of the field (running forward) who had run the straight dash.[9]

The Giants and the Black Sox split before as many as 20,000 fans. The Brotherhood announced a profit of $3,500 (an amount with $48,000 in purchasing power in 2013).[10] Then the Lincolns made a mid-September appearance at the Stadium for a doubleheader against the Cuban Stars, another New York club playing, as were the Lincolns, as an independent outfit following the collapse of East Coast Negro League ball the year before. The games only drew about 3,000 fans, however.

But then, during the last week of September, a 10-game matchup between the Giants and the Homestead Grays of Pittsburgh, the "race championship" of that year, included six games at the Stadium. Since league ball had folded in the East no one could prevent any two teams from calling their competition a "championship series," though in fact these were clearly two of the strongest Black squads in the East. The Grays had won three of the four games played in Pittsburgh and Philadelphia, but the Lincoln Giants split each of the three Yankee Stadium doubleheaders on September 21, 27, and 28 to make the series competitive down to its very last innings.

The teams were so razor close in the New York games that an injury to one of the Lincolns' stars in the final contest may well have tipped the series in the Grays' favor. The Giants had won the first game of the final doubleheader on September 28, 6-2, led by ace starter Bill Holland, and were trailing by only 1-0 in the fifth inning of the nightcap when second baseman Rev Cannady and right fielder Smith collided on a short fly ball. Smith was hurt, and he was replaced in the lineup by Luther "Red" Farrell, a left-handed pitcher who played the outfield when not on the mound. Farrell was a prodigious slugger, but not a particularly adept fielder. With two out in the top of the eighth he misjudged a fly ball that Smith likely would have caught, which turned into a double. Then Homestead third baseman Judy Johnson ripped a triple between the lumbering Farrell and center-fielder Clint Thomas, and the Grays were on their way to a four-run inning and the championship.[11]

Homestead owner Cumberland Posey had equivocated for weeks about accepting the challenge of Lincoln owner James Keenan, but finally agreed to the series in early September. According to the Negro sporting press, Jacob Ruppert was impressed enough by the Lincolns' play to make the Stadium available to them again. This may have been true, but there were some more important angles to this agreement. Use of the Stadium was no longer free, for example. With no charity involved now blackball would pay the Yankees' standard rates.

The team regularly rented its park for other profit-making sporting events (college football, championship boxing, and track and field, for example), and had taken $1,000, 40 percent of the gate, for the Giants-Cubans doubleheader. The requirement to pay rent was actually a positive recognition of Black baseball's growing status in New York—it was seen by the Yankee organization as a professional endeavor that could stand with the other sports using the Stadium.[12]

Ruppert may have admired Jim Keenan's Giants, but a more likely explanation for the championship series landing at the Stadium was that Roy Lancaster was again involved on the business side. He seems to have served as "match-maker" and promoter and took away a share of the profits. Attendance ran to more than 10,000 for the first and third doubleheaders, both on Sunday, traditionally the big day for Black baseball attendance. Importantly for the future of Negro ball in the Bronx, the teams and the promoter walked away with $9,100. Posey's Grays got a little more than $3,335, Keenan's Giants took $3,964 and Lancaster was paid $1,799, although he would have incurred advertising and other promotional expenses out of that share that do not show up on the Yankee ledgers. The Yankees' share of $4,243 ($3,237 after paying for ticket printing and game day payroll expenses), was 31 percent of the gross gate. This was very good money for the Black teams and a nice "bonus" for the Yankees for use of the park while the team was on the road.[13]

Black ball at the Stadium was off to a good start for everyone. The venerable ex-player and manager Sol White, now writing on baseball for African American newspapers, opined that "now is the time for men of the race to take hold of this grand old game and push it up to where it belongs… We know of no safer investment for a few thousand dollars at this time than stock in a team of race players that can and would strut their stuff on grounds of the Yankee Stadium."[14] White was a venerated baseball man, but his advice failed to take the Depression into account. Negro baseball was about to take a calamitous nosedive. Before the 1932 season major league Black baseball had folded everywhere, not just in the East, and the pickings were as slim for Black ballplayers as for many other Americans.

The Yankee Stadium results reflected this. The Harlem Stars, a successor team to the Lincoln Giants, who had gone out of business shortly after their 1930 series against Homestead, played three doubleheaders in 1931 that drew only about 13,000 fans in all. The final date, on August 16, was another Sleeping Car Porters benefit, which flopped. Almost all the advantages the union had in its 1930 benefit vanished the next year. Internal union politics had cost

Lancaster his officer's job the previous September. Romeo Dougherty, the sports editor of the *New York Amsterdam News*, who was to replace Lancaster, reportedly became ill, and afterwards had little good to say about the less-experienced people who had stepped in for him: "In the account of expenses we found items calling for certain sums which we would not have sanctioned had the Statue of Liberty decided to give an imitation of Snakehips [Black dancer Earl Tucker, the "Human Boa Constrictor"] at the Polo grounds [sic] for our personal benefit." The planners also made a serious error in picking the day of the game—it was staged head-to-head with a New York Giants' doubleheader at the Polo Grounds, just across the East River, which drew 58,000 fans. The game at Yankee Stadium drew only 1,975 paid admissions and the final balance sheet showed the Porters had lost $187.97 on the undertaking. The losses would have been substantially greater except that the Harlem Stars, who unwisely had agreed to play for a percentage of the profits, didn't get paid, since there were no profits. The visiting team, Hilldale of Philadelphia, was paid a $500 visitors' guarantee and the Yankees made $687, one-third of the gate, as stadium rental.[15]

After that debacle there were no Black games at the Stadium until 1934. Then William "Gus" Greenlee, who led the revival of league baseball by founding the second Negro National League, which included his Pittsburgh Crawfords, began to rent the Yankees' home. Greenlee had also spearheaded the annual East-West games in Chicago. Historian Neal Lanctot says that "perhaps more than any other owner, Greenlee realized the importance of presenting Black baseball in a major league venue, transcending the usual White perception of Black baseball as semiprofessional in caliber."[16]

The return to the Stadium was on September 9 with a doubleheader that was a fundraiser for the Colonel Charles Young American Legion post in Harlem. About 25,000 fans turned out, reportedly from as far away as Pennsylvania. Unsurprisingly, Greenlee's Pittsburgh Crawfords were represented—they played the Philadelphia Stars to a 1-1 tie, called due to darkness. That game featured the Stadium debut of the best draw throughout Negro baseball's entire run there. Satchel Paige pitched for the Crawfords and dueled Slim Jones of the Stars in the nine-inning tie. Jones only gave up three hits and struck out nine men, while Paige, yielding six hits, fanned 12.

The opening game that day also had some significance. It was the Stadium debut of the Yankees' black namesake, the New York Black Yankees. A successor to the Lincoln Giants and Harlem Stars, the Black Yanks had been in existence since 1932, and were part of a tradition in which Negro League teams laid claim to the name of a strong local White professional club, amending it by inserting the word "Black" at the beginning of the name. The Birmingham Black Barons and the Atlanta Black Crackers are other examples. In this case, though, the tie between the White and Black teams was strengthened by the fact that one of the reasons for the Black Yankees deciding on this name was the team's first set of uniforms, secondhand suits originally worn by their White counterparts.[17]

The Black Yankees joined the second Negro National League in 1936 and remained a member until the league went out of business after the 1948 season. Despite the distinguished origin of the team name, they were never a very good squad. Proving that clothes don't, in fact, make the man (or team of men), in the 13 seasons they were in the NNL their White namesakes won the American League pennant eight times, while the Black Yankees never copped a flag. Nonetheless, the Black Yanks, sometimes claiming the Stadium as one of their home parks, played in 93 games there between 1934 and 1948, the most appearances of any Black team. But their .432 winning percentage was the worst of the Eastern Negro League teams that regularly played at the Stadium.

The two matchups from September 9 were repeated on the 30th, and Paige and the Crawfords topped Jones and the Stars, 3-1. Paige gave up only five hits, while Jones yielded only seven. The Black Yankees squeezed out a 3-2 win over Chicago in the second game.

From 1935 through 1938 Greenlee's Negro National League booked one or two doubleheaders a season. Three of the dates functioned as fundraisers for civic purposes that either directly involved the New York African American community (a Black Elks lodge) or institutions that significantly contributed to Blacks (the Police Athletic League and the Greater New York Fund, a predecessor to the city's current United Way charity). The games were well attended and competitive, averaging from 15,000 to 20,000 fans per date, except when Paige came to town again on September 26, 1937. Satchel, the pitching mainstay of Greenlee's Crawfords, had deserted with other stars that spring for a rich offer from the Dominican Republic's league. The departure of Paige and the others was the beginning of the end for Greenlee's team, and his Crawfords were out of business by 1938.

But Paige and his fellow defectors were still useful to Greenlee, who paid $3,000 to the Yankees to stage a game between a team of Negro National League All-Stars that included future Baseball Hall of Famers Biz Mackey and Jud Wilson and the "Santo Domingo Stars," the players who had jumped south that spring. As many as 30,000 fans attended as Paige and the Dominican stars won, 9-4, and a second game ended in a 1-1 five-inning tie called by darkness.[18]

Although Greenlee faded from the Black big-league scene, his idea of playing Negro League games in Yankee Stadium persisted. His arrangement with the Yankees had one major drawback—the Yanks charged from $2,500 to $3,000 per date. But prior to the 1939 season the Negro National League hired Philadelphia sports figure Ed Gottlieb as its booking agent for Stadium games. Gottlieb, although White, was as a part owner of the NNL's Philadelphia Stars, an insider at the league's councils. He also was one of the leading bookers of semiprofessional games on the East Coast and could walk into Yankee President Edward Barrow's office and work out a deal that reduced the Yanks' rental charge in exchange for many more playing dates. Although no written agreements between Gottlieb and the Yankee organization appear to survive, analysis of the date-by-date financial transactions from 1939 on appear to show that the Yankees changed their financially challenging flat-rate rent to 25 percent of gross revenue, with a $1,000 minimum charge.[19]

The Yankees also offered the Ruppert Memorial Trophy, named after the recently-deceased team owner, to the Negro National League team winning the most games at the Stadium each year. It was hardly a selfless gesture since the Yankee organization was profiting from the games, too. But the combination of Gottlieb's new deal and the trophy caused Black usage of the park in 1939 to leap to six dates, a total of 11 games, with an estimated total attendance of about 79,000. And use of the Stadium just kept increasing. From 1940 through 1946, the financial heyday of the Black leagues, there were a total of 145 games played on 75 different dates, drawing an estimated 984,000 fans. The World War II seasons were difficult for White professional baseball—major league attendance declined and many minor leagues suspended play for the duration of the war as young potential players were drafted or enlisted instead. But paradoxically the Negro Leagues never had it better in terms of attendance and profits, although they, too, lost many of their best players to the military. The turning of the mighty manufacturing sector in Northern cities into a defense industry drew new workers, including African Americans, from the less-industrialized South, providing a large increase to blackball's fan base.

Harlem's population had been growing even before the war. In 1940, 65 percent of New York's Black population lived in the borough of Manhattan, mostly in Harlem. The number of Blacks in Manhattan had increased by more than 30 percent between the 1930 and 1940 U.S. censuses, and the number of Black males 21 and over—the demographic group most likely to be fans, had jumped by more than 20 percent.[20] The Stadium was well located to attract the Black New York baseball fan, only four subway stops north of 125th Street, Harlem's business and entertainment center. Experience proved that the closer a Black ballgame in New York City was to Harlem, the better its chance of making money.

The New York Giants' Polo Grounds, opposite Yankee Stadium on the Manhattan side of the East River, was actually one subway stop closer. Many games were played at the Polo Grounds when Negro League ball in the city was in its heyday during World War II, (Gottlieb said the park came into use when the Stadium couldn't meet the increased demand for dates).[21] But the Negro National League usually turned to the Yankees when making up its New York schedule, certainly in part because of Gottlieb's close relationship with management there. As to the Brooklyn Dodgers' Ebbets Field, Black baseball there was tried seriously twice, by the Bacharach Giants in the early 1920s and the Brooklyn Eagles in 1935, but it never prospered due to the park's distance from the fan base in Harlem and heavy competition from nearby prime White semipro teams.

Negro League games at Yankee Stadium were mostly a showcase for the National League, the only ones, for example, competing for the Ruppert Trophy. But as the annual number of games steadily increased, from 11 (on six different dates) in 1939 to 30 (on 14 dates) in 1946, teams from the Negro American League, located in the Midwest and South, got onto the schedule when they made Eastern barnstorming swings, playing their National League counterparts in exhibition games. The first appearance of the American League was August 27, 1939, when the Negro Leagues staged a second East-West All-Star Game in New York, a money-making follow-up to the main East-West game played in Chicago on August 6. The East team, composed of NNL stars, avenged an earlier loss in Chicago with a 10-2 victory as Ed Stone of the Newark Eagles had three hits and Bill Wright of the Baltimore Elite Giants and Buck Leonard of the Homestead Grays two each. The attendance of 20,000 was the best for a Black game at Yankee Stadium that year. The two leagues again reprised the East-West game at the Stadium in 1948, the NNL's last year of existence, and the Easterners again won, 6-1.

The leagues would also occasionally use this big venue for important championship games. The Baltimore Elite Giants beat the Grays, 2-0, on September 24, 1939, to wrap up the NNL pennant playoffs, and the Negro World Series, which was usually partially played in cities other than the homes of the contenders, visited the Stadium in 1942 and 1947. Individual NAL teams began to play there in the latter part of the 1940 season when the Memphis Red Sox and St. Louis Stars showed and were regularly appearing at the Stadium by 1941. The most important Midwestern visitors were the Kansas City Monarchs. The Monarchs were one of the strongest teams in the NAL, it was true, but the real reason they were so welcome is that they brought Satchel Paige, a major drawing card all by himself, back to Yankee Stadium.

The legendary Paige made 20 starts in Yankee Stadium for Black teams. (He made one more, against the Yankees as a Cleveland Indian in 1949, after major league integration.) Crowds for those games averaged about 20,400 per date, nearly double the 11,600 average for the rest of the dates. When he pitched on May 11, 1941 (on loan from his Kansas City Monarchs to the New York Black Yankees), the Negro League game at the Stadium outdrew the New York Giants contest at the Polo Grounds across the East River by 6,000, an occurrence repeated more than once in later games that featured Paige. On August 2, 1942, a four-team doubleheader including Satchel and the Monarchs drew 30,000, more than either the Giants at the Polo Grounds or the Dodgers at Ebbets Field. A reappearance at the Stadium on August 26, 1944, produced a crowd of 28,000 that nearly tripled the attendance at a Dodgers-Giants game across the river at the Polo Grounds.

Paige was so in demand that he was able to command his own fee for showing up, separate from his team's share of the gate. For example, he received a personal fee of $500 for pitching "on loan" from the Monarchs for the Black Yankees in 1941. Not only was his very presence notable, but so was his absence. Greenlee's new program of Yankee Stadium promotions suffered a setback on September 22, 1935, when his Crawfords arrived for a doubleheader, but Satchel was not with the club. Paige was engaged in continuing salary battles with Greenlee, who was forced to explain to the New York baseball press that the pitcher had "stopped off in Chicago en route east and while there was offered $500 to pitch for the Kansas City Monarchs on Sunday. This caused him to forget all about his agreement to appear in New York."[22]

Satchel had three dominating games at the Stadium in the 1930's, (two complete-game wins and the 1-1 tie against Slim Jones in 1934), but he was in his own mid-30s by the beginning of the 1940s and rarely went a full nine innings anymore. He only threw a complete game in two of his 17 Stadium starts in the '40s, usually yielding to a reliever after five or six innings. Nonetheless, very little enemy offense blossomed when he was on the mound. He allowed less than two runs and seven hits per nine innings in the 19 starts for which statistics exist. His teams won 13 of his 20 starts (there were two ties, and only five losses). Paige himself got credit for 11 wins, against only two defeats.

But he was not the only Negro League workhorse at the Stadium. Little right-hander Dave Barnhill was the New York Cubans staff ace in the early 1940s. The Cubans, owned by Alejandro Pompez, born in Florida to well-off Cuban immigrants, were the team with most of the good dark-skinned Latin American players in the NNL. But Pompez would gladly sign United States-born talent, too, as witnessed by his recruitment of North Carolinian Barnhill in 1941. Like the Black Yankees, the Cubans claimed Yankee Stadium as one of their home parks in the New York area and played 71 games there from 1935 through 1948. From

1941 through 1943 Barnhill was the regular Cuban starter for the coveted Sunday dates at the Stadium. He made 20 starts and one relief appearance in those three years, earning 11 wins against eight losses and a save. His pitching was curtailed by injuries for the rest of the war years, but he pitched in the Stadium again in 1946 and 1948, splitting four more decisions for a career record of 12-10 in the big ballpark. Barnhill, who unlike Paige was in his physical prime during the '40s, finished 17 of his 23 starts, which included two two-hitters, two four-hitters and three five-hitters. He won five of seven starts in 1943, his last start a head-to-head matchup with Paige in which Barnhill produced a two-hit shutout with nine strikeouts for the victory.

Josh Gibson was another legendary Negro Leaguer who excelled at the Stadium. He made several appearances, the first in the championship series of 1930 and the last in August 1946. In the mythology of Black baseball Gibson is famous for something he didn't actually do—hit a fair ball out of the cavernous park. This failure puts him in good company though, since no one else ever did, either. But Josh, historically the Negro Leagues' most prolific home run hitter, crashed seven homers there. His second, on September 27, 1930, the next-to-last day of the big Grays-Lincoln Giants series, was among the longest shots there by any player. He was an 18-year-old rookie with the Grays and while he was the regular catcher he hadn't yet graduated to the position of "main man" in the Homestead batting order. He batted sixth on this day. Gibson had hit an opposite-field homer to right in the first game, which the Lincolns won, 9-8. Homestead jumped right on Giants starter Connie Rector in the first inning of the nightcap and the young catcher came up with two men on. Rector pitched, and Gibson launched a shot to left field that the *Chicago Defender* reporter pegged at 460 feet.[23] Gibson went out at the Stadium in 1946 with the same sort of flourish, bombing a 430-foot shot to center to help beat the Black Yankees, 7-0, in the May 26 game, and doubling in a run in his last appearance there August 30. Josh, who could still hit for power although his all-around skills were decaying at only age 34, was closer to the end than anyone imagined. He suffered a stroke in early January of 1947, and never played again.

The career path of Gibson, who reportedly was gravely disappointed in not being chosen to help integrate the White majors, parallels the late 1940s history of the Negro Leagues, which went into sudden and irreversible decline after the color barrier was broken in 1947. Black baseball at Yankee Stadium went down with it, as attendance plummeted to about 7,000 per date in 1947 and 8,000 in 1948. The Negro National League went out of business after the 1948 season, with most surviving teams huddling in the Negro American League and the New York Cubans surviving as an independent. Pompez, the Cubans owner, had become a Latin American scout for the New York Giants, and his team played at their Polo Grounds. From then on the Negro League presence at the Stadium was intermittent, at best. A search of the sports pages after 1948, hampered by the lack of coverage in the major Black weeklies, themselves in decline, turns up only a pair of doubleheaders in each of 1950 and 1954. By then opportunities for the best Black players were steadily becoming available in the formerly White major and minor leagues, and the one surviving Black league, the American, could no longer be considered to have top-level ball.

Of the 450 team appearances at Yankee Stadium through the end of the 1948 season (the 225 games times two teams per game), 415 of them, 92 percent of the total, were Negro League or equivalent teams, plus the Negro League all-star teams. The two local teams that played there the most, the Black Yankees (48-50-5) and the Cubans (35-34-2), only had middling records. Among the regular Negro League competitors, the top won-lost marks were held by the Homestead Grays (26-11-1) and the Elite Giants from Nashville and then Baltimore (23-11-1).

In the last three years of high-quality Black games, lesser-ranked regional Black teams such as the Richmond Giants; Jacksonville Eagles; and Asheville, North Carolina, Blues played, usually in the preliminary game of a four-team Sunday doubleheader. Occasionally, a White team would provide an opponent. The 1946 season ended on October 6 with a game between the Satchel Paige and Bob Feller all-star squads as the two well-known hurlers brought their 20-game postseason barnstorming show, top Black players against top Whites, to New York. Although Feller's team had the better overall record, the Paige All Stars won, 4-0, at the Stadium. Paige threw five shutout innings before more than 27,000, the largest crowd of the year there for a Black game.

It's clear that the games at the Stadium added a great deal to the competitive nature of Negro baseball, and helped popularize it in what was then the biggest city in the U.S. But what were they worth, financially, to all involved? Anything approaching precise information on Negro League finances is sorely lacking today, even more so than complete player statistics. Financial records were usually lost when the Black teams went out of business, and sports page accounts of the business of the Negro Leagues were usually confined to "it was a good year," or "it was a bad year" types of reports. But, in two donations in 1955 and 1970 the New York Yankees gave the National Baseball Hall of Fame many of their business and financial records, plus many of those of the team's minor league affiliates, the whole run of data ranging from 1913 to 1950. These gifts have been enthusiastically mined by researchers for salary figures and other data helping to reconstruct the front office life of the Yankees.

But the Yankee cash ledgers also contain reports of cash receipts and expenditures for nearly all the blackball games played at the Stadium. Cash accounting for the Black games runs from 1930 through 1944. When compared to the game accounts found in the major Black weeklies consulted for this project (*Pittsburgh Courier, Chicago Defender, New York Amsterdam News,* and *New York Age)*, plus the *New York Times*, which covered many games, the cash ledgers seem to include financial data for each playing date. The Yankee data stops after 1944, but Negro League ball was still very popular for the next few years, and the newspapers still provided strong coverage, so the assumption is made here that the papers continued to report every contest at the Stadium. After the Negro National League folded following the 1948 season games at the Stadium became much fewer and far between, since many of the Eastern teams had gone out of business and Pompez had moved the Cubans to the Polo Grounds.

The erosion of the Negro Leagues, combined with the lack of Yankee ledger information, led to the decision to cut off the games included in this project at the end of the 1948 season. For the record, a doubleheader was discovered in each of 1950 and 1954. On May 28, 1950, the Philadelphia Stars beat the Kansas City Monarchs twice, 3-0 and 3-1, before a reported 4,000 fans. On July 11, 1954, the Indianapolis Clowns defeated the Monarchs, 5-1, and then the Monarchs turned the tables, 6-4, before 7,500 fans.

An accompanying table uses the Yankee financial records available in the Hall of Fame Library as a base for calculations. It also depends upon attendance figures to help reach financial results, since in the years before Gottlieb began representing Black baseball in 1939 the team ledgers sometimes only record what the Yankees were paid for the Stadium's use. A total revenue figure in those instances was established by averaging reported game day attendance from the major Black weeklies, plus that from the *New York Times*, which frequently carried shorter stories on the games. After establishing an attendance figure for each date and making some assumptions based on what the average ticket price might have been for Black games, it appears that through 1944, the last full year of Yankee records, the collaboration brought in a gross amount of about $426,000 dollars. After subtraction of the federal 10 percent entertainment tax on each ticket sold and Stadium game day expenses, there was a net of about $372,000. Of that amount, the Negro Leagues and the independent teams that sometimes played took away about 70 percent, $255,000. The Yankee organization kept about 30 percent. The $115,000 the Yankees made over 13 years isn't much for a team that was usually leading its league in attendance each season, but the money was a windfall, a small profit made while the Stadium would otherwise be sitting idle.

On the other hand, the money going to the Negro Leagues was an impressive sum for them. During the heyday years of 1939 through 1944 the Black leagues had an estimated income from the Stadium of $32,500 per season. In comparison the Newark Eagles, considered one of the higher salaried Black teams, and one of the few clubs whose records survive, had an annual payroll of $22,500 toward the end of that period. So, a relative handful of games at Yankee Stadium in the prime seasons cleared more than the entire Eagles payroll for players and other employees, with plenty left over.[24]

All of this is not to say that Yankee Stadium clearly was the most important venue for Negro League baseball. It shares the honor with Comiskey Park, the site of the East-West Games. From the first game in 1933 through 1948, the last year included in this study, the East-West game in Chicago drew an average of 36,500 fans per game. This was more than three times the average attendance at the Stadium's Black games (a figure even more impressive when it is taken into account how much greater the Stadium attendance was than that for the average Negro League game elsewhere). More people went to an East-West game than attended a game at Yankee Stadium even when the matchless Paige was starting. And the East-West Game produced dozens of thrilling games and individual performances that have become part of Black baseball lore.[25]

But the Stadium games, held in the leading city in the United States, in the park of the leading baseball team, provided important prestige for the Negro Leagues in addition to a financial shot in the arm for the Black majors. Essentially, the title for most influential Negro League game of the year was regularly won by Chicago, while the crown for sustained influence rested in New York.

ATTENDANCE AND PROFITS

Year	Games	Dates	Attendance	Gross Rev	Net Rev	NYY Share	Black Share**
1930*	10	5	39,700	$15,898	$14,660	$3,989	$10,671
1931	6	3	12,200	$4,666	$3,747	$1,376	$2,323
1934	4	2	50,000	$31,241	$27,367	$5,000	$22,367
1935	4	2	37,500	$15,000	$12,775	$6,000	$6,775
1936	2	1	15,000	$6,000	$5,273	$3,000	$2,273
1937	4	2	42,500	$17,000	$14,729	$5,500	$9,229
1938	4	2	31,700	$12,667	$11,189	$5,000	$6,189
1939	11	6	79,100	$30,611	$26,758	$6,554	$17,744
1940	14	7	75,000	$28,537	$24,814	$7,153	$17,662
1941	16	8	144,000	$58,429	$51,696	$11,929	$39,768
1942	19	10	170,900	$68,333	$59,907	$20,712	$39,195
1943	20	10	135,900	$57,389	$49,566	$17,750	$31,816
1944	24	12	139,300	$80,563	$69,244	$20,588	$48,656
1945	22	12	131,300	—	—	—	—
1946	30	16	188,400	—	—	—	—
1947	20	13	56,800	—	—	—	—
1948	15	8	57,300	—	—	—	—
	225	119	1,406,600	$426,333	$371,726	$114,550	$254,668
						31%	69%

* Not including Sleeping Car Porters benefit

** Includes a few payments to White opponents

BLACK BASEBALL AT YANKEE STADIUM: THE HOUSE THAT RUTH BUILT AND SATCHEL FURNISHED (WITH FANS)

BLACK GAMES AT YANKEE STADIUM, 1930-48

YEAR BY YEAR

1930

Date	Winner	Loser	Score	Est Att	Comments
5-Jul	Lincoln Giants	Baltimore Black Sox	13-4	16,700	1st Porters' games
5-Jul	Baltimore Black Sox	Lincoln Giants	5-3	—	1st Porters' games
11-Sep	Cuban Stars, East	Lincoln Giants	13-3	3,000	
11-Sep	Lincoln Giants	Cuban Stars, East	5-1		
21-Sep	Lincoln Giants	Homestead Grays	6-2	10,000	"Race Championship"
21-Sep	Homestead Grays	Lincoln Giants	3-2	—	"Race Championship"
27-Sep	Lincoln Giants	Homestead Grays	9-8	—	"Race Championship"
27-Sep	Homestead Grays	Lincoln Giants	7-3	—	"Race Championship"
28-Sep	Lincoln Giants	Homestead Grays	6-2	10,000	"Race Championship"
28-Sep	Homestead Grays	Lincoln Giants	5-2		"Race Championship"
				39,700	

1931

Date	Winner	Loser	Score	Est Att	Comments
10-May	Harlem Stars	Lancaster Giants (W)	17-0	8,500	
10-May	Harlem Stars	Philadelphia Pros (W)	8-6		
12-Jul	Harlem Stars	Brooklyn Royal Giants	7-2	1,200	
12-Jul	Harlem Stars	Brooklyn Royal Giants	4-3		
16-Aug	Harlem Stars	Hilldale	3-1	2,500	2nd Porters' games
16-Aug	Harlem Stars	Hilldale	11-3	—	2nd Porters' games
				12,200	

1934

Date	Winner	Loser	Score	Est Att	Comments
9-Sep	Chicago American Giants	New York Black Yankees	4-3	25,000	American Legion Fundraiser
9-Sep	Pittsburgh Crawfords	Philadelphia Stars	1-1		A.L. fundraiser; Paige start; tie game
30-Sep	Pittsburgh Crawfords	Philadelphia Stars	3-1	25,000	Paige start
30-Sep	New York Black Yankees	Chicago American Giants	3-2		
				50,000	

1935

Date	Winner	Loser	Score	Est Att	Comments
9/22	Nashville Elite Giants	New York Cubans	4-3	20,000	
9/22	Pittsburgh Crawfords	Philadelphia Stars	12-2		
13-Oct	Major League All-Stars (W)	Negro National All-Stars	3-0	17,500	
13-Oct	Major League All-Stars (W)	Negro National All-Stars	1-0		
				37,500	

1936

Date	Winner	Loser	Score	Est Att	Comments
16-Aug	Philadelphia Stars	Newark Eagles	15-7	15,000	Police Athletic Lg. benefit
16-Aug	New York Black Yankees	New York Cubans	2-1		
				15,000	

1937

Date	Winner	Loser	Score	Est Att	Comments
16-Aug	New York Black Yankees	Pittsburgh Crawfords	4-1	12,500	Elks benefit
16-Aug	Pittsburgh Crawfords	Philadelphia Stars	5-0	—	Elks benefit
26-Sep	Santo Domingo All-Stars	Negro National All-Stars	9-4	30,000	Paige start
26-Sep	Negro National All-Stars	Santo Domingo All-Stars	1-0		
				42,500	

1938

Date	Winner	Loser	Score	Est Att	Comments
26-Jun	Philadelphia Stars	Baltimore Elite Giants	8-7	16,700	Greater NY Fund benefit
26-Jun	Pittsburgh Crawfords	New York Black Yankees	5-3	—	Greater NY Fund benefit
31-Jul	Newark Eagles	Birmingham Black Barons	7-5	15,000	
31-Jul	Homestead Grays	Memphis Red Sox	9-1		
				31,700	

1939

Date	Winner	Loser	Score	Est Att	Comments
4-Jun	Baltimore Elite Giants	New York Cubans	7-3	12,300	
4-Jun	New York Black Yankees	Philadelphia Stars	5-4		
2-Jul	Newark Eagles	Philadelphia Stars	8-1	12,500	
2-Jul	Baltimore Elite Giants	New York Black Yankees	4-0		
23-Jul	Homestead Grays	Philadelphia Stars	11-2	12,500	
23-Jul	New York Black Yankees	New York Cubans	4-0		
13-Aug	Baltimore Elite Giants	New York Cubans	11-1	12,500	
13-Aug	Homestead Grays	New York Black Yankees	11-5		
27-Aug	Negro National All-Stars	Negro American All-Stars	10-2	20,000	2nd All-Star Game
24-Sep	Baltimore Elite Giants	Homestead Grays	2-0	9,300	NNL Championship
24-Sep	Negro National All-Stars	Minor League All-Stars (W)	1-1		Tie game
				79,100	

1940

Date	Winner	Loser	Score	Est Att	Comments
19-May	New York Black Yankees	New York Cubans	4-2	11,000	
19-May	New York Cubans	New York Black Yankees	8-0		
26-May	Baltimore Elite Giants	New York Black Yankees	8-1	6,000	
26-May	Homestead Grays	Philadelphia Stars	8-3		
16-Jun	Baltimore Elite Giants	New York Cubans	5-4	8,800	16 innings
16-Jun	New York Black Yankees	Philadelphia Stars	5-3		
7-Jul	Homestead Grays	New York Black Yankees	5-3	11,000	
7-Jul	Philadephia Stars	New York Cubans	4-0		
28-Jul	Homestead Grays	Baltimore Elite Giants	5-0	11,700	Elks Day
28-Jul	Baltimore Elite Giants	Homestead Grays	15-6		
4-Aug	Memphis Red Sox	New York Black Yankees	3-0	11,800	
4-Aug	St. Louis Stars	Baltimore Elite Giants	6-4		
8-Sep	Homestead Grays	Memphis Red Sox	3-1	14,700	
8-Sep	Baltimore Elite Giants	New York Cubans	3-0		
				75,000	

BLACK BASEBALL AT YANKEE STADIUM: THE HOUSE THAT RUTH BUILT AND SATCHEL FURNISHED (WITH FANS)

1941

Date	Winner	Loser	Score	Est Att	Comments
11-May	New York Black Yankees	Philadelphia Stars	5-3	19,300	Paige start for Yanks
11-May	Philadelphia Stars	New York Black Yankees	4-1		
30-May	New York Black Yankees	Newark Eagles	6-5	22,000	Memorial Day; Joe Louis threw 1st pitch
30-May	New York Cubans	Baltimore Elite Giants	6-3		
8-Jun	New York Black Yankees	New York Cubans	3-2	12,000	Gehrig Memorial Service
8-Jun	Philadelphia Stars	Newark Eagles	6-3		
29-Jun	Baltimore Elite Giants	Philadelphia Stars	4-0	12,000	
29-Jun	Homestead Grays	New York Cubans	3-2		
20-Jul	Kansas City Monarchs	New York Cubans	7-2	27,200	Paige start
20-Jul	New York Black Yankees	Philadelphia Stars	3-1		
10-Aug	Birmingham Black Barons	New York Black Yankees	2-1	16,500	Elks Day
10-Aug	New York Cubans	Memphis Red Sox	7-4	—	Elks Day
24-Aug	Kansas City Monarchs	Newark Eagles	6-1	22,500	Paige 1-hitter
24-Aug	New York Cubans	Philadelphia Stars	4-3		
11-Sep	Homestead Grays	New York Cubans	20-0	12,500	
11-Sep	Homestead Grays	New York Cubans	5-0		
				144,000	

1942

Date	Winner	Loser	Score	Est Att	Comments
17-May	New York Black Yankees	New York Cubans	5-3	12,000	
17-May	New York Cubans	New York Black Yankees	5-0		
24-May	Homestead Grays	New York Black Yankees	9-2	30,000	
24-May	New York Black Yankees	Homestead Grays	3-2		
31-May	Baltimore Elite Giants	Philadelphia Stars	5-3	14,500	
31-May	Newark Eagles	New York Cubans	8-3		
21-Jun	Homestead Grays	Philadelphia Stars	3-2	12,000	
21-Jun	New York Cubans	Baltimore Elite Giants	3-2		
28-Jun	Philadelphia Stars	New York Cubans	3-0	12,000	
28-Jun	Baltimore Elite Giants	New York Black Yankees	7-3		
4-Jul	Baltimore Elite Giants	Newark Eagles	8-4	12,000	
4-Jul	New York Cubans	New York Black Yankees	7-2		
26-Jul	New York Black Yankees	Chicago American Giants	8-0	18,700	Elks Day
26-Jul	New York Cubans	Birmingham Black Barons	5-2	—	Elks Day
2-Aug	Philadelphia Stars	Baltimore Elite Giants	7-4	30,000	
2-Aug	Kansas City Monarchs	New York Cubans	9-0		Paige start
16-Aug	Memphis Red Sox	New York Black Yankees	2-2	4,000	10 inning tie, called by rain
13-Sep	Kansas City Monarchs	Homestead Grays	9-3	25,700	World Series, Paige start
13-Sep	Kansas City Monarchs	Homestead Grays	5-0		7-inning exhibition
				170,900	

1943

Date	Winner	Loser	Score	Est Att	Comments
16-May	New York Cubans	New York Black Yankees	12-2	11,000	
16-May	New York Cubans	New York Black Yankees	5-5	—	Tie game, called darkness
23-May	New York Cubans	Baltimore Elite Giants	9-2	7,500	
23-May	New York Cubans	Baltimore Elite Giants	10-3		

13-Jun	St. Louis Stars	New York Black Yankees	12-0	7,000	
13-Jun	St. Louis Stars	Philadelphia Stars	6-3		
27-Jun	New York Cubans	New York Black Yankees	6-2	22,000	
27-Jun	Kansas City Monarchs	New York Cubans	6-3	—	Paige start
4-Jul	Baltimore Elite Giants	New York Black Yankees	13-0	9,500	
4-Jul	New York Cubans	Philadelphia Stars	10-0		
11-Jul	Baltimore Elite Giants	Philadelphia Stars	4-1	6,000	
11-Jul	Newark Eagles	New York Black Yankees	6-5		
8-Aug	New York Cubans	Philadelphia Stars	7-0	24,700	
8-Aug	New York Cubans	Kansas City Monarchs	8-5	—	Paige start
15-Aug	New York Black Yankees	Atlanta Crackers	9-1	16,700	Elks Day
15-Aug	New York Black Yankees	St. Louis Stars	7-2	—	Elks Day
22-Aug	Birmingham Black Barons	New York Black Yankees	3-1	12,000	
22-Aug	New York Cubans	Birmingham Black Barons	5-0		
12-Sep	New York Cubans	Baltimore Elite Giants	7-1	19,500	
12-Sep	New York Cubans	Kansas City Monarchs	2-0	—	Paige start
				135,900	

1944

Date	Winner	Loser	Score	Est Att	Comments
30-Apr	Homestead Grays	New York Black Yankees	15-3	16,700	
30-Apr	Homestead Grays	New York Black Yankees	10-0		
28-May	Philadelphia Stars	New York Cubans	9-3	8,500	
28-May	New York Cubans	Philadelphia Stars	6-3		
4-Jun	Birmingham Black Barons	Philadelphia Stars	9-0	12,000	
4-Jun	Birmingham Black Barons	New York Black Yankees	13-0		
11-Jun	New York Black Yankees	Philadelphia Stars	4-3	8,000	
11-Jun	Cincinnati Clowns	New York Black Yankees	3-1		
25-Jun	Baltimore Elite Giants	New York Cubans	9-8	5,000	
25-Jun	New York Cubans	Baltimore Elite Giants	4-3		
23-Jul	New York Cubans	Philadelphia Stars	3-2	9,100	
23-Jul	New York Cubans	Philadelphia Stars	13-4		
30-Jul	Philadelphia Stars	Baltimore Elite Giants	5-1	14,000	
30-Jul	Newark Eagles	New York Cubans	6-2		
6-Aug	Atlanta Black Crackers	New York Black Yankees	6-0	7,000	
6-Aug	New York Black Yankees	Atlanta Black Crackers	6-5		
26-Aug	Kansas City Monarchs	New York Cubans	4-2	28,700	Paige start
26-Aug	New York Cubans	Birmingham Black Barons	4-3		
10-Sep	New York Black Yankees	Boston Colored Giants	9-0	11,000	
10-Sep	Philadelphia Stars	Jacksonville Red Caps	6-1		
24-Sep	New York Black Yankees	N. Carolina All-Stars	6-3	7,000	
24-Sep	Philadelphia Stars	S. Carolina All-Stars	12-0		
1-Oct	Homestead Grays	Birmingham Black Barons	5-2	12,300	
1-Oct	Homestead Grays	Birmingham Black Barons	8-5		
				139,300	

BLACK BASEBALL AT YANKEE STADIUM: THE HOUSE THAT RUTH BUILT AND SATCHEL FURNISHED (WITH FANS)

1945

Date	Winner	Loser	Score	Est Att	Comments
6-May	Homestead Grays	New York Black Yankees	13-3	3,700	
13-May	Philadelphia Stars	New York Cubans	5-2	8,000	
20-May	Baltimore Elite Giants	New York Black Yankees	8-2	8,400	
20-May	Baltimore Elite Giants	New York Black Yankees	4-0		
17-Jun	Philadelphia Stars	New York Black Yankees	7-1	13,700	
17-Jun	Kansas City Monarchs	Philadelphia Stars	3-1	—	Paige start
1-Jul	Philadelphia Stars	Newark Eagles	4-1	9,000	
1-Jul	New York Black Yankees	Philadelphia Stars	8-5		
8-Jul	Miami Giants	Boston Giants	11-9	14,000	
8-Jul	New York Black Yankees	Cincinnati Clowns	6-0		
5-Aug	Boston Giants	Miami Giants	10-0	11,500	Elks' Day
5-Aug	New York Black Yankees	Philadelphia Stars	4-2	—	Elks' Day
12-Aug	Birmingham Black Barons	Philadelphia Stars	5-1	19,000	
12-Aug	Kansas City Monarchs	New York Black Yankees	4-1	—	Paige start
19-Aug	Chicago American Giants	New York Black Yankees	1-0	16,000	
19-Aug	Baltimore Elite Giants	Memphis Red Sox	5-0		
2-Sep	Philadelphia Stars	Cincinnati Clowns	4-1	10,000	
2-Sep	New York Black Yankees	Birmingham Black Barons	3-2		
3-Sep	New York Black Yankees	Philadelphia Stars	5-4	10,000	
3-Sep	Cincinnati Clowns	Birmingham Black Barons	5-0		
23-Sep	Homestead Grays	Cleveland Buckeyes	7-1	8,000	
23-Sep	Homestead Grays	Cleveland Buckeyes	7-1		
				131,300	

1946

Date	Winner	Loser	Score	Est Att	Comments
27-Apr	Homestead Grays	New York Black Yankees	10-0	8,000	
27-Apr	Homestead Grays	New York Black Yankees	10-0		
19-May	New York Cubans	New York Black Yankees	5-1	7,000	
19-May	New York Black Yankees	New York Cubans	2-1		
26-May	Homestead Grays	New York Black Yankees	7-0	12,000	
26-May	New York Black Yankees	Newark Eagles	3-1		
23-Jun	Nashville Cubs	Jacksonville Eagles	12-11	12,000	
23-Jun	Baltimore Elite Giants	New York Black Yankees	11-3		
4-Jul	Newark Eagles	New York Black Yankees	3-1	10,000	
4-Jul	Asheville Blues	Boston Giants	15-8		
7-Jul	New York Black Yankees	Philadelphia Stars	4-1	15,000	
7-Jul	New York Black Yankees	Kansas City Monarchs	4-3	—	Paige start
28-Jul	Cincinnati Crescents	House of David	13-2	16,000	
28-Jul	New York Cubans	New York Black Yankees	6-2		
1-Aug	Kansas City Monarchs	New York Black Yankees	10-0	8,900	Paige start, night game
4-Aug	Newark Eagles	Cleveland Buckeyes	3-2	13,000	
4-Aug	Memphis Red Sox	New York Black Yankees	1-0		
18-Aug	Philadelphia Stars	New York Cubans	6-0	12,000	

18-Aug	New York Black Yankees	Indianapolis Clowns	3-1		
30-Aug	Philadelphia Stars	Homestead Grays	3-1	9,000	1st Twi-Nite Doubleheader
30-Aug	New York Cubans	New York Black Yankees	10-7		
1-Sep	Newark Eagles	New York Black Yankees	3-2	11,000	
1-Sep	New York Cubans	Philadelphia Stars	6-5		
10-Sep	New York Black Yankees	Indianapolis Clowns	8-2	10,000	
10-Sep	New York Black Yankees	Kansas City Monarchs	6-3		
15-Sep	Philadelphia Stars	Indianapolis Clowns	5-1	11,000	
15-Sep	New York Black Yankees	Kansas City Monarchs	3-1		Paige start
29-Sep	Philadelphia Stars	Asheville Blues	7-4	6,000	
29-Sep	New York Cubans	New York Black Yankees	2-0	—	5 innings, darkness
6-Oct	Paige All-Stars	Feller All-Stars (W)	4-0	27,500	Paige, Feller start
				188,400	

1947

Date	Winner	Loser	Score	Est Att	Comments
20-Apr	New York Black Yankees	Homestead Grays	3-3	4,000	9-inning tie, called darkness, cold
11-May	New York Cubans	New York Black Yankees	7-0	9,300	
11-May	New York Black Yankees	New York Cubans	4-3		14 innings
27-May	Homestead Grays	New York Black Yankees	7-1		
29-Jun	Newark Eagles	New York Black Yankees	9-8	7,000	
29-Jun	New York Black Yankees	Newark Eagles	6-5		
11-Jul	Baltimore Elite Giants	New York Cubans	6-3	—	Twi-nite Doubleheader
11-Jul	Baltimore Elite Giants	New York Cubans	0-0	—	Tie game, 7 innings
13-Jul	New York Cubans	New York Black Yankees	8-0	7,500	
13-Jul	New York Cubans	Memphis Red Sox	9-1		
18-Jul	New York Black Yankees	Homestead Grays	9-8	—	Night game
20-Jul	Philadelphia Stars	New York Black Yankees	16-1	7,000	
20-Jul	Philadelphia Stars	Birmingham Barons	4-3		
8-Aug	New York Cubans	Kansas City Monarchs	8-3	7,500	Paige start
10-Aug	Asheville Blues	Tampa Rockets	2-1		
10-Aug	Memphis Red Sox	New York Black Yankees	2-2		12 inning tie, darkness
24-Aug	New York Black Yankees	Philadelphia Stars	6-4	5,500	
24-Aug	New York Black Yankees	Kansas City Monarchs	0-0	—	9 inning tie; Paige start
27-Aug	Indianapolis Clowns	New York Black Yankees	5-2	—	Urban League benefit
21-Sep	Cleveland Buckeyes	New York Cubans	10-7	9,000	World Series game 2
				56,800	

1948

Date	Winner	Loser	Score	Est Att	Comments
2-May	New York Cubans	Homestead Grays	7-1	10,300	
2-May	Philadelphia Stars	New York Black Yankees	5-2		
23-May	Baltimore Elite Giants	New York Cubans	3-2	5,000	
23-May	Baltimore Elite Giants	New York Cubans	9-6		
20-Jun	San Juan Stars	Winston-Salem Giants	8-6	9,000	
20-Jun	New York Cubans	Asheville Blues	7-6		

5-Jul	New York Black Yankees	Philadelphia Stars	9-8	7,000	10 innings
5-Jul	New York Cubans	Newark Eagles	2-0		
11-Jul	San Juan Stars	Richmond Giants	7-6	5,000	
11-Jul	Philadelphia Stars	New York Cubans	8-3		
8-Aug	Harlem Globetrotters	Honolulu Hawaiians	7-4	5,000	
8-Aug	Philadelphia Stars	New York Cubans	4-3		
24-Aug	Negro National All-Stars	Negro American All-Stars	6-1	16,000	2nd All-Star Game
12-Sep	Philadelphia Stars	New York Cubans	10-8		
12-Sep	Madison Colonials	Miami Hobos	4-1		
				57,300	

YANKEE STADIUM WON-LOST RECORDS: NEGRO LEAGUE TEAMS

	Games	W	L	T	PCT
Atlanta Black Crackers	3	1	2	0	.333
Baltimore Black Sox	2	1	1	0	.500
Baltimore/Nashville Elite Giants	35	23	11	1	.676
Birmingham Black Barons	14	5	9	0	.357
Brooklyn Royal Giants	2	0	2	0	.000
Chicago American Giants	4	2	2	0	.500
Cincinnati/Indianapolis Clowns	8	3	5	0	.375
Cleveland Buckeyes	4	1	3	0	.250
Cuban Stars, East	2	1	1	0	.500
Harlem Stars	6	6	0	0	1.000
Hilldale	2	0	2	0	.000
Homestead Grays	38	26	11	1	.703
Kansas City Monarchs	17	10	6	1	.625
Lincoln Giants	10	5	5	0	.500
Memphis Red Sox	9	2	5	2	.286
NY Black Yankees	93	38	50	5	.432
NY Cubans	71	35	34	2	.507
Newark Eagles	18	9	9	0	.500
Philadelphia Stars	58	25	32	1	.439
Pittsburgh Crawfords	6	4	1	1	.800
St. Louis Stars	4	3	1	0	.750
	406	200	192	14	.510

Other Teams

	Games	W	L	T	PCT
Asheville Blues	4	2	2	0	.500
Boston Giants	4	1	3	0	.250
Cincinnati Crescents	1	1	0	0	1.000
Dominican All-Stars	2	1	1	0	.500
Feller All-Stars	1	0	1	0	.000
Harlem Globetrotters	1	1	0	0	1.000
Honolulu Hawaiians	1	0	1	0	.000
House of David	1	0	1	0	.000
Jacksonville Eagles	1	0	1	0	.000

Jacksonville Red Caps	1	0	1	0	.000
Lancaster, PA, Giants	1	0	1	0	.000
Madison Colonials	1	1	0	0	1.000
Major League All-Stars	2	2	0	0	1.000
Miami Giants	2	1	1	0	.500
Miami Hobos	1	0	1	0	.000
Minor League All-Stars	1	0	0	1	
Nashville Cubs	1	1	0	0	1.000
Negro American All-Stars	2	0	2	0	.000
Negro National All-Stars	7	3	3	1	.500
North Carolina All-Stars	1	0	1	0	.000
Paige All-Stars	1	1	0	0	1.000
Philadelphia Pros	1	0	1	0	.000
Richmond Giants	1	0	1	0	.000
San Juan Stars	2	2	0	0	1.000
South Carolina All-Stars	1	0	1	0	.000
Tampa Rockets	1	0	1	0	.000
Winston-Salem Giants	1	0	1	0	.000
	44	17	25	2	.405
Total	**450**	**217**	**217**	**16**	

Notes

1 Michael Gershman, *Diamonds: The Evolution of the Ballpark* (Boston, New York: Houghton Mifflin, 1993), 138.

2 Philip J. Lowry, *Green Cathedrals, The Ultimate Celebration of Major League and Negro League Ballparks*, (New York: Walker & Company, 2006), 110, 142, and 235.

3 "Ruppert, Owner of Yankees and Leading Brewer, Dies, *New York Times*, January 14, 1939; Dan Levitt, "Jacob Ruppert," SABR Baseball Biography Project, http://sabr.org/bioproj/person/b96b262d; Elizabeth L. Bradley, *Knickerbocker, the Myth Behind New York,* (New Brunswick, NJ: Rivergate Books, 2009), 121-23.

4 Larry Tye, *Rising from the Rails: Pullman Porters and the Making of the Black Middle Class* (New York: Henry Holt and Company, 2004), 114.

5 Tye, *Rising from the Rails*, 112-13; "Randolph Leads Fight for Porters," *New York Amsterdam News*, August 26, 1925; "500 Enthusiastic Porters Loudly Cheer Proposed Porters' Union," *New York Amsterdam News*, September 2, 1925.

6 Willliam Hamilton Harris, *Keeping the Faith: A. Philip Randolph, Milton P. Webster, and the Brotherhood of Sleeping Car Porters, 1925–1937* (Urbana, IL: University of Illinois Press, 1977), 26, 73.

7 C.L. Dellums, interview by Joyce Henderson, oral history transcript for The Bancroft Library, University of California, Berkeley, CA, at Online Archive of California (http:www.oac.cdlib.org); "Roy Lancaster 'Puts Over' Big Benefit Event," *New York Age,* July 19, 1930.

8 Al Monroe, "The Big League," *Abbott's Monthly*, April 1933, 7.

9 "'Bojangles' Wins, But Phil Edwards is Beaten in Half-Mile Handicap at Yankee Stadium Porters' Benefit," *New York Age*, July 12, 1930; "Thousands at Yankee Stadium," *New York Amsterdam News*, July 9, 1930.

10 http://www.measuringworth.com/uscompare.

11 "Grays Win Eastern World Series, *Pittsburgh Courier*, October 4, 1930.

12 "Posey Signs With Keenan for the Championship Series Between Lincoln Giants and Homstead (sic) Grays at Stadium," *New York Amsterdam News*, September 10, 1930; "Lincolns in Yankee Bowl Next," *Pittsburgh Courier*, September 6, 1930; American League Base Ball Club of New York. Records. 1913–1950. A. Bartlett Giamatti Research Center, National Baseball Hall of Fame and Museum, Cooperstown, NY.

13 American League Base Ball Club records.

14 Sol White, "Baseball Notes," *New York Age*, December 20, 1930.

15 Romeo L. Dougherty, "In the Whirl of Sport, *New York Amsterdam News*, August 19, 1931; William E. Clark "A. Philip Randolph Explains Why Stars Got No Money from Porter's Benefit," *New York Age*, August 29, 1931.

16 Neil Lanctot, *Negro League Baseball: The Rise and Ruin of a Black Institution* (Philadelphia: University of Pennsylvania Press, 2004), 38.

17 Lanctot, 15.

18 American League Base Ball Club records.

19 Art Rust Jr., *"Get that Nigger Off the Field!": A Sparkling, Informal History of the Black Man in Baseball* (New York: Delacorte Press, 1976), 55; American League Base Ball Club records.

20 Historical Census Browser, University of Virginia Library, (http://mapserver.lib.virginia.edu/).

21 Rust, *"Get That Nigger Off the Field,"* 55.

22 Nat Trammell, "Satchel Likes Jim Semler's Personality," *New York Amsterdam News*, May 17, 1941; William E. Clark, "Satchel Paige Fails to Show Up," *New York Age*, September 28, 1935.

23 "Homestead Grays Defeat Lincoln Giants 6 Out of 10 Games for Eastern Title," *Chicago Defender*, October 4, 1930.

24 Newark Eagles Business Papers, Newark Public Library, Newark, NJ.

25 *The Negro Leagues Book*, Dick Clark and Larry Lester, eds. (Cleveland: Society for American Baseball Research, 1994), 242-254.

THE RISE AND FALL OF GREENLEE FIELD

Geri Driscoll Strecker

This article appeared in Black Ball: A Negro Leagues Journal*, Fall 2009.*

THE STORY OF GREENLEE FIELD

Any story requires plot, characters, and setting. In reconstructing the history of Black baseball box scores give us the basic outline of the plot, and biographical records tell us who the players were. But until now, the setting—where teams actually played their legendary games—has been left mostly to our imagination, even for great clubs like the 1930s Pittsburgh Crawfords. The only detail we have known about the exterior of Greenlee Field is that its brick façade had three arched entryways. These are clearly visible in the background of the 1935 team photograph, behind the famous Mack bus and underneath a sign that reads "ENTRANCE." The park's interior has also been a mystery. Teenie Harris's photographs[1] show a few interior details, but not enough to imagine the big picture, leaving us wondering about the ballpark's appearance both inside and out, its orientation on the site, and the playing field's dimensions.

GUS GREENLEE

Pittsburgh's Hill District businessman Gus Greenlee began investing in the Crawfords by 1931, hoping to build the team from a local semiprofessional club to contenders in a professional league.[2] Initially, the team was mediocre, with no superstars but some decent players: Robbie Williams, Moe Harris, "Jap" Washington, Sam Streeter, and Bill Harris. The *Pittsburgh Courier* called the 1931 Crawfords "a disorganized team of temperamentals…without a single brainy pitcher." But the same writer assessed, "before the season ended [the] Crawfords were ranked in the first division." Robbie Williams was the team's player-manager, and Cum Posey's brother See was business manager. Sportswriter W. Rollo Wilson declared, "Gus Greenlee has built an exceptional good team in the short while he has owned the former sandlotters." Yet the Crawfords were still no match for the Homestead Grays, who in 1931 won 33 games against major Black teams and lost just 18, leading Cum Posey to claim his team "undisputed champions." That season, the Grays featured sluggers Josh Gibson and Oscar Charleston, men who had shared the nickname "the Black Babe Ruth." But great things were in store for the Pittsburgh Crawfords in 1932, and Rollo Wilson predicted Greenlee was "going into the proposition in a big way."[3]

BUILDING A NEW BALLPARK

During the 1931 season, the Crawfords had to rent grounds for their home games, playing most at Ammon Field on Bedford Avenue (now Josh Gibson Field) in the Hill District,[4] but leasing Forbes Field from the National League Pirates for important games. While the major league stadium was certainly superior, Black teams were not allowed to use its clubhouse facilities. Plus, Forbes Field was in Oakland, almost two miles away from the African American neighborhoods where most of the Crawfords' fans lived, and Greenlee recognized the "disadvantage which [they] had to undergo to reach it."[5] Frustrated with the "high rental price charged for parks with inadequate accommodations…[Greenlee] concluded that an enclosed field within walking distance would be attractive to sport fans." During the summer of 1931, he began searching for a suitable Hill District location to build his ballpark and settled on a site owned by the Entress Brick Company, occupying an entire city block on the north side of Bedford Avenue between Junilla Street and Watt Street.[6]

An abundance of cheap natural gas and prime clay made southwestern Pennsylvania ideal for brick manufacturing, so such businesses were common around Pittsburgh. The

(Courtesy of NoirTech Research, Inc.)

In August of 1932, Gus Greenlee added permanent lights to the Crawford home field.

Entress Brick Company had been operating since 1882, using three large kilns to produce about 20,000 bricks per day during the late 1890s.[7] Although the company had been quite profitable, when the Great Depression began, construction projects dwindled, so Entress stockholders were ready to sell the Bedford Street property.

In 1931, Entress Brick Company's principal stockholder was Dr. Joséph F. Thoms, a White physician who also held the deed to the land. To broker the deal with Entress and gather sufficient funds for building a quality ballpark, Greenlee and Thoms formed the Bedford Land Company, with Latrobe Brewery owner Joe Tito (also White) as their third partner. Prior to this venture, Tito had reportedly been connected with Greenlee's less legitimate businesses, including his numbers organization. Greenlee only owned 25 percent of the ballpark and held no office in the company. Thoms served as president, and Tito as treasurer. The secretary for the Bedford Land Company was Robert F. Lane, former bookkeeper of the Entress Brick Factory. Lane handled money, kept records, and arranged contracts for renting the park to other users. Tito's brother Ralph leased the concession stand, and their relative Tony Christiano was official groundskeeper.[8]

Understanding business structure and ownership roles in the Bedford Land Company is important. Many contemporaries charged that Greenlee Field failed economically because Greenlee refused to include African Americans in the daily operations. However, this accusation neglects that he was not sole owner and in fact had little control over staffing. Greenlee was the charismatic front man but greatly relied on his White partners for funding and logistical support to book events, maintain the facility, and generate revenues. In return, they controlled most of the ballpark's staffing and supply arrangements.

THE ARCHITECT

One of the most interesting untold stories behind the construction of Greenlee Field is the identity of its African American architect: Louis Arnett Stuart Bellinger. A few *Pittsburgh Courier* articles about the ballpark mention his last name, but none explain who he was or his role in Pittsburgh's African American community.

Bellinger was born September 29, 1891, in Sumter, South Carolina, about 100 miles north of Charleston. His father, George, and a few other male relatives were carpenters. After graduating from a local academy in 1910, Bellinger enrolled in Howard University and received his bachelor of science degree in architecture in June 1914.[9] His first job was teaching mathematics and science at Fessenden Academy in Ocala, Florida, from 1914 to 1915.[10] In 1916, Bellinger accepted a new position in Columbia, South Carolina, teaching mathematics at Allen University, an institution which the Methodist Episcopal (AME) Church had founded in 1870 to educate freed slaves.[11] When the United States entered World War I in 1917, Bellinger immediately registered for the draft and served a short time in the army. Around this time, he also married Ethel Connel, a music teacher. They had no children.

After the war, Bellinger moved to Pittsburgh and is listed as an architect in the 1919 city directory. The 1920 Federal Census lists him renting a residence at 611 Chauncey Street, less than two blocks south of the future Greenlee Field site. In 1922, Bellinger opened his own practice with a downtown office at 525 Fifth Avenue. Among his first commissions was an apartment building on Junilla Street, in the Hill District. The following year, he took a job as an assistant to the city architect, working on projects to remodel public buildings. Bellinger returned to private practice in 1926 and in 1927 designed the Pythian Temple, which later became the New Granada Theatre. The building still stands at 1909 Centre Avenue, with its rear entrance on Wylie Avenue, and has been nominated to the National Register of Historic Places. It is one of very few remaining examples of Bellinger's work.[12]

In 1928, the Harmon Foundation honored Bellinger by including his work in a national exhibition of African American Artists. His featured piece was "Proposed Plan for Church and Apartments." He was invited to participate in another Harmon Foundation exhibition in 1933, but his materials were damaged in transit. Invitations to participate in these events mark Bellinger's status not just in Pittsburgh, but in the larger African American creative community.

In 1928, Bellinger designed the $19,000 home he and Ethel occupied at 530 Francis Street.[13] However, when his business faltered during the Great Depression, he had to close his downtown office and sell the house. In 1932, he unsuccessfully ran for Congress as a Republican candidate. In 1936, Bellinger secured a position as Inspector in the City of Pittsburgh Bureau of Building Inspection; he held this job until 1939 and then again from 1941-42. During the break in between, he again attempted to restart his private practice. Bellinger was elected to the American Institute of Architects (AIA) on July 10, 1945, and work began to pick up after World War II. But then Bellinger died suddenly on February 3, 1946, of a cerebral hemorrhage. His obituary appeared with his photograph on the front page of the *Pittsburgh Courier*.[14]

Before beginning the Greenlee Field project in 1931, Bellinger and Greenlee were certainly acquainted, and their wives actually shared advertising space in the *Pittsburgh Courier*: Mrs. Bellinger offering private music lessons, and Mrs. Greenlee seeking tenants for a boarding house she owned. Later, in 1933, Bellinger drafted plans to remodel a "storeroom" at Greenlee's Crawford Grill, 1401 Wylie Avenue.[15]

Bellinger's association with Greenlee Field appears to have begun early on in planning the project. As one of only 60 African American registered architects then working in the United States, he was an ideal choice to design the ballpark. He and his wife were also prominent in Pittsburgh's African American community, serving leadership roles at the YMCA and in several fraternal and other organizations. This added an air of legitimacy to Greenlee's project. Bellinger's relationship with Pittsburgh government also ensured construction would follow local regulations and hopefully prevent the city from closing the park for code violations. Such tactics were common in cities where Black businessmen tried to gain social and economic strength.

ZONING

Because Greenlee Field required more land than just the acres between bordering streets, the Bedford Land Company worked with the city and adjacent properties—Lincoln Memorial Cemetery to the west and Municipal Hospital to the east—to request zoning variances. This included closing Junilla and Watt Streets north of Bedford Avenue so the ballparks' exterior structure could be built directly on top of the former roads. During this era, zoning appeals and requests for building permits were typically listed in *Builders' Bulletin*, the weekly newsletter of the Pittsburgh Builders Exchange. The following listings relate to Greenlee Field:

August 8, 1931

Zoning Appeal Denied

Bedford Land Corporation, 2509 Bedford Avenue, 5th Ward. Occupy property as athletic field.

November 28, 1931

5th Ward. Bedford Land Co., 2408 Bedford Ave., owner; Guibert Steel Co., McKees Rocks, Contractor. Steel bleachers, 2408 Bedford Ave., $3,000

December 26, 1931

5th Ward. Bedford Land Co., 2408 Bedford Ave., owner and builder. Concrete and steel ball stand, 2515 Bedford Ave., $32,000.

January 23, 1932

5th Ward. Bedford Land Co., 2408 Bedford Ave., owner and builder. Grandstand, 2515 Bedford Ave., $5,000[16]

Aside from showing a location change for the Bedford Land Company's business offices, the building permits also reveal an interesting shift from the company being listed merely as owner to both owner and builder. This would have enabled the partners to conceal funding and other business matters. Hence, while the building permits only total $40,000, it is still possible that the ballpark cost closer to the $100,000 that Greenlee claimed, especially when we consider costs of acquiring the land, appealing zoning decisions, and grading the site.

Unfortunately, it is not clear how or when Greenlee and his partners managed to reverse the initial zoning denial, since no further mention of this appears in the *Builders' Bulletin* or Pittsburgh newspapers. However, this was certainly a delicate arbitration since the Bedford Land Corporation was not only changing the use of the site, but also closing off two streets and developing the ballpark snugly between a cemetery and hospital, entities which would have had genuine concerns about their new neighbor. Bellinger's previous role in the City Architect's office would certainly have been an asset in negotiating this process.

GRADING THE SITE

Although the Entress Brick property was the best-suited available site for a ballpark in the Hill District, the land was certainly not flat; in fact, it had elevation changes of up to 20 feet. Workers broke ground for Greenlee Field on Monday July 20, 1931.[17] To create a level playing field, they used steam shovels to excavate 21,000 cubic yards of soil[18] and remove the section of Watt Street between the ballpark and the hospital and the section of Junilla Street between the ballpark and Lincoln Memorial Cemetery.[19] Much of the steepest topographical change—a sudden 20-foot drop—was already along part of what would become the right field line, so contractors extended this wall of earth northward along the property line, using additional earth from a 20-foot hill which stood between the future pitcher's mound and short right field. Adding a wooden fence on top of the earthen wall created a bowl effect for the ballpark and prevented home runs from flying into Municipal Hospital. Later, the sloped wall also held a few rows of additional bleachers.[20]

THE BRICK FAÇADE

Aerial and ground photographs taken in 1938 provide a clear picture of Greenlee Field's physical appearance. The brick façade extended the full length of Bedford Avenue between Junilla Street and Watt Street.

The southwest corner of the building behind home plate was two stories tall allowing room for offices on the second floor and ample space on the first floor to accommodate concessions, locker rooms, storage, and other functions. Upper rows of the grandstand extended above the southwest corner of the façade, and a brick chimney rose above the top seats. Moving east from the corner, the façade had two windows and a doorway (likely the office entrance), followed by six ticket windows and three arched entryways under a White "ENTRANCE" sign.[21] Further east are another arched entry/exit, two gated pedestrian exits, and a wide double gate for vehicle access to the field. Besides maintenance equipment, this last gate was also used for cars when Greenlee Field hosted auto races. Beginning in 1934, Greenlee also allowed parking in the outfield during boxing events an "innovation…[that] made a hit with fans."[22]

Reflecting economic conditions of the Great Depression, the ballpark's architecture was quite plain. The façade used locally-kilned red brick with simple corbelling along the top of the two-story section and along the lower section between the arched entrances and the two exit gates. Concrete coping capped the entire length of the wall. The archways were unadorned, lacking limestone keystones and details that were typical of the time.

INSIDE THE PARK

From these aerial photographs, we can also use the standard 90-foot basepaths to estimate dimensions of the entire playing field:

Right Field 338 feet

Center Field 410 feet

Left Field 342 feet

These dimensions are on par with or just slightly shorter than typical major league ballparks of the time.[23]

Bellinger initially designed Greenlee Field to seat 6,000 spectators for baseball games, but the grandstands were eventually expanded to hold over 7,000. For boxing events, portable seating was brought in to accommodate up to 12,000. The field lights were added in September 1932, but an electric public address system was already functioning for the opening game in April. The 1938 photographs show the speakers mounted halfway up the light poles. While the sound system was first rate, the announcer who called out batters was not. In June 1932, the *Courier* advised, he "should know whereof he speaks. An error now and then is pardonable, but continual mistakes...are disconcerting to fans who are trying to follow the game.[24]

One of the park's impressive features was a large scoreboard in left field. Early in the first season, the *Courier* identified the person who ran it: "Eddie Bryant, a popular uptown youth who...is doing his job efficiently...[and] goes about his task just like they do at Forbes Field, and eleven times out of ten he is right."[25] The 1938 photographs show a Latrobe Beer advertisement along the bottom. This endorsement for Joe Tito's brewery was certainly added after December 1933 when the 21st Amendment repealed prohibition.

SIGNING A NEW MANAGER

With his new ballpark well under way, Greenlee focused on improving his team. He had already acquired Satchel Paige during the 1931 season, and in December, rumors spread that the Crawfords might have a new manager in 1932. Greenlee said he found "no fault with Robbie Williams" but had "been requested to consider [Oscar] Charleston and [Bill] Pierce." Greenlee did not specify the source of this "request," but by then his business partners were surely eager to insure their investments. Responding to the prospect of the Crawfords acquiring Charleston as manager, the *Courier* remarked, "as a fielder and batter he is the best gate attraction in Negro baseball." Soon, Dizzy Dismukes was added to the list of potential managerial candidates. William E. Nunn declared in the *Courier*, "Whether the Crawford threat materializes into anything definite, or not, depends on the next few moves Greenlee and his associates make." On January 23, 1932, the *Courier* printed a credible rumor that Greenlee was trying to hire Charleston. Two weeks later, Greenlee announced he had signed his "new pilot," and that Charleston was already in town making arrangements and assembling a team.[26] One of the manager's acquisitions was Josh Gibson.

PREPARING TO PLAY

On February 5, 1932, M.E. Goodson, owner of the New York Black Yankees, held a reception to honor "present and veteran baseball players." Among the attendees were Gus Greenlee and Oscar Charleston. During the event, Goodson agreed to bring his team to Pittsburgh for the opening game at Greenlee Field.[27] But this was still almost three months away, and much work remained to be done on the field and with the team.

The first of the Crawfords left for spring training at Hot Springs, Arkansas, on February 23, knowing that their new ballpark would be ready upon their return to Pittsburgh.[28] The team was traveling in style because in addition to securing a new field, a great manager, and Josh Gibson, Gus Greenlee also provided quality transportation. On February 20, 1932, manager Charleston announced: "A seventeen-passenger Mack bus is now in the paint shop, where the sign man will 'do his stuff.' It is a Mack B. G. six-cylinder, 79-horsepower affair, with vacuum booster foot brakes...capable of 60 miles per hour. It is upholstered in genuine grain leather." This bus was rumored to have cost $10,000, which was a fortune in 1932, when most Negro League players did not even earn a tenth of that sum in a whole season.[29]

FINISHING TOUCHES

While the players were boiling out and limbering up in Hot Springs, "the busy hum of mortar-mixing machines" continued on Bedford Avenue as "the speedy activity of efficient colored bricklayers and their helpers" worked to finish "the fresh-looking, neat brick" structure. On April 9, the *Courier* reported, "The spacious new…home of the Pittsburgh Crawfords is almost completed. The imposing high red brick wall which surrounds the park has just about reached its topmost point." The only section of the brick exterior still unfinished was "the triangular corner behind the home plate. And this sector will soon be entirely completed." The grandstands, "erected upon a strong concrete base and built with the very finest supporting steel beams, are getting their finishing touches." Beneath the stands were "modern…dressing rooms…where several teams can be easily accommodated." Bellinger's design also included "plenty of space for storing…equipment and for the…field business headquarters." The ballpark "promises to be the finest and largest…ever built in this city for a colored club to cavort upon." Groundskeepers were still smoothing out a "few remaining minor irregularities," but the *Courier* reassured its readers, "Architect Bellinger, who has been kept busy on the project, feels sure that everything will be in readiness for the opening."[30] In all, constructing the ballpark required 75 tons of steel, 14 carloads of cement, and 1,100 linear feet of steel fencing."[31]

PLAY BALL!

After training in Hot Springs, then playing 22 exhibition games across eight states in six weeks and logging over 5,000 miles in their new bus, the Crawfords were ready to open their new ballpark.[32] The first game at Greenlee Field—Friday, April 29, 1932—pitted the Crawfords against the New York Black Yankees. Opening day featured many "dedicatory exercises," and the schedule for events was as follows:

3:45 Black Yankees batting practice

4:15 Crawfords batting practice

4:45 Team photographs

5:15 Black Yankees workout

5:30 Crawfords workout

5:45 Flag-raising exercises

6:00 Play Ball[33]

The *Courier* reported that a "capacity crowd of 4,000 [witnessed the] dedication of Greenlee Park."[34] It is unclear whether this attendance figure fell below the previously estimated capacity of 6,000 because some of the seating was not yet completed or because hundreds of complimentary passes were not counted in the gate receipts. Scores of prestigious people attended, including Pittsburgh's "mayor, councilmen, county commissioners, and other prominent city and county officials."[35] Gus Greenlee made a grand entrance: "Clad in a white silk suit, shirt, tie, and buck shoes, [he rode into] the park standing inside a red Packard convertible."[36] Before the game, "The teams lined up behind the band and marched to the flagpole in deep center field, where the American flag was unfurled and raised to the strains of the national anthem." Next, *Pittsburgh Courier* editor Robert L. Vann "made a short address…calling attention to the man, Mr. Gus Greenlee, whose investment, vision, and civic pride had made the wonderful park possible." The crowd gave Greenlee a standing ovation.[37] Then Vann took the mound and "…[showed] rare form as he pitched…the opening ball." The umpire declared it "a STRIKE! (on first bounce)."[38] *Courier* sports editor Chester L. Washington declared, "All the color, glamour and picturesqueness that usually attends the opening of a big league ball park was in evidence."[39]

After the inaugural ceremonies, manager Charleston led his team to the field against the Black Yankees, managed by George "Tubby" Scales. Unfortunately, the contest did not end as Pittsburgh fans wished. The game was close and exciting, a true pitchers' duel with a double shutout until the top of the ninth inning. The *Courier* reported the action: "Burning 'em across with all the speed and zip of mid-season form, and with the unerring aim of a machine gunner, Jesse Hubbard of the Black Yankees mowed down the Crawfords, 1-0, in a game that fairly sizzled with action." Satchel Paige, "the local rifleman," pitched well but allowed six hits to Hubbard's three. "So effective was the pitching on both sides that it was the first half of the ninth before the one and deciding marker was rushed across the pan." Ted Page scored the run; earlier in the game, he had also registered the first hit in Greenlee Field. Pittsburgh fans were hoping Josh Gibson would provide some opening day fireworks, but he went hitless and played left field rather than catching because he was still recovering from an appendicitis operation he had undergone in Hot Springs.[40] After the game, a group of local sports fans led by "former athlete" Joe Williams held a "reception and dance in honor of Gus Greenlee and the Pittsburgh Crawfords." A "high class orchestra" provided music in the Princess Hall ballroom, at the corner of Center Avenue and Miller Street. The event was open to the public, and organizers expected a crowd of 1,000.[41]

The next afternoon, the Crawfords took their revenge at Greenlee Field, defeating the Black Yankees, 2-1, in the bottom of the 10th inning.[42] And when New York returned to Pittsburgh on July 8, 1932, fans who braved the heat at Greenlee Field witnessed a spectacular game: Satchel Paige pitched a no-hit shutout against the Black Yankees, winning 6-0 and becoming "the first Crawford moundsman to pitch a no-hitter at the new Greenlee Field."

Paige repeated this no-hit feat against the Homestead Grays on July 4, 1934, striking out 17 batters in a 4-0 victory.[43]

TROUBLE FILLING THE GRANDSTANDS

Baseball games at Greenlee Field drew large crowds throughout May 1932, but once summer temperatures started to rise, gate receipts dwindled. One theory for this was that the uncovered grandstands provided no shade during afternoon games. In the sagging economy, covering the stands offered no guarantee that games would draw more spectators, so Greenlee and his partners decided not to invest in the additional construction. In 1934, Greenlee proposed adding a simple awning over the grandstand, but the other investors balked and declined the suggestion.[44]

In late summer 1932, Greenlee found a different solution to avoid afternoon heat: he invested a reported $6,000 for lights so the Crawfords could play at night. In early September, while the team was out of town, electricians installed a lighting system that fully equipped the field for night games. The first of these was held on September 16, between the Crawfords and the Grays. This caused a sensation because few ballparks had lights, and no major-league teams were yet playing night baseball. The Pittsburgh Pirates did not play their first night game at Forbes Field until June 4, 1940.[45]

Greenlee Field's new lighting system also solved another economic obstacle: the inability to play baseball on Sunday, the only day many Hill District residents had free to attend afternoon or early evening games. To challenge the Pennsylvania State Blue Law prohibiting Sunday baseball, Greenlee scheduled a night game between the Crawfords and the Grays, to begin at 12:01 a.m. Monday, September 19, 1932, less than three days after the field's first game under lights. This midnight affair provided plenty of glamour, bright lights, and color." The game "proved to be a real novelty attraction and drew out nearly 3,000, including most of the died-in-the-wool night-lifers and many of those who had to go to work in the morning." Chester L. Washington observed, "there is 'something new under the sun' and folks will go for it—if it is a real attraction."[46] The Crawfords repeated this midnight promotion on Saturday, August 11, 1934, with a game against the Birmingham Black Barons. The *Courier* heralded these events as "the most entertaining baseball novelty the Bedford Avenue enclosure has offered."[47]

More than lack of shade and Sunday games, the largest influence on shrinking attendance at the ballpark was the economic impact of the Great Depression. Most Hill District residents simply could not afford the luxury of attending baseball games, so Greenlee introduced other promotions to attract people to the ballpark. During a "Ladies' Night" on June 5, 1933, Satchel Paige struck out 15 in a 3-1 win over the Chicago American Giants. That night, women accounted for over 2,000 of the nearly 5,000 fans in attendance.[48] At the start of the 1936 season, Greenlee announced that the Crawfords were trying "two experiments at Greenlee Field...with a view to stimulating interest in the game and increasing attendance." The first "experiment" was an $8 season pass, which would "admit the holder to a grandstand seat to any game played at Greenlee Field by the Crawfords, whether opposed by a league or independent club." Spectators could purchase these passes at the Crawford Grill. The other promotion was raffling off a new 1936 Ford sedan. Fans received an entry for the drawing every time they purchased a game ticket, and the drawing was held on July 4. Greenlee noted that "Both innovations [were] launched for the purpose of raising finances to make needed improvements at Greenlee Field. Such as: a second tier of seats, or a cover over the present grandstand, reconstructed floodlight system for night attractions, portable dance floor, etc. These possible enhancements were an attempt to improve public relations. At the time, some local "race men" were faulting Greenlee for not involving enough African Americans in daily operations at the park and not adequately supporting the Hill District community. Greenlee noted "the Bedford Avenue park will solve many problems for religious, fraternal, [and] civic organizations."[49]

Turbulence between Greenlee and Homestead Grays owner Cum Posey also affected business at the ballpark. The Crawfords owner accused Posey of limiting his access to star players and trying to keep them out of the East-West League in 1932.[50] Then after the Negro National League revived in 1933, Posey accused Greenlee of forcing a stranglehold on Black baseball, expecting the Grays to lease Greenlee Field for their home games. The epic feud resulted in Posey deliberately seeing other grounds and even scheduling some of his team's games on the same days that the Crawfords were playing. These sour exchanges weakened leagues and helped erode local support of Black baseball in Pittsburgh.

Posey also accused Greenlee of trying to monopolize the best players, evidenced by his luring Oscar Charleston and Josh Gibson from the Grays in 1932. But Posey himself was certainly not innocent in this and seduced his own share of players away from other teams. Black baseball was, after all, a business; and with resources becoming increasingly scarce during the Great Depression, it is not surprising that key stakeholders fought to protect their shares. Writing in the *Courier* at the end of the 1932 season, W. Rollo Wilson noted, "The Crawfords have taken the play away from the Grays and no longer do Smoky City fans consider Cum Posey's bunch the penultimate in baseball. A lot of them have a deep suspicion that the Crawfords are now the chosen people." Wilson further recognized the precarious situation with two teams competing for support within the same city: "The Crawfords...are in Pittsburgh to stay and when the Grays face them this weekend, Cum Posey will be fighting for his baseball life...If there is room for only one team in [Pittsburgh]—I am very much of the opinion that the Grays are closing their books." Wilson believed Greenlee Field was the key to the Crawfords' increasing stature: "Whatever doubt there might have been in the minds of the bugs as to the permanence of the Crawfords ought to be dissipated by that fine park...out on Bedford Avenue."[51] Such intense rivalries were nothing new in Black baseball. Since the formation of the original Negro National League in 1920, repeated meetings and treaties had attempted to settle disputes over raiding teams, scheduling games, and sharing profits.

OTHER USES FOR GREENLEE FIELD

From the outset, Gus Greenlee and his partners intended to use Greenlee Field for more than just Crawfords baseball games. Even before the park opened, Greenlee "declared that no club would be barred from playing in Greenlee Field...[and] any baseball team which would make satisfactory arrangements would be allowed to stage their games at [the park]."[52] This included the rival Homestead Grays but also amateur and semiprofessional baseball and softball teams, plus other sporting and non-sporting events.

Because even uncovered grandstands are cooler than an overcrowded arena with no air conditioning, Greenlee Field almost immediately replaced Motor Square Garden as Pittsburgh's primary venue for professional boxing during the summer. In mid-May, the *Courier* announced that Jules Beck of Motor Square Garden would arrange the matches, and Greenlee Field brought in the Garden's boxing ring and floor seating. Light heavyweights Larry Johnson and Maxie Rosenbloom topped the ballpark's opening fight card on June 9.[53] After the initial event, weekly Thursday night matches of four to six bouts typically featured local amateurs and boxers from the Allegheny Mountain Association. Unlike baseball, professional boxing was not segregated, so Greenlee Field saw fighters of all races "[throwing] the leather mittens fast and furious." One bout in 1934 even featured a Chinese boxer, Mon Woo.[54]

Announcing "Pittsburgh's Amateur Boxing Classic,... sponsored by the Amateur Athletic Union," to be held at Greenlee Field on Tuesday, July 17, 1934, the *Daily News Standard* of Uniontown, Pennsylvania, noted, "The big ball park...seats upwards of 10,000 people." The feature of this event was the anticipated appearance of William "Rabbit" Eley, "crack negro 135-pounder," who was scheduled to make his last amateur appearance before going professional two days later at Greenlee Field's weekly Thursday Night boxing match. However, Eley's manager kept him away from the amateur match so that he would be in top shape for his professional debut, which drew more advance ticket sales than any previous bout in Pittsburgh. The bet paid off and Eley scored a fourth-round knockout against Paddy Gray. Eddie Zivic, a boxer praised by Jack Dempsey, was also scheduled to appear.[55]

As Greenlee's involvement in boxing grew, he expanded promotions to host professional bouts affecting national championship standings. These matches generated more income than baseball. For a professional bout in June 1935, promoters offered 5,000 general admission seats at $1.10 each, and reserved ringside seats for $2.20. By 1936, Greenlee himself was managing light-heavyweight title holder John Henry Lewis. However, as the Great Depression worsened, Greenlee had to lower prices to fill the stands at boxing matches too. In 1937, the first outdoor bout of the season offered "the lowest admission prices in local history." Since fighting was to be staged at the ballpark every Thursday throughout the summer, it was important to start with strong attendance.[56]

Since baseball and outdoor boxing seasons only lasted through late September, Greenlee and his partners found football teams to lease the field during the fall. Pittsburgh's professional football team—also called the Pirates—played their National Football League games at Forbes Field but used Greenlee Field at various times from 1934 to 1937 for preseason training, exhibition games, and midweek practices during the regular season."[57] The ballpark also served as temporary training grounds for the Pirates' opponents. For example, in 1935 the Chicago Cardinals of the National Football League played against the Pirates on October 18, then in New York against the Giants on October 25. Rather than traveling back to Chicago between games, the Cardinals spent the week in Pittsburgh practicing at Greenlee Field. In November 1935, the ballpark hosted a semiprofessional National-American Football Conference game with the St. Rosalia Preps, a team associated with the Pirates.[58]

During its seven-year lifespan, Greenlee Field also held many amateur football games featuring high school and college teams, which were particularly successful on Thanksgiving. The first of these "football classics" was a college game on Thanksgiving Day 1932, between Wilberforce and West Virginia. Over 500 tickets had already been sold by November 5, and the game sold out. Box seats cost $2.50, reserved seats $2.00, and general admission $1.00. On November 24, over 5,000 turned out for the game, and it became such a social event that the *Courier* ran a special "Classic Visitors" column to list some of the people who had come to town. The game ended in a 0-0 tie.[59]

To fill the gap between the football and baseball seasons, Greenlee Field also hosted amateur and semiprofessional soccer matches and mid-winter tournaments from December through April. In 1937, the Pittsburgh Steel semiprofessional soccer club occasionally used Greenlee Field for its games, and on June 2, 1937 the semiprofessional Pittsburgh District All-Stars played the professional Charlton club of Great Britain, which was touring the United States. Charlton won, 2-0.[60]

The spacious ballpark was also suitable for track and field events, such as the Amateur Athletic Union meet on Friday, September 6, 1935.[61] But racing of another sort was perhaps the strangest competition held at Greenlee Field. On July 26, 1933, the ballpark was converted to a race track, and "Auto racing patrons of Pittsburgh got their first glimpse of speed demons in action at Greenlee Field." The races were less spectacular than anticipated due to "a damp track and an unseasoned racing course." The first two events were 10-mile races, with the winner of the first clocking 12:02, and the victor in the second finishing a minute faster. The third race was "originally advertised as a 25-mile event, but was cut [to 15 miles] because of the hazardous condition of the track." Although the event drew a large crowd, auto racing did not catch on at Greenlee Field. Testing whether smaller cars would have better luck, on Saturday August 30, 1936, the ballpark hosted a national championship event for midget auto racing.[62] The ballpark's earthen right-field wall and bermed center-field curve were undoubtedly assets for these races, though it is unclear how cars were contained around the rest of the track.

With grandstand seating for over 7,000 people, Greenlee Field provided an ideal outdoor venue for non-sporting events, such as major community and church functions. On Monday, June 27, 1932, Ebenezer Baptist Church held a "Field Day" at the ballpark, with "a bazaar, songfest and...[a] women's baseball game." After the other events, a gospel chorus with 200 members sang spirituals."[63]

On December 16, 1933, the ballpark was the site of a formal social protest to raise financial support for the legal appeals of "the Scottsboro Boys"—Haywood Patterson and Clarence Norris—who were wrongly accused of raping two White girls in Arkansas and had been sentenced to death. In protest, the International Labor Defense, the League of Struggle for Negro Rights, and other organizations united to hold a parade through the Hill District, ending at Greenlee Field for a formal presentation and mass. It was the first social protest for which the city of Pittsburgh granted official police permits.[64]

But most non-sporting events at Greenlee Field were of a less serious nature, such as "Bob McKenzie and His Hollywood Suicide Circus," which performed at the ballpark on July 19, 1938, as a fundraiser for the Iron City Elks Lodge.[65]

THE FALL OF GREENLEE FIELD

In 1938, with Joe Tito and his family now fully occupied with their growing business at Latrobe Brewery, the Bedford Land Company investors turned over daily operations at Greenlee Field to Gus Greenlee. In hindsight, this was certainly too late since by then the city of Pittsburgh had other plans for the ballpark.[66]

Because of its geographic location at the intersection of three major rivers and abundant natural resources, Pittsburgh was ideal for developing major industries, most notably U.S. Steel, founded through a corporate merger in 1901. As such companies flourished, job growth attracted waves of new residents: first immigrants from Eastern Europe, then African Americans from the south pursuing a better life during the Great Migration after World War I. As a result of this influx of new residents the city's population doubled in less than 30 years.

1900	321,616
1910	533,905
1920	588,343
1930	669,817
1940	671,659[67]

Unfortunately housing did not keep up with this swelling city. In the Hill District, thousands of people lived either in decaying wood frame houses or dangerously substandard tenements. Even into the late 1930s, many residences lacked basic necessities like running water, indoor bathrooms, and functional kitchens. Oil lamps were still the main means of lighting.[68] The continuing effects of the Great Depression escalated these problems. Without jobs, people could not afford to maintain their homes or build new ones and as the economy worsened, absentee landlords walked away from crumbling properties they had no funds to repair or pay taxes on.

By the start of 1938, the city began searching for solutions to construct new sanitary public housing. Dramatically fluctuating topography in the Hill District made finding a suitable site for a large development difficult, since grading the land would be considerably expensive. Unfortunately, the most attractive site was a full city block of perfectly level land: Greenlee Field. Moderate topography of the adjacent Lincoln Memorial Cemetery made the site even more attractive. Thus, by mid-summer 1938, the Pittsburgh Housing Authority was aggressively pressuring the Bedford Land Company to sell their ballpark.

On Wednesday, July 20, Federal Housing Administrator Nathan Strauss announced that he had approved a nearly $7 million federal grant for three low-income housing developments in Pittsburgh. The previous day, the Pittsburgh Housing Authority had offered $50,000 for the Greenlee Field property, and the three Bedford Lan Company stockholders—Greenlee, Tito, and Thoms—had met to discuss the offer. The *Courier* noted that "No report of the meeting was given out, but it is understood that the stockholders were favorable to the…offer." The newspaper further added, "It is known that the Authority is bidding on other parcels of real estate contiguous to Greenlee Field, and it is believed that the baseball park would be taken in condemnation proceedings should the stockholders decline to sell." The *Courier* predicted the ballpark's future:

> If the plans of the Pittsburgh Housing Authority carry through, Greenlee Field, scene for the last [seven] years of the Hill District's most spectacular outdoor spectacles, including championship baseball, will blossom within a few months with a low-income housing project, fertilized by a Federal Government grant and a city loan.[69]

Greenlee and his partners did eventually accept the $50,000 offer but after the deal had been settled the Housing

Authority dropped the amount to $38,000. "[T]he stockholders had no alternative but to accept."[70]

Ironically, during the time of these negotiations, Greenlee Field's architect, Louis A.S. Bellinger, was working for the city building inspector, though it remains unclear whether he had any involvement in the ballpark's demise. In another strange twist, in February 1940, the Pittsburgh Housing Authority named Everett E. Utterback manager of the 432-unit Bedford Dwellings, a position he held until August 1942, when the city promoted him to manage 888-unit Wadsworth Terrace. Utterback had attended the University of Pittsburgh on a track scholarship and became the team's first African American captain. After graduating from Duquesne Law School, his most prestigious legal client was Gus Greenlee. Utterback had written player contracts for men like Satchel Paige and Greenlee's managerial agreements with boxing champion John Henry Lewis. Utterback later served as general counsel for the Pittsburgh Housing Authority.[71]

THE END DRAWS NEAR

The 1938 baseball season and other events carried on through the rest of the summer, but crowds continued to dwindle as the Depression dragged on. After losing money all season, the Crawfords and other Negro League teams resorted to playing many late-summer games on the road, hoping to attract more spectators in other cities. The last Crawfords game at Greenlee Field was scheduled for Saturday, September 3, 1938, against the Homestead Grays. It was the first of a planned four-game series, but the *Courier* lamented: "Those hectic ball games which give Greenlee Field fans their biggest thrill will be enjoyed by two of our sister states!" Games on September 4, 5, and 6 were scheduled at parks in Ohio and West Virginia. It is unclear who won the last Crawfords game at Greenlee Field, or if it was ever played, because neither the *Courier*, nor any other newspaper—Black or White—published a score.[72]

After the Crawfords' season was over, other events continued at Greenlee Field. On Sunday, September 4, the ballpark hosted the Western Pennsylvania Softball Tournament, with eight teams competing for the Western Regional title. The winner would compete in the national tournament in Chicago.[73] On September 9, 1938, heavyweight boxing champion Joe Louis brought his Brown Bombers all-star softball team to play the Smoky City All-Stars.[74]

But most importantly, sometime during 1938, architect Edward B. Lee and his associates at Marlier, Lee, Boyd, and Prack took aerial and ground photographs of Greenlee Field and surrounding properties, in preparation for their commission to design the Pittsburgh Housing Authority's Bedford Dwellings public housing project. Today, these photographs are the best images we have of Greenlee Field.

THE END

In early December 1938, workers started dismantling the ballpark. "The steel [was] junked, bricks destroyed, lumber and floodlights stored until an attractive bid [was] made." Eulogizing the ballpark in his December 10, 1938, *Courier* article "The Rise and Fall of Greenlee Field," John L. Clark wrote "Seven years ago, 1932 to be exact, Greenlee Field... was recognized and talked about as one of the best baseball diamonds in the United States, not excepting those used by major and minor league clubs." The park was "hailed to be a welcome answer to a long prayer of baseball fans in the tri-state district." Yet even though Greenlee Field was "situated within 10 minutes walk of over 10,000 colored voters...The Housing Authority, using all its vested power, selected this site...for its colored colony."

The ceremonial groundbreaking for Bedford Dwellings was held on December 19, and radio station KDKA broadcast the event.[75] The original borders of the 18-acre Bedford Dwellings property were Kirkpatrick and Watt Streets, Bedford Avenue, and Bigelow Boulevard, an area which also included Lincoln Memorial Cemetery. Before excavation could begin, remains of about 200 people were disinterred and relocated to a special section of Woodlawn Cemetery in Penn Hills. In late November 1938, "masked men" began the work using a giant steam shovel, picks, and shovels. Family members of the deceased stood by to watch the process, but few of the new graves at Woodlawn retained their original markers.[76] Old Municipal Hospital on the east side of Greenlee Field was also eventually demolished after the city received Works Progress Administration funding in 1939 to build a new Municipal Hospital at the corner of Darragh and Terrace Streets.

The Pittsburgh Housing Authority began accepting bids for construction work in March 1939. The "first formal application for a building permit for Bedford Dwellings" was filed on August 2, 1939, and work was expected to begin two days later. The lead contractor was Ring

Construction Company of Minneapolis, Minnesota, which meant that much of the financial profits for this $3 million project would not remain in the Hill District—nor even in Pennsylvania.[77]

The first residents began moving into Bedford Dwellings at the end of the summer in 1940, and the Housing Authority expected all of the apartments to be full by October when President Roosevelt toured the public housing development and praised this great community improvement project. The 432 new apartments were certainly more sanitary and were even equipped with Westinghouse refrigerators. However, many Hill District residents questioned the fairness of this project. Some displaced by the new development either could not afford to live there or had incomes too high to qualify for public housing. Plus, removing acquired properties from the tax rolls put more burden on other property owners in the Hill District. When the Housing Authority claimed Greenlee Field, Pittsburgh not only lost a ballpark, but a major tax-paying commercial property.[78]

Over time, local memories of specific details about the Crawfords' Bedford Avenue ballpark have faded, and much of Greenlee Field's story will always remain a mystery. But at least now we can again visualize the field where the amazing Pittsburgh Crawfords and so many of their Negro League opponents battled for supremacy on the Hill from 1932 to 1938. Today, only a shadow of the ballpark remains, visible in satellite images which show four of the original buildings at the northeastern end of Bedford Dwellings fanned out across the old playing field.[79]

During their seven-year occupancy of Greenlee Field, the Crawfords included seven future Hall of Famers: Oscar Charleston, Josh Gibson, Satchel Paige, Cool Papa Bell, Judy Johnson, Willie Foster (Rube's younger half-brother from their father's remarriage, also known as Bill), and Jud Wilson. But without his ballpark, Gus Greenlee could no longer afford to keep the Crawfords in Pittsburgh, so in 1939, Oscar Charleston took a handful of willing players to Toledo, Ohio, and tried to rebuild a team while the rest scattered to other clubs. The Toledo Crawfords lasted only a year and moved to Indianapolis in 1940 but then disbanded before the 1941 season.

Notes

1 Several of these images are now available online through the Carnegie Museum of Art's Charles "Teenie" Harris Archive: http://www.cmoa.org/searchcollections.

2 Sources vary on when exactly Greenlee bought interest in the team, but the *Pittsburgh Courier* first mentions the connection in 1931. "Grays Prime for Crawfords and Cleveland," *Pittsburgh Courier*, June 20, 1931, 4.

3 "Grays Prime for Crawfords and Cleveland," *Pittsburgh Courier*, June 20, 1931, 4; W. Rollo Wilson, "Sports Shorts," *Pittsburgh Courier*, August 8, 1931, 4; Cum Posey, "Grays Undisputed Champs," *Pittsburgh Courier*, October 10, 1931, 5.

4 Today this site is behind the Ammon Recreation Center and Macedonia Baptist Church at 2217 and 2225 Bedford Avenue. In May 2009, a refurbished Ammon Field was rededicated as Josh Gibson Field, providing a quality ballpark for teams in the Josh Gibson Little League. Fittingly, the first game at the new park featured children's teams playing as the Pittsburgh Crawfords and the New York Black Yankees, the same match-up as the inaugural game at Greenlee Field in 1932. "Battered Hill District Ball Yard Reborn as Josh Gibson Field" *Pittsburgh Post-Gazette*, May 26, 2009.

5 W.A. Greenlee, "Crawfords' Owner Makes First Statement about the Team, New Park and Plans," *Pittsburgh Courier*, February 27, 1932, 4.

6 John L. Clark, "The Rise and Fall of Greenlee Field," *Pittsburgh Courier*, December 10, 1938, 17. Sanborn Insurance and other historical maps show the Entress Brick Company's location and the original configuration of streets around the site. Prior to its use for brick manufacturing, the site had been a small Carmelite cemetery. The bodies had been relocated to Mt. Carmel Cemetery during the 1880s. American Historical Society, *History of Pittsburgh and Environs* (New York: American Historical Company, 1922), 291; the Rev. Anthony C. Dressel, "Rev. Angelus Forrestal, O. Carm., 1845-1879," undated, http://carmelnet.org/necrology/obits/ ForrestalAngelus1845-1879.pdf.

7 Pennsylvania State College Agricultural Experiment Station, *Annual Report of the Pennsylvania State College for the Year 1897* (Harrisburg: Wm. Stanley Ray—State Printer of Pennsylvania, 1898), 144.

8 Clark, "The Rise and Fall of Greenlee Field." The 1930 U.S. Federal Census lists Ralph Tito's occupation as truck driver for a transfer company and Tony Christiano's as landscape gardener.

9 Albert M. Tannler, "Louis Arnett Stewart Bellinger," *African American Architects: A Biographical Dictionary, 1865–1945* (New York: Routledge, 2004), 30-32. Unless otherwise noted, all biographical information about Bellinger is from this essay. Special thanks to Albert Tannler, Historical Collections Director at the Pittsburgh History and Landmarks Foundation, for also graciously providing access to his Bellinger files. U.S. Federal Census and military records accessed through Ancestry.com. Bellinger's first cousin Mamie Fields Garvin discusses their extended family in South Carolina in *Lemon Swamp and Other Places: A Carolina Memoir* (New York: Free Press, 1983).

10 Fessenden Academy was founded by the American Missionary Association of the Congregational Church in 1892, specifically for educating African American children. In January 1914, 225 students were enrolled at the school, being instructed by twelve teachers (three male, nine female), also all African American. Curriculum included "agriculture, mechanics, domestic science, sewing, and…literary subjects." The school stressed racial pride, and its Carnegie Building was built entirely by African American labor. The school is now a designated historic district in Ocala. United States, Dept. of the Interior, Bureau of Education, *Negro Education: A Study of the Private and Higher Schools for Colored People in the United States, 1916*, vol. 2 (Washington, DC: GPO, 1917), 174.

11 "Allen University Historical Background," Allen University, http://www.allenuniversity.edu/dnnweb4/AllenHistory/tabid/140/Default.aspx.

12 The Historic Pittsburgh Image Collections digital archive includes a June 7, 1935, photograph of the Pythian Temple (http://digital.library.pitt.edu/pittsburgh, search Image Collections for Pythian Temple, or identifier: 715.3524662.CP).

13 The 1930 U.S. Census reported the home's value.

14 "Louis A. Bellinger, Architect, Buried," *Pittsburgh Courier*, February 9, 1946, 1. Bellinger's grave in Allegheny Cemetery is just up the hill from Josh Gibson's.

15 Albert M. Tannler also provided information on the Crawford Grill storeroom project. It is unclear what part of the establishment was renovated.

16 These entries appear on pages 1, 11, 9, and 11, respectively

17 "Plan New Baseball Park Here," *Pittsburgh Courier*, July 18, 1931, 4.

18 "Greenlee Field Data Released," *Pittsburgh Courier*, July 9, 1932, 4.

19 Some historians have said that Greenlee also moved some of the Lincoln Memorial Cemetery, but aerial photographs suggest that he merely covered Junilla Street with the Eastern wall of the park, without disturbing any graves.

20 Topographical maps of this site from 1929 and 1959 are available online: "City of Pittsburgh Geodetic and Topographic Survey Maps, 1923–1961," Historic Pittsburgh, http://images.library.pitt.edu/cgi-bin/i/image/image-idx?c=geotopio&page=index (select plate 10 from the key map). Dramatic variations between these two maps show extensive excavations for the ballpark and later uses of the site.

21 The same sign and arched entrances are in the background of the 1935 Crawfords team photograph with the bus.

22 "Good Bouts at Greenlee Field," *Monessen* (PA) *Daily Independent*, July 14, 1934, 3.

23 Philip J. Lowry lists known dimensions for fields in *Green Cathedrals: The Ultimate Celebration of Major League and Negro League Ballparks* (New York: Walker & Company, 2006). He lists the dimensions of Forbes Field, home of the Pittsburgh Pirates, as left 365 (in 1930), center 435 (in 1930), and right 375 (in 1925). In 1932, Bellinger said the distance to the left field corner was 350. "Crawfords Back, Set for Test," *Pittsburgh Courier*, April 30, 1932, 5.

24 "Gleanings from Greenlee Field," *Pittsburgh Courier*, June 11, 1932, 4.

25 Ibid.

26 "Pittsburgh Crawfords May Have New Manager Next Season," *Pittsburgh Courier*, December 19, 1931, 4; William Nunn, "Sport Talks," *Pittsburgh Courier*, December 26, 1931, 4; "Oscar Charleston May Manage 1932 Crawfords," *Pittsburgh Courier*, January 23, 1932, 5; "New Pilot," *Pittsburgh Courier*, February 6, 1932, 5.

27 "Old-time and Present Ball Stars Meet," *Pittsburgh Courier*, February 13, 1932, 5. Other attendees included Frank Miller, George "Tubby" Scales, Smokey Joe Williams, Larry Brown, Fats Jenkins, Tex Burnett, Frank Grant, and Sol White.

28 "Crawford Vanguard Off for Hot Springs," *Pittsburgh Courier*, February 23, 1932, 5.

29 "Crawfords Secure 17-Passenger Bus," *New York Amsterdam News*, February 24, 1932, 13; "Pittsburgh Team to Start Tour," *Chicago Defender*, February 27, 1932, 9. The *Defender* article includes a photograph of the bus, which is not the same as the one in the 1935 team photograph.

30 "Greenlee Ball Park Preps for Opener," *Pittsburgh Courier*, April 9, 1932, 5.

31 "Greenlee Field Data Released," *Pittsburgh Courier*, July 9, 1932, 4.

32 "Crawfords Back, Set for Test," *Pittsburgh Courier*, April 30, 1932, 5.

33 Chester L. Washington, "Sportively Speaking," *Pittsburgh Courier*, April 30, 1932, 5.

34 "Hubbard Pitches Three-Hit Game To Beat Page (sic), 1 to 0," *Pittsburgh Courier*, May 7, 1932, 5. The misspelling is ironic since Ted Page actually scored the winning run against Satchel Paige.

35 "Pittsburgh's Crawfords to Open Friday," *Chicago Defender*, April 30, 1932, 8.

36 Mark Ribowsky, *The Power and the Darkness: The Life of Josh Gibson in the Shadows of the Game* (New York: Simon & Schuster, 1996), 91.

37 "Hubbard Pitches Three-"Hit Game To Beat Page (sic), 1 to 0," *Pittsburgh Courier*, May 7, 1932, 5. Interestingly, the opening of Greenlee Field also set the tone for "Negro Trade Week," May 8-15, which the Business and Professional Association of Pittsburgh sponsored to "Encourage Negro Business." The May 7, 1932 *Pittsburgh Courier* includes several articles about this event.

38 "*Courier* 'Chief' in Action," *Pittsburgh Courier*, May 7, 1932, 5. This article also includes a photograph of Vann pitching the ball.

39 Washington, "Sportively Speaking," *Pittsburgh Courier*, May 7, 1932, 5.

40 Washington, "Crawfords, Black Yanks Break Even in Series," *Pittsburgh Courier*, May 7, 1932, 5.

41 "Plan Dance to Honor Crawfords," *Pittsburgh Courier*, April 9, 1932, 5; "Crawfords Reception on April 28," *Pittsburgh Courier*, April 16, 1932, 6. It is not clear whether the "Joe Williams" organizing this event could have been the future Hall of Fame pitcher, still with the Homestead Grays at the beginning of 1932.

42 Washington, "Crawfords, Black Yanks Break Even in Series," *Pittsburgh Courier*, May 7, 1932, 5.

43 "New York Yanks Win Series from Crawfords," *Pittsburgh Courier*, July 16, 1932, 5; William G. Nunn, "Paige Hurls No-Hit Classic," *Pittsburgh Courier*, July 7, 1932, 1.

44 Clark, "The Rise and Fall of Greenlee Field."

45 "Greenlee Field Installs Lights," *Pittsburgh Courier*, September 10, 1932, 5; W. Rollo Wilson, "Baseball War In Pittsburgh," *Pittsburgh Courier*, September 17, 1932, 14; "Sidelights on Sports," *Pittsburgh Post-Gazette*, May 21, 1938, 157; "First Night Ball Game at Pittsburgh Tuesday," *Daily Courier* (Connellsville, PA), June 3, 1940, 7.

46 Washington, "2,000 Watch Big Midnight Tilt," and Washington, "Chez Says," *Pittsburgh Courier*, September 24, 1932, A5. Washington also noted that starting the "floodlight battle" soon after midnight and ending at 2:40 emphasized the problem of Negro League games taking too long to play. He wrote, "Two hours and twenty-five minutes is too much time for an ordinary ball game—and it was quite noticeable as the clock neared 3 Ah-Hem."

47 "The First Night Game of Its Kind," *Evening Gazette* (Indiana, PA), August 11, 1934, 3; "Cleveland and Barons Meet Crawfords Here," *Pittsburgh Courier*, August 11, 1934, 5.

48 Satchell (sic) Supreme in Craw Victory, *Pittsburgh Courier*, June 10, 1933, 5.

49 "Free Ford, Season Passes Offered at Greenlee Field," *Pittsburgh Courier*, May 9, 1936.

50 W.A. Greenlee, "Crawfords Owner Makes First Statement about the Team, New Park and Plans," *Pittsburgh Courier*, February 27, 1932, 4.

51 Wilson, "Baseball War In Pittsburgh," *Pittsburgh Courier*, September 17, 1932, 14.

52 "Greenlee Ball Park Preps for Opener," *Pittsburgh Courier*, April 9, 1932, 5.

53 "Boxing Opens at Greenlee Field June 1," *Pittsburgh Courier*, May 14, 1932, 5; "Gleanings from Greenlee Field," *Pittsburgh Courier*, June 11, 1932, 4 (contains a photograph of the ballpark rigged out for boxing); "Larry Johnson, Maxie Rosenbloom To Clash Here," *Pittsburgh Courier*, June 4, 1932.

54 "Speigal Loses to Negro Pug," *Daily News Standard* (Uniontown, PA), August 19, 1932, 12; "Bittner to Box Christof in One Feature Match," *Daily News Standard* (Uniontown, PA), July 17, 1934, 8.

55 P.V.A.C. Boys in Big Classic," *Daily News Standard* (Uniontown, PA), July 11, 1934, 8; Arnold Goldberg, "Sport Chatter," *Daily News Standard* (Uniontown, PA), July 17, 1934, 8; "Pittsburgh Boxing," *Daily News Standard* (Uniontown, PA), July 20, 1934, 14; "Good Bouts at Greenlee Field," *Daily Independent* (Monesson, PA), July 14, 1934, 3.

56 "Billy Nichy Tries Another Step Up Ladder," *Charleroi* (PA) *Mail*, June 18, 1935, 5; First Outdoor Fight Card Thursday Night at Greenlee Field," *Daily Courier* (Connellsville, PA), May 18, 1937, 7.

57 "New Back Joins Pro Grid Team," *Daily News Standard* (Uniontown, PA), September 14, 1934, 12; "Pirate Pros To Play Exhibit Game Sunday," *Charleroi* (PA) *Mail*, August 23, 1935, 7; "Pirate Pros Meet Chicago Bears at Pittsburgh Sunday," *Daily Courier* (Connellsville, PA), September 28, 1935, 8; "Pirate Gridders Start Practice," *Morning Herald* (Uniontown, PA), August 19, 1937, 14.

58 "Chicago Cards Start Here Tomorrow," *Pittsburgh Post-Gazette*, October 17, 1935, 51; "Ravens Prepare to Battle St. Rosalia Preps Sunday," *Daily Independent* (Monessen, PA), November 21, 1935, 7.

59 Floyd G. Snelson, "Gus Greenlee (Big Mogul of Pittsburgh)" *Pittsburgh Courier*, November 19, 1932, 8; "Over 500 Tickets Sold for Turkey Day Classic Here," *Pittsburgh Courier*, November 5, 1932, 1; Wilson, "Force, W. Va. In 0-0 Deadlock," and "Classic Visitors," *Pittsburgh Courier*, December 3, 1932, 4.

60 "Professional Team Will Offer Stiff Competition," *Charleroi* (PA) *Mail*, June 3, 1937, 7; "Charlton Club Tops District All-Stars at Greenlee Field," *Charleroi* (PA) *Mail*, June 3, 1937, 7; "Charlton Soccer Team Meets All-Stars Tonight," *Daily News Standard* (Uniontown, PA), June 2, 1937, 9.

61 "Sports Gleanings," *Daily Courier* (Connellsville, PA), September 4, 1935, 7.

62 "Auto Races Staged at Greenlee Field Last Nite," *Monessen* (PA) *Daily Independent*, July 27, 1933, 6; "Uniontown Race is Semi-Final for Midgets Saturday," *Daily Courier* (Connellsville, PA), August 13, 1936, 10. Interestingly, Indianapolis's Bush Stadium, home field of the Indianapolis Indians and Clowns, was briefly used for similar auto racing purposes after the construction of Victory Field in 1996.

63 "Ebenezer Field Day," *Pittsburgh Courier*, June 25, 1932, 19.

64 "Death Sentences to be Protested," *Pittsburgh Post-Gazette*, December 16, 1933, 5.

65 A photograph in the Teenie Harris archive at the Carnegie Museum of Art clearly shows an advertising banner for this event (accession number 2001.35.7834).

66 Clark, "The Rise and Fall of Greenlee Field," 17.

67 U.S. Census records.

68 "Big Demand Evident for PHA Homes" *Pittsburgh Post-Gazette*, December 6, 1939, 26.

69 "Greenlee Field!" *Pittsburgh Courier*, July 23, 1938, 6.

70 Clark, "The Rise and Fall of Greenlee Field."

71 "Housing Project Manager Resigns," *Pittsburgh Post-Gazette*, August 14, 1942, 6; "Memento Recalls a Different World," *Pittsburgh Post-Gazette*, November 17, 1983, 14.

72 "Craws Battle Grays in Holiday Series," *Pittsburgh Courier*, September 3, 1938, 17.

73 "Yezbaks Entered in West Penn Meet," *Morning Herald* (Uniontown, PA), September 1, 1938, 10.

74 Washington, "Sez Ches," *Pittsburgh Courier*, September 10, 1938, 16; "Talk O' Town," *Pittsburgh Courier*, September 10, 1938, 9.

75 "Start Housing Project Today," *Pittsburgh Post-Gazette*, December 19, 1938, 2.

76 "Masked Men Begin Job of Digging Up 'City of the Dead,' " *Pittsburgh Courier*, November 26, 1938, 6. In January 2001, Tom and Nancy McAdams compiled a list of some of those whose remains were moved to Woodlawn, and this list can be found online at the Woodlawn Cemetery Association website: http://freepages.genealogy.rootsweb.ancestry.com/~tandmnca/woodlawn/lincoln.html.

77 "Housing Bids Asked, Work Will Start Soon on Bedford Dwellings," *Pittsburgh Post-Gazette*, March 4, 1939, 13; "Housing Job Permit Asked," *Pittsburgh Post-Gazette*, August 3, 1939.

78 "Home Project To Be Opened," *Pittsburgh Post-Gazette*, September 16, 1940, 12; "Trip Arranged by President," *Pittsburgh Post-Gazette*, October 3, 1940, 3; "Buy Refrigerators for Home Projects" *Pittsburgh Post-Gazette*, January 31, 1940, 13; "The People Speak," *Pittsburgh Post-Gazette*, November 3, 1941, 8.

79 Online satellite images such as Google Earth clearly show this pattern. The approximate location of home plate was 40° 27' 4.46"N and 79° 58' 21.96"W. Using the Carnegie Mellon University Architecture Archive photographs, the author helped determine the exact location for the historical marker placed by the Pennsylvania Historical and Museum Commission, July 17, 2009. The marker, located directly where Greenlee Field's arched entry gates had been, was erected during the Society for American Baseball Research's annual Jerry Malloy Negro League Conference.

Integration and Black Baseball Socio-Economics

CAN YOU READ, JUDGE LANDIS?

Larry Lester

This article appeared in Black Ball: A Negro Leagues Journal, *Fall 2008*

PREMISE

By the late 1930s, and particularly during the years of US involvement in World War II, segregation in sport and society was a topic of increasing public interest. Nationalism had at least briefly trumped racism when Joe Louis and Jesse Owens emerged triumphant against the Germans. Within baseball, members of the media had loudly called for integration, which some major league managers, players, and even owners publicly supported. And as big leaguers went off to war, leaving behind diluted rosters and flagging attendance, calls for the signing of Black players grew more persistent. In spite of these facts, some researchers contend that Commissioner Kenesaw Mountain Landis must be held blameless for extending the color line; segregation, they argue, was a cultural wrong, and the time was not yet ripe to change it. This article advances a counter-argument, presenting evidence that Landis repeatedly disregarded calls for integrated play and in some instances acted to perpetuate segregation.

> "The only thing necessary for evil to triumph is for good men to do nothing."
>
> —Edmund Burke (1729–97)

This commentary is a counter response to Norman Macht's "Does Baseball Deserve Its Black Eye?" at SABR's 37th annual convention in St. Louis. His presentation looked at the attitudes and societal restrictions on racial integration prevailing in the era of Judge Landis's baseball leadership, giving Landis and other team owners an excuse from America's social ills. Meanwhile he stated there was no proof that Landis was against the integration of baseball and added, if there was, David Pietrusza's extensive biography would have indicated this. Macht also argued that team owners were "businessmen, not social reformers" and therefore exempt from their responsibility as laissez-faire thinkers. A request for a printed copy of Mr. Macht's presentation from SABR's research library was not honored. Also note, minutes of the leagues' executive board meetings, currently housed at the National Baseball Hall of Fame, are unavailable to researchers, as Major League Baseball has not "signed off" on their release.[1] This counterargument to Landis's position on integration is based on the premise of Nobel Prize–winning author Toni Morrison that "Racism is a scholarly pursuit, it's taught, it's institutionalized."[2]

The nation's credo, "All men are created equal," was a revolutionary idea which became the core of American beliefs. Somewhere along the way, these self-evident truths that were endowed by our Creator lost their way. As Americans strayed from this creed, Hall of Fame writer Sam Lacy said, "Some people were created more equal than others."[3] Nine score and seven years since the Declaration of Independence, these unalienable rights are still a dream for some, as some are reminded by Dr. Martin Luther King, Jr.'s "I Have a Dream" speech.

One such dream was to play the game of baseball. "Next to religion, baseball has furnished a greater impact on American life than any other institution," boasted President Herbert Hoover.[4] Several years before dreamer Jackie Robinson crossed the imaginary but real color line, there was a campaign initiated by wartime activists and writers to integrate this institution, known as the national pastime. This crusade to integrate baseball targeted Judge Kenesaw Mountain Landis, named after a Civil War battle of Confederate victory. For almost a quarter of a century, Commissioner Landis ruled apartheid baseball with a dictatorial influence that, among other things, prevented any man with a suntan from playing in his sandbox.

You were not welcomed if your name had ethnic overtones like Tyrone, Torriente, Clemente, Miñoso,

Dihigo, Ichiro, or Nomo. However, you would receive an invitation if you were in the image of the owners.[5] The *Baseball Register* would humbly display one's ancestry as Slovenian (Erv Palica), Scotch-Irish (Eddie Robinson), Irish Lithuanian (Barney McCosky), Irish Dutch (David Jolly), French Scotch-Irish (Ransom Jackson), French Canadian (Buddy Rosar), Czech German (Hal Newhouser), Danish Irish (Jack Jensen), Swiss English German (Dick Sisler), and Austrian-Hungarian (Hank Bauer).[6]

For someone looking at one's self through the eyes of another, race often becomes a creature defined by one's mind and twisted for its own discriminating purposes. Racism in baseball was not a static force. It transformed itself as it went from host to host, infecting our beloved game of peanuts and crackerjacks.

THE FORMATIVE YEARS

A central figure in our segregated game was Kenesaw Mountain Landis. He was meagerly educated and minimally trained for the profession of law. Landis was described by historian Harold Seymour as a "scowling, white-haired, hawk-visaged curmudgeon who affected battered hats, used salty language, chewed tobacco, and poked listeners in the ribs with a stiff right finger."[7]

Born in Millville, Ohio, Landis grew up in Logansport, Indiana. After failing an algebra class the Hoosier dropped out of high school. Later he taught himself dictation to secure a job as a courtroom reporter for the Cass County (Indiana) circuit court. Landis earned his high-school diploma in night school and later received his bachelor-of-law degree, in 1891, from the Union Law School in Chicago, now part of Northwestern University. Landis boasted to Tom Swope of the *Cincinnati Post*, "You Know, Tom, I never went to college myself. Mighty few persons know that, but it's a fact. I started my law course at the Y.M.C.A. Law School in Cincinnati and finished it at a similar school in Chicago."[8]

In 1905, President Theodore Roosevelt appointed high-school dropout Landis as a federal judge for Illinois. In 1907, Landis gained national fame when he ordered the nation's wealthiest man, John D. Rockefeller, to testify in the highly publicized suit against his Standard Oil Company for conspiring with railroads to fix prices. Landis smacked the Rock with an unprecedented fine of more than $29.4 million. Rockefeller won the case on appeal and never paid the fine.

In 1914 and 1915, Landis sat on the antitrust suit brought against the National League by the outlaw Federal League. Trustbuster Landis suddenly found himself on the side of monopoly and strategically withheld a decision in the case, eventually forcing the Feds to accept a settlement and fold their tents, thus preserving the hegemony of the two leagues. Baseball kept its monopoly and Landis was the hero of the club owners.

Seymour added: "Landis had a deep affection for baseball and looked upon the players more as heroes than as employees. He had a keen aversion to organized labor, liquor, and the New Deal. The rub was that he permitted his personal dislikes to warp his judicial objectivity."[9]

With damage to the national pastime's brand and image brought on by the infamous Black Sox Scandal in the 1919 World Series, baseball sought a remedy. Although the eight players suspected of fixing the series had been acquitted in court, the Judge used his subjectivity to argue that the need to clean up baseball's reputation took precedence over any legal judgments. His no-nonsense approach to matters made him an ideal choice to preside over baseball's kangaroo court. His salary rose from $7,500 as a judge to $50,000 as baseball commissioner. However, Landis would only take the difference of $42,500 for his sovereignty.[10]

Landis restored America's faith in baseball, but at the price of making the game paternal and sacred. In his first years as commissioner, the monarch of segregated baseball, with complete authoritative influence, banished for life 19 players, two owners, and one coach,[11] and at one time he ruled 53 players ineligible. Often accused of a restricted outlook on America's game, particularly in matters of race relations, Landis in 1921 issued a decree to prevent completely White major-league teams, especially the Babe Ruth All-Stars, from competing against Black teams in the post-season.[12] The commissioner threatened to ban the Bambino, Bob Meusel, and Wild Bill Piercy if they played against Oscar Charleston's Colored All-Stars (in the Southern California League). After the club lost to the Charleston club, Landis withheld their World Series pay and suspended the Yankee bad boys Ruth and Meusel (the team's second leading hitter) and Piercy (a third-string pitcher) for 39 days, or until May 20 of the 1922 season, for not adhering to his dictum.[13]

Landis's new ruling prevented more than three players from a single team to compete against the Black teams, with such games being promoted as "exhibition" games, to diffuse any inherent meaning of a meaningful contest. The 1922 postseason revealed the Bacharach Giants beating the New York Giants twice and the St. Louis Stars defeating the Detroit Tigers two out of three games. Meanwhile the Hilldale Club (of Darby, Pennsylvania) took five of six games from the Philadelphia Athletics, and the Chicago American Giants split two games with the Detroit Tigers.[14]

The commissioner's policies were often accepted, if not applauded, by the baseball nation. While writers often viewed Landis as harsh and narrow-minded, he was generally popular because of his steadfast efforts to maintain the integrity of the game, which was seriously questioned during the World Series scandal. His rule became nearly absolute with the 1922 Supreme Court decision that exempted the major-league cartel from antitrust legislation.

By 1926, *Washington Post* writer Shirley Povich summed up the icon's growing legacy in his column "Following Through":

> There is a man of mystery. Mysterious in the manner that he so completely dominates his associates, who, in his present undertaking, are his employers. And he makes them like it. Sixteen major league magnates, supposed to be business men and drivers of hard bargains, are so completely under the thumb of the man with the funny name and the well-deserved title that it is strange if not mysterious or weird. . . .
>
> Judge Landis is either the possessor of some spark of personality indescribable that puts him far ahead of his time or he is a grand hoax.

Landis had an uncanny capacity to influence and intimidate people and major league baseball "clothed him with the full power of his office." However, Povich observed,

> Why the sixteen major league magnates fear the displeasure of the man whom they elected to arbitrate in their own cause is strange.... What sort of a man is he who, by his mere presence and demeanor and the dignity that goes with age, turns such an adverse situation into a rout of his enemies? Surely, he is no ordinary personage. It may be the very audacity of his methods in flaunting the authority of his employers that gains him their respect. They clothed him with the full power of his office . . . Judge Landis, some man.[15]

THE MOVEMENT STARTS

In his SABR presentation, Macht made the dubious claim that America was "not socially ready" for integrated play. In fact, history holds many examples of peaceful contests between Black and White teams as well as fully-integrated games. In 1925, the Ku Klux Klan No. 6 of Wichita, Kansas, played the local colored Monrovians, in a contest officiated by two Irish Catholics to avoid preferential treatment.[16] There was no reported violence on or off the field in a victory for the Monrovians.[17] Further evidence reveals that integrated team play in Wichita's National Baseball Congress tournaments (in 1935, with extensive coverage by *The Sporting News*) and the Denver Post Tournament (in 1934) occurred without incident.[18] There are numerous examples of incident-free integrated play throughout Landis's tenure as commissioner.

In 1939 the National Baseball Hall of Fame opened in Cooperstown, New York, to honor baseball's greatest (White) players, managers, and executives. Meanwhile, some members of the mainstream press were outraged at the absence of African American ballplayers that were not invited to "The Show" and had no hope for Cooperstown fame. Jimmy Powers for the *New York Daily News* wrote to Bill Terry, manager of the New York Giants, who had finished in fifth place in 1939 with a 77–74 won-lost record: "Get yourself a batch of Satchel Paiges, Josh Gibsons and other truly great ball-busters. You'd find the Polo Grounds jammed with new and enthusiastic rooters. . . . Bill, you can make yourself the biggest man in baseball and I mean big. There is absolutely no law on your books barring a decent, hard-working athlete simply because his skin is a shade darker than his brother's. . . . You've got a pennant at your fingertips."[19]

A few months later, the *Philadelphia Record* made the same request to their local teams: "The Athletics and Phillies can be pennant contenders—not next year or the year after or five years from now—but immediately. Experienced players are available who could strengthen the A's shaky pitching staff, give the Phillies the batting punch they need. These players could make potential champions out of any of the other also-rans in either major league. . . . But they are Negroes, and organized baseball says they can't come in. . . . But no vote is ever taken on the subject, no manager or owner dares defy the Jim Crow tradition which in the past has been the most inflexible unwritten law in the game."[20]

The unwritten law generously allowed the 1939 Phillies to finish last with a 45–106 won-lost record, 50 1/2 games back. Their offense generated a paltry .317 on-base percentage. They failed to produce a batter with at least 70 RBIs or double-digit homers. On the other side of Philly, the A's pitching staff had a 5.79 ERA and only one 10-game winner (Lynn Nelson), as they finished in seventh place in the American League with a 55–97 won-lost record. Yet the city of Brotherly Love did not extend any love for their Black brothers.

As more attention than ever was focused on the integration issue, the last year of the decade proved to be a pivotal point for baseball in America, particularly Black baseball. With the exclusion of the Negro Leagues from the national pastime, it became a symbolic rip in the American flag. More press coverage and more campaigns questioned the so-called "gentlemen's agreement" imposed by major league owners.

Another thought came from Shirley Povich in his *Washington Post* column "This Morning":

> There's a couple of million dollars worth of baseball talent on the loose, ready for the big leagues yet unsigned by any major league clubs. There are pitchers who would win 20 games this season for any big league club that offered them contracts, and there are outfielders who could hit .350, infielders who would win quick recognition as stars, and there is at least one catcher who at this writing is probably superior to Bill Dickey. . . .
>
> Only one thing is keeping them out of the big leagues—the pigmentation of their skin. They happen to be colored. That's their crime in the eyes of big league club owners. Their talents are being wasted in the rickety parks in the Negro sections of Pittsburgh, Philadelphia, New York, Chicago and four other cities that comprise the major league of Negro baseball. They haven't got a chance to get into the big leagues of the White folks. It's a tight little boycott that the majors have set up against the colored player.

Povich directed responsibility at the commissioner: "It's definitely understood that no club will attempt to sign a colored player. And, in fact, no club could do that, because the elasticity of Judge Landis' authority would forbid it."[21] Since Landis had such absolute authority from the owners no one would defy this unwritten rule without some indication from the commissioner that is would be acceptable.

TRUTHS, LIES, & ALIBIS

In the summer of 1939, Wendell Smith launched a series of eight articles, in the *Pittsburgh Courier*, covering interviews with 40 players and eight managers requesting their opinions on integration. Smith strongly felt that Landis "never used his wide and unquestionable powers to do anything about the problem" and instead played a subtle "fence game." [22]

Selected interview excerpts support this premise.

> If the question of admitting colored baseball players into organized baseball becomes an issue, I would be heartily in favor of it. I think the Negro people should have an opportunity in baseball just as they have an opportunity in music or anything else.
>
> —William E. Benswanger, president, Pittsburgh Pirates[23]

> Yes, if given permission I would use a Negro player on my team. I have seen at least 25 Negro players who could have made the grade.
>
> —Deacon Bill McKechnie, Cincinnati Reds manager, later Larry Doby's coach (1947–49) with the Cleveland Indians[24]

> A few years ago, we played an exhibition game in Oakland, California, against a Negro all-star team. Satchel Paige, the fast ball wizard, pitched against

us, and I'm telling you he was great. I said right there that he was as good as Dizzy Dean.

—Ernie Lombardi, Reds catcher, 1938 National League Most Valuable Player[25]

I grew up in Philadelphia which was the hotbed of colored baseball. I saw any number of Negroes who should have made the big leagues. They had some of the best players I have ever seen on those teams.

—Bucky Walters, Reds pitcher, 1939 National League MVP[26]

I certainly wouldn't object to a good Negro ball player on our team. They have some of the best ball players I have ever seen. Although it's none of my business, I don't see why they are barred.

—Johnny Vander Meer, Reds pitcher who hurled back-to-back no-hitters in 1938[27]

Two years ago, I played in some exhibition games out on the Coast. I played in at least five-games and I guess I saw at least six colored players whom I thought I could use in the big leagues.

—Doc Thompson Prothro, manager of the last-place Philadelphia Phillies[28]

I saw two of the greatest ball players that ever lived, Rube Foster and Smokey Joe Williams. They were both pitchers and although I was just a kid, I was convinced that they were certainly good enough for the majors.

—Gabby Hartnett, Chicago Cubs manager, 1935 National League MVP and future Hall of Famer (1955) [29]

If some of the colored players I've played against were given a chance to play in the majors they'd be stars as soon as they joined up. Listen, Satchel Paige could make any team in the majors. He's got everything a pitcher can have. Shucks, only his color holds him back. He could be plenty of help to some of these big league teams—I'm tellin' you.

—Dizzy Dean, pitcher, 1934 National League MVP and future Hall of Famer (1953)[30]

I've seen plenty of colored boys who could make the grade in the majors. I have played against some colored boys out on the coast who could play in any big league that ever existed. Paige, [Cy] Perkins, Suttles and Gibson are good enough to be in the majors right now. All four of them are great players. Listen, there are plenty of colored players around the country who should be in the big leagues. I certainly would use a Negro ball player if the bosses said it was all right.

—Leo Durocher, manager, Brooklyn Dodgers[31]

Yes indeed, I've seen a number of Negro players whom I think were good enough for the majors. I rate Dick Lundy, Satchel Paige, Mule Suttles and [Robert] Clarke among the best players I have ever seen.

—Babe Phelps, Dodgers catcher, who hit .367 in 1936[32]

I've seen a whole gang who could make the grade. Paige, Gibson and Suttles are real big leaguers.

—Cookie Lavagetto, Dodgers third baseman, who would later play with Jackie Robinson in the majors[33]

Most of the great players I've seen are through. However, I'd name [Oscar] Charleston, [Martin] Dihigo and [Carlos] Torriente. They were good enough for any big league team that ever existed.

—Charley Dressen, coach, Dodgers[34]

The overall opinion of 48 men was in favor of the acceptance of Black players and included acknowledgment of some talented tan players. Managers McKechnie, Prothro, and Durocher appeared willing to accept Black players on their respective teams, if permitted. In turn Lester Rodney, a White writer for the Communist newspaper *New York Daily Worker*, explained his motivation to end racism in baseball:

> I belong to an organization which had as part of its party's platform the ending of discrimination—as a dream. Even long before I joined that party, I had been a red-hot baseball fan and got to know about some of the great players who were not allowed to play in America's national pastime.
>
> I would go out and see the Kansas City Monarchs and Satchel Paige pitch and all. You couldn't be a real baseball fan without knowing something was wrong there. Especially since my team, the Brooklyn Dodgers of the thirties was pretty pathetic.[35]

Rodney congratulated Smith for his efforts and noted the numerous statements by players and managers welcoming desegregation. Lambasting the apologists for blaming White fans and ballplayers for wanting the color line, Rodney and others also pointed out to the owners the mega-attendance at games between Negro League and MLB all-star teams.

Gate receipts at Negro League games also drew attention. In 1941, the East–West all-star game hit an all-time high in attendance with 50,256 fans and opened the curtains for Ed Harris of the Black-owned *Philadelphia Tribune* to pose the integration question to the moguls of major league baseball and their reasoning for ignoring Black players.

> You read about the 50,000 persons who saw the East-West game and the thousands who were turned away from the classic and you get to wondering what the magnates of the American and National League thought about it when they read the figures. Did any of them feel a faint stir in their hearts; a wish that they could use some of the many stars who saw action to corral some of the coin evidently interested in them? Or did they, hearing the jingling of the turnstiles in this, one of the good seasons baseball has had, just dismiss the notion and reserve the idea of Negro players in the big league until the next time there is a depression and baseball profits began to decline? Fifty thousand people at any baseball game, World Series included, is no small figure.[36]

As years went on, this economic argument began to overshadow major league owners' other reasons for rejecting Black players.

CAN YOU READ?

In 1942, a campaign called "Can You Read, Judge Landis?" was initiated by Rodney and the *Daily Worker*. With the war effort and national pride foremost in American minds, many socially activist groups campaigned for the inclusion of Blacks into baseball.

Joining the fight was columnist Eddie Gant of the *Chicago Defender*. In his column "I Cover the Eastern Front" he claimed Landis had always *"disliked the colored player and colored baseball"* and had attempted to prevent the upcoming Satchel Paige All-Stars from playing against a White all-star team, saying it was a phony relief game to benefit the war effort. Interracial games earlier that year had attracted 29,755 fans in Chicago, and 22,000 in Washington, D.C. Landis told major-league park owners not to rent their parks for these fundraisers.[37] There was a conscious strategy to maintain apartheid baseball.

Concurrently, the Greater New York Industrial Union Council, representing more than half a million CIO trade unionists from more than 250 locals, unanimously passed a resolution to end apartheid in baseball. The resolution was sent to Judge Landis with a challenge to other trade unions to follow their example. The council's resolution in part read:

> Whereas, in the spirit of national unity, Americans from all sections of the country have united to end the discrimination against race, color or creed. . . . Whereas, President Roosevelt in his address to the nation has stressed the importance of ending discrimination to insure victory. . . . Be it resolved that we, the Greater New York Industrial Union Council . . . demand that Judge Landis end jim-crow in the big league baseball now.[38]

Another union, the United Packinghouse Workers of America, Local 347, sent four resolutions to Judge Landis asking that the discrimination against Black players end as "it is the expression of Hilterism we are all seeking to destroy."[39] In June of 1942, a "Can You Read?" message was sent by the largest trade union in the United States, Ford Local 600 of the United Auto Workers (UAW). The Ford factory workers producing tanks and planes to defeat Nazism sent out telegrams and letters stating their belief that "National Unity embracing all races, colors and creeds is particularly necessary at this point in order to win the war against Fascism." The Ford local had 15,000 Black workers, including board members and union leaders. More than 80,000 workers approved the resolution to Judge Landis, which read in part:

> Whereas, Ford Local 600 UAW-CIO is opposed at all times to all forms of discrimination anywhere because of race, color or creed, and Whereas, Negroes are barred from playing in Major League baseball and Whereas, such leading baseball players as Joe DiMaggio, Bob Feller, Dizzy Dean and others have claimed that such Negro stars as Satchel Paige, Josh Gibson and others are capable of playing Major League ball, and Therefore be it resolved that Ford Local 600 goes on record against the ban of Negro ball players . . . and petition baseball commissioner Kenesaw Mountain Landis to use his powers to lift this ban.[40]

By the middle of July, more than one million signatures had been gathered on a petition to Judge Landis to lift the color barrier. "I would say the petition drive was a success when a million signatures landed on Landis' desk," said Lester Rodney. "And we didn't have a million Communists. These were people who were going to the ballpark and wanted to see justice. It played a role, but that didn't make the difference. A lot of great people started to join in and making noise."[41]

The "Can You Read?" campaign continued at movie houses. The debut of the motion picture *Pride of the Yankees*, about Lou Gehrig's career, was bombarded with pamphlets titled "In the Spirit of Lou Gehrig," calling for an end to Jim Crow. Roughly 20,000 leaflets were distributed to ten New York theaters with a statement that Gehrig made in 1938: "I have seen and played against many Negro players who could easily be stars in the big leagues. I could name just a few of them like Satchel Paige, Buck Leonard, Josh Gibson and Barney Brown who should be in the Majors. I am all for it, 100%."[42] And there still came no response from the commissioner's office.

The Communist Party was diligent in its campaign to bring racial equality to the forefront. Historian Henry D. Fetter noted, "The Communist paper's sports staff approached the breaking of baseball's color line with the belief that class, not race, provided the determinative fault line on American social life, and that racism was instigated by the bosses to foment division between White and Black workers, including baseball's working class: the players."[43]

Meanwhile, marching activists, organized by the Harlem-based League for Equality on Sports and Amusements, routinely picketed downtown Manhattan with signs that read: "IF WE CAN STOP BULLETS, WHY NOT BALLS?" and "WE CAN PAY, WHY CAN'T WE PLAY."[44]

JIM CROW MUST GO!

For years, similarly black ink came from Joe Bostic (*Harlem People's Voice*), Ches Washington (*Pittsburgh Courier*), Wendell Smith (*Pittsburgh Courier*), Jimmy Powers (*New York Daily News*), Sam Lacy (*Chicago Defender*, *Baltimore Afro-American*), Ed Harris (*Philadelphia Tribune*), Eddie Gant (*Chicago Defender*), Shirley Povich (*Washington Post*), and others to further the cause of "one-game-for-all."

On May 6, 1942, the day before the highly-attended Satchel Paige-Dizzy Dean matchup in Chicago, Rodney addressed Judge Landis, pressuring the commissioner to officially react to the apartheid issue in baseball. "We had always pointed to Landis as the one who had the authority to end the color line. But now we really put the spotlight on him," said Rodney. "The war was on and Blacks were being sent overseas and were among the casualties. So I decided to write Landis an open letter using that as a theme. We ran it under the headline 'TIME FOR STALLING IS OVER, JUDGE LANDIS.' This was about a month before I was drafted."[45]

> Judge Kenesaw Mountain Landis
> Commissioner of Baseball
> 333 North Michigan Ave.
> Chicago, Illinois
>
> The first casualty lists have been published. Negro soldiers and sailors are among those beloved heroes of the American people who have already

died for the preservation of this country and everything this country stands for—yes, including the great game of baseball.

So this letter isn't going to mince words.

You may file this away without comment as you already have done to the petitions of more than a million American baseball fans. You may ignore it as you have ignored the clear statements of the men who play our National Pastime and the men who manage the teams. You may refuse to acknowledge and answer it as you have refused to acknowledge and answer scores of sports columns and editorials in newspapers throughout the country—from Coast to Coast, Philadelphia, New York and down to Louisville and countless smaller cities.

Yes, you may again ignore this. But at least this is going to name the central fact for all to know.

You, the self-proclaimed "Czar" of Baseball, are the man responsible for keeping Jim Crow in our National Pastime. You are the one who, by your silence, is maintaining a relic of the slave market long repudiated in other American sports. You are the one who is refusing to say the word which would do more to justify baseball's existence in this year of war than any other single thing. You are the one who is blocking the step which would put baseball in line with the rest of the country, with the United States government itself.

There can no longer be any excuse for your silence, Judge Landis. It is a silence that hurts the war effort. You were quick enough to speak up when many Jewish fans asked for the moving back the World Series opening by one day to avoid conflict with the biggest Jewish holiday of the year . . . quick to answer with a sneering refusal. You certainly made it clear then that you were the one with the final authority in baseball. You certainly didn't evade any responsibility then.[46]

America is against discrimination, Judge Landis.

There never was a greater ovation in America's greatest indoor sports arena than that which arose two months ago when Wendell Willkie [a liberal-minded Republican who lost the presidential election to FDR in 1940], standing in the middle of the Madison Square Garden ring [after Louis defeated Buddy Baer the night of January 9, 1942], turned to Joe Louis and said, "*How can anyone looking at the wonderful example of this great American think in terms of discrimination for reasons of race, color or creed?*

Dorie Miller, who manned a machine gun at Pearl Harbor when he might have stayed below deck, has been honored by a grateful people.[47] "The President of our country has called for an end to discrimination in all jobs."[48]

Your position as big man in our National Pastime carries a much greater responsibility this year than ever before and you can't meet it with your alliance. The temper of the worker who goes to the ball game is not one to tolerate discrimination against 13,000,000 Americans in this year of the grim fight against the biggest Jim Crower of them all—Hitler.

You haven't a leg to stand on. Everybody knows there are many Negro players capable of starring in the big leagues. There was a poll of big league managers and players a couple of years ago and everybody but Bill Terry agreed that Negro players belonged in the big leagues. Terry is not a manager anymore and new manager Mel Ott, who hails from Gretna, Louisiana, is one of the players who paid tribute to the great Negro stars.

Bill McKechnie, manager of the Cincinnati Reds, set the tone for all the managers when he said, "*I could name at least 20 Negro players who belong in the big leagues and I'd love to have some of them on the Reds if given permission.*" If given YOUR permission, Judge Landis.

Manager Jimmy Dykes of the Chicago White Sox this spring was forced to tell two fine young Negro applicants for a tryout at the Pasadena training camp, "*I know you're good and I'd love to have you. So would the rest of the boys and every other manager in the big leagues I'm sure. But it's not up to me."* It's up to YOU, Judge Landis.

Leo Durocher, manager of the Brooklyn Dodgers, who were shut out in Havana this spring by a Negro pitcher, has said, *I wouldn't hesitate a minute to sign up some of those great colored players if I got the OK.* YOUR OK, Judge Landis. Get that?[49]

That's the sentiment of player, manager and fan.

The *Louisville Courier Journal*[50] of a month ago, entering the nationwide demand for the end of Jim Crow in our National Pastime said, "*Baseball, in this war, should set an example of democracy. What about it, Mr. Landis?"* Yes, what about it, Mr. Landis?

The American people are waiting for you. You're holding up the works. And the first casualty lists have been published.

Yours,

Lester Rodney, Sports Editor, *Daily Worker*

NEW YORK CITY

One of the incidents Rodney refers to occurred on March 22, 1942, when Jackie Robinson and pitcher Nate Moreland appeared at Brookside Park in Pasadena, California, unannounced. Robinson, then 23, and Moreland, 25, requested a tryout from White Sox manager Jimmy Dykes. Dykes allowed them to go through the motions of fielding and pitching, giving words of encouragement, with no incentives of employment. Dykes claimed, "Personally, I would welcome Negro players on the Sox, and I believe every one of the other fifteen big league managers would do likewise. As for the players, they'd all get along too." Dykes added he felt that Robinson would be worth $50,000 to any major-league team and suggested they talk with Commissioner Landis and team owners about the possibility of gainful employment. Dykes wrote: "There is no clause in the baseball constitution, nor is there anyone in the by-laws of the major league which prevents Negro baseball players from participating in organized baseball. Rather, it is an unwritten law. The matter is out of the hands of us managers. We are powerless to act and it's strictly up to the club owners and in the first place Judge Landis to start the ball a rolling. Go after them!"[51] The *Daily Worker*, under the banner "'Get After Landis, We'd Welcome You,' Sox Manager Tells Negro Stars," was the only newspaper to cover the event.)

Lester Rodney was not finished with the baseball czar:

After [the letter to the commissioner] we kept blasting away at Landis every chance we got. 'Can You Read, Judge Landis?' 'Can You Hear, Judge Landis?' and 'Can You Talk, Judge Landis?' in huge headlines. . . .

One time I noticed the attendance figures for a game between the Kansas City Monarchs and a team of former Big League All-Stars at Wrigley Field in Chicago. So out of curiosity, I checked the attendance of the White Sox-Detroit doubleheader being played in Chicago the same day. Well, the Monarchs-All-Star game, with Satchel Paige pitching, had outdrawn the White Sox-Tiger doubleheader by more than ten thousand fans. We turned that into a "Can You Count, Judge Landis?" piece. All these [articles] ran with our biggest headline type, above the masthead.[52]

A juggernaut of Black journalists, including Joe Bostic, Eddie Gant, Ed Harris, Sam Lacy, Alvin Moses, Ches Washington, Rollo Wilson, Fay Young, Dan Burley, and others, supported Wendell Smith's strong effort in the early thirties to end segregated baseball. Following Smith's lead, the *Daily Worker* published more articles about the need to integrate baseball than any other newspaper.[53] In fact, in 1937, the *Daily Worker* published more than fifty articles on the issue and nearly a hundred more in 1938.[54] Rodney's published letter to Landis and headline articles, along with signed petitions, had perhaps encouraged Judge Landis to make his first official statement on the race question. On July 17, the *Los Angeles Times* and several newspapers released Landis's duct-tape testament to end the debate:

There is no rule against major clubs hiring Negro baseball players. I have come to the conclusion it is time for me to explain myself on this important issue. Negroes are not barred from organized

> baseball by the commissioner and have never been since the 21 years I have served. There is no rule in organized baseball prohibiting their participation to my knowledge.
>
> If Durocher, or any other manager, or all of them want to sign one or 25 Negro players, it is all right with me. That is the business of the manager and the club owners. The business of the Commissioner is to interpret the rules and enforce them.[55]

The above statement was provoked by an alleged statement by the often abrasive and fiery Durocher, manager of the Brooklyn Dodgers: "I would hire Negro players if permitted."[56]

Headlines across America read "Landis's O.K. on Negro Stars Is a Great Democratic Victory for All America,"[57] "Commissioner Landis's Emancipation Proclamation,"[58] and "Landis Clears Way for Owners to Hire Colored."[59] Fay Young of the *Chicago Defender* called Landis's statement a "smokescreen for owner bigotry."[60]

In response to the *Los Angeles Times* article, White writer Gordon Macker of the *Los Angeles News* asked Landis: "What does that mean? Not a damn thing. He has merely stated that there is no rule against Negroes playing in organized baseball. There never has been any rule against them playing." Macker added, "The statement of the high commissioner is just a lot of words . . . just another case of hypocritical buck passing."[61]

An explicit Jim Crow rule was unnecessary if major league owners silently agreed to keep non-White players out of the game. In effect, Landis was the only man in baseball with the power to end discrimination. His unwillingness to change the status quo or even address the racial climate is his true legacy, not because he acted but because he refused to take action. Landis defended baseball's lack of a rule, when he should have been making a rule saying that baseball "shall not discriminate."

Perhaps seeing a need to protect Judge Landis, *The Sporting News*'s J. G. Taylor Spink, who wrote the 1947 best-seller *Judge Landis and 25 Years of Baseball*, immediately claimed in an editorial, "No value would come from discussing the race issue as the color line was in the best interests of both Black and White folks."[62]

Courageous New York Giants all-star hurler Carl Hubbell, replying to Landis's statement, said, "Yes, sir, I've seen a lot of colored boys who should have been playing in the majors. First of all I'd name this big guy Josh Gibson for a place. He's one of the greatest backstops in history, I think. Any team in the big leagues could use him right now. Bullet Rogan of Kansas City and Satchel Paige could make any big league team. Paige has the fastest ball I've ever seen."[63]

Alva Bradley, owner of the Cleveland Indians concurred, "Cleveland would consider Negro players."[64] His manager, Lou Boudreau (Larry Doby's first major-league manager), mentioned that he had played with Negroes in competition and had no objection to having them on his team, but added, "It's all up to Alva Bradley—he owns the team."[65]

THE TRYOUTS

Taking the initiative, William E. Benswanger, president of the Pittsburgh Pirates, scheduled a tryout for New York Cubans' ace Dave Barnhill (actual age 28, reported to be 24), catcher Roy Campanella (age 20), and second baseman Sammy T. Hughes (actual age 31, reported to be 27), the latter two of the Baltimore Elite Giants. The tryout was originally scheduled for August 4 but was postponed accommodating the Pirates' return from a road trip that day. "Negroes are American citizens with American rights and deserve all the opportunities given to a White man," said Benswanger. "They will receive the same trials given to White players."[66]

Homestead (Pittsburgh) Grays owner Cum Posey had expressed his skepticism about the proposed tryouts. In an interview with sportswriter John P. McFarlane of the *Pittsburgh Post-Gazette*, Posey excused the Pirates' president: "We've known Bill Benswanger for years. It was through his father-in-law, the late Barney Dreyfuss, that we got into baseball. Bill is sincere and he may go through with this thing, but we imagine that he will not try out colored players until he is sure some of the other teams will do the same, and I hardly think this will be before next spring, if then."[67]

Added approval appeared to come from National League president Ford Frick, who declared: "If a contract for a colored player came across my desk today, I would approve it, providing it was otherwise in order. There is nothing in the rules of baseball that I know of that would permit any other action.

"I state unequivocally that there is no discrimination against Negroes or anybody else per se, in the National League. And you can quote me on that."

Frick pointed out that African Americans had a false impression of baseball's attitude toward race relations, adding that "This is really a social problem, not a baseball problem. And it would be unfair to call on 'organized' baseball to solve it now or any other time.

"I don't think that racial or any other kind of discrimination is right. In fact if I thought that the inclusion of Negroes in baseball would end racial discrimination in America, I would start right out today and crusade for it."

Unwilling to step up to the plate, Frick would backslide with thoughts of entertaining the issue of equal access to public accommodations for Black players, explaining:

> Baseball has nothing to do with discrimination against Negroes in hotels, on trains, in restaurants, training camps and other public places.
>
> A colored player traveling with a White club would be subject to all kinds of embarrassments and humiliations which he would not ordinarily have to face while playing with his own people.
>
> It should also be realized that a ball club is a highly trained group of athletes who live, sleep two in a room, eat, travel and fight their team battles in the ball parks of the nation for eight months a year. They play 154 games in all, 77 at home and 77 on the road. In addition, they have to spend from a month to six weeks in the South during a strenuous training period so that the players can quickly develop into a smooth-running athletic machine. Absence of one or more players from training camp might prove an insurmountable problem.
>
> With some of these obstacles in view, however, I still say colored ball players will find no barriers in my office. They are welcome anytime.[68]

After three weeks of excuses and delays, the Pittsburgh Pirates asked Negro League officials, sportswriters, managers, and owners to select four players from the East–West game for tryouts. The short list became Campanella, Hughes, and Barnhill, along with Josh Gibson, Ted Strong, Hilton Smith, Satchel Paige, Willie Wells, Leon Day, Sammy Bankhead, Howard Easterling, Thomas "Pee Wee" Butts, Pat Patterson, and Bill Wright. The tryout was rescheduled for September 1, with Gibson, Wells, Day, and Bankhead as the chosen ones. The owners also selected eight alternates, which included the original trio of Campanella, Hughes, and Barnhill plus Strong, Smith, Easterling, Patterson and Butts.[69] Paige and Bankhead did not make the cut. With a change in the "game" plan, the Black press began to heavily advertise the attributes of the foursome.

Lacking skilled players like Paige, Bankhead, and other Black stars on August 22, the National League standings showed the Pirates in fifth place, four games behind the fourth-place Cincinnati Reds. Catching for the Pirates was 34-year old Al Lopez, batting .250 with 21 RBIs and a home run. Lopez was no competition for Gibson, who was hitting around .375 in his league. At shortstop the Pirates had Pete Coscarart, a utility player who hit for a .129 average for the Dodgers in 1941. It is doubtful Coscarart would have been a serious challenger to an all-star performer like Wells. Leon Day, who reportedly won 24 games the previous year, could really have helped the Pirates pitching staff. Truett "Rip" Sewell, already 35, had the top Pirates won-lost record, at 12–10. In their outfield, Maurice Van Robays, Vince DiMaggio, and Jimmy Wasdell all batted under .260. Bankhead would have been a welcome addition to this weak outfield, with his all-around power and speed.

The Homestead Grays proceeded to lose to the Kansas City Monarchs in the 1942 Negro World Series, as the Pirates finished up their season. Although Gibson would bat less than .200 in the series, he claimed, "I am in good shape for my try out with the Pittsburgh Pirates."[70] After several postponements, the tryouts never materialized. The Pirates management offered no excuses to the press, as they finished in fifth place (66–81), 36 1/2 games behind the pennant-winning St. Louis Cardinals.

The Cleveland Indians announced on September 2 they would offer tryouts to Cleveland Buckeyes manager and third baseman Parnell Woods (age 30, reported to be 26), outfielder Sam Jethroe (25, reported to be 22) and pitcher Gene Bremer (26), in the near future. John Fuster, sports editor of the Black-owned *Cleveland Call & Post* had arranged the tryouts. Indians vice president Roger Peckinpaugh would not give a definite date for the tryouts. Eventually, like the promised tryout by the Pirates, the Cleveland organization walked the plank of solidarity.[71]

New hope reigned during a September 15 meeting at the offices of the Brooklyn Dodgers. William T. Andrews, an assemblyman, and Father Raymond Campion, a Catholic Priest, met with Dodgers president Larry MacPhail for almost two hours. Others in attendance were former Negro League commissioner Ferdinand Q. Morton, Fred Turner of the NAACP, Dan Burley of the *Amsterdam News*, George Hunton of the *Catholic Interracial Review*, and Joe Bostic of the *People's Voice*. As the race issue was presented again to MacPhail, he responded with a different tone: "Plenty of Negro players are ready for the big leagues. In five minutes I could pick half a dozen men who could fit into major league teams." MacPhail added that he thought that "Negroes should have the opportunity not only to play in the leagues, but should have a lot of other opportunities, in employment, housing and other things."[72]

MacPhail also said he was willing to book his Dodgers against the Negro League winner for a postseason championship if his Bums won the National League pennant. He also suggested use of Ebbets Field, along with a 60–40 split of the gate receipts between the winners and losers. Father Campion and Assemblyman Andrews emphasized that Cleveland and Pittsburgh had failed in their commitment to grant players an opportunity to make their teams. MacPhail voiced his criticism of those owners: "It's not necessary to try them out. They're ready and willing to go into the majors [now]."[73] The sports section of the *Daily Worker* boasted in large, one-inch type on September 19, "DODGERS MAY PLAY MONARCHS, NEGRO LEAGUE CHAMPS, IN POST SEASON TILTS." [74] Like many earlier promises, this one failed to materialize, as the Dodgers finished two games out of first place.

The 1942 season brought success and failure. During the course of this season, 31-year-old Rodney became a private in the US Army. *Daily Worker* writer Nat Low took over command of Rodney's fight and wrote his analysis of the battlefield: "We DID get the Landis statement, and whereas we DID get the campaign much favorable national publicity and whereas we DID get promises of tryouts from two major league owners—William Benswanger of the Pittsburgh Pirates and Alva Bradley of the Cleveland Indians—we DID NOT succeed in our main objective—to get Negro stars onto major league teams, in uniform."[75]

Despite all the efforts of the press, writers found the patriotic pool too shallow to drown the gatekeepers in self-acknowledgment of righteousness, as they often provided a lifejacket of alibis. "If you ask any honest sportswriter, he will tell you Landis was a racist," claimed Lester Rodney. "He was a cold man. He could at any time as Commissioner, have said 'something is wrong with this game.'"[76] The owners pointed fingers at the commissioner, while Landis held the owners accountable to hire whomever. The skeptics were right; the promised tryouts never took place.

Sam Lacy, a Spink Award Winner and the first African American member of the Baseball Writers Association of America (1948), summed up the situation best:

> Baseball in its time has given employment to known epileptics, kleptomaniacs, and a generous scattering of saints and sinners. A man who is totally lacking in character has often turned up to be a star in baseball. A man whose skin is white, or red, or yellow has been acceptable. But a man whose character may be of the highest and whose ability may be Ruthian has been barred completely from the sport because he is colored.[77]

FROM AN END, A BEGINNING

Before the public ever knew whether Judge Landis would "learn how to read" the signs of change, the commissioner died on November 25, 1944, with the color curtain still tightly drawn. His rule had been absolute. Although generally regarded as the perfect man to bring integrity back to baseball after the Black Sox scandal, Landis held the throne too long.

In general, mainstream Americans accepted the racial exclusion of African American players because baseball executives claimed there was no color line issue to address. In effect, they chose the path of least resistance by ignoring that a "gentleman's agreement" needed to be addressed. With fear as a constant companion and controller of emotions, the Black man was deathly afraid of White supremacists and rightfully so. But where were the White brothers of truth and justice in the fight against the white sheets that projected purification of their dastardly deeds? Landis and his businessmen were about the business of keeping the status quo, despite *prima facie* evidence of any injustice.

Accordingly, a reviewer of renowned historian David Pietrusza's 564-page biography *Judge and Jury: The Life and Times of Judge Kenesaw Mountain Landis* notes:

> The work does have one glaring deficiency . . . with regard to the book's chronicle of Landis and the efforts to integrate the game. I rather felt that this (certainly the most significant of any shortcoming of his reign) was given less than adequate coverage by the author. Others have written more authoritatively (including firsthand reporting of confrontations over the issue) about how intractable a foe Landis was of integration of the American pastime. This book not only ignores almost all of these, but glosses over the issue in general with little more than an apologist's dismissal. From my perspective, this is an unpardonable transgression.[78]

Pietrusza wrote 26 pages in chapter 25, "You Fellows Say I Am Responsible," to lightly touch on the race issue.

Another reviewer states:

> Not content with praising Landis's actions, Pietrusza also defends his omissions. For example, he absolves Landis of any significant degree of responsibility for preserving baseball's color line. Pietrusza asserts that if Landis was the most important man in baseball never to hit or throw a curve, not to mention ahead of the game on the gambling front, he was no worse than even with it on the integration issue. To see Landis as the 'George Wallace of baseball' is to 'oversimplify' things and 'exculpate' the rest of the game's hierarchy.[79]

Yes, the janitorial Judge cleaned up the game, but he held back the master key to apartheid baseball. This is confirmed by his successor, former Kentucky governor and senator Albert Benjamin "Happy" Chandler, who reported that,

> For twenty-four years Judge Landis wouldn't let a Black man play. I had his records, and I read them, and for twenty-four years Landis consistently blocked any attempts to put Blacks and Whites together on a big league field. He even refused to let them play exhibition games.
>
> I was named the commissioner in April 1945, and just as soon as I was elected commissioner, two Black writers from the *Pittsburgh Courier*, Wendell Smith and Ric Roberts, came down to Washington to see me. They asked me where I stood, and I shook their hands and said, "I'm for the Four Freedoms,[80] and if a Black boy can make it in Okinawa and go to Guadalcanal, he can make it in baseball."[81]

The story of America's unpardonable acceptance of racial weakness and our nation's lengthy obedience in segregated and discriminatory practices toward African Americans is well documented. Sadly, Landis and his clan were never able to transcend the social constraints of the period, despite the willingness of baseball executives like Bill Veeck and Branch Rickey, or of other sports executives and owners like Paul Brown (Cleveland Browns), Dan F. Reeves (Los Angeles Rams), or Red Auerbach (Boston Celtics). As Voltaire, the French philosopher of social reform, would say, "Every man is guilty of all the good he did not do."

Historically, the omnipotent Landis had unlimited authority, and tremendous influence, but he lacked the fortitude to put a little soul into the game. Landis and his converts controlled the monopoly of racial inclusion and exclusion, meanwhile providing a plethora of excuses for their refusal to act. Nonetheless, the quarter-century tenure of ultraconservative Landis as the Commish, in which he opposed night games, the farm system, and integration, was romanticized with a special selection to the Cooperstown Hall of Fame a month after his death in November of 1944.[82] His plaque reads: "His Integrity and Leadership Established Baseball in the Respect, Esteem and Affection of the American People." This appeared to be self-evident truth for some Americans, not all Americans.

As Landis lay on his deathbed in St. Luke's Hospital in Chicago, the joint committee of the two leagues recommended Landis for reelection. Yes, another seven-year term to begin January 12, 1946, on the expiration of his current term.[83] Before the one-year anniversary of Landis's death, Brooklyn Dodgers general manager Branch Rickey signed Jackie Robinson to a minor-league contract with the Canadian-based Montreal Royals, literally changing the faces of major-leaguers and the racial landscape of America forever. Some say Judge Landis and Babe Ruth changed baseball. Others believe two men with one voice, Branch Rickey and Jackie Robinson, changed America!

Notes

1 Email from Erik Strohl, curator at the National Baseball Hall of Fame in Cooperstown, NewYork, dated April 25, 2008. The author attempted to obtain a printed copy of Macht's presentation from SABR's Research Library, but it was not available. Hence, references to the talk are from the author's notes.

2 E.B. Washington, "Toni Morrison Now," *Essence*, October 1987, 58–60.

3 Sam Lacy, interview with author in Washington, D.C., October 14 , 1993.

4 Paul Dickson, *Baseball's Greatest Quotations* (New York: Harper Collins, 1992), 187.

5 The owners of major league teams in 1944 were Sam Breadon (St. Louis Cardinals), Bill Benswanger (Pittsburgh Pirates), Powel Crosley Jr. (Cincinnati Redlegs), Philip K. Wrigley (Chicago Cubs), Horace Stoneham (New York Giants), J. A. Robert Quinn (Boston Braves), James and Dearie Mulvey (Brooklyn Dodgers), Robert R. M. Carpenter (Philadelphia Blue Jays), Donald Lee Barnes (St. Louis Browns), Walter Briggs Sr. (Detroit Tigers), Larry MacPhail, Dan Topping, and Del Webb (New York Yankees), Tom Yawkey (Boston Red Sox), Alva Bradley (Cleveland Indians), Connie Mack (Philadelphia A's), Grace Comiskey (Chicago White Sox), Clark Griffith and George H. Richardson (Washington Senators). Minority owner and general manager William DeWitt of the American League champion St. Louis Browns, a one-time Branch Rickey aide with the Cardinals, was voted *The Sporting News* Executive of the Year. Our knowledge of individual owners' positions on integration has been limited because minutes of the leagues' executive board meetings have been unavailable to researchers.

6 *Baseball Register* (St. Louis: C. C. Spink & Son, 1953).

7 Harold Seymour, *Baseball The Golden Age* (New York: Oxford University Press, 1971), 367.

8 J. G. Taylor Spink, *Judge Landis and 25 Years of Baseball* (New York: Thomas Y. Crowell, 1953), 7–8.

9 Seymour, *Baseball: The Golden Age*, 368.

10 Spink, *Judge Landis and 25 Years of Baseball*, 72

11 Wikipedia, http://en.wikipedia.org/wiki/List_of_Major_League_Baseball_figures_that_have_been_banned_for_life#People_banned_under_Commissioner_Kenesaw_Mountain_Landis (accessed June 30 2008). Eight players for the Chicago White Sox were banned in 1920 for conspiring with gamblers to throw the 1919 World Series in the Black Sox scandal: "Shoeless" Joe Jackson, Eddie Cicotte, Lefty Williams, Chick Gandil, Fred McMullin, Swede Risberg, Happy Felsch, Buck Weaver. Other banned players included Joe Gedeon, St. Louis Browns; Eugene Paulette, Philadelphia Phillies; Benny Kauff, New York Giants; Lee Magee, Chicago Cubs; Hal Chase, New York Giants; Heinie Zimmerman, New York Giants; Joe Harris, Cleveland Indians; Heinie Groh, Cincinnati Reds; Ray Fisher, Cincinnati Reds; Dickie Kerr, Chicago White Sox; Phil Douglas and Jimmy O'Connell, New York Giants; William Cox and Horace Fogel, Philadelphia Phillies owners.

12 "Judge Landis Talks on Ruth's Status," *New York Times*, May 19, 1922.

13 Spink, *Judge Landis and 25 Years of Baseball*, 104–105.

14 Neil Lanctot, *Fair Dealing and Clean Playing: The Hilldale Club and the Development of Black Professional Baseball, 1910–1932* (Jefferson, NC: McFarland, 1994), 180.

15 *Washington Post*, December 18, 1926.

16 Brian Carroll, "Beating the Klan: Pre-integration Baseball Coverage in Wichita, 1920–1930," *The Baseball Research Journal* 37 (2008), 51–61.

17 Bob Rives, "Klan and Colored Team to Mix on the Diamond Today," *Baseball in Wichita* (Charleston, SC: Arcadia, 2004), 58.

18 In 1869, the Philadelphia Pythians become the first Black team to defeat an all-White squad, defeating the cross-town rival City Items, 27–17.

19 Jimmy Powers, "Memo to Bill Terry," *New York Daily News*, February 23, 1940. Earlier, Powers in his article of February 8, 1933, reportedly asked league and team officials if they objected to Black players in baseball. The only exception came from John McGraw, while John Heydler (NL president), Jacob Ruppert (Yankees owner), Gary Nugent (Phillies president), and ballplayers Lou Gehrig, Herb Pennock and Frankie Frisch welcomed the opportunity to have ballplayers join their teams if given permission by Judge Landis. With respect to Pennock, it's curious that he was so open to integration in 1933, as in 1947 he was outspoken in his distaste for Jackie Robinson. Many sources have quoted Pennock ordering Branch Rickey to leave Robinson behind when the Dodgers visited the Phillies. In 1998, his racist actions reverberated as there was an outcry against a statue being erected in Pennock's honor at his birthplace in Kennett Square, Pennsylvania.

20 *Philadelphia Record*, May 14, 1940.

21 *Washington Post*, April 7, 1939, 21

22 Brian Carroll, *When to Stop the Cheering? The Black Press, the Black Community, and the Integration of Professional Baseball* (New York: Routledge, 2007), 134.

23 *New York Daily Worker*, July 30, 1939.

24 *New York Daily Worker*, July 30, 1939..

25 *New York Daily Worker*, July 30, 1939..

26 *New York Daily Worker*, July 30, 1939..

27 *New York Daily Worker*, July 30, 1939..

28 *Pittsburgh Courier*, August 5, 1939.

29 *Pittsburgh Courier*, August 12, 1939.

30 *Pittsburgh Courier*, August 12, 1939.

31 *Pittsburgh Courier*, August 5, 1939.

32 *Pittsburgh Courier*, August 5, 1939.

33 *Pittsburgh Courier*, August 5, 1939.

34 *Pittsburgh Courier*, August 5, 1939.

35 Lester Rodney, telephone interview with author, October 31, 1997.

36 *Philadelphia Tribune*, August 7, 1941.

37 Eddie Gant, "I Cover the Eastern Front," *Chicago Defender*, June 13, 1942.

38 New York Daily Worker, June 8, 1942.

39 *Chicago Defender*, July 11, 1942.

40 *New York Daily Worker*, June 18, 1942.

41 Rodney, telephone interview with author, October 31, 1997.

42 *New York Daily Worker*, July 15, 1942.

43 Henry D. Fetter, "The Party Line and the Color Line: The American Communist Party, the Daily Worker, and Jackie Robinson," *Journal of Sports History*, 28, no. 3 Fall, 2001, 384.

44 *New York Times*, April 18, 1945; Baltimore Afro-American, April 28, 1945.

45 Irwin Silber, *Press Box Red* (Philadelphia: Temple University Press, 2003), 79.

46 Yom Kippur is probably the most important holiday of the Jewish year. Yom Kippur means "Day of Atonement," a day set aside to atone for the sins of the past year. The year before, 1941, two New York councilmen, Brooklyn Democrats Walter R. Hart and Joséph T. Sharkey, sent telegrams to National League president Ford Frick, American League president Will Harridge and Commissioner Landis, requesting movement of the first game of the subway series, between the Dodgers and the Yankees, to October 2 from October 1. The telegram read: "The Council of the City of New York unanimously passed resolution urging the postponement of the opening game of the World Series to Oct. 2, to enable thousands of sport-loving members of the Jewish faith to attend." Although the Council sent telegrams to the league presidents, the feeble Ford Frick cried, "It's entirely up to Judge Landis. It's his party and I have nothing to say about it." (New York Times, September 17, 1941, "Day's Delay Asked in Start of Series"). Four days later, from his Chicago office Landis ruled that the World Series would open on October 1 as scheduled. The autocratic Landis mentioned that any person of the Hebrew faith could have a complete refund, including tax and the cost of postage if they sent their tickets by registered mail to him, in care of the National City Bank of New York (*New York Times*, "Series Dates Unchanged; Landis Denies Request," September 21, 1941).

47 Miller was an African American cook in the United States Navy and a hero who went above and beyond the call of duty during the attack on Pearl Harbor on December 7, 1941. He dragged his dying captain, Mervyn Bennion, away from the shelling before manning a machine gun. The following year in June, Miller's rank was raised to Mess Attendant First Class. On May 27, 1942, Admiral Chester W. Nimitz, the commander in chief, Pacific Fleet, personally presented to Miller, on board aircraft carrier USS Enterprise, for his extraordinary courage in battle, the Navy Cross, second-highest honor awarded by the Navy, after the Medal of Honor. Sadly, Miller didn't survive the war. In November of 1943, he died during an attack on the USS Liscome Bay.

48 More accurately, Executive Order 8802, signed in June of 1941 by President Franklin D. Roosevelt, prohibited racial discrimination in national defense plants. This order required all federal agencies and departments involved with defense production to ensure that vocational and training programs were administered without discrimination as to "race, creed, color, or national origin." All defense contracts were to include provisions that barred private contractors from discrimination as well. The executive order was issued in response to pressure from pre-King civil-rights activists Bayard Rustin and A. Philip Randolph, founder of the Brotherhood of Sleeping Car Porters, who had planned the original march on Washington, D.C., to protest racial discrimination across America. Randolph suspended the march until Executive Order 8802 was issued. Some civil-rights critics felt betrayed by the suspension because Roosevelt's proclamation only pertained to defense industries and not all the armed forces. Seven years later, in July of 1948, President Harry Truman issued Executive Order 9981, expanding 8802 to include equality of treatment and opportunity in all the armed services, not just defense plants, becoming the first American institution to officially prohibit racial discrimination. The operative statement was: "It is hereby declared to be the policy of the President that there shall be equality of treatment and opportunity for all persons in the armed services without regard to race, color, religion or national origin. This policy shall be put into effect as rapidly as possible, having due regard to the time required to effectuate any necessary changes without impairing efficiency or morale." The order also established a committee to investigate and make recommendations to the civilian leadership of the military to realize the policy. In effect it eliminated all-Black Montford Point (New River, North Carolina) as a segregated Marine boot camp, with the last of the all-Black units in the United States military dismantled in September of 1954.

49 The *New York Daily News* had the largest circulation of any newspaper in the country at the time. In that paper on July 21, 1942, Hy Turkin wrote: "A casual remark made by Leo Durocher to Lester Rodney, Sports Editor of the *Daily Worker*, now in the Army, may do more for his place in history than all his shortstopping and managing histrionics. He said that he would hire Black players and this is like the tail of the tornado that has overwhelmed Judge Landis with two million signatures and threatens the democratization of our national pastime."

50 Tommy Fitzgerald, *Louisville Courier Journal*, April 12, 1942.

51 *New York Daily Worker*, March 23, 1942.

52 Silber, *Press Box Red*, 82.

53 Chris Lamb, *Blackout: The Untold Story of Jackie Robinson's First Spring Training* (Lincoln: University of Nebraska Press, 2004), x, xi.

54 Kelly Rusinack, "Baseball on the Radical Agenda: The Daily and Sunday Worker on the Desegregation of Major League Baseball, 1933–1947" (master's thesis, Clemson University, 1995), 31, 57.

55 *Los Angeles Times*, July 17, 1942.

56 *Los Angeles Times*, July 17, 1942.

57 *New York Daily Worker*, July 18-20, 1942.

58 *Pittsburgh Courier*, July 25, 1942.

59 *Baltimore Afro-American*, July 18, 1942.

60 *Chicago Defender*, July 25, 1942.

61 "White Writer Hits Landis," *Chicago Defender*, August 15, 1942, 21.

62 *The Sporting News*, August 6, 1942.

63 *Los Angeles Times*, July 17, 1942.

64 *Cleveland Call and Post*, July 24, 1942.

65 *Cleveland Call and Post*, July 24, 1942.

66 *New York Daily Worker*, July 28, 1942.

67 *Pittsburgh Courier* August 22, 1942.

68 *Pittsburgh Courier*, August 8, 1942.

69 *Pittsburgh Courier*August 22, 1942.

70 *Pittsburgh Courier*, September 17, 1942.

71 *Cleveland Call and Post*, September 2, 1942.

72 *New York Daily Worker,* September 19, 1942.

73 *New York Daily Worker,* September 19, 1942.

74 *New York Daily Worker,* September 19, 1942.

75 *New York Daily Worker*, December 2, 1942.

76 Rodney, telephone interview with author, October 31, 1997.

77 *Baltimore Afro-American*, November 10, 1945.

78 Eric C. Moye, http://www.amazon.com/review/product/1888698098/ref=dp_top_cm_cr_acr_txt?%5Fencoding=UTF8&showViewpoints=1 (accessed June 30, 2008).

79 John C. Chalberg, review of *Judge and Jury: The Life and Times of Judge Kenesaw Mountain Landis*, by David Pietrusza, *Journal of Sport History* 27, no. 2, 350.

80 The four freedoms were given by President Franklin D. Roosevelt's address to Congress on January 6, 1941. They were freedom of speech and expression, freedom of every person to worship God in his own way, freedom from want, and freedom from fear.

81 Peter Golenbock, *Bums: An Oral History of the Brooklyn Dodgers, Breaking Baseball's Color Barrier*, (New York: G. P. Putnam's Sons, 1984), 122.

82 "Senators' Plea for More Night Games Denied as Landis Casts Deciding Vote," *New York Times*, July 7, 1942.

83 "Judge Landis Dies; Baseball Czar," *New York Times*, November 26, 1944, 78.

JACKIE ROBINSON'S SIGNING: THE REAL UNTOLD STORY

John Thorn and Jules Tygiel

This article appeared in The National Pastime No. 10, *1989.*

Jules Tygiel and I collaborated on this story for SPORT magazine in June 1988. Subsequently it appeared in SABR's The National Pastime, *in several editions of* Total Baseball, *and in Jules's* Extra Bases: Reflections on Jackie Robinson, Race, and Baseball History. *Despite this drumbeat of evidence, the legend surrounding Jackie Robinson's signing has persisted. Jules and I believed that the real story was not only more interesting than the schoolboy version but also made Jackie's pioneering mission even more heroic. —John Thorn*

October 1945. As the Detroit Tigers and Chicago Cubs faced off in the World Series, photographer Maurice Terrell arrived at an almost deserted minor-league park in San Diego, California, to carry out a top-secret assignment: to surreptitiously photograph three Black baseball players.

Terrell shot hundreds of motion-picture frames of Jackie Robinson and the two other players. A few photos appeared in print but the existence of the additional images remained unknown for four decades. In April 1987, as Major League Baseball prepared a lavish commemoration of the fortieth anniversary of Robinson's debut, I unearthed a body of contact sheets and unprocessed film from a previously unopened carton donated in 1954 by *Look* magazine to the Baseball Hall of Fame in Cooperstown, New York. This discovery triggered an investigation which led to startling revelations regarding Branch Rickey, the president of the Brooklyn Dodgers, and his signing of Jackie Robinson to shatter baseball's longstanding color line; the relationship between these two historic figures; and the stubbornly controversial issue of Black managers in baseball.

The popular "frontier" image of Jackie Robinson as a lone gunman facing down a hostile mob has always dominated the story of the integration of baseball. But new information related to the Terrell photos reveals that while Robinson was the linchpin in Branch Rickey's strategy, in October 1945 Rickey intended to announce the signing of not just Jackie Robinson, but of several other Negro League stars. Political pressure, however, forced Rickey's hand, thrusting Robinson alone into the spotlight. And in 1950, after only three years in the major leagues, Robinson pressed Rickey to consider him for a position as field manager or front-office executive, raising an issue with which the baseball establishment grappled long after.

The story of these revelations began with the discovery of the Terrell photographs. The photos show a youthful, muscular Robinson in a battered cap and baggy uniform fielding from his position at shortstop, batting with a Black catcher crouched behind him, trapping a third Black player in a rundown between third and home, and sprinting along the basepaths more like a former track star than a baseball player. All three players wore uniforms emblazoned with the name "Royals." A woman with her back to the action is the only figure visible amid the vacant stands. The contact sheets are dated October 7, 1945.

The photos were perplexing. The momentous announcement of Jackie Robinson's signing with the Montreal Royals took place on October 23, 1945. Before that date his recruitment had been a tightly guarded secret. Why, then, had a *Look* photographer taken such an interest in Robinson two weeks earlier? Where had the pictures been taken? And why was Robinson already wearing a Royals uniform?

I called Jules Tygiel, the author of *Baseball's Great Experiment: Jackie Robinson and His Legacy,* to see if he could shed some light on the photos. Tygiel knew nothing about them, but he did have in his files a 1945 manuscript by newsman Arthur Mann, who frequently wrote for *Look.* The article, drafted with Rickey's cooperation, had been intended to announce the Robinson signing but had never been published. The pictures, Jules and I concluded, were to have accompanied Mann's article; we decided to find out the story behind the photo session.

The clandestine nature of the photo session did not surprise us. From the moment he had arrived in Brooklyn in 1942, determined to end baseball's Jim Crow traditions, Rickey had feared that premature disclosure of his intentions might doom his bold design. No Blacks had appeared in the major leagues since 1884 when two brothers, Welday and Moses Fleetwood Walker, had played for Toledo in the American Association. [In recent years an earlier African American major leaguer has been identified: William Edward White, a one-game first baseman for Providence of the National League in 1879.] Not since the 1890s had Black players appeared on a minor-league team. During the ensuing half-century all-Black teams and leagues featuring legendary figures like pitcher Satchel Paige and catcher Josh Gibson had performed on the periphery of White organized baseball.

Baseball executives, led by Commissioner Kenesaw Mountain Landis, had strictly policed the color line, barring Blacks from both major and minor leagues. Rickey therefore moved slowly and secretly to explore the issue and cover up his attempts to scout Black players during his first three years in Brooklyn. He informed the Dodger owners of his plans but took few others into his confidence.

In the spring of 1945, as Rickey prepared to accelerate his scouting efforts, advocates of integration, emboldened by the impending end of World War II and the recent death of Commissioner Landis, escalated their campaign to desegregate baseball. On April 6, 1945, Black sportswriter Joe Bostic appeared at the Dodgers' Bear Mountain training camp with Negro League stars Terris McDuffie and Dave

Terrell photographs of Jackie Robinson, October 7, 1945.

"Showboat" Thomas and forced Rickey to hold tryouts for the two players. Ten days later Black journalist Wendell Smith, White sportswriter Dave Egan, and Boston city councilman Isidore Muchnick engineered an unsuccessful ninety-minute audition with the Red Sox for Robinson, then a shortstop with the Kansas City Monarchs; second baseman Marvin Williams of the Philadelphia Stars; and outfielder Sam Jethroe of the Cleveland Buckeyes. In response to these events the major leagues announced the formation of a Committee on Baseball Integration. (Reflecting White baseball's true intentions on the matter, the group never met.)

In the face of this heightened activity, Rickey created an elaborate smokescreen to obscure his scouting of Black players. In May 1945 he announced the formation of a new franchise, the Brooklyn Brown Dodgers, and a new Negro League, the United States League. Rickey then dispatched his best talent hunters to observe Black ballplayers, ostensibly for the Brown Dodgers, but in reality for the Brooklyn National League club.

A handwritten memorandum in the Rickey Papers at the Library of Congress offers a rare glimpse of Rickey's emphasis on secrecy in his instructions to Dodger scouts. The document, signed "Chas. D. Clark" and accompanied by a Negro National League schedule for April-May 1945, is headlined "Job Analysis," and defines the following "Duties: under supervision of management of club":

1. To establish contact (silent) with all clubs (local or general).
2. To gain knowledge and [sic] abilities of all players.
3. To report all possible material (players).
4. Prepare weekly reports of activities.
5. Keep composite report of outstanding players. To travel and cover player whenever management so desire.

Clark's "Approch" [sic] was to "Visit game and loose [sic] self in stands; Keep statistical report (speed, power, agility, ability, fielding, batting, etc.) by score card"; and "Leave immediately after game."

Clark's directions, however, contain one major breach in Rickey's elaborate security precautions. According to his later accounts, Rickey had told most Dodger scouts that they were evaluating talent for a new "Brown Dodger" franchise. But Clark's first "Objective" was "To Cover Negro teams for possible major league talent." Had Rickey confided in Clark, a figure so obscure as to escape prior mention in the voluminous Robinson literature? Dodger superscout and Rickey confidante Clyde Sukeforth had no recollection of Clark when Jules spoke with him, raising the possibility that Clark was not part of the Dodger family, but perhaps someone connected with Black baseball. Had Clark himself interpreted his instructions in this manner?

Whatever the answer, Rickey successfully diverted attention from his true motives. Nonetheless, mounting interest in the integration issue threatened Rickey's careful planning. In the summer of 1945 Rickey constructed yet another facade. The Dodger president took into his confidence Dan Dodson, a New York University sociologist who chaired Mayor Fiorello LaGuardia's Committee on Unity and requested that Dodson form a Committee on Baseball ostensibly to study the possibility of integration. In reality, the committee would provide the illusion of action while Rickey quietly completed his own preparations. "This was one of the toughest decisions I ever had to make while in office," Dodson later confessed. "The major purpose I could see for the committee was that it was a stall for time. . . . Yet had Mr. Rickey not delivered . . . I would have been totally discredited."

Thus by late August, even as Rickey's extensive scouting reports had led him to focus on Jackie Robinson as his standard bearer, few people in or out of the Dodger organization suspected that a breakthrough was imminent. On August 28 Rickey and Robinson held their historic meeting at the Dodgers' Montague Street offices in downtown Brooklyn. Robinson signed an agreement to accept a contract with the Montreal Royals, the top Dodger affiliate, by November 1.

Rickey, still concerned with secrecy, impressed upon Robinson the need to maintain silence. Robinson could tell the momentous news to his family and fiancée, but no one else. For the conspiratorial Rickey, keeping the news sheltered while continuing arrangements required further subterfuge. Rumors about Robinson's visit had already spread through the world of Black baseball. To stifle speculation Rickey "leaked" an adulterated version of the incident to Black sportswriter Wendell Smith. Smith, who had recommended Robinson to Rickey and advised Rickey on the integration project, doubtless knew the true story behind the meeting. On September 8, however, he reported in the *Pittsburgh Courier* that the "sensational shortstop" and "colorful major-league dynamo" had met behind "closed doors. . . . The nature of the conference has not been revealed," Smith continued. Rickey claimed that he and Robinson had assessed "the organization of Negro baseball," but Smith noted that "it does not seem logical [Rickey] should call in a rookie player to discuss the future organization of Negro baseball." He closed with the tantalizing thought that "it appears that the Brooklyn boss has a plan on his mind that extends further than just the future of Negro baseball as an organization." The subterfuge succeeded. Neither Black nor White reporters pursued the issue.

Rickey, always sensitive to criticism by New York sports reporters and understanding the historic significance of his actions, also wanted to be sure that his version of the integration breakthrough and his role in it be accurately portrayed. To guarantee this he persuaded Arthur Mann, his close friend and later a Dodger employee, to write a 3,000-word manuscript to be published simultaneously with the announcement of the signing.

PART TWO

Although it was impossible to confirm in 1987, when I found Maurice Terrell's photos, it seemed to Jules and me highly likely that, inasmuch as they had been commissioned by *Look*, they were destined to accompany Mann's article. (Once we located Terrell himself, he confirmed the linkage.) Clearer prints of the negatives revealed that Terrell had taken the pictures in San Diego's Lane Stadium. This fit in with Robinson's autumn itinerary. After his August meeting with Rickey, Robinson had returned briefly to the Kansas City Monarchs. With the Dodger offer securing his future and the relentless bus trips of the Negro League schedule wearing him down, he left the Monarchs before season's end and returned home to Pasadena, California. In late September he hooked up with Chet Brewer's Kansas City Royals, a postseason barnstorming team which toured the Pacific Coast, competing against other Negro League teams and major- and minor-league all-star squads. Thus the word "Royals" on Robinson's uniform, which had so piqued our interest as a seeming anomaly, ironically turned out to relate not to Robinson's future team in Montreal, but rather to his interim employment in California.

SPORT Magazine, August 1949

For further information Jules contacted Chet Brewer, who at age eighty still lived in Los Angeles. Brewer, one of the great pitchers of the Jim Crow era, had known Robinson well. He had followed Robinson's spectacular athletic career at UCLA and in 1945 they became teammates on the Monarchs. "Jackie was major-league all the way," recalled Brewer. "He had the fastest reflexes I ever saw in a player."

Robinson particularly relished facing major-league all-star squads. Against Bob Feller, Robinson once slashed two doubles. "Jack was running crazy on the bases," a Royals teammate remembered. In one game he upended Gerry Priddy, Washington Senators infielder. Priddy angrily complained about the hard slide in an exhibition game. "Any time I put on a uniform," retorted Robinson, "I play to win."

Brewer recalled that Robinson and two other Royals journeyed from Los Angeles to San Diego on a day when the team was not scheduled to play. He identified the catcher in the photos as Buster Haywood and the other player as Royals third baseman Herb Souell. Souell was no longer living, but Haywood, who like Brewer lived in Los Angeles, vaguely recalled the event, which he incorrectly remembered as occurring in Pasadena. Robinson recruited the catcher and Souell, his former Monarch teammate, to "work out" with him. All three wore their Kansas City Royals uniforms. Haywood found neither Robinson's request nor the circumstances unusual. Although he was unaware that they were being photographed, Haywood described the session accurately. "We didn't know what was going on," he stated. "We'd hit and throw and run from third base to home plate."

The San Diego pictures provide a rare glimpse of the pre-Montreal Robinson. The article which they were to accompany and related correspondence in the Library of Congress offer even more rare insights into Rickey's thinking. The unpublished Mann manuscript was entitled "The Negro and Baseball: The National Game Faces a Racial Challenge Long Ignored." As Mann doubtless based his account on conversations with Rickey and since Rickey's handwritten comments appear in the margin, it stands as the earliest "official" account of the Rickey-Robinson story and reveals many of the concerns confronting Rickey in September 1945.

One of the most striking features of the article is the language used to refer to Robinson. Mann, reflecting the racism typical of postwar America, portrays Robinson as the "first Negro chattel in the so-called National pastime." At another point he writes, "Rickey felt the boy's sincerity," appropriate language perhaps for an 18-year-old prospect, but not for a 26-year-old former Army officer.

"The Negro and Baseball" consists largely of the now familiar Rickey-Robinson story. Mann recreated Rickey's haunting 1904 experience as collegiate coach when one of his Black baseball players, Charlie Thomas, was denied access to a hotel. Thomas cried and rubbed his hands, chanting, "Black skin! Black skin! If I could only make 'em White." Mann described Rickey's search for the "right" man, the formation of the United States League as a cover for scouting operations, the reasons for selecting Robinson, and the fateful Rickey-Robinson confrontation. Other sections, however, graphically illustrate additional issues Rickey deemed significant. Mann repeatedly cites the costs the Dodgers incurred: $5,000 to scout Cuba, $6,000 to scout Mexico, $5,000 to establish the "Brooklyn Brown Dodgers." The final total reaches $25,000, a modest sum considering the ultimate returns, but one sufficiently large that Rickey must have felt it would counter his skinnortheastern image.

Rickey's desire to show that he was not motivated by political pressures also emerges clearly. Mann had suggested that upon arriving in Brooklyn in 1942, Rickey "was besieged by telephone calls, telegrams and letters of petition in behalf of Black ball players," and that this "staggering pile of missives [was] so inspired to convince him that he and the Dodgers had been selected as a kind of guinea pig." In his marginal comments, Rickey vehemently wrote "No!" in a strong dark script. "I began all this as soon as I went to Brooklyn." Explaining why he had never attacked the subject during his two decades as general manager of the St. Louis Cardinals, Rickey referred to the segregation in that city. "St. Louis never permitted Negro patrons in the grandstand," he wrote, describing a policy he apparently had felt powerless to change.

Mann also devoted two of his twelve pages to a spirited attack on the Negro Leagues, repeating Rickey's charges that "they are the poorest excuse for the word league" and documented the prevalence of barnstorming, the uneven scheduling, absence of contracts, and dominance of booking agents. Mann revealingly traces Rickey's distaste for the Negro Leagues to the "outrageous" guarantees demanded by New York booking agent William Leuschner to place Black teams in Ebbets Field while the Dodgers were on the road.

Rickey's misplaced obsession with the internal disorganization of the Negro Leagues had substantial factual basis. But Rickey had an ulterior motive. In his September 8 article, Wendell Smith addressed the issue of "player tampering," asking, "Would [Rickey] not first approach the owners of these Negro teams who have these stars under contract?" Rickey, argued Smith in what might have been an unsuccessful preemptive strike, "is obligated to do so and his record as a businessman indicated that he would." As Smith may have known, Rickey maintained that Negro League players did not sign valid contracts and so became free agents at the end of each season. Thus the Mahatma had no intention of compensating Negro League teams for the players he signed. His repeated attacks on Black baseball, including those in the Mann article, served to justify this questionable position.

The one respect in which "The Negro and Baseball" departs radically from the common picture of the Robinson legend is in its report of Robinson as one of a group of

Blacks about to be signed by the Dodgers. Mann's manuscript and subsequent correspondence from Rickey reveal that Rickey did not intend for Robinson to withstand the pressures alone. "Determined not to be charged with merely nibbling at the problem," wrote Mann, "Rickey went all out and brought in two more Negro players," and "consigned them, with Robinson, to the Dodgers' top farm club, the Montreal Royals." Mann named pitcher Don Newcombe and, surprisingly, outfielder Sam Jethroe as Robinson's future teammates. Whether the recruitment of additional Blacks had always been Rickey's intention or whether he had reached his decision after meeting with Robinson in August is unclear. But by late September, when he provided information to Mann for his article, Rickey had clearly decided to bring in other Negro League stars.

During the first weekend in October, Dodger coach Chuck Dressen fielded a major-league all-star team in a series of exhibition games against Negro League standouts at Ebbets Field. Rickey took the opportunity to interview at least three Black pitching prospects—Newcombe, Roy Partlow, and John Wright. The following week he met with catcher Roy Campanella. Campanella and Newcombe, at least, believed they had been approached to play for the "Brown Dodgers."

At the same time, Rickey decided to postpone publication of Mann's manuscript. In a remarkable letter sent from the World Series in Chicago on October 7, Rickey informed Mann:

> We just can't go now with the article. The thing isn't dead,—not at all. It is more alive than ever and that is the reason we can't go with any publicity at this time. There is more involved in the situation than I had contemplated. Other players are in it and it may be that I can't clear these players until after the December meetings, possibly not until after the first of the year. You must simply sit in the boat. . . .
>
> There is a November 1 deadline on Robinson,—you know that. I am undertaking to extend that date until January 1st so as to give me time to sign plenty of players and make one break on the complete story. Also, quite obviously it might not be good to sign Robinson with other and possibly better players unsigned.

The revelations and tone of this letter surprised Robinson's widow, Rachel, forty years after the event. Rickey "was such a deliberate man," she recalled in our conversation, "and this letter is so urgent. He must have been very nervous as he neared his goal. Maybe he was nervous that the owners would turn him down and having five people at the door instead of just one would have been more powerful."

Events in the weeks after October 7 justified Rickey's nervousness and forced him to deviate from the course stated in the Mann letter. Candidates in New York City's upcoming November elections, most notably Black Communist City Councilman Ben Davis, made baseball integration a major issue in the campaign. Mayor LaGuardia's Democratic party also sought to exploit the issue. The Committee on Baseball had prepared a report outlining a modest, long-range strategy for bringing Blacks into the game and describing the New York teams, because of the favorable political and racial climate in the city, as in a "choice position to undertake this pattern of integration." LaGuardia wanted Rickey's permission to make a pre-election announcement that, as a result of the committee's work, "baseball would shortly begin signing Negro players."

Rickey, a committee member, had long since subverted the panel to his own purposes. By mid-October, however, the committee had become "an election football." Again unwilling to risk the appearance of succumbing to political pressure and thereby surrendering what he viewed as his rightful role in history, Rickey asked LaGuardia to delay his comments. Rickey hurriedly contacted Robinson, who had joined a barnstorming team in New York en route to play winter ball in Venezuela and dispatched him instead to Montreal. On October 23, 1945, with Rickey's carefully laid plans scuttled, the Montreal Royals announced the signing of Robinson, and Robinson alone.

Mann's article never appeared. *Look,* having lost its exclusive, published two strips of the Terrell pictures in its November 27, 1945, issue accompanying a brief summary of the Robinson story, which was by then old news. The unprocessed film and contact sheets were loaded into a box and nine years later shipped to the National Baseball Hall of

SPORT Magazine, October 1952

Fame, where they remained, along with a picture of Jethroe, unpacked until April 1987.

PART THREE

Newcombe, Campanella, Wright, and Partlow all joined the Dodger organization in the spring of 1946. Jethroe became a victim of the "deliberate speed" of baseball integration. Rickey did not interview Jethroe in 1945. Since few teams followed the Dodger lead, the fleet, powerful outfielder remained in the Negro Leagues until 1948, when Rickey finally bought his contract from the Cleveland Buckeyes for $5,000. Jethroe had two spectacular seasons at Montreal before Rickey, fearing a "surfeit of colored boys on the Brooklyn club," profitably sold him to the Boston Braves for $100,000. Jethroe won the Rookie of the Year Award in 1950, but his delayed entry into White baseball foreshortened what should have been a stellar career. Until I informed him of how he had been part of Rickey's 1945 plan, Jethroe had been unaware of how close he had come to joining Robinson, Newcombe, and Campanella in the pantheon of integration pioneers.

For Robinson, who had always occupied center stage in Rickey's thinking, the early announcement intensified the pressures and enhanced the legend. The success or failure of integration rested disproportionately on his capable shoulders. He became the lightning rod for supporters and opponents alike, attracting the responsibility, the opprobrium and ultimately the acclaim for his historic achievement.

Beyond these revelations about the Robinson signing, the Library of Congress documents add surprisingly little to the familiar story of the integration of baseball. The Rickey Papers copiously detail his post-Dodger career as general manager of the Pittsburgh Pirates, but are strangely silent about the critical period of 1944 to 1948. Records for these years probably remained with the Dodger organization, which in 1988 claimed to have no knowledge of their whereabouts. National League Office documents for these years have remained closed to the public.

In light of the controversy engendered by former Dodger General Manager Al Campanis's remarks about Blacks in management, however, one exchange between Rickey and Robinson becomes particularly relevant. In 1950, after his fourth season with the Dodgers, Robinson appears to have written Rickey about the possibility of employment in baseball when his playing days ended. Robinson's original letter cannot be found in either the Rickey papers or the Robinson family archives. However, Rickey's reply, dated December 31, 1950, survives. Rickey, who had recently left the Dodgers after an unsuccessful struggle to wrest control of the team from Walter O'Malley, responded to Robinson's inquiry with a long and equivocal answer.

"It is not at all because of lack of appreciation that I have not acknowledged your good letter of some time ago," Rickey began. "Neither your writing, nor sending the letter, nor its contents gave me very much surprise." On the subject of managing, Rickey replied optimistically, "I hope that the day will soon come when it will be entirely possible, as it is entirely right, that you can be considered for administrative work in baseball, particularly in the direction of field management." Rickey claimed to have told several writers that "I do not know of any player in the game today who could, in my judgment, manage a major-league team better than yourself," but that the news media had inexplicably ignored these comments.

Yet Rickey tempered his encouragement with remarks that to a reader today seem gratuitous. "As I have often expressed to you," he wrote, "I think you carry a great responsibility for your people . . . and I cannot close this letter without admonishing you to prepare yourself to do a widely useful work, and, at the same time, dignified and effective in the field of public relations. A part of this preparation, and I know you are smiling, for you have already guessed my oft repeated suggestion—to finish your college course meritoriously and get your degree." This advice, according to Rachel Robinson, was a "matter of routine" between the two men ever since their first meeting. Nonetheless, to the thirty-one-year-old Robinson, whose non-athletic academic career had been marked by indifferent success and whose endorsements and business acumen had already established the promise of a secure future, Rickey's response may have seemed to beg the question.

Rickey concluded with the promise, which seems to hinge on the completion of a college degree, that "It would be a great pleasure for me to be your agent in placing you in a big job after your playing days are finished. Believe me always." Shortly after writing this letter Rickey became the general manager of the Pittsburgh Pirates. Had Robinson ended his playing career before Rickey left the Pirates, perhaps the Mahatma would have made good on his pledge. But Rickey resigned from the Pirates at the end of the 1955 season, one year before Robinson's retirement, and never again had the power to hire a manager.

Robinson's 1950 letter to Rickey marked only the beginning of his quest to see a Black manager in the major leagues. In 1952 he hoped to gain experience by managing in the Puerto Rican winter league, but, according to the *New York Post*, Commissioner Happy Chandler withheld his approval, forcing Robinson to cancel his plans. On November 30, 1952, the Dodgers star raised the prospect of a Black manager in a televised interview on *Youth Wants to Know*, stating that both he and Campanella had been "approached" on the subject. In 1954, after the Dodgers had fired manager Chuck Dressen, speculation arose that either Robinson or Pee Wee Reese might be named to the post. But the team bypassed both men and selected veteran minor-league manager Walter Alston, who went on to hold the job for more than two decades.

Upon his retirement in 1956, Robinson, who had begun to manifest signs of the diabetes that would plague the rest of his life, had lost much of his enthusiasm for the prospect of managing, but nonetheless would probably have accepted another pioneering role. "He had wearied of the travel," Rachel Robinson stated, "and no longer wanted to manage. He just wanted to be asked as a recognition of his accomplishments, his abilities as a strategist, and to show that White men could be led by a Black."

Ironically, in the early years of integration White baseball had bypassed a large pool of qualified and experienced Black managers: former Negro League players and managers like Chet Brewer, Ray Dandridge, and Quincy Trouppe. In the early 1950s Brewer and several other Negro League veterans managed all-Black minor-league teams, but no interracial club at any level offered a managerial position to a Black until 1961, when former Negro League and major-league infielder Gene Baker assumed the reins of a low-level Pittsburgh Pirate farm team, one of only three Blacks to manage a major-league affiliate before 1975.

This lack of opportunity loomed as a major frustration for those who had broken the color line. "We bring dollars into club treasuries while we play," protested Larry Doby, the first Black American Leaguer, in 1964, "but when we stop playing, our dollars stop. When I retired in '59 I wanted to stay in the game, to be a coach or in some other capacity, or to manage in the minors until I'd qualify for a big-league job. Baseball owners are missing the boat by not considering Negroes for such jobs." Monte Irvin, who had integrated the New York Giants in 1949 and clearly possessed managerial capabilities, concurred. "Among retired and active players [there] are Negroes with backgrounds suited to these jobs," wrote Irvin. "Owning a package liquor store, bowling alley or selling insurance is hardly the vocation for an athlete who has accumulated a lifetime knowledge of the game."

Had Robinson, Doby, Irvin, or another Black been offered a managerial position in the 1950s or early 1960s, and particularly if the first Black manager had experienced success, it is possible that this would have opened the doors for other Black candidates. As with Robinson's ascension to the major leagues, this example might ultimately have made the hiring and firing of a Black manager more or less routine. Robinson dismissed the notion that a Black manager might experience extraordinary difficulties. "Many people believe that White athletes will not play for a Negro manager," he argued in 1964. "A professional athlete will play with or for anyone who helps him make more money. He will respect ability, first, last, and all the time. This is something that baseball's executives must learn—that any experienced player with leadership qualities can pilot a ballclub to victory, no matter what the color of his skin."

On the other hand, the persistent biases of major-league owners and their subsequent history of discriminatory hiring indicated that the solitary example of a Jackie Robinson regime would probably not have been enough to shake the complacency of the baseball establishment. Few baseball executives considered hiring Blacks as managers even in the 1960s and 1970s. In 1960 Chicago White Sox owner Bill Veeck, who had hired Doby in 1947 and represented the most enlightened thinking in the game, raised the issue, but even Veeck defined special qualifications needed for a Black to manage. "A man will have to have more stability to be a Negro coach or manager and be slower to anger than if he were White," stated Veeck. "The first major-league manager will have to be a fellow who has been playing extremely well for a dozen years or so, so that he becomes a byword for excellence." The following year Veeck sold the White Sox; other owners ignored the issue entirely.

Jackie Robinson himself never flagged in his determination to see a Black manager. In 1972, at the World Series at Riverfront Stadium in Cincinnati, baseball commemorated the twenty-fifth anniversary of his major-league debut. A graying, almost blind, but still defiant Robinson told a nationwide television audience, "I'd like to live to see a Black manager."

"I would have eagerly welcomed the challenge of a managerial job before I left the game," Robinson revealed in his 1972 autobiography, *I Never Had It Made*. "I know I could have been a good manager." But despite his obvious qualifications, no one offered him a job.

On Opening Day 1975, African American star player Frank Robinson took the reins of the Cleveland Indians. But Jackie had not lived to see that; he died nine days after his remarks at the 1972 World Series.

NEGRO LEAGUE BASEBALL, BLACK COMMUNITY, AND THE SOCIO-ECONOMIC IMPACT OF INTEGRATION

Japheth Knopp

This article was published in the Baseball Research Journal*, Spring 2016.*

This essay will explore the subject of racial and economic integration during the period of approximately 1945 through 1965 by studying the subject of Negro League baseball and the African American community of Kansas City, Missouri, as a vehicle for discussing the broader economic and social impact of desegregation. Of special import here is the economic effect desegregation had on medium and large-scale Black-owned businesses during the postwar period, with the Negro Leagues and their franchises serving as prime examples of Black-owned businesses that were expansive in size, profitable, publicly visible, and culturally relevant to the community. Specifically, what we are concerned with here is whether the manner in which desegregation occurred did in fact provide for increased economic and political freedoms for African Americans, and what social, fiscal, and communal assets may have been lost in the exchange.

The Kansas City Monarchs baseball club and the Kansas City African American community serve as a focal point for a number of reasons, including access to sources, the stature of the Monarchs as a preeminent team, the position of Jackie Robinson as the first openly Black player to cross the color barrier in the modern period, and the vibrancy of the Kansas City Black community. Also, Kansas City is unique in that it was the westernmost major metropolis in a border state, straddling the line between North and South and taking on aspects of both.[1] However, in most respects the setting for this essay could have been any urban Black area in the United States in this period, with Kansas City being quite representative of the time. St. Louis or Chicago, Newark or Pittsburgh, across the country a general theme emerges of increased political and economic freedoms for African Americans, at least within segregated communities that in many ways were lost after increased contact and competition with White-owned businesses.[2] All of these communities would in this period struggle with the ramifications of "White Flight," decapitalization of urban areas, prejudicial hiring and housing policies, and increased economic competition.[3] The story of Black enterprise in America follows a close parallel to what happened to the Negro Leagues.

AUGUST 28, 1945; 18TH & VINE, KANSAS CITY, MO

The headlines of the *Kansas City Call*, the local Black newspaper, were still filled with postwar optimism but also with trepidation over continuing economic and civic issues in the months following the end of the war. From the Friday, August 31, 1945, edition we find that the S & D Process Company, an all-Black mail order distribution house, had been abruptly closed, laying off its last 60 workers, most of whom were women. At the height of the war the firm had employed some 245 Black workers.[4] In the same issue it was announced that the local office of the Federal Employment Practices Commission (which sought to provide more fair hiring and employment standards for minorities, especially in heavy industry and manufacturing) had been closed and was being incorporated in the St. Louis office.[5] The writer had some concerns for what this meant for the Black workers in the area.

Perhaps the most troubling news item from this issue was the case of Seaman First Class Junius Bobb, a Black sailor arrested for allegedly starting an altercation with a White Marine at Union Station rail depot. At press time the Navy would not disclose details, saying only that the incident was under investigation and that Seaman Bobb would stand trial for assault at Great Lakes Naval Training Center outside of Chicago. According to eyewitnesses, the Marine began the exchange by verbally and physically assaulting Seaman Bobb. The Shore Patrol arrived shortly thereafter and several military policemen began to beat Seaman Bobb with batons in full view of the public. The Marine in question was not arrested. Seaman Bobb's condition was unknown and he was being held incommunicado. The NAACP had announced that they would be providing legal counsel if Seaman Bobb did not prefer a Navy lawyer.[6]

On the whole, however, the general tone of the paper was upbeat and optimistic. While issues involving economic and legal inequality dominated the front page, there were many more stories celebrating success stories from the Black community. Local girl Yolanda Meek had been awarded a $5,000 scholarship by the Delta Sigma Theta Sorority.[7] Op-ed columnist Lucia Mallory wrote about the importance of continuing to support the government by buying bonds even after the war had ended, and appealed to her readers to donate clothes and other supplies to the relief effort for victims of war-torn Europe.[8] Even though the local office was being closed, the FEPC was scheduled to hold a meeting October 14 at Municipal Auditorium called "An Industrial Job for all who Qualify," focusing on retaining Black employment in the industrial sector after shifting to a peace-time economy.[9]

Many of the same sentiments were echoed in another local Black newsletter, which on the front page expressed concern about the unemployment rate of the African American community and what postwar demobilization would mean for the Black worker. While employment rates among Black workers had doubled between 1940 and 1943, there had already been numerous layoffs in the various wartime industries, where Black workers faced a "last hired, first fired" mentality.[10] Companies such as Remington Arms, North American Aircraft, Aluminum Company of America, and Pratt and Whitney Aircraft had increased their employment of Black workers by some 200% during the war, 30% of whom were women.[11] What would become of these jobs in peacetime was a major concern. However, the inside fold of the circular contained stories of decorated Black service members from the area, making special note of how many of them had been commissioned officers. These consistent themes of concern over civil liberties and economic opportunities intermixed with a sense of community pride and optimism seem to have been pervasive at this time.

This same general pathos is reflected in *The Call's* sports pages. No fewer than four articles were dedicated to the Kansas City Monarchs of the Negro National League and one of the most storied Black teams in baseball history. After dutifully reporting game summaries giving details of two lost games in a doubleheader to the Chicago American Giants by scores of 15–1 and 2–1, the writer moved on to more pleasant aspects of the club. There was a small writeup about the antics of legendary pitcher and showman Satchel Paige, who was equally famous both for his abilities as a player and for his on-field theatrics that dazzled the crowd and added to his already mythic persona. Another item advertised for the upcoming Labor Day doubleheader against the Memphis Red Sox in which ace pitcher and future Hall of Famer Hilton Smith was scheduled to pitch.[12] Somewhat surprisingly, there was no mention of star rookie shortstop Jackie Robinson, who was having one of the finest seasons of any player in the league.[13] While the official announcement would not be made until October, this was the first issue of the Monarchs' local paper following the historic signing of Robinson by Branch Rickey and the Brooklyn Dodgers on August 25, becoming the first Black player in the twentieth century to have signed with a major league team.[14]

In the immediate wake of World War II, economic prosperity was permeating all levels of society (though admittedly distributed unequally) and Kansas City's African American community was no exception. Having weathered the Great Depression with unemployment and business failure rates much higher than their White counterparts, businesses were booming in the early postwar period. More than half of all businesses in Kansas City's Black section were owned and operated by African American proprietors. While most of these were small-scale service sector operations, there were also banks, insurance agencies, doctors' offices, and law firms. More than 200 local Black-owned businesses provided hundreds of jobs and an average weekly salary of $23.81, which was still below the national median, but much improved from just a few years prior.[15] Returning veterans were taking advantage of the Servicemen's Readjustment Act of 1944 and other benefits to open new businesses and purchase their own homes.[16] Employment opportunities for African American women had improved in this area to such an extent that there was a shortage of domestic workers available to work for wealthy White households.[17]

Increased economic opportunities and a sense of empowerment from wartime achievements (combined to a smaller degree with new government programs) fostered a zeitgeist of activism more commonly ascribed to the Civil Rights Movement of a decade later. Instead of maintaining the status quo, there were numerous new groups organized to push for expanded rights in the fields of healthcare, housing, employment, and access to advanced education and other public amenities. Organizations such as the Urban League were becoming increasingly vocal and insistent upon equal opportunity as well as instilling a sense of civic pride in the accomplishments of local African Americans.[18]

The epicenter of the African American community was located around 18th Street between Vine and The Paseo. Businesses of all types, from barber and shoe repair shops to doctors' and lawyers' offices were found in this neighborhood. This section of town was perhaps best known for its night life, with patrons packing clubs with colorful names such as the Cherry Blossom, the Chez Paree, Lucille's Paradise, and the Ol' Kentuck' Bar-B-Q.[19] Kansas City was a regular tour stop for many of the biggest names in blues and jazz from this period. Count Basie and his orchestra, Cab Calloway, Billie Holliday, and Louis Armstrong, among many others, could frequently be found playing the many venues in this district.[20]

And of course, there were the Monarchs, arguably the greatest team of the Negro League era and perhaps one of the finest clubs in baseball history. With perennially winning teams built around future Hall of Famers like Satchel Paige, Cool Papa Bell, and Jackie Robinson, as well as Buck O'Neil, whose bronze image stands near the Cooperstown shrine's entrance, the Monarchs were consistently one of the top drawing teams in baseball (Black or White) and nearly always in championship contention. Established shortly after the turn of the century as a barnstorming team, they had been a central element of the Black community for years before the establishment of the Negro National League in 1920, and would go on to dominate that circuit for several years before playing as an independent club for a number of seasons and then becoming a charter member of the Negro American League in 1937.[21]

Besides fielding a consistently competitive team, playing in one of the newest and nicest ballparks in the Negro Leagues also helped attract fans. Muehlebach Field, which opened in 1923 and would go through a number of name changes before settling on Municipal Stadium in 1955, was shared by the Monarchs and the Kansas City Blues, the top minor league club in the Yankees farm system. Located on Brooklyn Avenue a few blocks south of 18th Street, the stadium straddled the dividing line between the Black and White sections of town and attracted spectators from both. Being as the Monarchs were nearly always in contention for the pennant, Municipal Stadium would host several Negro League World Series, beginning with the first one in 1924. By the 1940s shifting demographics placed Municipal Stadium squarely in the African American area of town and would remain the home of the Monarchs for the rest of their tenure in Kansas City.[22]

The question becomes why, then, if social and economic conditions were improving exponentially in the African American community some ten years before what is nominally considered the beginning of the Civil Rights Era, were circumstances at the culmination of this period (and to an extent, today) practically unchanged, if not worse? The answer lies in how integration occurred, with White-owned businesses able to expand their market share at the expense of Black-owned businesses, while at the same time cherry-picking the best-educated and most-qualified Black workers and controlling the methods, timing, and public perception of desegregation.

ROLE OF BASEBALL AND BLACK BUSINESSES AS COMMUNITY TOUCHSTONE

One point that has been fairly well developed in the literature is the concept of baseball as community focus. While this model does not apply to African Americans exclusively, one of the most recurring points made in the various histories of the Negro Leagues in particular and Black baseball generally was how these teams served a communal purpose. Baseball functioned as a critical component in the separate economy catering to Black consumers in the urban centers of both the North and South. While most Black businesses struggled to survive from year to year, professional baseball teams and leagues operated for decades, representing a major achievement in Black enterprise and institution building.

Kansas City in this period was known not only for its ball club, but also as a hotbed of the jazz scene, and of course for its world famous barbeque. All of these elements merged in the Kansas City Black community, centered in the inner-city area of 18th and Vine. According to Monarchs manager and first baseman Buck O'Neil, this was an exciting time and place to be a part of:

"[P]laying for the Monarchs in the late thirties and early forties, staying in the Streets Hotel at 18th and Paseo, and coming down to the dining room where Cab Calloway and Billie Holiday and Bojangles Robinson often ate. 'Course, some of them were having supper while we were having breakfast and vice-versa. 'Good morning, Count,' I'd say. 'Good evening, Buck,' Mr. Basie would say. As somebody once put it, 'People are afraid to go to sleep in Kansas City because they might miss something.'

"Nowadays that downtown neighborhood is kind of sleepy, though we have some plans to wake up the ghosts. But we could never bring it back to its glory days."[23]

While Kansas City may have been somewhat unusual in the variety of activities available and the prominence of its Black celebrities, these themes can be found in urban Black communities throughout the North during this period. As desegregation gained momentum throughout the postwar era, many Black-owned businesses were unable to effectively compete with White-owned firms who were now serving, and in some cases employing, African Americans. During the 1950s and 1960s, "White Flight" to the suburbs would continue to draw capital away from urban centers where Black communities tended to congregate, leading to large-scale vacancy, plummeting property values, and blighted areas where crime became more frequent. As O'Neil notes, there have been many plans for urban renewal to help reinvigorate these areas. In the case of the 18th and Vine district in Kansas City, these efforts have been largely successful; however, other cities have met with more limited success.

In Jack Etkin's *Innings Ago: Recollections by Kansas City Ballplayers of their Days in the Game*, O'Neil discusses how Black teams provided a community focus for groups of African Americans living outside of cities with Negro League teams and in rural areas with small Black populations.[24] According to O'Neil, when a team such as the Kansas City Monarchs barnstormed through small towns in the South and Midwest, often the entire Black population in the area would turn out, wearing their Sunday best. For these fans, the attraction was perhaps not so much the game itself, but rather the expression of African Americans being treated with something like equality (as in playing on equal terms against White teams) and often demonstrating their ability to compete successfully. For many, these exhibitions were a highlight of the yearly social calendar.[25]

Baseball was of course not the only type of business to serve as a communal focal point. Many businesses, most notably barber shops, beauty parlors, and, perhaps to a lesser extent, night clubs and restaurants also filled this role. The financial stability these businesses provided, in conjunction with a safe and separate space, led to business owners (and beauticians in particular) being leaders and activists in the Black community with these shops being at the center, like a base of operations for these activities.[26] With increased competition from businesses outside the Black community coupled with decapitalization of inner-city areas, the importance of African American owned and operated businesses as a unique space for organization and communal fellowship began to erode.

ECONOMIC IMPACT OF BLACK BASEBALL

By the early 1920s, with a booming economy generally, and a fast growing and racially aware Black population in Northern and Midwestern urban centers, the stage was set for professional African American baseball leagues to successfully develop, and this was certainly the case in the Kansas City community. Between the 1920s and 1950s there would be ten professional Black leagues, though the most successful were the Negro National League (NNL) which operated between 1920 and 1931 and then from 1933 through 1948 and the Negro American League (NAL) from 1937 to 1960.[27] It is hardly coincidental that successful organized Black baseball began in this period. Black populations in Northern cities boomed during the 1910s with the Great Migration from the South and relatively plentiful job opportunities in defense industries during World War I. This was also the period of Garveyism, the Harlem Renaissance, and the first wave of Black Nationalism. This combination of expendable income, leisure time, and racial awareness all helped to make Negro League baseball popular within the African American community and for the first time profitable for its proprietors. Throughout the 1920s Black teams continued to make money, and while paid substantially less than their White counterparts, African American players earned about twice the national median income.[28]

However, by the end of the decade Black baseball was in steep decline. The reason for this reversal of fortunes was primarily economic. While national unemployment rates during the Great Depression would peak at about 25% and White baseball saw substantial decreases in attendance, the jobless rate among African Americans was considerably higher.[29] With deteriorating economic conditions, fans attended far fewer games, and teams and leagues began to fail. It was during this period that illegal money, particularly from gambling interests, began to be a major influence in the Negro Leagues. At least two teams were financed entirely by illegal gaming, though it is believed that several other teams may have also been involved.[30] What the true intentions of the gamblers were remains a source of debate. While it is undoubtable that some teams, such as the Newark Eagles owned by Abe and Effa Manley and Gus Greenlee's Pittsburgh Crawfords, served as fronts for laundering money, these owners also claimed to have had a genuine desire to keep their teams afloat and to continue to serve as a community focal point. There is some evidence to support these claims as these owners were well known within the Black community and were frequent donors to charities and social causes.[31] Whatever the intent, it is unlikely that the Negro Leagues could have survived the Depression without this influx of capital. Also, the sources of capital and intentions of White owners of major and minor league teams were likely not always completely pure. Several teams were owned by beer barons, and there is much speculation that some of these teams were used as a means of washing monies.[32] While Black owners were criticized (sometimes fairly) for being connected with illegal gaming and numbers-running, there were major league owners during the same period who actually owned casinos and horse tracks.[33]

This trend in Black baseball was mirrored in African American owned businesses more broadly. In 1932, there were 103,872 Black owned businesses in the United States. While most of these were small "mom and pop shops," there had also been growth during the 1920s in larger-scale operations such as insurance companies, publishing houses, and banks. However, even with diversification of business types owned by African Americans, these businesses continued to depend almost exclusively on Black customers. With widespread unemployment during the Great Depression (made worse in the African American community due to prejudicial hiring practices), there was less disposable income for Black customers to spend. Predictably, Black-owned firms began to fail and by 1940 the number of Black-owned businesses had declined by 16% to 87,475.[34]

The situation in Kansas City was different and unique in the league, as the Monarchs had a White owner, J.L. Wilkinson, who had long sponsored integrated (both by race and sex) barnstorming teams based out of Kansas City. He became one of the charter owners of the Negro National League. While this was a source of conflict for some of the owners, including league founder Rube Foster, Wilkinson's reputation for fairness (plus the fact that he held the lease on the one suitable ballpark) persuaded the owners to accept him into the fold.[35]

After narrowly surviving the 1930s, the Negro Leagues were in resurgence during the first half of the 1940s. Nearly full employment due to the war effort once again gave many African Americans disposable income. For the first time in more than a decade, teams consistently made money, and attendance was at an all-time high. Some teams were assessed as being as valuable as major-league franchises.[36] As the postwar period of economic prosperity set in and all sectors of the population saw rising income levels and standards of living, indications were Black businesses, including the Negro Leagues, were finally about to fulfill their potential. This was not to be.

Somewhat paradoxically, for many Negro League teams the years between 1947 and 1950 would be their most financially successful, but this was due almost exclusively to selling the contract rights of their players to White-owned teams in both the major and minor leagues.[37] Whereas the postwar period began very promising for the Negro Leagues with growing attendance, within just a few years most Black fans had taken to following their favorite players in the major leagues, and ticket sales fell off precipitously.

To complicate matters further, a number of White teams refused to honor the contracts of the Negro Leagues and pirated the players outright without compensating the team owners.[38] At other times owners sold the rights to players at below-market prices, finding it better to get some return rather than risk having the player signed outright. By 1948 only the NAL was still in operation, and it was relegated to minor league status. In the early 1960s there were only a few teams left and the league disbanded, though some clubs—like the Monarchs—continued to barnstorm. The Indianapolis Clowns were the last Negro League team in business and played their final game in 1988.[39]

WHITE FLIGHT, DECAPITALIZATION, AND THE AFRICAN AMERICAN COMMUNITY

Another important element during this period concerns the decapitalization of urban areas (and especially parts of cities where African Americans tended to congregate) and migration of White families to suburban communities from the late 1940s through the early 1960s. Again, Kansas City serves as a model, with several large industries leaving the center-city area in the 1950s and relocating to suburban areas where most White workers continued to be employed while laying off most of the Black workforce. The change began in earnest in the early 1950s with the decline of the railroad industry, chiefly due to competition from automobile and air travel. Union Station, which had been the second busiest rail terminal in America after Chicago and employed large numbers of African Americans in various capacities, declined rapidly and fell into disrepair. Another blow to the economy came with the Great Flood of 1951 which destroyed much of the stockyards located in the West Bottoms section. The stockyards, which were also second nationally to Chicago in size, never fully recovered as the cattle industry moved away from urban centers. With both of these industries went many comparatively well-paid and often unionized jobs.

As in baseball, in many middle- and large-scale industries, Black-owned firms were unable to compete with their White counterparts after racial integration. Many skilled Black workers were lured away to work at better-paying and more prestigious White-owned businesses. This clearly happened in baseball, where the very best Black and Latino players went to the major leagues, forcing the Negro Leagues to try to compete with less talented players.

This was again the case in Kansas City. In 1955 the Philadelphia Athletics moved into Municipal Stadium, where the Monarchs played, and though they were always near the bottom of the American League standings and moved on to Oakland after a number of seasons, this increased competition for entertainment dollars and use of public facilities forced the Monarchs out. In the min-1950s the Monarchs were sold, and while they retained the name "Kansas City Monarchs," this was a device used as a draw at the gate. The team was headquartered out of Grand Rapids, Michigan, until it finally folded in the min-1960s, only occasionally playing in Kansas City.[40]

"White flight" also affected baseball as new stadiums for almost every major-league team during the 1960s and 1970s were nearly always located away from inner-city areas whereas previous stadiums had been almost exclusively located in downtown areas. This would happen in Kansas City, where the aging Municipal Stadium was abandoned and the Truman Sports Complex—with stadiums for both the new Kansas City Royals and Kansas City Chiefs of the National Football League (NFL)—was built in 1972 near the interstate many miles away from the city's downtown area and much closer to the then predominately White suburbs.

ECONOMIC COSTS OF DESEGREGATION ON NEGRO LEAGUE BASEBALL

While the integration of professional baseball is often seen as a benchmark in the history of civil rights, this did not come without great cost—financial and otherwise—to Black baseball and the African American community broadly. Again, this is in keeping with what happened in other large-scale Black-owned businesses such as banks, newspapers, and insurance companies.[41] As events unfolded, the best Black players were cherry-picked by major-league clubs, leaving the Negro Leagues to try to compete for fan dollars with fewer quality players and less cultural significance.

Of the 80 players who would jump from the Negro Leagues to the majors, eight would be inducted into the Hall of Fame. Between 1947 and 1959, former Negro Leaguers would supply six Rookies of the Year and nine Most Valuable Player winners.[42] Black baseball, like many other African American-owned businesses, now had to compete against White-owned businesses for Black clientele and with less talent, capital, and cultural privilege than their

White counterparts. The result would be the collapse of the Negro Leagues (and many other Black-owned enterprises) which in conjunction with White Flight left many urban areas much less economically viable and with fewer opportunities for capitalization. From the middle 1950s through the 1970s most major-league teams left their inner-city ballparks for new stadiums closer to the predominately White suburbs, which further removed Black fans from the game.[43]

Making matters worse for the Black-owned teams was the practice of pirating Black players without compensating their former teams. Citing a lack of proper contracts (which is to say, contracts that had been approved for use in the White major and minor leagues), teams simply ignored the vested interests of Black clubs and signed the many of the best players outright without any financial consideration of Negro League owners.[44] Denouncing Black-owned businesses as being illegitimate and therefore ethical to deal with in an inequitable manner had long been a common practice among White business owners. This view was both obviously exploitative and paternalistic, harkening to the nineteenth-century stereotypes of Black people being unsophisticated and childlike and their efforts being seen as cargo cult-like mimicry of Whites rather than legitimate expressions of capitalism.

It is also important to remember that the failure of the Negro Leagues economically impacted many more people than the players on the field. An entire support staff of front-office personnel, groundskeepers, concessionaires, ticket-takers, bus drivers, and so forth were all necessary to put a game on the field. These workers in turn then patronized local businesses. When the teams began to struggle and finally collapsed, many people besides the players also lost their livelihoods. Similarly, as African Americans lost market share of industrial and manufacturing jobs, the service sector also suffered as their regular clientele had increasingly less disposable income. Coupled with increased competition with White-owned businesses, many Black-owned urban enterprises began to go under.

ALTERNATIVE PATHS TO INTEGRATION

The manner in which integration in baseball—and in American businesses generally—occurred was not the only model which was possible. It was likely not even the best approach available, but rather served the needs of those in already privileged positions who were able to control not only the manner in which desegregation occurred, but the public perception of it as well in order to exploit the situation for financial gain. Indeed, the very word integration may not be the most applicable in this context because what actually transpired was not so much the fair and equitable combination of two subcultures into one equal and more homogenous group, but rather the reluctant allowance—under certain preconditions—for African Americans to be assimilated into White society.

Another negative aspect of the manner in which baseball was integrated was the unofficial, but common, practice of using racial quotas. Beginning with Rickey's Dodgers, most major league teams—with a few notable exceptions such as Bill Veeck's Cleveland Indians, who became a powerhouse behind several Black stars—kept roster spots for African American players to a minimum. Black players were nearly always signed in even numbers, so that their White teammates would not have to share rooms with them on the road.[45] It was not at all unusual to see a Black player traded or sent to the minors if there were "too many" Black players on the squad.[46] Additionally, while Black players often made more money than their White colleagues, this was mostly because almost every Black player of the 1940s and 1950s was a star. Slots for journeymen and utility players were the exclusive territory of White players. The message was clear; produce more than the average White player or leave.

After Jackie Robinson broke the color line, executives and owners from the Negro Leagues met with their counterparts from the major leagues and proposed a number of options for mergers and cooperation. At first it was suggested that the better clubs with large fan bases from the Negro Leagues, such as the Monarchs and Crawfords, be allowed in as expansion franchises.[47] Several of these teams operated in cities without major league teams to compete with, already had large followings and the logistical infrastructure in place, and were perfectly positioned to help the major leagues take advantage of postwar prosperity and newly expendable income. The proposal was unanimously voted down. When this was rejected, the possibility of the Negro Leagues becoming a AAA circuit was raised. This too was summarily dismissed.[48] White owners had no interest in cooperating with their Black counterparts, and instead of engaging in a business enterprise which would have most likely proved beneficial for all parties, the major leagues made a deliberate choice to put the Negro Leagues out of business after obtaining their best players and wooing away much of their fan base.

SEPTEMBER 1965; 18TH & VINE, KANSAS CITY

Twenty years later the tone was considerably more pessimistic. The headlines of *The Call* still carried stories about violence and inequality within the Black community but gone was the sense of optimism or increasing opportunity. The lead story from the September 1965 issue (at this point, *The Call* had become a monthly rather than weekly publication) led with a story titled, "Vicious Attack on Farmer: Admits Cutting Man's Tongue Out," in which a young Black man killed an elderly Black farmer while attempting to keep him from being able to testify against him regarding a crime the older man had witnessed by removing his tongue.[49] Other headlines include, "Three Whites Arrested in Brewster Killing," "Slain Priest Buried in Home Town," "2,200 Still in Jail from L.A. Rioting," and "NAACP Official Injured in Bombing."[50] The paper also ran a two-page summary of a study analyzing the underlying causes of racial violence. The story, titled "New Study Tells Why Riots Occur," examined fifty years of data and concluded that riots occur when Whites feel economically threatened and local authorities, particularly the police, are not adequately trained to properly handle the situation.[51] Clearly, racially related violence had by the middle 1960s become a pervasive issue, and other concerns seemed secondary. There are no mentions of scholarships being awarded, mass meetings for employment opportunities, or patriotic calls for donations and privation here.

The sports page is no less bleak. There is no mention of the hapless Kansas City Athletics who were stumbling to another disappointing finish. The only mention of baseball at all was an incident on August 22 when Juan Marichal of the San Francisco Giants beat L.A. Dodgers catcher Johnny Roseboro in the head with a baseball bat, leading to a fine and suspension by the National League.[52] Even in baseball, violence seemed to permeate. There was also no mention of the Monarchs, long a source of civic pride, who probably played their last game about this time.[53]

A return visit to what had been the heart of the Black community reiterates this theme. Whereas 20 years before, 18th Street was a vibrant center for art and commerce, it had by this time become little more than a ghost town with nearly all the buildings abandoned and left to deteriorate. The first blow came under the guise of reform, when a number of new "blue laws" made it increasingly difficult for the night clubs to operate profitably. Similarly to many other inner-city areas, urban renewal projects that were intended (at least in theory) to help revitalize the area had the exact opposite effect. In the middle 1950s five acres of historic buildings were razed in order to make room for new building projects. However, due to poor financing this area sat vacant for many years and became known as a dangerous place to walk through. With new public accommodation laws came increased competition with other businesses outside of the traditional Black section of the city, and many African American owned shops—which generally had less access to capital, and prohibitive conditions attached when it could be found—were in most cases no longer able to operate profitably.[54] By 1964, only two large buildings anchored the area, with the *Kansas City Call* still operating in the same space since 1922 on the east end, and the Lincoln Building housing several professional offices to the west. The corridor between the two comprised a few bars and a handful of shops, with nearly all of the storefronts boarded up in disuse and disrepair.[55]

Municipal Stadium would continue to be used on and off by various teams and for different events until the early 1970s, but little effort or funding was put into maintaining the structure. The primary reason given for moving the Athletics to Oakland was Kansas City's lack of commitment to building a new ballpark.[56] According to owner Charles O. Finley, the neighborhood had become too dangerous for night games, and he blamed the aging and inadequate facility for low attendance numbers (though one might argue that the club being at the bottom of the standings for more than a dozen years contributed more to low turnout). The promise of a new publicly financed stadium helped secure Kansas City an expansion team, the Royals, in 1969 and Municipal Stadium was finally abandoned after the 1972 baseball season.[57] It sat unused and dilapidated until 1976 when it was demolished for being a danger to public safety.[58] Professional baseball had left Kansas City's African American community for the last time.

This seeming trend of negativism within the Black community at this time would seem paradoxical, at least in the traditional framework of American history. The Voting Rights Act of 1965 had been signed into law on August 6 of that year, and the Civil Rights Act of 1964, outlawing discrimination based on race, sex, or religion and segregation of public accommodations, was barely a year old. Why then, at a time of such apparent progress, does the record suggest such unfavorable conditions for many in the African American community? One would argue that despite the legal gains made during this period, which were substantial and should not be dismissed, the larger issue was access to economic opportunities. Indeed, the evidence reveals that levels of education and income in the early 1960s were essentially unchanged since World War II.[59] These stagnant levels of earnings and upward mobility are all the more telling being as this period witnessed some of the fastest and most widespread economic growth in American history. Increased competition, lack of capital, and the withdrawal of industry from inner-city areas all contributed to a rather bleak social and economic prognosis that no legislation could mitigate and which is still with us today.[60]

CONCLUSION

In many ways the story of Negro League baseball in general and the Kansas City Black community and ball club in particular provide an excellent example of the economic and social changes occurring in urban African American communities during the postwar era. While on the one hand the end (at least officially) of legal segregation and prejudicial hiring policies was clearly a victory for the cause of progress and many people have undoubtedly been able to succeed and have had opportunities that would not have otherwise been afforded them, it must be remembered that this came at a cost, and many of the long-term issues that have plagued inner-city areas are residual damage caused in large part by the manner in which integration occurred. The reality is that much of the African American community was largely unaffected economically by the successes of the Civil Rights Era. Black workers lacking higher education and job skills, mostly due to an inadequate and unequal education system, remained trapped in low-paying jobs and neighborhoods with increasingly few amenities.[61] While there was growth in this period among the Black middle class, these new jobs were almost exclusively in White-owned firms. Large-scale Black-owned businesses, unable to find new clients, sources of revenue, and at a competitive disadvantage for the patronage of their traditional customers, failed.

This is not to imply that segregation, economic or otherwise, was in any way beneficial to the African American community. The current face of American society would have been almost unimaginable at the beginning of the Civil Rights Movement. The fact remains, however, that in spite of discrimination and disadvantage, many Black entrepreneurs were able to find a niche market and achieve financial success. In the end desegregation happened on what were essentially the terms of the White majority, which in many ways benefited economically from the new arrangement, rather than honest assimilation combining the best qualities of both communities and building a more just and equal society.

Notes

1. Urban League of Kansas City. "The 'Northern City with a Southern Exposure,'" *Matter of Fact: Newsletter of the Urban League of Kansas City, Missouri*. Vol. I; No. 1, July, 1945, 1.
2. Robert H. Kinzer and Edward Sagrin, *The Negro in American Business: The Conflict Between Separatism and Integration* (New York: Greenburg, 1950), 100–1.
3. Thomas J. Sugrue, *Sweet Land of Liberty: The Forgotten Struggle for Civil Rights in the North* (New York: Random House, 2008), 177–79.
4. "All-Black Company Closes Suddenly," *Kansas City Call*. Vol. 27; No. 16, August 31, 1945, 1.
5. "Kansas City FEPC Office Closed," *Kansas City Call*. Vol. 27; No. 16, August 31, 1945, 1.
6. I subsequently did some research on the matter, but was unable to discover the outcome of the trial or what became of Seaman First Class Bobb.
7. "Local Girl Awarded Scholarship," *Kansas City Call*. Vol. 27; No. 16, August 31, 1945, 3.
8. Lucia Mallory, "Keep Buying War Bonds!" *Kansas City Call*. Vol. 27; No. 16, August 31, 1945, 4.
9. "FEPC to Hold Meeting," The *Kansas City Call*. Vol. 27; No. 16, August 31, 1945, 5.
10. Urban League of Kansas City. *Matter of Fact: Newsletter of the Urban League of Kansas City, Missouri*. July, 1945, 1.
11. Census Bureau. *1950 United States Census of Population Report; Kansas City, Missouri* (U.S. Govt. Printing Office; Washington, 1952), 17–19.
12. "Smith to Start Labor Day Double-Header," *Kansas City Call*. Vol. 27; No. 16, August 31, 1945, 9.
13. Statistics for Negro League players are notoriously difficult to find exact figures for. Baseball-Reference.com, usually considered to be authoritative, lists Robinson as having a .414 batting average in 63 games that season, though this is probably incomplete.
14. Frank Foster, *The Forgotten League: A History of the Negro League Baseball* (BookCaps; No city given, 2012), 55.
15. Urban League of Kansas City. "Local Survey Made," *Matter of Fact: Newsletter of the Urban League of Kansas City, Missouri*. Vol. I; No. 6, April–May, 1946, 2

16 Urban League of Kansas City. "Clinic for Small Business Draws Much Interest," *Matter of Fact: Newsletter of the Urban League of Kansas City, Missouri*. Vol. I; No. 6, April 1946, 2–3.

17 Urban League of Kansas City. "'You Just Can't Find Good Help Anymore,'" *Matter of Fact: Newsletter of the Urban League of Kansas City, Missouri*. Vol. II; No. 1, August, 1946, 2.

18 Urban League of Kansas City. "It's a Matter-of-Fact that:" *Matter of Fact: Newsletter of the Urban League of Kansas City, Missouri*. Vol. 1; No. 1, July, 1945, 2.

19 Chuck Haddix, "18th & Vine: Street of Dreams," in *Artlog*. Missouri Arts Council. Vol. XIII; No. 1, January –February, 1992, 3.

20 Chuck Haddix, "18th & Vine: Street of Dreams," in *Artlog*. Missouri Arts Council. Vol. XIII; No. 1, January –February, 1992, 4.

21 Janet Bruce, *The Kansas City Monarchs: Champions of Black Baseball* (University of Kansas Press; Lawrence, 1985), 117.

22 Bruce, 126

23 Buck O'Neil, *I Was Right on Time: My Journey from the Negro Leagues to the Majors* (Simon & Schuster; New York, 1996), 75–76

24. Jack Etkin, *Innings Ago: Recollections by Kansas City Ballplayers of their Days in the Game* (Walsworth Publishing; Marceline, MO, 1987), 18.

25 Etkin, 19.

26 Tiffany Gill, *Beauty Shop Politics: African American Women's Activism in the Beauty Industry* (University of Illinois Press; Chicago, 2010), 2.

27 Leslie Heaphy, *The Negro Leagues, 1869–1960* (McFarland & Co; Jefferson, North Carolina, 2003), 224.

28 Rob Ruck, *Raceball: How the Major Leagues Colonized the Black and Latin Game* (Beacon Press, Boston, Massachusetts, 2011), 101.

29 William Sundstrom, "Last Hired, First Fired? Unemployment and Urban Black Workers during the Great Depression" in *The Journal of Economic History* (Vol. 52, No. 2, June, 1992), 485.

30 Bob Luke, *The Most Famous Woman in Baseball: Effa Manley and the Negro Leagues* (Potomac Books; Dulles, Virginia, 2011), 11.

31 Luke, 45.

32 Peter Golenbock, *The Spirit of St. Louis: A History of the St. Louis Cardinals and Browns* (HarperCollins; New York, 2000), 352.

33 Bill Veeck, *Veeck–As in Wreck* (University of Chicago Press; Chicago, 1962), 246-247.

34 Michael Woodward, *Black Entrepreneurs in America: Stories of Struggle and Success* (Rutgers University Press; New Brunswick, NJ, 1997), 18.

35 O'Neil, 77–78.

36 Ruck, 78.

37 Bruce, 118–19.

38 Veeck, 176.

39 Heaphy, 227.

40 Bruce, 126.

41 Robert E Weems Jr., *Black Business in the Black Metropolis: The Chicago Mutual Assurance Company, 1925–1985*. (Indiana University Press; Indianapolis, 1996), xv.

42 Larry Lester and Wayne Stivers, *The Negro Leagues Book. Volume 2: the Players*, 1862-1960 (Kansas City, MO, NoirTech Research, 2020) 233-238.

43 Lanctot, 395–96.

44 Mitchell Nathanson, *A People's History of Baseball* (University of Illinois Press; Urbana, IL, 2012), 86–87.

45 Nathanson, 99.

46 Ibid, 103–104.

47 Ruck, 115

48 Ibid, 116

49 "Vicious Attack on Farmer: Admits Cutting Man's Tongue Out," The *Kansas City Call*, Vol. 46; No. 22, September 3, 1965, 1.

50 "NAACP Official Injured in Bombing," The *Kansas City Call*, Vol. 46; No. 22, September 3, 1965, 1.

51 "New Study Tells Why Riots Occur," The *Kansas City Call*, Vol. 46; No. 22, September 3, 1965, 1.

52 Bill James, *New Historical Baseball Abstract* (Simon & Schuster; New York, 2001), 253.

53 The exact date has proven impossible to track down after extensive research. By this point the team had been playing out of Grand Rapids, Michigan for several seasons, only keeping the name as a source of revenue. It is known that the team played most of the 1965 season and folded near the end of the year. S

54 Woodward, 26

55 Haddix, 5.

56 Herbert Michelson, *Charlie O: Charles Oscar Finley vs. the Baseball Establishment* (Bobbs-Merrill; New York, 1975), 125, 127–28.

57 Mark Stallard, *Legacy of Blue: 45 Years of Kansas City Royals History & Trivia* (Kaw Valley Books; Overland Park, KS, 2013), 6.

58 Lawrence Ritter, *Lost Ballparks: A Celebration of Baseball's Legendary Fields* (Penguin; New York, 1994), 136.

59 United States Department of Labor. *Home, Education, and Unemployment in Neighborhoods; Kansas City, Missouri*, January 1963.

60 Andrew Brimmer, "Small Business and Economic Development in the Negro Community," in *Black Americans and White Business*, Edwin Epstein and David Hampton, ed., (Dickinson Publishing, Encino, CA., 1971).

61 Woodward, 30–31.

EARLY TWENTIETH-CENTURY HEROES: COVERAGE OF NEGRO LEAGUE BASEBALL

in the Pittsburgh Courier and the Chicago Defender

Brian Carroll

This article appeared in Journalism History, *Spring 2006.*

Had baseball card collecting been popular in the 1920s, fans of the nascent Negro leagues likely would have coveted the cards of Andrew "Rube" Foster, C.I. Taylor, Ed Bolden, and John Blount. Because these men were team owners and not players, the backs of the cards would have presented lists of businesses owned and positions held in the local Black church and in business and social federations like the Persian Temple of Mystic Shriners. There would have been no baseball cards of the players, who were considered mere employees. Players would not supplant owners as heroes to and role models for the Black community until the mid-1930s.

It should not surprise to find Black baseball's owners rather than the athletes portrayed as champions in the weekly newspapers. During the first two decades of Negro League history, leading Black newspapers such as the *Chicago Defender, Kansas City Call*, and *Pittsburgh Courier* considered themselves important partners with Black professional baseball in creating minority-owned, minority-run businesses. These owners were community leaders to be admired, with status in the community to which to aspire.[1] Based on Black press coverage during the period, it is clear that newspaper writers believed their readers had a vested interest in the decisions and activities of these owners, a connection Barbara Molette has noted a community must perceive with those it has identified as its heroes.[2]

This paper explores the role of the Black press in creating and portraying role models to the largely urban Black community of the 1920s, 1930s, and the first half of the 1940s leading up to the selection of Jackie Robinson as the breaker of White major league baseball's color barrier. The paper seeks a better understanding of the daily reality for this community by looking at Black press coverage of these exclusively male figures. By examining the values, goals, and actions held up by the Black press as those to model and mirror, it is perhaps possible to better understand what the Black community of the period sought in its hero figures and important people and, therefore, how its members saw themselves and who they hoped to become. Finally, this study assumes a scope and function of the hero in society as a phenomenon of mass media communication.[3]

One of the first scholars to comment on American notions of hero and hero-worship, Thomas Carlyle noted that "great men" were recurrent, prominent subjects of scholarship as "modelers, patterns . . . even creators, of whatsoever the general mass of men contrived to do or to attain."[4] Still widely cited, Carlyle's 1840 lecture suggests that a look at the world's heroes is a look "into the very marrow of the world's history," justifying in some ways an historical approach to the study of any one community's heroes.[5]

Molette argued that for a figure to become an important person in the Afrocentric framework, the person's actions must transcend the needs and reality of the individual. The Black community's members must see that hero as a "prototypical manifestation of their own hopes, aspirations, and values."[6] Though this examination is not definitive in analyzing the beliefs of Black newspaper readers in the quarter-century leading up to Jackie Robinson's entry into previously segregated Major League Baseball, it does seek to reveal some of their shared beliefs and the context in which they were formed and held. The heroic portrayals can be seen as an effort to influence the process of projecting and, to a lesser extent, creating Afrocentric heroes for what was during the period studied an entirely segregated society.

It is also important to study African American notions of heroism and heroic figures because of the institutionalized racism that defined life in the 1920s and 1930s. This systemic discrimination created or at least contributed to an environment of oppression, pain, and hardship that would seem to add yet more luster to the Black community's heroes since these figures had to demonstrate an uncommon strength merely to survive. Finding ways to endure, in fact, is one of the hallmarks of Afrocentric heroes throughout the last 300 years.[7]

The Black press is a useful record of the time period, at least when looking at the middle-class, mostly urban, mostly northern Black communities of the 1920s, 1930s, and 1940s. Since what constitutes heroism and who is recognized as a hero can be seen as functions of cultural values that are negotiated and, therefore, change over time, Black newspapers as a communication medium provide a convenient Petri dish, or preservation method for information and, equally important to this study, for how that information was prioritized and presented.[8] As Frankie Hutton found, since its inception, the Black press has focused on "vindication, uplift, and acceptance of Blacks into mainstream America despite racism, violence, harsh personal problems, and discord," portraying the Black community as a "resilient, idealistic, persecuted" group.[9]

The *Chicago Defender* and *Pittsburgh Courier* are logical choices for the study. By 1920 the nation's largest Black weekly, the *Defender* distributed more than two-thirds of its issues outside of Chicago, mainly by using Pullman porters. This increasingly national influence and awareness among Blacks would dramatically expand the impact of a crusading Black press. By 1925, the *Defender* had a circulation of 250,000, which set a new standard for Black newspapers. With a pass-around readership of between four and five people, the true number of readers perhaps numbered more than a million, explaining in part how the *Defender* could inspire and persuade so many Blacks to leave the South and flee northward as part of the Great Migration of 1915–1919.[10]

The *Courier* took its cues from the *Defender* in building a national circulation and distribution network. Founded in 1910, the Pittsburgh paper was by the late 1930s the most widely read Black newspaper and remained so through the 1950s. In 1947, for example, the paper represented a $2 million business with a circulation of about 330,000. In the 1930s the *Courier* operated 12 branches and published 14 editions.[11]

Little research has been done on Black press coverage of and involvement in Negro League baseball. Even less has been published in journalism and mass communication scholarship. Because members of the Black press are prominent in the narrative of Negro League history, and since the mainstream press largely ignored Black baseball, Black newspapers provide an important primary source for scholarship on the Negro Leagues and professional baseball's integration. Rarely, however, has the Black press itself been the subject of research in the context of its relationship with and intimate involvement in Black baseball.

Douglas Porpora noted that considerable scholarly attention has been paid to heroes as created and promoted by media, but virtually all of the research has examined mainstream society and, therefore, mainstream media.[12] The Black press has not been examined as a projector or creator of hero figures, though consideration has been given to Booker T. Washington's hero status.[13] This is significant, for as Lance Strate has argued, the nature and function of a hero in any society is dependent upon the dominant medium.[14] For African-Americans in the 1920s through 1940s, weekly newspapers such as the *Defender* and the *Courier* were among the principal communication media.

Janice Hume, who has done a series of studies on heroic women in mid-century mainstream media, found that mass media tell heroic stories to mass audiences and, therefore, become tools for defining American heroism.[15] Susan J. Drucker and Robert S. Cathcart, who were among the first to consolidate scholarship on heroes portrayed by and in contemporary mass media, also determined that media attention is the agency that makes contemporary heroes and found that it also *unmakes* them. Media satisfy the public's demand for supermen and every bit as relentlessly chronicle their human faults and failings.[16]

An important distinction must be made, however. As Drucker has argued, sports heroes are more about the illusion of heroism than the embodiment of truly heroic values. The ways that playing fields, photography, publicity, and media coverage construct myths of heroes and heroism point to a celebrification process that turns modern-day athletes into "pseudo-heroes."[17] In this study, when the newspapers' heroes become the athletes on the field and are, therefore, no longer true community leaders, Drucker's descriptions of celebrification and the fabrication of heroism become important.

Unlike football, boxing, or basketball, the game of baseball in the 1920s was covered by the Black press as a Black-owned, Black-run business offering job- and income-creation. The sport was not merely a source of diversion and entertainment. Baseball in the pages of the Black press, therefore, served as a point of pride for the Black community. Early in the decade, the *Defender,* for example, routinely boasted of its participation in the league, promising its readers a "correct version" of the comings and goings of the Negro National League, the first enduring Black league, and claiming itself to be "the newspaper which has done more for baseball and sports among our people than any three papers published."[18]

This boosterism explains how the *Defender* could elect not to criticize the league or its owners even though they failed to solve or meaningfully address the league's persistent problems. At least through the decade's first half, the newspaper described what it called the owners' "church-like harmony," a description that could not qualify as objective reporting by any definition.[19] Selective reporting was necessary. Communities need heroes; communities can, in fact, form around heroes.[20] Black press historian Frankie Hutton found that Black newspaper editors since the beginnings of the Black press in America made themselves "overseers of uplift" and their papers mediators of style.[21]

An early researcher into how America creates its popular heroes, Orrin E. Klapp, observed that writers ascribe hero status to figures by honoring them, giving them special status, commemorating their accomplishments, and venerating them over time. This gradual, accretive process confers hero status on a figure "who evokes the appropriate attitudes and behavior" and who is seen as a personage of idealized virtues, admired and honored.[22] He is set apart, in this context by newspaper writers, by "deference, precedence, decorations."[23] All three means are on display in the *Defender*'s sports pages of the 1920s.

Weekly newspapers had the power and reach, as Elizabeth Eisenstein observed, to "supplement tales of great men teaching by example."[24] Hero creation was a collective process, one that selected, honored, and cast individuals as symbols for the larger community. Explaining in large part why the Black press chose them, businessmen excelled in fields of endeavor that the community's members admired, an excellence that Klapp argued a public's heroes must demonstrate.[25] Socially, culturally, and economically, baseball occupied pre-eminent status for the Black community of the 1920s and 1930s—a status difficult to comprehend in the context of the variegated sports and entertainment landscapes of contemporary American culture.

Baseball was pre-eminent in part because other sports did not have the commercial impact within the Black community that baseball provided. A page one editorial by *Pittsburgh Courier* publisher Robert Vann published in December 1923 described the sport as one of "America's big business enterprises . . . both an economic and civic institution." He contrasted baseball with football, which could "not assume the economic proportions known to baseball."[26] Most importantly, baseball represented a point of pride and an outlet for leisure for a segregated society striving to hold up its collective head. As social and cultural critic Amiri Baraka wrote, the Negro Leagues were:

> Like a light somewhere. Back over your shoulder. As you go away. A warmth still, connected to laughter and self-love. The collective Black aura that can only be duplicated with Black conversation or *music* . . . these were professional ballplayers. Legitimate Black heroes. And we were intimate with them in a way and they were extensions of all of us, there, in a way that the Yankees and Dodgers and whatnot could never be! . . . It was like we all communicated with each other and possessed ourselves at a more human level than was usually possible out there in cold whitey land.[27]

Evidence of the extent of segregation is found in the complete absence in coverage during the 1920s of the major leagues. Absent, too, are the experiences and perspectives of individual players, a gap closed in the 1930s with the arrival of pitching great Satchel Paige, the popularity of boxing, an individual sport, and the success of Black athletes like Jesse Owens in the 1936 Olympics. The priority during this early phase of the leagues' existence was establishing baseball's businesses on stable terms and, therefore, keeping control of the sport within the Black community.

The White major leagues were not discussed, and that sport's color ban was not debated or protested.[28] Even on the many occasions when Negro league teams and squads of major league players competed against each other, exclusively in exhibition games, the fact that Black players were prohibited from joining the big league circuit generated little discussion.[29] These exhibition games for the Black press were instead reasons to celebrate. White big league players were portrayed as celebrities and attractions but, significantly, not as heroes as the term is defined and used in this paper. Babe Ruth and pitching great Dizzy Dean, for example, were portrayed in much the same way as the prime minister of France or emperor of Japan might have been—as important people to be revered, but individuals with little or no cultural relevance to a segregated community.

In October 1922, the Kansas City Monarchs beat the city's professional White team, the Kansas City Blues of the American Association, and the Negro League team did so with some emphasis. The Monarchs won five out of six games. For the *Defender,* these victories were not an indictment of racism or even of segregation. Rather, they were cause for the Monarchs to get from White writers and White fans "what they deserved—much praise."[30]

To challenge major league baseball, the Black press and Black businessmen partnered to build the Negro Leagues. The first lasting product of this partnership and the focus of coverage during the 1920s was the Negro National League founded in 1920. This pioneering league, which operated under the motto, "We are the ship; All else is the sea," did not find success easy or lasting, despite almost uniform support from the larger Black newspapers. Through 1925, the league had the unwavering support of sportswriters, many of whom had official roles with the league. Newspaper coverage glossed over baseball's problems, both in the box office and on the field. The writers encouraged and in some cases demanded support from "the Race," for the good of the Race, because baseball was to be a showcase for the accomplishment of the race.[31]

The Negro National League's president, Rube Foster, who also owned and managed the Chicago American Giants baseball team, took great pride in what he and his fellow Black team owners were able to accomplish given the scant resources they had to work with, particularly when compared to their counterparts in the White leagues. Where big league owners had "wealth counted in millions," Foster and his fraternity had "only the faith in the weather man . . . We are willing and know what can be done but have nothing to do it with."[32]

The partnership was on prominent display in the close-knit business fraternities in Black baseball's cities, particularly in their many banquets and smokers. Coverage of these occasions provides examples of what Klapp described as deference, precedence, and decoration. At one such banquet in honor of Foster in early 1923, the guests gathering at Cleveland's Coleman Restaurant included officials of the Cleveland Tate Stars baseball team; the editor of the Black newspaper, the *Cleveland Whip;* a director of the Empire Bank; a vice president of the Starlight Realty Co.; and other local businessmen.[33] For Y.W.C.A. Day at Chicago's Schorling Park that same year, the organizing committee united Robert S. Abbott, the *Defender*'s publisher; Jesse Binga, owner of Chicago's pre-eminent Black-owned bank, the Binga State Bank; a real estate broker; the founder and president of the Liberty Life Insurance Co.; and Frank A. Young, the *Defender*'s sports editor.[34]

Foster, C.I. Taylor, owner of the Indianapolis ABCs, and Edward Bolden, owner of the Hilldales in Philadelphia, were businessmen and community leaders first and baseball men second. The "magnates," as the Black press routinely referred to them, also were deeply involved in civic and community life. As employees of these entrepreneurs, both in season and out, the players were inferior to owners in social and economic status.[35]

The emphasis in coverage on baseball as a business overshadowed wins and losses and the season-long horse race. In a January 1922 column in the *Defender*, Dave Wyatt supported Foster's desire to weed out the league's lesser businessmen and to find "those who are fit," a common theme in both the *Defender* and *Courier*.[36] Wyatt's zealousness in portraying Foster as the pre-eminent Black community hero of the time perhaps blinded the sports writer to his portrayals of the players. A former player himself, Wyatt repeated Foster's own critiques when he described the athletes as greedy and self-serving.

Wyatt was not alone. When players groused over pay in 1923, the *Defender* called them "Monshine [*sic*] drinkers" slated to be either cut or traded.[37] In a February 1922 article, Young refers to outfielder Clarence Smith as the "property of Detroit Stars."[38] Players existed in newspaper coverage largely as chits or game pieces and rarely as individuals with a vested interest in the fate of the leagues themselves. This treatment would continue into the mid-1930s. Evidence of the marginal status of players is found in coverage of the first Colored World Series played in 1924. The newspapers focused on gate receipts and the financial impact of the games, not on the performances on the field or the outcomes of the games. Detailed accounts of the series' receipts and disbursements were published by the *Defender* and the *Courier*, which sided with the owners in a controversy over whether the series' players could have made more money barnstorming.[39]

Even holding the series was hailed mainly for its potential fiscal impact in the Black community. The *Courier*'s Philadelphia-based correspondent, W. Rollo Wilson, wrote during the first Colored World Series that, "like the White man, the 'brother' is beginning to see the folly of falling out of things that concern his financial well-being."[40] Another *Courier* article, published on page one in September in anticipation of the series is remarkable in the detail it provides of the financial arrangements, including which parties were entitled to a share of the revenues, how expenses would be assigned, and even who should receive complimentary game tickets.[41]

Despite modest attendance figures and paltry payouts to the teams and players, for Foster the series proved a commercial success. He claimed a lion's share of credit for making the event possible, and the Black newspapers supported this claim. Foster wrote in the papers that anyone could see the "mutual benefits to the whole Race that come from the able and courageous business ability of this baseball leader." The series symbolized for Foster the "successful development" of Black baseball, a "gift" to the Race from Foster "the philanthropist."[42]

The business-owner-as-hero model marks a sharp contrast to sports writing common in the mainstream or White press of the period. Writers such as Grantland Rice and Jimmy Cannon helped usher in the era of the "Big Event" and the "Famous Sports Hero," an era that coincided with the celebration of Black baseball's businessmen in the pages of the Black press.[43] In the mainstream press, the athlete often provided the focus; Babe Ruth, boxer Jack Dempsey, and golfer Bobby Jones are prime examples. They were among mainstream society's heroes, and their chroniclers have been called myth makers. For the big city dailies, these "heroes" made the 1920s a "Golden Age for sport."[44]

The Black press model does, however, bear a striking and provocative resemblance to fifth century B.C. epinician poetry, particularly Pindar's Olympian odes. Pindar and his contemporaries praised the owners of the chariots but never their drivers. Even the horses got more poetic attention than the "athletes" of the period. These poets, according to one classical poetry scholar, "read into the poetic record the great power and wealth of their patrons, but they seek to do so while implying that their patrons do not pursue the wealth for its own sake." The criteria and context for heroic action were similar for the Black press in the first half of the 1920s, which portrayed the owners as patrons uninterested in their own gain but instead in the uplift of the entire Black community.[45]

The close press-baseball partnership began to fracture in late 1924 and 1925 as the league's financial problems proved stubborn and as an internecine blame game forced owners and writers to pick sides. Dependence on a working-class clientele and the absence of stadium lights necessary for night games meant the economy of Black baseball depended on weekend day games. Without ballparks of their own, Negro league team owners also were at the mercy of major league team owners and, perhaps most mercilessly of all, the vagaries of weather.

By September 1926, even the *Defender*'s long-time sports editor Fay Young wrote that at last he was fed up with the Negro National League's dissension. He lashed out, challenging owners to "lay their petty ambition and jealousy aside and get down to business."[46] This criticism marks a significant shift in coverage and a break from the boosterism that characterized most of the first seven seasons of Negro League play. Rather than give owners the benefit of the doubt, the assumption among Black press writers became instead that the primary motivation for any action by an owner was greed and self-protection. Criticism became more frequent and increasingly personal. It is as if the writers felt betrayed by the owners in the joint struggle for at least one integrated sporting field in America.

Never again would the Black team owners be able to use the Black newspapers as their own personal soapboxes from which to strike out at adversaries and rivals. Just as the metropolitan dailies had the "get tough" school of journalism to balance Grantland Rice and his fellow myth makers, the Black press, too, had a sober strain in its Negro League coverage. Young in Chicago and Wilson in Pittsburgh would from this point cheer far less and instead make demands that Black baseball do better at organizing and in consistently providing its fans with a good product on the field.

Race was increasingly an issue during the period, and society more rapidly segregated along racial lines. The practice for many major league teams of hiring Blacks as trainers and mascots, and only as trainers and mascots, is emblematic. It is possible these subservient roles fueled racial prejudice; it is certain they helped foster stereotypes that later players, including Jackie Robinson, would find difficult to challenge. In the 1920s and 1930s, major league trainers served only as equipment managers, with no medical, nutritional, dietary, or physical training responsibilities whatsoever.[47] Yet, based on newspaper coverage of the time, these limited roles were important, even heroic. Bill Buckner, a long-time trainer for the Chicago White Sox, was portrayed as a celebrity in the pages of the *Defender,* which regularly reported on his travels with the White Sox. When he was reappointed trainer for the White Sox in February 1922, fans flooded the *Defender* with letters of congratulations.[48]

Blacks also joined major league teams in the role of mascot, a subservient role that often involved a comic entertainment element. Mascots served as good luck charms and resembled circus clowns in dress and appearance. The *Courier*'s Wendell Smith described the New York Giants' mascot in 1939, Cecil Haley, as a 13-year-old "new luck piece" who was expected to "put his mystic powers to work by some supernatural method."[49] Nashville of the American Association employed a Black mascot nicknamed "Rubber," and the Philadelphia Athletics had a Black bat boy and mascot nicknamed "Black Cat."[50]

Like the trainers, mascots were celebrated in the Black press—an indication of how much the newspaper writers would have to change philosophically before any crusade for baseball's integration could be embraced. The hiring of "Black Cat" was hyperbolically hailed in the *New York Amsterdam News* as "the most radical move any major leaguer has made in the annals of baseball."[51] That the trainers and mascots were gainfully employed by mainstream society was in no small measure a reason for their status.

The Depression of the late 1920s proved crippling for the Black community, which began feeling the downturn's full effects in mid-decade. The Depression devastated a people already hard-pressed to lift themselves out of the pits of poverty, oppression, and under-development. A scarcity of jobs, scuttled savings accounts, and dwindling discretionary income ravaged Black baseball to make the sport vulnerable to and even dependent on what Donn Rogosin has termed "gangster capital."[52] Kingpins in gambling, including runners of the numbers games so popular in urban Black ghettoes in the 1930s and 1940s, became more prominent as power brokers in Negro League baseball during the 1930s. In owning a baseball team racketeers found respectability and a convenient way of laundering money.

The likes of Rube Foster and C.I. Taylor—Black church and civic leaders outspoken in their moralist proscriptions—had yielded to a decidedly less respectable, less heroic ilk in Gus Greenlee, Rufus "Sonnyman" Jackson, and Abe Manley, among others. "Big Red" Greenlee, who became chairman of a re-formed Negro National League in 1932, was a numbers king hard-wired into Pittsburgh's political, social, and civic scenes.[53] Because these new owners were needed if Black baseball was to resurrect itself, the Black newspapers got behind them, but not to the extent they did during the first Negro League push beginning in 1920.

Greenlee's famous Crawford Grill, a three-story restaurant and cabaret, flourished as a social and entertainment hub on Wylie Avenue much as the Cotton Club brightened Harlem. Grill patrons included Miles Davis, Dizzy Gillespie, and Louis Armstrong.[54] Eager for a heroic figure like Foster, the *Defender* and *Courier* frequently mentioned Greenlee's proprietorship of the Crawford Grill and his involvement in boxing promotions. Without exception writers avoided reference to his illicit numbers businesses. In the pages of the Black newspapers, it is as if they did not exist. A tribute in *Courier* columnist Rollo Wilson's "Sports Shots" is typical. Praising Greenlee on the 1933 season, Wilson thanked the magnate for sacrificing time and money "all because he feels he is honor bound to keep faith even though his associates fall by the wayside." Wilson made no mention of Greenlee's main source of income.[55]

Similarly, references to Newark Eagles' owner Abe Manley were universally positive and did not mention his gambling concerns. To the *Courier* he was "the man who has invested more in the game, as a sport and as an investment, than anyone," a "quiet-spoken business man," and a "lover of the game [with] unbounded faith in the future of the game."[56] What the newspapers omitted is as important as what they included and emphasized. In ignoring the new owners' links to organized crime, the Black sportswriters were not unlike their counterparts in mainstream media, who routinely omitted from their reports the many indiscretions of White major league players such as Babe Ruth and Ty Cobb.

After a brief honeymoon for the new Negro National League started in 1932, a period of partnership much briefer than that enjoyed by the first Negro National in the early 1920s, Black newspapers distanced themselves somewhat from political and commercial power brokers. This philosophical change during the decade's first half took the *Defender* and *Courier* away from unbridled boosterism and optimism toward a more neutral stance vis-à-vis Black baseball. Mainstream sports journalism was being transformed, as well, also becoming more objective, but the reasons were different. For mainstream papers, new competition from radio for game accounts put more emphasis on the athletes by relying more on pre- and post-game interviews.[57] Black newspapers, however, remained the exclusive source for Negro League game reports.

At least to some degree the switch in the Black press was deliberate, not merely a reaction to the greed and malice among a fickle fraternity of Black businessmen and an awareness of the group's financial difficulties. Signaling the switch, Dan Burley used his column in the *Defender* to promise readers "impartiality, unbiased opinion and clear-cut, straightforward presentation of the game," a pledge of objectivity meant to replace "the partisan spirit that used to characterize all athletic comment by writers of our group."[58] Burley claimed the readers themselves demanded non-partisan coverage.

For the most part, Burley and *Defender* sports editor Al Monroe, who replaced Fay Young, adhered to the new philosophy, as did Chester Washington and W. Rollo Wilson at the *Courier*, at least in their papers' regular baseball coverage. Always the province of opinion and proscription, columns varied, with some, like Wilson's, remaining unapologetically partisan. Others, such as those of Burley, Monroe, and Washington, attempted to stay on the sidelines. Monroe would remain fairly neutral in all matters throughout the decade.[59]

This promise of more objective reporting coincided with the emergence of some of the biggest names in sporting's history. The late 1930s introduced Black and White audiences to heavyweight fighter Joe Louis and *the* hero of the 1936 Berlin Olympics, Jesse Owens.[60] Add to this elite group Black baseball's Satchel Paige, who, like Louis, had a personality to match his extraordinary athletic talent, and newspapers had impetus to begin showcasing athletes rather than owners or businessmen.

This passing of a hero's baton, from businessman to athlete, can be seen in the illustrations Black newspapers ran with their columns and stories. In the early 1920s, studio portraits of baseball's team owners routinely appeared in the sports pages. An image of the American Giants' Rube Foster regally sitting on a throne-like chair, wearing a three-piece suit, bowler hat, and gold watch and chain, and holding the kind of cigar reserved for celebrating back-room business deals frequently ran in Black newspapers.[61] In the 1930s, however, gone were the owners and in their place ran cartoon caricatures of the athletes striking heroic poses. Satchel Paige and heavyweight boxing champion Joe Louis were perhaps the most frequently drawn athletes.[62]

There was no larger story in the 1930s than Louis, the prototypical Black hero whose personality and performances lifted the spirits and pride of Blacks throughout the country. Owens, too, proved a heroic figure in challenging and defeating the world's best sprinters during Hitler's Berlin Olympics, winning four gold medals in six days of competition.[63] The *Courier* helped cast Owens as a hero; *Courier* publisher Robert Vann covered the games himself and contributed $500 to help pay for the Olympic team's travel.[64]

Vann cabled stories to the *Courier* on Owens' gold medals in the 100- and 200-meter sprints, the 400-meter relay, and the broad jump. Owens, too, sent cables to *Courier* readers through Vann for publication in the newspaper.[65]

Prior to the emergence as a mediated hero of pitching great Satchel Paige in 1936, newspaper coverage of games consisted of straightforward accounts of play, with little on individual players and only on the rarest of occasions a feature story on a player. Paige changed this. He was so clearly superior to Black and White opposition, and his personality commanded attention both on and off the field. In fact, a content analysis revealed that Paige received more coverage during the season than a majority of the teams.[66] Paige became Exhibit A in the case that Negro League talent belonged in the White big leagues.

Of undetermined age, Paige rarely lost to White major league all-star teams, and he often dominated them. His appearance in a February 1936 tune-up against White major league all-stars attracted a sellout in Oakland and equaled "one of the greatest exhibitions of pitching witnessed by the writer in nearly a score of years," White sportswriter Eddie Murphy wrote.[67] Paige struck out a dozen and allowed but three hits, one of them to New York Yankee great Joe DiMaggio, who later described Paige as the greatest pitcher he had ever faced.[68] This was significant; one of White baseball's biggest stars and best hitters had hailed Black baseball's premier pitcher.

Paige continued to be the biggest baseball story in the early 1940s, as well. A superstar by any definition, who without exception drew the season's largest crowds, Paige was promoted heavily in the Black newspapers whenever he came to town. He single-handedly raised the profile of Black baseball during a career that spanned five decades.[69] He remains the Negro Leagues' most recognizable veteran and in 1971 he became the first Negro Leaguer to be inducted into the National Baseball Hall of Fame.

Mainstream society took note. Paige was the subject of a lengthy feature article in a 1940 *Saturday Evening Post,* the first instance of Negro League coverage in a leading magazine.[70] A year later, *Life* magazine featured the pitcher.[71] WGN Radio hosted Paige on a December show in 1941, the year Paige began being episodically covered by several White dailies.[72]

The cumulative effect of Paige coverage on his sport was not unlike that of Michael Jordan on professional basketball in the 1990s, which signals the celebrification process Drucker described. The 1943 season, for example, featured "Satchell [*sic*] Paige Day" at Wrigley Field.[73] His divorce that same season made the *Defender*'s front page, and when he returned to Chicago in December 1943 to judge a big band contest, the *Defender* championed his celebrity and called Black baseball's highest-paid player "the greatest single drawing card in baseball today."[74]

Paige served also as precursor to the penultimate Black baseball hero, Jackie Robinson, who was recommended to Branch Rickey by *Courier* sports editor Wendell Smith as the man to bring down baseball's color barrier. Smith lobbied Rickey on behalf of Robinson and scouted the player for Rickey, not because Robinson was the best Negro League player. He clearly was not, and he had only played one season in the Negro Leagues. Rather, Smith liked Robinson's profile as a model citizen in the Black community.[75] The Kansas City Monarch shortstop was an army officer, a college man (though he did not graduate), a four-sport letterman at UCLA, and, most importantly, a name the American public already recognized. He fit the hero mold Smith and Smith's fellow Black press sportswriters felt the task required.[76] Also important to Smith, Robinson had already played on integrated teams and against major leaguers on the West Coast.[77]

When Robinson broke into the major leagues in 1947, the Black press immediately shifted resources to coverage of Robinson and the Dodger organization and away from the Negro Leagues.[78] The Black press realized what the White mainstream dailies did not, that the signing of Robinson cleaved baseball history into periods of "before" and "after" just as Brown v. Board of Education in May 1954 marked eras in the nation's schools. The *Pittsburgh Courier, Chicago Defender*, and *Washington Afro-American,* among other Black papers, reported with emotion and as participants in the Robinson drama, framing the event as part of the narrative of segregation in professional baseball that began with Moses Fleetwood Walker's exclusion from the American Association in 1889.[79]

Robinson and Brooklyn Dodgers president Branch Rickey were to some extent cast by the Black press as heroes in the bitter battle for equal access and equal participation.[80] Robinson's status was memorialized in 1982 when he became the first baseball player of any race to appear on an American postage stamp.[81] In 1997 Major League Baseball retired Jackie Robinson's number 42 for all teams, and in 2004 the date Robinson broke baseball's color barrier in 1947—April 15—became Jackie Robinson Day.[82] These commemorations are reminders of how in integrating baseball and forcing the game to adapt to him and to a style of play common in the Negro Leagues, Robinson was for Blacks, in Molette's words, the "prototypical manifestation of their own hopes, aspirations and values."[83]

Twentieth-century scholars write about heroes as embodiments of popular virtues. The characteristics of heroes portrayed in the Black press evolved as the cultural values of the community those newspapers served also changed. In the early part of the century, the values had everything to do with self-help and, in the tradition of Booker T. Washington, with collaboration in the Black community lifting itself out of poverty.[84] For the Black press, the Negro Leagues provided an important test case in entrepreneurism and self-help, which was a major reason the newspapers co-founded the leagues with leading Black businessmen.

Demands for societal change, for equality, or for an end to racial discrimination were not made by Black baseball during this period. In the late 1930s and early 1940s, as the Black community's goals shifted more toward challenging and competing against mainstream society, these demands began to be made. This community's heroes naturally became those who could compete with the best that mainstream society could offer. DiMaggio struck out trying to hit Paige and then called him the best he had ever faced. Robinson extended into October the seasons of the previously all-White, April-to-September Brooklyn Dodgers, a team nicknamed "Dem Bums" for their habitual ineptitude.[85]

This study is limited. By relying on the major Black newspapers of the period, the study focuses on a mostly middle-class Black readership concentrated in America's northern cities, though the national weeklies examined were circulated throughout the country. It is important to note that the Black middle class did not fit mainstream socio-economic definitions of the term, but rather it represented a significantly lower earning power and status, particularly in such a comprehensively segregated age.[86]

Because of the social strictures of the period, gender is almost completely ignored. The heroes studied, therefore, are exclusively male. As a heroine both to Black baseball and to the Black community, Effa Manley is a subject ripe for future research. With her husband, Abe Manley, she owned the Newark Eagles, from which Larry Doby emerged to integrate the American League in 1947. The Manleys, however, were also members of the Black baseball world. Future research could and perhaps should examine the realms of boxing and Olympic sports, arenas where Black athletes asserted themselves as individuals in the 1930s.

Finally, it is acknowledged that sports heroes are more about the illusion of heroism than its reality. The appearance of heroism in professional sports, including Negro League baseball, is connected to performance and play and not to truly heroic acts. To the extent that sports heroes are in fact celebrities and not real or true heroes, this study is limited in the connections it can make between the Black community and its role models, particularly after the shift away from business leaders to baseball players is complete.

Notes

1 Lance Strate, "Heroes, Fame and the Media," *Mass Media* (Spring 1985), 47.

2 Barbara Molette, "Black Heroes and Afrocentric Values in Theater," *Journal of Black Studies* 15, no. 4 (June 1985), 447.

3 Susan J. Drucker and Robert S. Cathcart, eds., *American Heroes in a Media Age* (Cresskill, NJ: Hampton Press, 1994), vii.

4 Thomas Carlyle, *Heroes, Hero Worship and The Heroic in History* (New York City: A.L. Burt Company, no date), 1.

5 Ibid., 2.

6 Molette, 449.

7 Ibid., 457. Andrew Kaye also notes that for Blacks the triumphs and trials of their heroes "carried extra significance, in that these challenges often took place under the same Jim Crow conditions with which they grappled on a daily basis" (Andrew Kaye, "The Canonisation of 'Tiger' Flowers: A Black Hero for the 1920s," *Borderlines: Studies in American Culture* 5 [1998], 156).

8 Drucker and Cathcart, "The Hero as a Communication Phenomenon," *American Heroes in a Media Age,* ed. Drucker and Cathcart (Cresskill, NJ: Hampton Press, 1994), 2.

9 Frankie Hutton, *The Early Black Press in America, 1827-1860* (Westport, CT: Greenwood Press, 1993), 27.

10 Armistead S. Pride and Clint C. Wilson, *A History of the Black Press* (Washington, D.C.: Howard University Press, 1997), 137.

11 Armistead S. Pride and Clint C. Wilson, *A History of the Black Press* (Washington, D.C.: Howard University Press, 1997), 139, 155.

12 Douglas V. Porpora, "Personal Heroes, Religion, and Transcendental Metanarratives," *Sociological Forum* 11, 2 (June 1996): 210.

13 See, for example, Louis Harlan's *Booker T. Washington: The Wizard of Tuskegee, 1901–1915* (Oxford: Oxford University Press, 1986).

14 Lance Strate, "Heroes: A Communication Perspective," in *American Heroes in a Media Age*, 15.

15 Janice Hume, "Changing Characteristics of Heroic Women in Midcentury Mainstream Media," *Journal of Popular Culture* 34, 1 (Summer 2000): 9-29.

16 Drucker and Cathcart, "The Hero as a Communication Phenomenon," 12.

17 Drucker, "The Mediated Sports Hero," in *American Heroes in a Media Age,* 82.

18 "Magnates To Meet Here Last of January," *Chicago Defender,* January 7, 1922. Present at the meeting were Ira F. Lewis of the *Courier*, Elwood Knox of the *Freeman,* and several *Defender* writers.

19 "Baseball Men and Scribes Gather For League Meetings," *Chicago Defender,* January 28, 1922.

20 Drucker, "The Mediated Sports Hero," 84.

21 Hutton, *The Early Black Press in America, 1827-1860*, 87.

22 Orrin E. Klapp, "The Creation of Popular Heroes," *The American Journal of Sociology* 54, 2 (September 1948): 135. The other three ways of conferral are by spontaneous popular recognition and homage; by formal selection, as in canonization and military decoration; and by the gradual growth of popular legends.

23 Klapp, "Hero Worship in America," *American Sociological Review* 14, 1 (February 1949): 61. Other than for the sake of simplicity, the exclusivity of males as heroes in the Black press during the period studied is the sole reason for use of the male pronoun and why, therefore, there are no female pronouns.

24 Elizabeth Eisenstein, *The Printing Press as an Agent of Change* (Cambridge, England: Cambridge University Press, 1979), 229.

25 Klapp, "Hero Worship in America," 62.

26 Robert L. Vann, "Football As A Vehicle," *Pittsburgh Courier,* December 1, 1923, 1.

27 Amiri Baraka, *The Autobiography of Leroi Jones* (Chicago: Lawrence Hill Books, 1997), 46.

28 One of the only references to the exclusion of Blacks from "organized baseball" was made by the *Courier*'s Ira F. Lewis in Robert Vann's short-lived monthly *The Competitor* magazine. Lewis observed that major league baseball seemed to approve of Cubans, "provided they do not come too Black," Chinese, Indians, "and everyone else under the sun... except the Black man." He mused that, "Perhaps, someday, a Regular American baseball man will establish a precedent—maybe" (Ira Lewis, "Who'll Be The Next," *Competitor,* October/November 1920, 221).

29 Frank A. Young, "The American Giants-Detroit Tigers Games," *Chicago Defender,* October 27, 1923.

30 "National League To Meet In Chicago," *Chicago Defender*, October 28, 1922.

31 One owner, C.I. Taylor of the Indianapolis ABCs, wrote of the need for baseball as the race's showcase and that "the sooner we as a race recognize this fact, the quicker we will be acknowledged by other people; and the greater will be our strides in the game of life" ("The Future of Colored Baseball," *The Competitor*, February 1920, 76). The Competitor was published by the *Pittsburgh Courier*.

32 Andrew "Rube" Foster, "Rube Foster Has A Word To Say To The Baseball Fans," *Chicago Defender,* January 5, 1924.

33 "Rube Foster Banqueted by Cleveland Business Men," *Chicago Defender,* February 17, 1923.

34 "Y.W.C.A. Day Sunday, June 24," *Chicago Defender,* June 16, 1923.

35 See "C.I. Taylor And His A.B.C. Base Ball Club," *Indianapolis Freeman*, December 23, 1916. ABC players worked for Taylor during the offseason in his billiards parlor. Ed Bolden, owner of the Hilldales in Philadelphia, also hired his players in winter, "Hilldale Successful in Seeing Improved Trolley Service," *Philadelphia Tribune,* June 29, 1918.

36 David Wyatt, "Players Developed, Need Trained Officials Now," *Chicago Defender,* January 7, 1922.

37 "Foster's Ire Aroused Over Ball Player's Charges," *Chicago Defender,* November 24, 1923.

38 Frank A. Young, "Lloyd Goes to Connors," *Chicago Defender,* February 4, 1922.

39 "World Series Report," *Chicago Defender,* November 1, 1924. Barnstorming refers to the custom of many ballplayers to join traveling teams in the off-season, teams that would tour a region and play local clubs of varying sophistication for a share of the gate.

40 Rollo Wilson, "The Sportive Realm," *Pittsburgh Courier,* September 6, 1924.

41 "Arrangements Complete For Big Series," *Pittsburgh Courier,* September 6, 1924.

42 Andrew "Rube" Foster, "Rube Foster Reviews The World Series And Tells A Little Baseball History," *Chicago Defender,* November 15, 1924. Foster's praise of himself is incredible by any standard. The article's opening sentence: "It is impossible to enjoy a work of art without being mindful of the artist whose skill brought the treasure into existence." In fact, the tone and language of the article suggests that Foster intended the article to run without his byline, as if the *Defender* were praising him for the world series.

43 William Harper, *How You Played the Game, The Life of Grantland Rice* (Columbia, MO.: University of Missouri Press, 1999), 18.

44 Charles Fountain, *Sportswriter: The Life and Times of Grantland Rice* (New York: Oxford University Press, 1993), 343.

45 Quote from Joséph Farrell, "Classical Genre in Theory and Practice," *New Literary History* 34, 3 (Fall 2003): 399. Pindar's *Olympian* Odes were composed in honor of victories "won" by rulers and chariot owners such as Hieron and Theron (quote from Charles Paul Segal, "God and Man in Pindar's First and Third *Olympian* Odes," *Harvard Studies in Classical Philology* 68 [1964]: 211). Segal puts the competitions in the year 476. A sample from Pindar's "Olympian 1" ode, written to honor Hieron of Syracuse for a single-horse race in 476 B.C.: "The rich and blessed hearth of Hieron, who wields the scepter of law in Sicily of many flocks, reaping every excellence at its peak, and is glorified by the choicest music, which we men often play around his hospitable table . . . the king of Syracuse who delights in horses. His glory shines in the settlement of fine men" (Pindar, *Olympian Odes*, Olympian 1).

46 Fay Young, "Directors of National League Hold Future of Our Baseball in Their Hands," *Chicago Defender,* September 11, 1926. Young wrote under the bylines Frank A. Young, Frank Young, and Fay Young.

47 See "Bill Buckner in Texas," *Chicago Defender*, March 4, 1922. Buckner, Black trainer for the Chicago White Sox, was a barber during the off-season, owner of Chicago's Colonial Barbershop.

48 "Fans Glad To See Buckner Back As White Sox Trainer," *Chicago Defender,* February 11, 1922.

49 Wendell Smith, "Smitty's Sports Spurts," *Pittsburgh Courier,* August 5, 1939.

50 Neil Lanctot, *Fair Dealing and Clean Playing: The Hilldale Club and the Development of Black Professional Baseball, 1910–1932* (Jefferson, NC: McFarland & Co., 1994), 185.

51 Neil Lanctot, *Fair Dealing and Clean Playing: The Hilldale Club and the Development of Black Professional Baseball, 1910–1932* (Jefferson, NC: McFarland & Co., 1994), 185.

52 Donn Rogosin, "Black Baseball: The Life in the Negro Leagues" (Ph.D. diss., University of Texas at Austin, 1981), 8.

53 Rob Ruck, *Sandlot Seasons: Sport in Black Pittsburgh* (Urbana: University of Illinois Press, 1987), 135, 151.

54 Jim Bankes, *The Pittsburgh Crawfords* (Jefferson, NC: McFarland Press, 2001), 17, 70. When Satchel Paige married Janet Howard, a waitress at the Grill, in 1934, Bill "Bojangles" Robinson served as best man and provided tap dancing for entertainment. Lena Horne, among others, began her career at the Crawford, where she first sang "Stormy Weather," her signature song.

55 Rollo Wilson, "Sports Shots," *Pittsburgh Courier*, October 7, 1933.

56 "Future Of Baseball Is Bright, Says Man Who Invested Most," *Pittsburgh Courier*, June 6, 1936.

57 Fountain, *Sportswriter: The Life and Times of Grantland Rice*, 256.

58 Dan Burley, "Just A Word," *Chicago Defender*, May 3, 1930.

59 For a comprehensive comparison and analysis of the shifts in coverage by these writers, see Brian Carroll, "When to Stop the Cheering? The Black Press, the Black Community, and the Integration of Professional Baseball," Ph.D. diss. (University of North Carolina, 2003).

60 One reason Louis enjoyed hero status within and beyond the Black community was the contrast he marked with previous Black heavyweight champion Jack Johnson, who was described as Louis' "distasteful predecessor" (Kaye, "The Canonization of 'Tiger' Flowers," 148). Tiger Flowers, a Black middleweight champion from Georgia, also was revered in part because he was not Jack Johnson, which "alone commend[ed] him to decent Americans" (from the *Pittsburgh Courier*, March 6, 1926).

61 Foster's portrait frequently appeared in the *Defender*. See, for example, Rube Foster, "Pitfalls of Baseball," *Chicago Defender*, January 3, 1920; "Kansas City Selected for Meeting of Baseball Magnates," *Chicago Defender*, February 7, 1920; Ira F. Lewis, "Baseball Men Hold Successful Meeting," *Competitor*, January/February 1921, 51.

62 No empirical study of the drawings and caricatures was conducted. A reading of the *Defender* and *Courier* for the period under study, however, strongly suggests that renderings of Paige and Louis were more common than those for any other athlete or sporting figure.

63 "Olympic Stars Get Welcome of City; 121 From the American Team, Headed by Owens, Parade Through Cheering Crowds," *New York Times*, September 4, 1936.

64 Robert L. Vann, "*Courier* Sends $500 To Aid American Athletes Go To Berlin Olympics," *Pittsburgh Courier*, July 18, 1936.

65 See Robert L. Vann, "'Proud I'm An American,' Owens Says; Sends Message 'Back Home,'" *Pittsburgh Courier*, August 8, 1936. In the brief article, Vann writes of Owens' message "sent to Americans through the *Pittsburgh Courier* Monday afternoon directly after he had won America's second championship in the 100-meter dash."

66 Brian Carroll, "When to Stop the Cheering: A Content Analysis of Changes in Black Press Coverage of the Negro Leagues," in *The 14th Annual Cooperstown Symposium on Baseball and American Culture*, William Simons (ed.) (Jefferson City, NC: McFarland Press, 2001).

67 Eddie Murphy, "Daily Scribe Tells Majors Of Value Of Satchel Paige," *Chicago Defender*, February 8, 1936. Murphy's newspaper was not identified.

68 Lester Rodney, "DiMaggio Calls Negro Greatest Pitcher," *Daily Worker*, 13 September 1937.

69 See Buck O'Neil, *I Was Right On Time* (New York: Simon and Schuster, 1996), 107-108. O'Neil, discussing a 1941 *Saturday Evening Post* article about Paige, wrote that it was "the first time a magazine like the *Post* had ever written about Black baseball." Negro leaguers were not resentful of the publicity Paige routinely got, O'Neil wrote, because "it meant that we were getting publicity, too." See also William G. Nunn, "Satchell [*sic*] Paige Is Magnet at E-W Game," *Pittsburgh Courier*, August 29, 1936.

70 Ted Shane, "Chocolate Rube Waddell," *Saturday Evening Post*, July 27, 1940.

71 "Satchelfoots," *Life*, June 3, 1940, 44.

72 See *Chicago Defender*, November 28, 1942; Fay Young, "Through The Years," *Chicago Defender*, July 24, 1943. According to Young, Paige was "the greatest single drawing card in baseball" and its highest paid player, Black or White. See also "Satchel Paige Day at Wrigley Field," *Chicago Defender*, July 3, 1943.

73 "Satchel Paige Day At Wrigley Field July 18," *Chicago Defender*, July 3, 1943.

74 "Satchel Paige Here Dec. 8 With Three Dance Bands," *Chicago Defender*, November 28, 1943.

75 Brian Carroll, "When to Stop the Cheering? The Black Press, The Black Community and The Integration of Professional Baseball" (Ph.D. diss., University of North Carolina at Chapel Hill, 2003), 193-248.

76 While more accomplished than Robinson, Paige was not seriously considered, primarily because of his age. Though no one knew for sure his age, Paige was believed to have been 42 when he did make it to the major leagues in 1948, with Bill Veeck's Cleveland Indians (Negro League Players Association biography, accessible at http://www.nlbpa.com/paige__satchel.html). It was also Paige's disadvantage to have been a starting pitcher and, therefore, someone who would play only every fifth day or so.

77 See Herman Hill, "Robinson Sparkling On Coast," *Pittsburgh Courier*, October 13, 1945. As Robinson scholar Arnold Rampersad pointed out, Robinson played also on the racially integrated Pasadena Sox, an all-star team sponsored by the Chicago White Sox, in 1939, leading that team to the California State Amateur Baseball championship (64). Robinson previously played on the baseball team of Pasadena Junior College, which was racially mixed, and he played for a dreadful but interracial UCLA baseball team in 1940, becoming that year the first UCLA student to letter in four sports (74). *Jackie Robinson: A Biography*, (New York City: Alfred A. Knopf, 1997).

78 See Brian Carroll, "When to Stop the Cheering: A Content Analysis of Changes in Black Press Coverage of the Negro Leagues," 228-9.

79 Baseball historians are trying to determine whether William Edward White, a Brown University student who played in the late nineteenth century, was the first Black baseball player in the major leagues. White is thought to have played one game for the Providence Greys of the National League on 21 June 1879 (for more on White, who was from Milner, Georgia, see the *Macon Telegraph*, February 8, 2004, available: www.macon.com/mld/macon/7902848.htm; accessed May 5, 2004). It has been generally accepted that Moses Fleetwood Walker was the first, playing for the Toledo Blue Stockings of the American Association in 1884. Walker was the last Black player in the major leagues until Jackie Robinson, cut from the Blue Stockings in 1889.

80 One example is a column in which Wendell Smith places Robinson in the context of baseball's history by tracing that history back to Walker, who, like Robinson, was also "well educated and a gentleman of the highest quality" ("The Sports Beat," *Pittsburgh Courier*, November 3, 1945). This description conveniently omits Walker's legendary drinking problems and his jailing on charges of murder.

81 "A Stamp of Recognition," *New York Times*, June 16, 1982.

82 Dick Heller, "Why Not Hail the Grays?," *Washington Times*, July 30, 2004.

83 Molette, 449.

84 See Kevin K. Gaines, *Uplifting the Race: Black Leadership, Politics, and Culture in the Twentieth Century* (Chapel Hill, NC: UNC Press, 1996). African American cultural elites during the violent racism at the turn of the twentieth century articulated a positive Black identity and a middle-class ideology of racial uplift, according to Gaines. These Black elites espoused an ethos of self-help and service to the Black masses, hence the phrase "uplifting the race." Gaines draws on the work of W. E. B. Du Bois, Anna Julia Cooper, Alice Dunbar-Nelson, Hubert H. Harrison, and others.

85 For more on the history of the nickname, see Peter Golenbock's *Bums: An Oral History of the Brooklyn Dodgers* (New York: McGraw Hill, 2000).

86 See St. Clair Drake and Horace R Clayton, *Black Metropolis: A Study of Negro Life in a Northern City* (New York: Harcourt Brace, 1970).

1933–1962: THE BUSINESS MEETINGS OF NEGRO LEAGUE BASEBALL

Duke Goldman

This article, originally published in Baseball's Business: The Winter Meetings, 1958-2016 *(SABR, 2017), was honored as a 2018 McFarland-SABR Baseball Research Award winner.*

Although the first organized and sustainable Negro League, the original Negro National League (NNL), founded by Rube Foster in 1920, did not survive the Great Depression, it was the forerunner of several other Negro Leagues. In the 1920s, the Eastern Colored League (ECL) was formed as a counterpart to the NNL. It lasted from 1923 through the early part of 1928, then was succeeded by the American Negro League (ANL) for one year in 1929. The first NNL, largely based in the Midwest, continued its operations into the 1930s, but was replaced in 1932 by another short-lived organized league called the East-West League. Like the ANL, the East-West League survived only one year.

In 1933, several events of marked importance occurred: Franklin Delano Roosevelt started his 12-year presidency, Adolf Hitler became chancellor of Germany—and the second NNL began operations. This incarnation of the NNL was a hybrid of Eastern and Western clubs, including the developing twin powerhouse Pittsburgh franchises the Pittsburgh Crawfords and the Homestead Grays, along with Midwestern mainstay the Chicago American Giants (at that time referred to as Cole's American Giants as Robert Cole took over ownership in 1931), the team that Rube Foster pitched for and owned while he started the original NNL.[1] Though this NNL began operations during the depths of the Great Depression, it managed to survive the 1930s, thrive during the wartime 1940s, and then begin to struggle as soon as Jackie Robinson signed a contract with the Brooklyn Dodgers in 1945 to begin playing with the Montreal Royals in 1946.

It is important to note here that the second NNL started right after "the most harrowing four months" of the Depression, when the US economy had hit rock-bottom.[2] According to historian David Kennedy, African-Americans during the Depression represented one-fifth of the people on federal relief, approximately twice their population percentage at the time.[3] That the 1933 NNL was able to get off the ground during these difficult times for all Americans (but especially for the Black population) is a testament to the determination of the owners who were committed to re-establishing organized Black baseball at a level at least comparable to the original Negro National League.

As referred to by the Negro Leagues Baseball Museum, the "Golden Years" of Negro League Baseball that began in 1933 with the re-established NNL and was augmented by a second competing Negro League, the Negro American League (NAL), starting in 1937, began to slowly close as the NNL ended operations after the 1948 season.[4] The NAL, however, survived, with yearly fluctuations in the number of teams it fielded, through the 1950s. Many commentators consider 1960 to be the last year of the NAL's operations, but others point to limited activity among NAL teams through 1962.

This article is not meant as a complete history of the 30 seasons of Negro League competition through 1962; although references to the on-field performance of the NNL and NAL during this period will be made, along with the star players who populated the legendary teams in each league, the primary focus will be an examination of the often contentious business dealings of team owners within the NNL and NAL as well as the internecine conflicts between the two leagues for their 12-year coexistence. Although what follows will include yearly reports of winter and, when available, in-season meetings of the NNL, NAL, and joint meetings of the two leagues, it will also group the analysis into four distinct periods:

- • Birth and Growth (1933–1940): The New NNL and the beginnings of the East-West (E-W) Game (1933) and the birth of the NAL (1936) and fledgling years of two-league play (1937–1940).
- • War and Prosperity (1941–1945): The heyday of Black league baseball—the two leagues profit and the Negro World Series (NWS) and E-W Game thrive.
- • Integration and Storm Clouds—The NNL's Demise (1945–1948): Jackie Robinson signs with Brooklyn and Negro League owners see drastic business decline, culminating in the end of the NNL.
- • The Surviving NAL—The End of the Negro Leagues (1949–1962): League membership expands and contracts from the late 1940s through the early 1960s as the Negro Leagues struggle to survive—through the last E-W Game on August 26, 1962.

The primary source material for this article is the Black press; however, as referenced by several reporters and columnists who were frustrated by Negro League owner practices, the owners could be secretive about their boardroom discussions; this meant that sometimes the press reported that a meeting was upcoming along with the planned agenda but then did not cover the meeting afterward. Over time, though, this began to change, especially as those involved wrote their own columns describing conflicts between owners in self-serving ways.[5] It is those columns, as well as several excellent secondary sources that have delved into Negro League operations and the correspondence and meeting minutes found in Newark Eagles owner Effa Manley's files that form the basis of this chronicle.

PART 1: BIRTH AND GROWTH (1933–1940)

PRE-1933

Even though Rube Foster, the founder of the first NNL in 1920, had ceased to be involved in its operations by late in the 1926 season due to his own mental breakdown, the league managed to survive—barely—through 1931.[6] It did not take long, however, for "Eastern and Western cities east of Chicago" to plan a meeting in Cleveland for January 20 and 21 of 1932. The cities to be included in this meeting were New York, Newark, Philadelphia, Baltimore, Washington, Pittsburgh, Cleveland, and Detroit. A "Cuban team representative" was also expected, while Kansas City's Monarchs were there to join the league as an associate member.[7] As an associate member, Kansas City would pay a smaller franchise fee and be included in league scheduling, but would not be counted in league standings and therefore could not play in any postseason games.[8] The resulting league, named the East-West League, operated through mid-1932, when it also foundered despite the best efforts of team owners like Cumberland Posey of the Homestead Grays, J.L. Wilkinson of the Kansas City Monarchs, and Syd Pollock of the Cuban House of David.

In addition to the short-lived E-W League, 1932 saw a previously minor-league Negro Southern League (NSL) achieving short-lived major-league status. Though incarnations of the NSL existed prior to 1932, they were exclusively constituted by Southern teams; in 1932, in addition to the Monroe, Louisiana, Monarchs, Louisville Black Caps, Nashville Elite Giants, and teams in Houston, Birmingham, and Pittsburgh, the last of which was an associate member that quit before the end of the season, the league included former NNL teams like the Chicago American Giants, the Indianapolis ABCs, and the Cleveland Cubs. Unlike the E-W League, the 1932 NSL struggled through a fragmented second half to a conclusion culminating in a "World Series" between NSL champion Monroe and E-W League member Pittsburgh Crawfords.[9] The loose, ragged nature of league competition in Black baseball in 1932 raised a very simple question: What league or leagues, if any, would there be in 1933?

1933

The remnants of the aborted E-W League and the non-Southern 1932 NSL teams met in the first months of 1933 to see if the NNL could be revived. For one thing, as pointed out by *Chicago Defender* writer Ben Diamond, those Northern teams that played in the NSL in 1932 learned a lesson—that it was futile to "cram inter-sectional games down the throats of 'up North fandom.'" Those fans, Diamond suggested, felt that the South "comprises minor league territory and you cannot make them see it differently."[10] Instead, by the end of 1932 there had already been two meetings including the Northern NSL teams, other E-W League teams, former NSL team representatives, and only one Southern team (albeit one that was reportedly considering moving North), the Nashville Elite Giants.[11]

And faithful reporter and former player and soon-to-be NNL manager of the Columbus Blue Birds William "Dizzy" Dismukes let it be known in the year-end edition of the *Pittsburgh Courier* that an organizing meeting of the new league, the first meeting of 1933, would be held in Chicago on January 10, 1933.[12] Dismukes had some strong opinions about what ailed the prior Negro Leagues, and what was needed going forward. For one thing, he believed that the new league should pick among its owners a single league president or a three-man commission, as hiring an outsider he deemed to be unaffordable. This viewpoint foreshadowed a repeated battle between changing ownership factions who favored an insider as league head and other factions who favored a theoretically unbiased outsider non-owner as the league's chief executive.

Dismukes had other opinions—that there should be no salary limit on an owner's payroll, that a 5 percent pool from league receipts should be awarded to the new league's 1933 pennant winner since there would not be two strong leagues to play a season-ending World Series, and that player averages should be reported twice a month, among other things.[13] Dismukes would get his say as he was chosen to be the secretary of the new NNL along with the league's statistician—he would be the one to report league averages—although he would eventually step down from this position to manage the short-lived Columbus team.[14]

Meanwhile, William A. "Gus" Greenlee, owner of the Pittsburgh Crawfords, was chosen as the temporary chairman of the new incarnation of the NNL at the organizing meeting in Chicago.[15] Greenlee had funded his operations—two hotels, the Crawford Grill restaurant, and his baseball team—through the illegal numbers lottery.[16] But there was another side to the story—Greenlee was seen by the Pittsburgh Black community as a benefactor, not a racketeer. There were countless stories of the help he gave poor Black citizens, including operating a soup kitchen during the Great Depression.[17] According to Negro Leagues historian Jim Overmyer, the funding derived from "numbers bankers" who enabled the "launching [of] a league in the teeth of the Depression. As Rufus Jackson's widow told an interviewer in Pittsburgh in the 1960s, "Well, of course they were involved—they were the only ones with any money."[18] Rufus Jackson later was recruited by Greenlee's "very bitter baseball rival" Cum Posey to fund the operations of his Homestead Grays, while other numbers operators like Alex Pompez and Abe Manley later became owners of the New York Cubans and Newark Eagles, respectively.[19]

It is fair to conclude that Branch Rickey's later characterization of Negro League baseball as a racket, in order to justify his signing of Jackie Robinson without compensation to his Negro League team, the Kansas City Monarchs, was based in part on the illegality of the numbers operations engaged in by owners like Greenlee and Pompez. Rickey, however, was willing to partner with Greenlee in the development of the United States League (USL) when it suited his purposes, as Rickey's involvement in that league provided a subterfuge for his scouting of Black players for Brooklyn. In the end, as Overmyer pointed out, the illegality of numbers games at that time was by state statute—whereas today, state governments make money through the lottery, a modern version of the numbers lottery.[20]

In the February 11, 1933, edition of the *Courier*, columnist W. Rollo Wilson reported that chairman Greenlee had recently met in Philadelphia with Eastern owners including teams from Philadelphia, New York, Baltimore, Washington, Harrisburg, and Newark to form an Eastern division of the new league who would play primarily within their division with some lesser number of games to be played against the "West division," culminating in a "world's title" match at season's end.[21] Several of these teams, including Philadelphia, Baltimore, New York, Newark, and Washington, were represented by proxy at a February 15 league meeting held in Indianapolis, with one more meeting scheduled prior to the league's commencement for schedule-making.

The Eastern division of the 1933 NNL never materialized; according to author Neil Lanctot, Greenlee "abandoned a tentative plan for a separate eastern league after encountering resistance and a general lack of enthusiasm."[22] Already, tensions between ownership factions were evident, as can be seen by contrasting reportage from "Eastern" (in this case, Pittsburgh) and Western (Chicago) sources. Rollo Wilson's *Courier* column of March 4, 1933, praised Greenlee as having the makings of a good president. Wilson suggested that Greenlee was anointed permanent chair of the NNL due to his hard work as the temporary head, spreading the word in various cities of the new league's advent. Wilson extolled Greenlee for the building of Greenlee Park in 1932 and for the force of his vision and willingness to spend to achieve it.[23]

Meanwhile, in a more oblique piece, Al Monroe of the *Chicago Defender*, in his "Speaking of Sports" column of February 25, 1933, questioned why the East was put in "direct control of the league even though its idea was conceived and its first meeting arranged by and in the West."[24] While conceding that the East had more experienced hands for running the ship of the NNL, Monroe also cast a wary eye backward to the failed E-W League operations of 1932 and saw a "mark of similarity" in the 1933 setup. If, Monroe said, the leadership did what they promised, success would ensue but the West had valuable resources ("players and managers") that must also be employed if this league would echo the success of Chicagoan Rube Foster's first NNL. Monroe therefore felt that the newly constituted NNL should be led but not dominated by Pittsburgh's Gus Greenlee and Homestead's Cum Posey.[25]

But enough of the machinations of power; let's talk business. At the Indianapolis meeting on February 15, all the league officials and some of the member teams were finalized. It was announced that Cleveland would not be able to field a team due to its inability to find a ballpark in which to play its home games. Meanwhile, Detroit's owner John Roesink was picked as a league member with Negro League great Bingo DeMoss to manage the team. Columbus, Ohio, was also given membership, and Cincinnati was voted an associate membership "to take care of the jumps from the East to the West."[26]

The unnamed columnist who wrote the *Defender*'s other February 25, 1933, column on the Indianapolis meeting of February 15 also reported (and editorialized) that "there was plenty talk of trades but little was actually done."[27] Although trades did occur at various Negro League meetings during the 1933-to-1962 period, it was more often the case that talk occurred without moves being made. In this case, new NNL president and Crawfords owner Greenlee could have pulled off a bombshell—he reportedly offered none other than Satchel Paige to the Nashville Elite Giants for pitcher Jim Willis but Nashville owner Tom Wilson "balked at the thought of sending this favorite of Nashville fans elsewhere."[28] As it turned out, both Paige and Willis were picked for the inaugural East-West All-Star Game that summer of 1933 although neither pitched in the game. For Paige it was the first of numerous All-Star berths, culminating in his appearance in the penultimate East-West Game on August 20, 1961; for Willis, it was his only time to be picked for the team. Clearly, Paige was in the early stages of establishing his stardom, while Jim Willis had reached his peak. For Greenlee, this was evidence supporting the baseball bromide that "the best trades are often the ones you don't complete."

As we shall see, more team maneuverings in and out of the fledging league were to come, presaging a 30-year history of such offseason—and in season, at times—franchise additions and deletions. But at this formative NNL meeting, league officials Dismukes, James Taylor, and Robert Cole, owner of the Chicago American Giants, were chosen as secretary, vice chairman, and treasurer, respectively. Now permanent chairman Greenlee was still angling for an Eastern division; he reportedly met with several Eastern owners for a two-hour conference in the days prior to a final preseason "Negro National Association" meeting in Detroit on Saturday, March 11.[29] According to Rollo Wilson, the uncertainty of Sunday baseball in Pennsylvania meant that schedules would not be finalized until early April but meanwhile, Greenlee was talking with Ed Bolden, John Dykes, Otto Briggs, and other Eastern club owners as well as the Baltimore Black Sox and Ben Taylor's Baltimore Stars and the New York Black Yankees.[30]

The *Chicago Defender*'s March 18, 1933, column reported on the March 11 meeting, omitting any mention of the Eastern teams, instead recounting that club owners from teams in Indianapolis, Chicago, Detroit, Pittsburgh (both Crawfords and Grays), Columbus, and Nashville were present and a tentative final schedule for the league's initial weeks was announced, as well as that of the various Southern spring-training sites and some players and managers on each team. Notably, future Hall of Famers Willie Wells, Turkey Stearnes, and Mule Suttles were announced as having signed with the Chicago American Giants; speedster James "Cool Papa" Bell was retained by Gus Greenlee: and "Gentleman Dave" Malarcher, Bingo DeMoss, and possibly Clint Thomas were reportedly going to manage Chicago, Detroit, and Columbus respectively.[31]

According to Neil Lanctot's seminal history of Negro League Baseball as a business institution, "a bizarre series of franchise shifts occurred soon after the outset of the season in May."[32] What it boiled down to, according to Lanctot and the Black press, was that the original Detroit franchise's unpopular White owner, John Roesink, withdrew before the season's commencement, but after one game with weak attendance in Indianapolis, the ABCs of that city moved to Detroit but were largely replaced there by the Chicago American Giants, who, having been forced out of Schorling Park in Chicago, relocated to play at Perry Field, home of the (White) minor-league Indianapolis Indians, after playing a few games at Mills Field in Chicago that were unsuccessful financially. However, the now Indianapolis-based team still wore Chicago American Giants uniforms.[33] And, to add to the confusion, in late May a seventh team, the Baltimore Black Sox, was added to the league.

There was clearly a need for a midseason meeting to sort out who was still viable to play the second half of the season. The meeting was held on June 23 at Greenlee Field in Pittsburgh. As reported in the July 8, 1933, edition of the *Norfolk Journal and Guide*, six of the seven teams were represented at the meeting, the glaring exception being the Homestead Grays. Neither Grays owner Cum Posey nor any other representatives of the team appeared to defend themselves against changes "involving violation of Section 7 and Section 28 of the Constitution."[34] Apparently, the membership (absent the Grays) voted unanimously to expel the Grays because they allegedly "acquired" Binder and Williams from Detroit without Detroit's permission. This was not the only charge raised at this meeting but it was the most important and most divisive. There were other player disputes between Baltimore and Nashville and between Columbus and nonleague team, the Kansas City Monarchs. And, as befits a fledgling league still figuring out how to operate, "methods of reporting and collecting fees, advertising changes and cancellation of games preceded the work of the schedule makers."[35]

The Grays were now banned from the league's second half but the argument about who caused the rift between the league and Posey and indeed whether Posey withdrew from the league prior to being suspended was waged in the Black press for weeks to come.

More importantly, the Black press and Greenlee were involved in a major development for the future of Negro League Baseball—the creation of an annual All-Star game which became the signature event of Negro League Baseball. What is undisputed is that the East-West Game did not originate at a meeting of NNL owners. The story of how the game originated is disputed; bitter rivals Posey and Greenlee each placed themselves in prominent roles in its conception, but it is generally acknowledged that sportswriter Roy Sparrow of the Pittsburgh Sun-Telegraph was the "driving force behind the game" and Bill Nunn of the *Courier* was instrumental in its realization; alternatively, some sources report that Black Cleveland sportswriter Dave Hawkins claimed to have inspired Greenlee and Cole by staging a game in League Park, home of the Cleveland Indians, between Eastern power Pittsburgh Crawfords and Western power Chicago American Giants.[36]

On the eve of the 10th East-West Game, Cum Posey, in his regular *Courier* column called "Posey's Points," recounted his version of the story—that he had invited sportswriters Sparrow and Nunn to a meeting at Pittsburgh's Loendi club to discuss an idea of Sparrow's that "two All-Star Colored Teams feature the Annual Milk Fund Day at Yankee Stadium, New York City." According to Posey, in the discussion "we suggested that the Milk Fund idea be forgotten and a game be staged at Yankee Stadium between the star players of the North versus the Star players of the South."[37] Supposedly, when Greenlee heard of this from Sparrow and Nunn, he changed both the venue and the name by enlisting Robert Cole of the Chicago American Giants to establish the game in Chicago's Comiskey Park as an East-West game, with Nunn and Sparrow helping to promote it. According to historian Lanctot, Greenlee then paid for an exorbitant ($2,500) rental of Comiskey Park which was essential in making the event happen.[38]

What is particularly remarkable in Posey's 1942 column is his parenthetical statement that Greenlee "was a very bitter baseball rival of everything and persons connected with the Homestead Grays" as he explained why Greenlee purportedly changed the game's name and venue.[39] Was the Posey of 1942 also remembering nine years later that Greenlee as NNL chairman banned the Grays from participating in the second half of the 1933 NNL around the same time of the conception of the East-West Game? In a July 8, 1933, letter published in the *Courier*, Posey claimed that rather than being expelled from the NNL, the Grays had withdrawn from the league because President Greenlee restricted league teams to getting 35 percent of gross receipts for league games, with 5 percent going to the league, when Posey had never accepted less than 40 percent.[40]

In a column headlined "Cum Posey's Pointed Paragraphs" appearing in the *Courier* a month after the just-mentioned letter, Posey expanded his charges against the league, now stating, "[W]e came out of the Negro National Association because it was not a fair league and was handled to a great extent under the sinister influence of the booking agent of the East. All we need at the head of an association of colored baseball clubs is a man with courage enough to fight for what is due the owners of colored clubs."[41] Posey was now contending that booking agents Nat Strong and Ed Gottlieb were strong-arming his team and others by insisting on 5 percent of the receipts of any league game between Eastern and Western clubs (Gottlieb) and blocking games from being played at Yankee Stadium (Strong). Posey obliquely alleged that these actions not only benefited Gus Greenlee's Pittsburgh Crawfords but also by extension the Columbus Blue Birds and Baltimore Black Sox, who stopped playing league contests and booked games independently in the second half of 1933.[42]

So what really happened at the league's June 23 business meeting at Greenlee Field? One firsthand account by a participant in that meeting was reported. After Dizzy Dismukes relinquished the NNL secretary's job to manage Columbus, John L. Clark took that position. Admittedly not an objective observer, as he was a Crawfords official as well, Clark nonetheless provided a detailed description of how and why the league expelled Posey while meeting at "Greenlee's Gardens." Clark charged that Posey's "case" was a subterfuge for his intention to a) appropriate players directly rather than legitimately acquire them from other league clubs and b) cancel league contests without notice.[43] It is a minor point, but still worth mentioning, that Clark explains why the meeting was held at Greenlee Field, arguably enemy territory for Posey, rather than a more neutral site. According to Clark, the meeting was originally scheduled for 10 A.M. at Center Avenue YMCA but was changed to 1:30 P.M. at the offices at Greenlee Field because several league members were not able to reach the city for the earlier scheduled time and location. In addition, Clark carefully documented that the meeting was not a "special session to pass decision of an unfaithful member"—rather, it was called primarily to draft a schedule for the season's second half and before charges were telegraphed by Greenlee to Posey on June 21 that Posey had taken players Binder and Williams without permission from or compensation given to Detroit. Clark further states that Posey had been requested to attend, but after five other items of business were taken care of, Posey's actions were deliberated without his presence. It was then contended by Chicago at the meeting that Posey had canceled upcoming scheduled league games with them on June 24-26 at Greenlee Field and that his actions were eroding the goodwill of the public.

In Clark's account, after a unanimous vote to expel the Grays at the June 23, 1933, meeting, Posey did appear but failed to satisfactorily explain his actions and evaded direct questions. Clark editorialized that Posey was against league play largely because he did not control the league. But Clark did present the argument that Posey left for financial reasons, with league-mandated player and salary limits having "a great deal to do with Posey's kidnapping of Binder and Williams."[44]

Whether one chooses to believe Posey's version or that of Clark (or a little of both), any observer, contemporary or in retrospect, should realize that a pattern had been established. Not only would Posey and Greenlee largely remain at loggerheads, but fierce battles, with accusations of league violations and decisions to expel teams and/or for teams to declare that they were abandoning the league schedule, would be common throughout the 30 seasons of Negro League play starting in 1933 and ending in 1962. Although there were certainly such issues (and many others) in the prior incarnation of the NNL, league President Rube Foster was such a powerful and revered figure that his rulings tended to be respected and followed. There are many reminiscences in the Black press about the "halcyon days" of the 1920s and the founding fathers of league play, indicating that many scribes found the ongoing ownership battles in the successor leagues to be tiresome, divisive, and destructive not only to league operations and league success, but also to the larger cause of promoting Black athletics with an eye toward eventual integration into White major league operations.[45]

In the final analysis, the 1933 NNL season was a limited success. Only three teams—Nashville, Chicago/Indianapolis, and Pittsburgh—completed the entire season. The first East-West All-Star Game was played with the West prevailing, 11-7, but seven of the 14 who played for the East were from the Pittsburgh Crawfords, and seven of the nine West players were from the Chicago American Giants. Attendance for the game has been variously reported as 19,568 and about 12,000, a pretty good turnout for the times and for a league limping along to the end of its inaugural season, but far less than several future East-West Games.[46]

Not only did the Homestead Grays, Columbus Blue Birds, Detroit Stars, and Baltimore Black Sox abandon (or in the case of the Grays, were also suspended from) league play, but top teams like the Kansas City Monarchs, the Philadelphia Stars, the New York Black Yankees, the Newark Browns, and the New York Cubans never joined the league. Additionally, there was a short-time member of the 1933 NNL, mostly in the season's second half, called the Akron Black Tyrites, who were 2-9 in league play.[47] Chicago protested a game played against Baltimore and when the protest was upheld, they won the league's first half by one game.[48] The second half was apparently a muddle—down to only three teams, Chicago was eliminated as a second-half contender as a compromise resulting from confusing and competing claims by Nashville and Pittsburgh regarding games each wanted counted in their favor as forfeits by disbanding teams. According to the September 27 edition of the *New York Amsterdam News*, Nashville and Pittsburgh were to play a five-game series, and the winner of that series would play Chicago for the 1933 league championship. This author has found no mention of any of those preliminary or championship games being played.

There was hope, though, for 1934. Even in Cum Posey's "Pointed Paragraphs" of August 12 in which he lambasted the NNL's White booking agents while he indicated that a stronger league leader than Greenlee was needed, Posey stated, "Colored baseball in 1934 will start on the upturn."[49] And Rollo Wilson, while noting that in his opinion the booking agents were against league baseball, seemed to believe that in 1934 the NNL would succeed where it failed in 1933 with a new alignment, including Eastern teams in New York and Philadelphia. "Next year," Wilson said, "always brings something new and better to some few…."[50] Which "few" would they be?

1934

At the end of 1933, it was hardly clear whether the wind was blowing in the direction of an established NNL that would continue operations in 1934 and beyond, or back toward an array of independent clubs like the Monarchs, Grays, and Philadelphia Stars and loose confederations like the NSL existing in an uncertain black baseball universe. After all, recent history involved aborted one-year leagues—the ANL and the E-W League did not survive beyond 1929 and 1932 respectively. Given the way the 1933 NNL season petered out, with only three of seven clubs finishing the season and no apparent postseason playoffs, what indications were there of a sustained NNL?

On the one hand, you had a successful start of an all-star franchise in the inaugural East-West Game; on the other hand, the *Pittsburgh Courier* reported that the Nashville Elite Giants, Chicago American Giants, and Pittsburgh Crawfords had very little communication between them during early winter of 1933-34.[51] According to the *Courier*, it was believed that the NSL would operate in 1934 but it was unclear whether that three-team NNL nucleus could join with other Eastern clubs and/or Western clubs to form a circuit, while it was doubtful that all three regions would form a complete confederation. The "moguls" behind all the clubs were operating in secrecy, but it was at least known that a January 13, 1934, meeting in Pittsburgh was planned. The invitation list constituted 12 teams from the East, West, and South which did not even include the Homestead Grays and representatives of Dayton, Columbus, Indianapolis, and Akron.[52]

The turnout was limited to Cum Posey, who was not formally invited but received an oral notification from Chairman and fierce rival Greenlee, and apparently, Greenlee himself and Prentice Byrd of the Cleveland Red Sox attending.[53] The 1933 league secretary (and Crawfords employee) John Clark called this meeting discouraging, as the lack of turnout indicated a desire by most potential league members to wait and see what developed.[54] Posey, on the other hand, seemed to think that the league had potential if Philadelphia, Baltimore, and Newark, who had their own parks and who had owners with experience in

Ed Bolden (Philadelphia), Joe Cambria (Baltimore), and Harry Passon (Bacharach Giants, formerly of Atlantic City but now playing in Philadelphia), could be included in the league. Otherwise, Posey planned for the Grays to continue the independent status they assumed when they were expelled in the second half of the 1933 season.[55]

Most importantly, however, Greenlee declared at the January meeting that there would be a subsequent league meeting on February 10 in Philadelphia. At the February meeting, six clubs attained full membership in a planned 1934 league—the three-team nucleus of 1933, the Cleveland Red Sox, Ed Bolden's Philadelphia Stars, and the Newark Dodgers. Bolden objected to there being another Philadelphia team in the league (Passon's Bacharachs), believing that he could not succeed with intracity league competition, and his wishes were granted. He did not succeed, however, in convincing the other owners that a good-faith financial deposit (also called a franchise fee or forfeit) was unneeded. Meanwhile, neither the Grays nor Cambria's Baltimore Black Sox were admitted to the league, in the latter case because he did not attend this meeting.[56]

Although little of substance was accomplished at the February 10 meeting, two important steps were taken—1) a third league meeting was announced for March in Philadelphia at which a schedule of playing dates was to be decided upon; and 2) 1933 Chairman Greenlee requested that Rollo Wilson operate as chair when the new league members were voted on.[57]

On March 10 and 11, the newly reconstituted league did in fact meet and chose *Courier* writer Wilson to be the commissioner of the NNL, although Greenlee was still voted chairman of the board, with Tom Wilson, owner of the Elite Giants, as vice chairman, John Clark as secretary, and Robert Cole as treasurer. According to sportswriter Randy Dixon, the choice of Wilson to head the league deserved high praise, as Dixon believed that Rollo had stellar credentials: "His long experience as a critic and follower of colored baseball, his keen insight of the game, and his wide acquaintanceship and contacts makes him ideally suited to the position."[58] Author Neil Lanctot indicated that it was commonly viewed that Wilson, who was an experienced operative from prior Negro Leagues and who was seen as impartial, could successfully arbitrate league disputes and counteract perceived bias in Gus Greenlee's 1933 league operation.[59]

Wilson Made 'Judge Landis' Of New Negro Ball League

— *New York Amsterdam News*, March 17, 1934

And disputes there were—immediately, Wilson became the judge of conflicts between the Homestead Grays (who were made associate members at the March meeting) and the Pittsburgh Crawfords over outfielder Vic Harris and catcher-infielder Leroy Morney, while pitcher Ted Trent was claimed by Chicago and the New York Black Yankees (who were still being debated as potential associate members). Meanwhile, at the meeting a schedule was adopted, with the season to be split into halves—the first half to be played from May 12 through July 4, and the second half ending September 9, to be followed by a playoff between the winners of each half-season. And the Negro Southern League, represented by Nashville owner Tom Wilson at this meeting, agreed to be a farm system for the NNL as NNL clubs could buy NSL players "on a trial basis" with the player chosen returning to the NSL club if he did not succeed in the higher league.

The final preseason meeting of 1934 was held in Pittsburgh on April 14. Along with routine business (booking issues, forfeit fees, authority for disbursements granted to league Secretary Clark), the few members present witnessed "representative" Nat Strong withdraw the application of the New York Black Yankees for membership and rejected Baltimore's application as they again did not appear at the meeting.[60]

But Cumberland Posey was not satisfied with his team's associate status. He still chafed about not being officially invited to the initial 1934 meeting, and he also was greatly dissatisfied with the league's decision not to offer Harry Passon's Bacharach Giants league membership.[61] League secretary Clark used his *Courier* column to answer Posey's "points" pointedly and at times, sarcastically. Clark simply said that Posey was left off the initial invitation list because of his actions giving rise to his team's expulsion in mid-1933 and that his other claims to players and criticisms of league choices on membership and on other matters did not merit equal consideration with opinions of full league members. Perhaps the league's biggest mistake, Clark sarcastically opined, was not picking Posey to be league commissioner, as "everybody has been 'picking' on the Homesteader ever since."[62]

Was it true, as Clark claimed, that Posey wanted that "his every claim should be honored, his views accepted without modification"?[63] Not according to Posey. In his view, the well-intentioned commissioner Wilson was being undermined by the power-hungry league secretary Clark, who, he believed, had no right to decide matters like disputed playing dates between clubs or even whether an associate member like the Grays had as much right to consideration as did a full member. Meanwhile, his rival Greenlee was being "strong-armed" by Nat Strong, White booking agent and part-owner behind the scenes; African American James Semler was the public franchise representative of the New York Black Yankees.[64] The result, according to Posey, was a league without monthly financial reports and an independent commissioner who could not stop the Crawfords from operating the league in their own best interests. [65]

Despite all the vitriol, the league finished its first half without losing any members. And, in a midseason meeting held in Philadelphia on June 28 and 29, right before the first half ended, the league expanded, adding the Bacharach Giants and Baltimore Sox as full members for the league's second half. Commissioner Wilson, in his June 30, 1934 *Pittsburgh Courier* column, indicated that the main order of business at this meeting was to settle on a second-half schedule but that "certain warring owners" would need to peacefully settle their disputes.[66] Settlement of the main battle, between Posey and Greenlee, was not going to come easily. During the meeting, Posey's "money man [and numbers man]" Rufus "Sonnyman" Jackson, turned down an opportunity for full membership for the Grays that was ostensibly offered by the other teams. Secretary Clark, in his July 14 *Courier* column stated that Commissioner Wilson put membership discussions ahead of the "regular order of business" to bring about harmony and to "perpetuate organized policies in Negro baseball."

In the end, according to Clark, Jackson turned down membership while his co-owner Posey's agenda—which, of course, included removing columnist Clark from his league secretary position—was turned down flat by the league.[67] Nevertheless, both the *Atlanta Daily World* and the *Chicago Defender* gave mostly positive reports of this meeting and the status of the league. The World characterized the meetings as "for the most part, amicable with the owners disposed to give and take."[68] Meanwhile, the *Defender* opined that "although the league machinery has not operated smoothly, it is a distinct improvement over performances of 1933."[69] Arguably, Posey's repeat performance was no worse and perhaps less disruptive to league operations than that of 1933; and adding rather than subtracting teams constituted distinct progress.

(NoirTech Research, Inc.)

Pittsburgh racketeer Rufus "Sonnyman" Jackson (at right) with Seward Posey (center) provided Grays' owner Cum Posey with the money he needed to lure many of the Negro Leagues' best players to Homestead in the 1930s and 1940s.

Pittsburgh racketeer Rufus "Sonnyman" Jackson (at right) with Seward Posey (center) provided Grays' owner Cum Posey with the money he needed to lure many of the Negro Leagues' best players to Homestead in the 1930s and 1940s. (Noir-Tech Research, Inc.)

The second half of the 1934 season had its fair share of successes, failures, and ultimately, disputes. The second East-West Game followed up successfully from the first one in 1933 with over 25,000 fans, up considerably from the attendance at the inaugural event, seeing East defeat West by a 1-0 score.[70] The league also staged a four-team doubleheader at Yankee Stadium on September 9 before over 20,000 fans, with the Chicago American Giants defeating the New York Black Yankees 4-3 in the first contest and Satchel Paige dueling Stuart "Slim" Jones to a 1-1 tie in the second game.[71] The American Giants, first-half pennant winner, played the second-half pennant-winning Philadelphia Stars for the league championship. The seven-game series, which ended with the Stars winning, 2-0 in Game Seven to take the Series four games to three, was marred by a series of protests, with Chicago saying that Hall of Famer Jud "Boojum" Wilson should have been ejected from Game Six for striking umpire Bert Gholston, and both teams protesting Game Seven.[72]

Nevertheless, columnist Ed Harris of the *Philadelphia Tribune* generally praised the league for its two "spectacles of sufficient proportion" (the Yankee Stadium doubleheader and the East-West Game) while noting that the league's biggest challenge was that it needed to book nonleague games to maintain its profitability, thereby undermining the integrity of the league schedule.[73] And columnist Romeo Dougherty of the *New York Amsterdam News* praised Greenlee for his successes in staging games in New York while suggesting that the best future path for the league would be to add two New York teams and form an Eastern association with Greenlee as president and have a Western association based in Chicago, with the league champions playing each other at the season's end for a national championship. The ambivalent fortunes of the league are captured well by Dougherty's statement near the end of his column that he was "looking forward with anxiety (emphasis added) to the meeting of the National Negro Baseball League in January.[74]

Before that January 1935 meeting, however, the league had one final abortive session in 1934. In it, only league treasurer and Chicago owner Robert Cole, Chairman Greenlee, and Posey and Jackson of ineligible-to-vote associate member Homestead appeared. The meeting was supposed to resolve the Game Seven protest as well as have members pay off their league obligations. When 5 o'clock came and went without any other members appearing, Greenlee expressed the opinion that league business could be conducted, including bill payments. Treasurer Cole refused to "sign a single check until all members were present—adding that there were several matters that he wanted to be clear on." Clearly, Cole was dissatisfied about the failure of his league to rule on his team's protest—and eventually, the protests by both teams were thrown out and the Stars were awarded the 1934 league championship.[75]

1935

Although 1934 was a successful year compared with 1933, NNL Commissioner (but not for long) Rollo Wilson admitted that "few, if any clubs made any money" while Chairman Greenlee cautioned that "in spite of the success of 1934, we have not arrived."[76]

One potentially lucrative opportunity beckoned. Although the NNL played two successful doubleheaders at Yankee Stadium in September of 1934, the second one interrupting the league championship series, they did not have any New York area teams represented in the 1934 NNL.[77] According to Neil Lanctot, NNL Chairman Greenlee realized that the Eastern market provided better moneymaking opportunities than did the Midwestern ones, in large part because of the sizable Black population in the Washington-New York corridor.[78] In addition, the *Atlanta Daily World*, in reporting on the upcoming initial 1935 meeting of the NNL on January 12, stated simply that Eastern clubs were reluctant to play in the West because "they almost lost their shirts when they made Western trips last year."[79]

But there was a potential roadblock in Nat Strong, the White powerhouse in the world of Black and semipro baseball in New York City. Strong ran a booking agency which had a virtual monopoly on the New York baseball booking business, charging 5 to 10 percent of the gate receipts to book games in venues like Yankee Stadium and Ebbets Field while offering minimal ($500-$600) flat guarantees to Black teams that played Sunday night games at Brooklyn's

Dexter Park.[80] Though it was clear that Strong would oppose it, the NNL nonetheless voted in November 1934 to add the Brooklyn Eagles to the 1935 NNL mix. The Eagles, owned by Abe and Effa Manley, were to play at Ebbets Field, thereby competing directly with games that Strong would book at Dexter Park.[81]

Suddenly and unexpectedly, that potential problem disappeared, and an even greater opportunity to expand into the New York market became viable because Nat Strong died of a heart attack on January 10. When the NNL met in New York shortly after Strong's death, the league voted to admit not only the Eagles but also the New York Cubans, owned by Cuban-American Harlem racketeer Alejandro "Alex" Pompez. The league was now a robust eight-team assemblage; in addition to the Eagles and the Cubans, the Homestead Grays were bumped up from associate to full membership, and Nashville, Pittsburgh, Philadelphia, Chicago, and Newark fielded teams as well.[82]

The January 12 meeting could be characterized as celebratory, even though the proceedings were "chilled a bit through the death of Nat Strong.[83] While the league members voted unanimously to include the Cubans, they also dropped the Baltimore and Cleveland teams from the roster. Pompez then spoke, "declaring himself ready to spend $35,000 to make New York baseball-conscious as far as Negro baseball is concerned," with plans for enlarging and improving Dyckman Oval in Upper Manhattan as the Cubans' home venue. In addition to perfunctory league business such as Secretary Clark's 1934 report and scheduling and player salary discussions, there was a radio broadcast Saturday afternoon and a dinner for over 100 people at Harlem's Small's Paradise on Saturday night, with a concluding session for player transactions Sunday afternoon.[84]

Baseball Men Gather For Annual Assembly

— *Atlanta Daily World*, January 23, 1935

The league got down to business in a three-day confab held in Philadelphia from March 8 to 10. The league's managers chose eight umpires out of 24 applicants for the 1935 season, including the umpires who worked the protested games of the 1934 league championship. They also submitted their player lists, with only a couple of players being claimed by more than one club, meaning that player disputes were at a minimum. As usual, a great deal of time and energy was devoted to scheduling, characterized by Cum Posey in his March 16, 1935, *Courier* column as "a matter of give and take all the way with a desire shown by all the members to aid the new clubs in their home cities."[85]

The bombshell revelation of this meeting, however, occurred on Sunday night when it was revealed that 1934 Commissioner Rollo Wilson was voted down for the 1935 post; instead Ferdinand Q. Morton—the first Black person chosen to be a New York City Civil Service commissioner—was chosen to succeed Wilson.[86] The choice was not unanimous, as Greenlee and Philadelphia Stars owner Ed Bolden still supported Wilson—but Robert Cole, still bitter about the controversial resolution of the 1934 league championship protests in favor of the Stars, and frequent Wilson (and Greenlee) critic Cum Posey joined the two New York teams in supporting Morton.[87] All the other 1934 league officials, including Chairman Greenlee, were re-elected.

Also at this meeting, it was finally resolved that the 1935 lineup of teams would not include the Bacharach Giants (who had attended the January 12 meeting) and would therefore have eight teams, as the "surprise of the meeting was the inability of the Bacharach Giants of Philadelphia to post the necessary forfeit."[88] All the other teams posted the necessary $500 forfeit, or franchise fee, a perhaps small but yet significant indicator of a newly established financial stability for the league.[89]

And then it all unraveled. This author has found no mention in the Black press or in several secondary sources of any formal league meetings during the 1935 season, although presumably some contact between owners happened as traditionally the schedule for the league's second half would have been arranged during the season. But, according to Ed Bolden, the league was in conflict. Bolden was quoted in the Amsterdam News of August 31 as follows: "There is too much politics in the league and we are dissatisfied with the way its business has been conducted. … We intend to have a show-down at the fall meeting and rip things wide open."[90] Unfortunately for Bolden, the league did not hold any fall meeting, even though Cum Posey pleaded for a meeting "so things could be ironed out."[91] Posey and the other owners clamored for the return of their $500 forfeits while various league owners, including Gus Greenlee and new owners Pompez of the Cubans and the Manleys of the Eagles experienced financial problems, in whole or in part due to poor league attendance."[92] The Cubans were successful on the field, winning the league's second-half pennant but losing to first-half winner Pittsburgh in an exciting seven-game championship series.[93] Yet despite the successful postseason series, the future of the second NNL seemed to hang in the balance.

1936

In the early days of 1936, Commissioner Morton called for a league meeting on January 10. Chairman Greenlee, however, was not planning to attend this meeting, and in the end it was not held. Since the nonmeeting followed the disarray and dissension of most of 1935, a fair characterization of the status of the league would be "in limbo" at best. Greenlee did finally call for a meeting that was held in Philadelphia on January 26 and 27. According to Courtney Smith's article covering the *Philadelphia Tribune*'s reportage on the Philadelphia Stars from 1933–1938, *Tribune* writer Ed Harris was one of seven writers who attended but were barred from this meeting. In a January 16, 1936, *Tribune* article, Harris expressed surprise that the NNL moguls did not realize that canceling league meetings as they did on January 10 undermined the league's legitimacy. Now Harris expressed a belief that ownership's blocking of press coverage of league operations left the fans lacking information about the league and was a foolish way to alienate the fan base.[94]

Since media could not therefore provide an unfiltered report of the meeting, the fans got a measure of the current league plans that was part conjecture, part observation of the comings and goings of prominent individuals, and part leaked information along with some apparently announced league determinations. Conjecture—there is rampant displeasure with the current slate of league officers, including the commissioner: "[A] clean sweep in the personnel officers is forecast." Observation—Greenlee left the meeting early, at the end of the first day, and then switched places with Secretary Clark, who missed day one. Commissioner Morton stayed away on Saturday "but gave them a very limited amount of his time on Sunday." Leaked information—unofficial word that Greenlee offered his resignation as chairman to Commissioner Morton while "varied opinions on the financial health of the body leaked out to the pressmen." Apparent announcements—Newark Dodgers owner Charles Tyler sold his team to heretofore Brooklyn Eagles owner Abe Manley, while Manley's Brooklyn Eagles were "thrown back into the lap of the parent body" and New York Black Yankees owner James Semler applied formally for membership but the league deferred a vote until a planned March 7 meeting. Conclusion? "Members of the Negro National League deferred until March 7 many important matters which intrigue the diamond fans of the country."[95]

Echoing Harris, this was no way to engage the willing but often impoverished Black fan base. So Candy Jim Taylor, manager of the Nashville (soon to be Washington) Elite Giants, spoke out. In a February 15, 1936, *Defender* column Candy Jim criticized the magnates: "[A]fter waiting all winter to call the meeting there was little done to get the clubs together and to get the fans interested."[96] Taylor felt that many leaders of Black baseball from its earlier days were missed—some like former manager C.I. Taylor, his older brother, and Rube Foster, had since passed away, but others like J.L. Wilkinson, owner of the independent Kansas City Monarchs, and St. Louis Stars owners Dick Kent, L.A. Brown, and G.B. Key, he thought should be invited to a general baseball conference. Finally, Candy Jim raised a sore point that would continue to be harped on throughout the history of Negro League operations: he suggested that the NNL pick a non-owner of a club, perhaps a sportswriter, as league president, pay him a salary and expect him to use his connections to publicize the game.[97] But why should the wise ownership of NNL franchises follow such eminently good advice?

Owners Are At Fault For Present Plight Of Baseball, Says Taylor

THEY BLEED GAME OF MONEY AND PLAYERS, MANAGER SAYS

— *Chicago Defender*, February 15, 1936

Instead, the *Defender* reported in its February 29, 1936, edition that Chairman Greenlee would reconsider his resignation and remain NNL president.[98] But they were wrong. At the March 7-8 meeting, Greenlee did indeed resign as president and "Chief" Ed Bolden was chosen to replace him. Commissioner Morton was retained for another year. But Abe Manley was chosen as vice president, with former VP Tom Wilson shifting to treasurer, replacing Robert Cole, who had remained league treasurer in 1935 even though he sold his interest in Chicago in mid-1935. Since new American Giants owner Horace Hall kept them independent in 1936, it clearly made no sense for Cole, no longer even affiliated with a team no longer in the league, to remain as treasurer—after all, officials outside of team employees were rarely involved in league operations! John Clark continued as league secretary.

Other decisions made at the March 7-8 parley included rejecting the Black Yankees' membership application, a determination to play another split-season schedule with a seven-game championship playoff between the winners of each half, and allowing Nashville to shift its operations to Washington and play at Griffith Stadium, the home park of the Washington Senators, while the now renamed and shifted Brooklyn Eagles would play in Newark's Ruppert Stadium as the Pittsburgh Crawfords and the Homestead Grays would play at Forbes Field, home of the National League Pirates.[99]

On June 18, 1936, the NNL held a midseason meeting in New York. The meeting followed private ones held between the now (Nat) Strong-less but still strong and independent Black Yankees, represented by African American owner James Semler and White owner/booking agent William Leuschner (former partner of Nat Strong), and Commissioner Morton, in which the Yankees were persuaded to drop damage suits against Eagles owner Abe Manley and New York Cubans owner Alex Pompez for using players under contract to the Yankees. In the subsequent league meeting, the Yankees, "stormy petrels of Negro baseball," were finally made a full member of the league.[100] This meant that, for the second half of the 1936 schedule, the league would have seven teams, with the Yankees joining the Nashville/Washington Elite Giants, Pittsburgh Crawfords, Homestead Grays, Philadelphia Stars, Newark Eagles, and New York Cubans in league competition.[101]

While mundane league business was also conducted at the June 18 meeting, including continuing the Worth baseball as the official NNL baseball, coming to terms with league umpires, and acknowledging a Homestead Grays protest of a May 24 game in Newark, the real league action was elsewhere. Though Greenlee was out as league chairman, Cum Posey was still at odds with him and league Secretary Clark. Posey refused to play his home games at Greenlee Field, resulting in no Grays-Crawfords contests during the league's first half. Meanwhile, a ruling that each league team had to play the others five times per half led to a dispute over the winner of the first-half pennant. In the end, the Elite Giants were declared first-half winner over the Philadelphia Stars but a "convoluted controversy" over rescheduling two Stars-Elites games was unsatisfactorily handled by Commissioner Morton.[102]

While the first-half controversy raged on, the Crawfords claimed the league's second-half crown. But the planned league championship series was canceled after the playing of only one game. A suggestion that the series be finished in the spring of 1937 was dismissed; meanwhile, Chairman Bolden expressed the opinion that "it is not mandatory that the two champions complete a World Series if it does not pay financially."[103] Not only does this statement of Bolden's indicate that the league's disordered and disputed affairs affected fan interest, he preceded it in his *Defender* column by an even more disturbing statement: "[I]t is news to me that the Negro World Series has been abandoned."[104] Did Bolden really not know what was going on in the league over which he presided?

1937

At the start of 1937, the NNL was in trouble. *Philadelphia Tribune* writer Ed Harris, a particularly strident league critic, had assessed the league thusly: "The league as a league is a flop. It seems that some of the teams in the group are in it the way some people are married—simply because it sounds nice."[105] And the marriage was fractious—according to Posey, the seven members of the league as 1936 ended were arrayed as follows: three pulling one way and four pulling opposite."[106]

In addition, they would soon have Western competition. In early October of 1936, a "Negro Western League" had an organizing meeting in Indianapolis, with attendees choosing Major Robert R. Jackson as league head, Kansas City Monarchs owner J.L. Wilkinson as treasurer, and *Chicago Defender* sports editor Al Monroe as secretary. Eight cities were awarded league membership at this meeting: Kansas City, Chicago, Indianapolis, Memphis, Birmingham, St. Louis, Cincinnati, and Detroit.[107]

A second meeting was held in Chicago in early December where the league officials were formally installed, a scheduling committee was formed, and statements were made indicating that players who had gone East to play for 1936 NNL teams would be returned to their rightful Western owners in time to prepare for the coming 1937 inaugural "Negro National League."[108] Was the *Defender* simply mistaken in labeling this new venture as a new "NNL," or were they expecting the 1936 NNL to cease operations—or were they harkening back to the original Western-based NNL of the 1920s by calling this new league the NNL and perhaps planning to refer to whatever Eastern association that continued in 1937 as the Negro National Association?

Despite its sagging fortunes, the NNL (Eastern variety) did hold a meeting on January 4, 1937, in Philadelphia. It was reported in one source that the NNL clubs were considering adding yet another New York club to the league, and were also interested in connecting with the nascent Western league, but neither of those initiatives would occur in 1937.[109] Instead, the meeting "produced little action for the Negro National League," reported embattled Secretary Clark.[110] Clark was himself taking action by declaring his resignation as league secretary effective at the end of January. Clearly, Posey's criticism of Clark's "double-dealing" (working for the league and the Crawfords simultaneously) had taken its toll, though why a secretary should be more unbiased than the other league officials, many of whom owned or worked for teams, remains puzzling.

Announcements involving the Grays, Crawfords, Cubans, and Black Yankees provided some hope that the most bitter disputes were abating, as the Grays said they would play 1937 games at Greenlee Field and the Black Yanks at Dyckman Oval, the home field of the Cubans. Additional news from the January 4 meeting included the announcement of a minimum ticket price of 35 cents for all league games, and that Commissioner Morton was running unopposed for another term and was simultaneously running for league chairman against *Courier* business manager Ira Lewis.[111]

A quick follow-up meeting in New York in late January decided the league officers for 1937. Commissioner Morton stayed on for a third term; instead of Ira Lewis, Leonard Williams, a reputed Pittsburgh underworld figure, was chosen chairman, with Elites owner and 1936 Treasurer Tom Wilson returning to the vice-chair position he held in 1934 and 1935 and Abe Manley, who had been vice chair in 1936, switching with Wilson and becoming treasurer. An important change from prior years (albeit one that was later rescinded) was the decision to play an undivided season from May 15 through September 15—could this be an attempt to avoid another controversy like the previous year's dispute over the first-half winner? Various player trades were discussed, with some rejected and others still pending. Finally, what the *Pittsburgh Courier* described as a highlight of the meeting was a unanimous vote by the members to be covered by the Major-Minor agreement of White Baseball. Baseball integration was not even a rumor at this point, but acquiring legitimacy by operating under the same structure as White baseball was a desperate hope of the struggling league.[112]

The NNL held its annual schedule-making meeting in New York in late March, a three-day affair punctuated by a blockbuster trade: The Crawfords sent legendary slugging catcher Josh Gibson and star third baseman Judy Johnson to their rival Homestead Grays for catcher Pepper Bassett, third baseman Henry Spearman, and $2,500, then sold pitcher Harry Kincannon to the Black Yankees for an undisclosed amount.[113] Superficially, the first deal was an equal exchange of players at two positions, but the cash element augmenting the meager return of talent for two future Hall of Fame players along with the sale of Kincannon demonstrated that Greenlee was in dire need of funds. Meanwhile, with Leonard Williams having declined the chairman/president position, the league returned the Crawfords owner to his former position.[114]

During the 1937 season, two major developments threatened the league's viability. First, New York Cubans owner Alex Pompez had to leave the country to avoid arrest for his prior involvements in New York's numbers rackets. While Pompez cooled his heels in Mexico City, he left Roy Sparrow and Frank Forbes in charge of his franchise.[115] At the same time, Dominican Republic dictator Rafael Trujillo commenced his raids on prominent Negro League players including luminaries Satchel Paige, Cool Papa Bell, and player-manager Martin Dihigo of the New York Cubans. Eventually, 18 Negro League players, many of them from the Crawfords and the Cubans, departed for the Dominican Republic in 1937, and by April, it was announced in the *New York Age* that the New York Cubans would not play ball in 1937, leaving the 1937 NNL as a six-team operation.[116]

The NNL did try to take action to either recover the Dominican jumpers or at least punish them and suspend them from the NNL for their actions, while gaining US government support in sanctioning the Dominican Republic. In its June 19, 1937, issue, the *New York Amsterdam News* reported that the NNL held a meeting in Philadelphia on May 27 for the purpose of condemning the raid of their players and to strategize about enlisting US government support in their efforts to get these players to return.[117] Several NNL officials and Negro American League President R.R. Jackson did indeed meet with a State Department official, leading to a fruitless discussion with an emissary of the Dominican government, and the players did not return to the NNL in 1937.[118]

Meanwhile, the newly organized Negro American League (as it was now referred to by the *Chicago Defender*) met in late February of 1937 with its primary purpose being to prepare the league's schedule. The NAL planned a split season and a playoff between winners of its first and second halves. To show that the NAL was for real, league President Jackson "ordered all clubs to post forfeit money to guarantee good faith and to assure the fans that no combats will be canceled at any time."[119] At the meeting, the NAL announced that Ted "Double-Duty" Radcliffe had been traded to Cincinnati by Indianapolis and hurler Thomas had been sent by Chicago to Detroit for an "infielder yet to be selected."[120] The NAL completed its 1937 season with a five-game series between Chicago and Kansas City to settle a tie in the standings of the league's first half. Kansas City won the playoff, which included a 17-inning tie, in the second game, and the league decided that there was no purpose to having another playoff series, as the Monarchs had won the season's second half.[121]

Despite the suggestion mentioned at an early 1937 NNL meeting of maintaining contact with the NAL, the two leagues had player disputes and therefore did not develop much of a working relationship in 1937.[122] The Monarchs, though, did play a nine-game series against a team of NNL pennant-winning Homestead Grays and second-place (in the season's first half) Newark Eagles players, with the Grays/Eagles taking seven of the nine games.[123] As *Defender* writer Frank "Fay" Young editorialized, "I cannot see where it can be called a World Series."[124] NNL President Greenlee chimed in by saying that the games were merely a promotion staged by the owners of the Newark Eagles and Homestead Grays and therefore not sanctioned by the NNL.[125] Nevertheless, the series signified the beginnings of interleague competition at the end of the first year of a fledgling two-league Black institution.

While the "World Series" was being played, the NNL held a final 1937 meeting in New York on September 27. Former NNL Secretary Clark characterized this meeting as of little moment. Clearly, ownership battles were evident. Clark reported charges being made by Posey and others that Greenlee refused to allow the Dominican contingent of NNL players to return to the NNL and also used some of these players himself in unofficial 1937 games.[126] Would Greenlee be allowed to continue to lead the NNL in 1938?

1938

As the year started, the NNL was on very shaky footing. According to historian Lanctot, "[B]y 1938 numerous African American sportswriters, owners, players and fans had begun to doubt whether professional Black baseball could ever fulfill its potential as a profitable enterprise."[127] Not only were the conditions of a continuing depression depressing fan turnout, but the weak financial conditions and limited business acumen of most NNL franchises also contributed toward maintaining a state of constant trouble in the league's attempt to remain viable. Figurehead Commissioner Morton called for the first 1938 NNL meeting to be held in New York in mid-January but, according to the *Pittsburgh Courier*, no one showed up. At least Greenlee could still get ownership to meet, which they did on January 28 and 29. In anticipation of the gathering, Greenlee maintained that the league, its teams and its players needed to operate in a more disciplined fashion, and salaries, which he claimed to be two-thirds of operating costs for the league's first five years, needed to be reduced.[128]

Modern Baseball Needs Another Rube Foster!

— *Pittsburgh Courier*, January 29, 1938

In the business files of Effa Manley, a document summarizing this January meeting was found. Following up on Greenlee's concerns, the six teams expected to form the 1938 NNL—Effa and Abe Manley's Newark Eagles, the New York Black Yankees, the Pittsburgh Crawfords, the Homestead Grays, the Elite Giants (who were in flux as to their location—which would explain the missing city next to their name), and the Philadelphia Stars were listed underneath a statement that "for the past seven years, Negro League Baseball has operated at a loss."[129] The document went on to declare that salaries would have to be cut so that even greater losses would not occur in 1938.[130]

But this agreement aside, the league was still seen as fundamentally divided: "[T]he Nashville [Elite Giants] Philadelphia, Pittsburgh Crawfords were aligned against Newark, Black Yanks, and Homestead Grays."[131] Not only the *Defender*, but the other leading Black newspaper, the *Pittsburgh Courier*, perceived the ongoing conflict, describing it as "petty quarreling, underhanded moves, factional fights and differences, and failure to meet obligations."[132] The NNL responded by electing a three-member board of Greenlee, Abe Manley and Thomas Wilson to head the league, and picked Cum Posey as secretary-treasurer. It was an attempt to bridge the gap between sides by picking two owners from each faction as league officials. In addition, the league declared efforts to reduce expenses other than salaries such as cutting down from six to three traveling umpires and attempting to eliminate the expense of middlemen by clubs doing their own promotions.[133]

On March 6 and 7, a final preseason NNL meeting was held in Philadelphia. Resolved—the league would consist of seven teams, including a new team in Washington called the Black Senators.[134] Postponed—the appointment of a commissioner to preside over both the NNL and the NAL. The NAL had picked a commissioner, their 1937 Chairman R.R. Jackson, at an earlier NAL meeting held in Chicago on Saturday, February 19 and had sent J.B. Martin of the Memphis club to Philadelphia to nominate Jackson to oversee the operations of both leagues.[135] After a heated debate, however, there was a deadlock in the NNL vote for commissioner between Jackson and Judge Joseph Rainey of Philadelphia. It had already been made clear that NNL Commissioner Morton was not under consideration for the job. There were many player sales and trades at this meeting, most notably involving pitcher Chet Brewer being sent to Washington from Pittsburgh and Judy Johnson also being obtained by Washington from Homestead—many of the transactions that were announced involving Washington as they were populating their roster. The league set a 16-player limit, and postponed a vote on a Buffalo team entering the league along with the choice of an NNL/NAL commissioner.[136] And, most importantly, players on the disbanded (in 1937) 1936 New York Cubans were distributed throughout the league while the rights to players who followed Trujillo's siren song to Santo Domingo in 1937 reverted to their former teams as their suspensions were lifted.[137] The players were supposed to pay fines, but they were never enforced, which led to criticism by fans and sportswriters of the league's lack of backbone.[138]

The Senators did not survive the 1938 season, disbanding in August; as Neil Lanctot described it, "[T]he failure of the Black Senators and yet another incomplete playoff series climaxed a nightmarish season for Black professional baseball."[139] As in 1937, no official NNL/NAL World Series was held; the Grays won both halves of the 1937 NNL season although the Cubans and Grays both claimed to have won the season's second-half pennant.[140] The rumor mill was busy with speculation that Gus Greenlee would be held accountable for NNL failures and in particular for his poor handling of the Dominican jumpers and would be asked to resign.

The NAL met prior to the 1938 season in Chicago in mid-December 1937. They elected Major R.R. Jackson to a second term as league president, and chose J.B. Martin vice president, *Defender* sportswriter Frank "Fay" Young secretary, and J.R. Wilkinson of Kansas City treasurer. The NAL admitted the Atlanta Black Crackers and Jacksonville Red Caps as associate members at this meeting.[141] When they reconvened on February 19, Atlanta had been raised to a full member, joining the Memphis Red Sox, Chicago American Giants, Indianapolis ABCs, Birmingham Black Barons, and the Kansas City Monarchs in a six-team circuit.[142] The NAL decided not to include franchises from Detroit, Cincinnati, or St. Louis as their representatives failed to attend this meeting and put up forfeit money. Rather than including "weak clubs" in an eight-team league, the members felt that "six fast clubs" would be better for the fans.[143] As far as postseason play was concerned, a two-game playoff was swept by first-half winner Memphis over second-half champion Atlanta.[144]

A joint NAL/NNL meeting was held on June 22, 1938 but did not solve the commissioner issue as the Eastern clubs, who met separately prior to the joint meeting, were now against electing one. What the leagues did agree on was "a set of rules by which both leagues could operate and respect territorial rights as well as forcing players to respect contracts."[145] Would the two leagues respect this agreement in their actions or in the breach?

1939

First, though, the two leagues would have to decide upon whether they planned to continue as two leagues or instead merge into one league with two divisions, one in the East and one in the West, much like the original concept of the second NNL in 1933. On Sunday, December 11, 1938, at Chicago's Appomattox Club, the NAL held its now "regular December meeting" (for the third straight year!) with the principal topic of discussion being the configuration of 1939 Negro League competition.[146] Faithful reporter Cum Posey's *Courier* column noted that the meeting, called to order by NAL President Jackson at "10:30 sharp (Negro National League owners, please take notice)" included re-electing 1938 NAL officers Jackson as well as Vice president J.B. Martin, Secretary Frank (Fay) Young and Treasurer J.L. Wilkinson, and Posey's own conveyance of an NNL proposal to merge into one league composed of the best cities, with regular league games between teams from each 1938 league. Posey reported that Jackson would decide by January 10 about forming one combined league.[147]

The January 14, 1939, edition of the *Chicago Defender* reported that Jackson's league would remain intact, specifying that a merger would have involved only four teams from each league and the NAL would not "desert the other four members and make them associate members for 1939."[148] The NNL would just have to move ahead and plan its own operations, without being joined by any NAL teams, for the 1939 season—and they would be doing it without Gus Greenlee.

Even before the NNL's February 1939 meeting, the rumblings of Greenlee's departure from the NNL were being felt. In December of 1938, Greenlee sold Greenlee Field. He considered operating elsewhere but financial setbacks, particularly in the boxing arena, leading to alleged unpaid debts and bouncing checks, meant that he ultimately decided to disband his team.[149] It was hardly a surprise, then, that Greenlee resigned as league chairman in February, (although he was really a member of a three-man board heading the NNL in 1938) and though the league passed a resolution naming him "honorary chairman," neither Greenlee nor any Pittsburgh Crawfords representative appeared at the meeting.[150] In a missive summarizing this meeting written by Cum Posey, he listed the following as team owners: Tom Wilson of the Baltimore Elite Giants, the Eds (Bolden and Gottlieb) of the Philadelphia Stars, Abe Manley of the Newark Eagles, Rufus "Sonnyman" Jackson of the Homestead Grays, Alex Pompez of the returning Cuban Stars, James Semler of the New York Black Yankees, and finally Hank Rigney of Toledo. The absence of any mention of Greenlee in this summary, along with subsequent events, suggests that Gus Greenlee was no longer a factor in the NNL's operations.[151]

The members also elected Tom Wilson as president, Ed Gottlieb recording secretary, and Posey corresponding secretary, with Abe Manley as treasurer, and Ed Bolden as vice president. Along with various resolutions and discussions involving time between doubleheaders, forfeits, and fines, the most intriguing development was a decision to "inaugurate 'streamline' baseball, that is, no player shall throw the ball around between innings, the pitcher shall be allowed to throw four warm-up pitches between innings."[152] Even in 1939, owners were looking for ways to speed up the game! But, just like twenty-first-century initiatives to limit batters stepping into and out of the batter's box, indications are that umpires were inconsistent in enforcing this "streamlined" format as is suggested by a memo written by Posey asking that owners "kindly see that it (streamline baseball) is enforced."[153]

The NAL also held a February meeting in which it announced its first-half schedule with teams in Chicago, St. Louis, Kansas City, Louisville, Cleveland, and Memphis. Newly elected NNL President Wilson attended and advised the NAL scheduling committee regarding open dates which would enable interleague play.[154]

By April, the NNL took action to finalize the replacement of the Pittsburgh Crawfords in the 1939 NNL, as Cum Posey traveled to Toledo in mid-April with the great Oscar Charleston to meet with the prospective Toledo owners. As Posey related in a letter to Effa Manley, Toledo wanted assurances that they would have all 1938 Crawfords players on their roster in return for their $250 fee, a demand which was agreed to by President Wilson.[155] Unfortunately, Toledo would only play five league games as their failure to get the NNL to fulfill its agreement on providing the Crawford players along with the readmission of the New York Cubans into the NNL ended their NNL membership. Instead, at its June 20 meeting, the NNL unanimously passed a motion to allow Toledo to join the NAL.[156]

The NNL and NAL clearly had conflicts in 1939. NAL President Jackson and NNL club owner Posey were trading charges that the other league was operating in bad faith by taking players from their respective league's teams. Major Jackson referenced a lack of a commissioner overseeing both leagues as part of the difficulty in resolving player disputes. After the NNL briefly met on June 20, they recessed prior to the convening of a joint NNL/NAL session. The most important outcome of this session was a signed agreement "which protects players under contract and a heavy fine is placed on owners who attempt to steal or entice players under contract with one club to another."[157] Specifically, ownership of both leagues agreed to a $50 fine for any club inducing a player to jump his club or league; a second such offense would be fined $100; and "any owner who accepts a player who is the property of another league shall be suspended indefinitely and banned from organized baseball."[158] Along with this attempt at interleague cooperation on respecting player contracts, both leagues agreed to an East-West game to be held on August 6 in Chicago and an all-star game in Yankee Stadium on August 27.[159]

On August 27, presumably in New York, another joint league meeting produced a motion to punish Toledo for using Homestead Grays outfielder Jerry Benjamin.[160] Along with other ongoing interleague player conflicts, the discord over Benjamin signified that the commitment to protecting player contracts was a "wobbly agreement [that] would not last past 1939."[161] The following day, the NNL met and agreed to two five-game semifinal playoff series between Homestead and Philadelphia and between Newark and Baltimore, the winners to meet in a final playoff.[162] In the end, the Homestead Grays defeated the Baltimore Elite Giants 2-0 in the final series while the Monarchs defeated the St. Louis Stars 3-2 in the NAL final playoff series.[163]

When you consider Cumberland Posey's belief, expressed in a letter to Abe Manley, that the two of them and Ed (presumably Ed Gottlieb) had saved the league when the three men met in Philadelphia in January 1939 and "faced things in a sensible manner," the 1939 season could be characterized as a modest success, considering a full slate of playoff series in each league, attendance of over 33,000 at the annual East-West Game, and a total of over 60,000 fans in attendance for five doubleheaders in Yankee Stadium.[164] Nevertheless, as the year came to an end, Newark owner Abe Manley sent his wife and co-owner Effa Manley to speak at a year-end NAL meeting on December 9 and 10, 1939 and convey his belief that "we must have a better understanding, and freindleir (sic) relations between our two leagues. If we hope to command the respect of the baseball loving public…"[165]

1940

In his thorough examination of the inner workings of Negro League baseball, historian Neil Lanctot opined that "Effa Manley provided a necessary stimulant to the often torpid and stagnant world of Black professional baseball."[166] There is no doubt that Effa Manley ignited sparks between and among competing factions of the Negro League owners as she sided first with one and then another of the varying (by the year, by the issue) interest groups debating how best to run the Negro Leagues.

While 1939 saw an effort to streamline night baseball, the NAL winter meeting on December 9, 1939 saw Effa Manley leading a "movement to streamline the administration of the industry through a commissioner to oversee both leagues."[167] Her solution to both interleague disputes and ineffectual league operating systems began with her putting the name of Judge William Hastie, at that time the dean of Howard Law School and previously the first Black federal judge to serve in the U.S. (albeit in the Virgin Islands) before the NAL as a potential commissioner of both leagues, assuring the meeting that Hastie was supported by the Cuban Stars, New York Black Yankees, and Newark Eagles. According to the meeting notes of NNL Secretary Cum Posey (hardly an unbiased observer, as we shall soon see, when the NNL voted on a 1940 president with Posey in opposition to Manley's choice), "the A.N.L. (sic.) did not accept Mr. Hastie on the grounds that this was not a joint meeting."[168]

What the league generally referred to as the NAL (although ANL is occasionally found in letters like Posey's and in the Black press) did do was vote 5-to-2 in favor of Dr. J.B. Martin, owner of the Chicago American Giants, to succeed Major R.R. Jackson after he had served three one-year terms as NAL president. But the NAL still had a place for Jackson, as Posey noted that at the December 9 meeting the league picked the major as NAL commissioner, an action which seemed to suggest that Jackson should be commissioner of both leagues—as well as underscoring that the NAL "wasn't ready to have a hand-picked candidate jammed down their throat."[169]

Before taking up the commissioner issue at a joint meeting of the two leagues in late February, the NNL held its first meeting of 1940 on February 2 in Philadelphia. In what was described by the *Chicago Defender* as "the stormiest meeting in the history of the Negro National League—and there have been many stormy ones…,"[170] the league owners split down the middle, deadlocking on choosing to either re-elect Tom Wilson as president or pick *New York Amsterdam News* publisher C.B. Powell as president. Not only were the NNL owners all at loggerheads, but they were being excoriated by members of the Black press for, among other items, being kept in the dark about their business proceedings. In the February 3, 1940, edition of the *Pittsburgh Courier*, columnist Randy Dixon asked a series of scathing, sarcastic questions and offered his own answers about the NNL and its February 2, 1940 meeting, a sample of which follows:

"What is the Negro National League? The Negro National League is much ado about nothing… Does the league accomplish anything at its meetings? No… What, then, does it do at its meetings? That's easy: The formula has been the same, year in and year out. It sees to it that all newspapers are excluded… How does the league accomplish excluding newspapermen?... by bluntly telling them they are neither wanted nor required, and then releasing canned copy from which the newspapermen are expected to erect a story…"[171]

Dixon was known for being particularly critical of the men who, he often referred to as "mag-nuts."[172] In contrast, sportswriter Art Carter, who seemingly reported "just the facts" in his *Baltimore Afro-American* column of February 10, 1940, about the conflict between Posey and Effa Manley regarding her seeking Wilson's dismissal, was nonetheless accused by Manley of misstating her reasons for her positions and enthusiastically criticizing her even though "you were not there to see what I did, or hear what I said."[173] In Manley's letter, she essentially acknowledged limits on access placed on the Black press as she stated that Carter was "at no time … in the outer office or the inner office, at the time the press was admitted to listen in on the proceedings."[174] The press heard and saw enough, however, to know that Manley 1) headed the effort by the three New York area clubs to oust Wilson, 2) argued that Wilson should be dismissed because he allowed a White booking agent, Philadelphia Stars co-owner Ed Gottlieb, a prohibitive 10 percent of revenues fee while booking games at Yankee stadium instead of him arranging for a Black entity to get the booking fees, and after being insulted by Manley, Posey "left the meeting in a huff, vowing that he would never return as long as Mrs. Manley was the Newark Eagles representative and charging that she, as a woman, took advantage of her sex in the deliberations."[175] From a twenty-first-century view, we can certainly censure the media, league ownership, and league officials for their obvious sexism, but we can also see that the media was hardly being enabled by secretive owners and operatives to do their job reporting and in some sense publicizing the league.

The February 2 meeting left matters unresolved; accordingly, the NNL scheduled a meeting on February 23 prior to a joint NNL-NAL meeting in Chicago on February 24. In the NNL meeting, the deadlock over the league presidency held; the league therefore decided to go along with the same officers as in 1939, retaining Wilson as president, at the recommendation of New York Cubans owner Alex Pompez.[176] Though a decision was made, the NNL was really only "kicking the can down the road" as bickering between the factions would resume at the next annual election of league officers. By then, a pattern of bickering, deadlocking, and ultimately keeping the same oftentimes ineffectual leadership had been well-established, especially in the NNL.

In the February 24 joint meeting, the leagues resolved several NNL/NAL player disputes but also entertained a motion by Posey to elect Major Jackson as commissioner of both leagues, in opposition to the position of the Manleys, but the NNL indicated it was not ready to vote on this and Posey withdrew his motion.[177]

On June 18 and 19 in New York, a midseason NNL meeting was followed by a rancorous joint night session, as the leagues battled over "that elongated individual, Satchel Paige" and whether he belonged to the Newark Eagles or not.[178] While the Manleys held the NAL responsible for Paige not reporting to them, Satchel was pitching for an independent team called the Satchell (sic) Paige All-Stars, who had their games booked by Lee Wilkinson, brother of Monarchs owner J.L. Wilkinson.[179] In retaliation, Abe and Effa Manley played infielder Bus Clarkson and pitcher Ernie Carter, who were owned by the now-NAL member Toledo Crawfords. Despite NNL President Wilson having earlier ruled that Clarkson and Carter belonged to the NAL, and NAL President J.B. Martin denying that the two players could be traded to the Eagles before being waived out of the NAL (as Abe Manley claimed that Toledo owner Hank Crawford had authorized them going to Newark), the Manleys later got their way in keeping Clarkson and Carter, although Paige became NAL property. At the meeting, however, "the fur flew" as Memphis owner B.B. Martin "stated that the Negro American League was 'sick and tired of having players taken by the Negro National League clubs and then threatening to break the agreement between the two leagues if the N.A. League did not allow this.'"[180]

Is it any surprise that a World Series between league pennant winners scheduled for mid-September did not materialize, given the contention between the two leagues? The powerhouse Homestead Grays and the Kansas City Monarchs won league pennants in the NNL and NAL respectively, although second half NAL standings were incomplete while the NNL played a "straight season through to September 9."[181] Cum Posey reported that the NNL had a final meeting in New York City on September 3 in which "there was a decided trend toward the idea of one Negro major league." In the same piece, Posey criticized the NAL for choosing an inexperienced owner, J.B. Martin, to succeed Major Jackson as NAL president, noted "internal strife amongst league owners causing irregularities in booking," stated that NNL President Wilson "did a fine job, considering the handicap of starting the season with three antagonistic members, "and concluded that "the 1940 baseball season was not a success, financial or otherwise." [182] One can only conclude that if, as Randy Dixon suggested, "1940 is SHOWDOWN year for National Negro League," the NNL and the NAL, if Posey is to be believed, failed the test.[183]

PART 2: WAR AND PROSPERITY (1941–1945)

As 1941 began, the institution of Negro League Baseball was at a crossroads. There were now two (somewhat) functional leagues—yet there was little cooperation between leagues, and no postseason play between them. But 1941 was a signal year for Negro League operation, even as America moved ever closer to entering the worldwide conflict between fascism and democracy. Although American democracy operated on dual tracks, the disadvantaged world of Black America received a boost from the wartime economy, and more citizens of color with money in their pockets meant more patronage of Negro League baseball. Ironically, the most profitable years for Negro League magnates simultaneously highlighted the rampant injustice of Black stars playing a segregated game, while a war to end injustice raged on abroad.

During this period Negro League owners and executives continued to be at loggerheads with each other and often with the Black media. Problems with White booking agents, players skipping out on their contracts to pursue lucrative adventures south of the border, and ongoing difficulties establishing effective stewardship of the leagues persisted—but Black baseball shined like it never had before—until October 23, 1945, when it all changed with a signed contract and the fortunes of the institution of Negro League baseball changed with it.

1941

The annual winter meeting of the NAL was held on Sunday, December 29, 1940, in Chicago, one week prior to that of the NNL. In describing the conduct of the meeting, the *Chicago Defender* mentioned that "the entire meeting was harmonious," a believable characterization in that previously a good deal of the conflict had been within the NNL and between the two leagues.[184] Principal business actions at this meeting were the re-election of 1940 officers J.B. Martin (president), Horace G. Hall (VP), Fay Young (secretary), and Major Jackson (NAL commissioner), a discussion about making an agreement with the NNL for the coming season including each league swinging through the other's territory, and the dropping of the Cleveland Bears because of poor 1940 attendance.[185]

The NNL followed with its first 1941 meeting, held in Baltimore on Friday and Saturday, January 3-4. *Baltimore Afro-American* columnist Art Carter echoed the *Defender's* NAL meeting depiction by describing the NNL meeting atmosphere as "harmony prevailing on the majority of the important issues at stake."[186] The harmony, though, was clearly relative—Carter saw it as a "striking contrast to last year's hectic session" while the *Courier* vividly characterized the meeting as having "started out in the same manner as a screaming bomb, but ended up as tranquil as the Pacific Ocean."[187] Since Carter and the *Afro-American* were hosts of a sumptuous dinner Friday night, with Carter welcoming guests and NL President Wilson awarding a trophy to the 1940 pennant-winning Homestead Grays, he perhaps viewed the *atmosphere* a bit more positively than did his *Courier* counterparts.

The *Courier* report, though, barely mentioned any club conflicts, recounting a treasurer's report that "showed the league with a clean slate, financially, as all bills were paid" and the agreement of five NNL clubs on lifting a ban against players who jumped their contracts in 1940. Additionally, the clubs defused prior anger at the practices of Ed Gottlieb in booking games at Yankee Stadium by agreeing on a "two percent kickback from the booking agent's fee" to go into the league's coffers.[188] Nevertheless, conflict, overt and implicit, still existed within the NNL ownership and between NNL and NAL positions, as a minority of NNL owners opposed the lifting of the contract-jumping-player ban, which meant that no decision on the ban would be reached until the next joint NNL/NAL session, even though NAL prexy J.B. Martin "stated emphatically that his group was against lifting the ban on the recalcitrant players."[189]

Additionally, the NNL's voting in Posey as a combined secretary-treasurer meant that Abe Manley had been voted out as treasurer, "which pushed Manley out of the so-called inner circle."[190] But the NNL re-elected Tom Wilson as president with no reported opposition while developing a robust interleague schedule of 24 out of 74 planned league games, awaiting the NAL's approval at the upcoming joint meeting of the two leagues.[191]

Philadelphia owner Ed Bolden was also re-elected as NNL VP, but without his presence at the January meeting. Bolden was proposing a new solution to the Negro League commissioner problem—a committee including Pennsylvania Judge Joseph Rainey, Philadelphia Elks official Edward Henry, and Philadelphia attorney Raymond Alexander would survey Negro League baseball, with one of them then becoming commissioner![192] In summation, then, three offered suggestions for commissioner were: a Philadelphia owner promoting Philadelphia officials to oversee Negro League operations, a New York area owner (Effa Manley) having recently (1940) promoted a New York newspaperman (C.B. Powell) to lead the NNL, and the NAL continuing to promote its (Midwestern) former president to become commissioner of both leagues—do we see a pattern here?

Bolden Threatens To Go On Warpath—

CLUB OWNER SAYS HE SMELLS A SKUNK

— *Chicago Defender*, January 18, 1941

Despite Bolden's expectations of a firestorm, the joint meeting in Chicago on February 23 successfully resolved key issues involving returning players, interleague scheduling, and settling on a date for the annual East-West Game. Ten out of 12 owners from both leagues agreed to an amended plan allowing jumping players to return to their original clubs if they paid a $100 fine by May 1. Cum Posey was then able to declare his previous signing of 1940 jumper Josh Gibson to play for the Grays in 1941. Both leagues agreed to add interleague play to their schedules, and to hold the East-West Game on July 27.[193] Meanwhile, the NNL held its own meeting in Chicago. In it, Newark officially rejoined the league as they resolved a dispute over payments allegedly withheld from the Grays for a 1940 contest they played in Newark. And Frank Forbes was picked to replace Roy Sparrow as "secretary to the promoter" of those lucrative and controversial Yankee Stadium games.[194]

Despite steps toward peaceful dispute resolution, there continued to be acrimony between the leagues, according to Cum Posey. In his "Posey's Points" column of March 29, 1941, the Grays owner observed conflict at the recent joint session, suggesting that he expected at one juncture that the joint agreement between the leagues would not be maintained. While the decision by both leagues to end the ban on jumping players preserved the joint agreement, Posey sounded an alarm over the possibility that NAL member Kansas City would play the Ethiopian Clowns, who he believed demeaned Negro League baseball with their clowning and playing to racist stereotypes. Posey suggested that the NNL would abrogate the joint agreement unless NAL president J.B. Martin stopped Kansas City from playing the Clowns. Naturally, the Monarchs went ahead and played two separate series against the Clowns during 1941, albeit without NAL approval.[195]

But the NAL had its own axe to grind as owner Jim Semler of the New York Black Yankees used Satchel Paige, under contract to play for the Kansas City Monarchs, to pitch his 1941 league opener against the Philadelphia Stars. This occasioned a "hurried meeting" by NAL owners in Chicago on Saturday, May 17, in which they agreed to ask NNL President Wilson to stop Paige from appearing again for the Black Yankees the following Sunday in Cleveland. In response, Wilson promised to suspend any NNL club using Paige or any other NAL player.[196] Placated, NAL owners eventually agreed to make Paige available to NNL teams for exhibition games.[197]

Clearly, another joint meeting, held in late June in New York, was needed to sort out and resolve league differences. As reported by the *Pittsburgh Courier*, this meeting "went a long way toward correcting some of the flaws in organized Negro baseball."[198] The East-West Game, which was ostensibly in doubt over Paige's antics, was confirmed at this meeting, and a related incipient controversy—over Harlem Globetrotters owner and Negro League promoter Abe Saperstein's role in promoting the game, was resolved in favor of retaining Saperstein. This decision accorded with NAL desires, although Cubans owner Pompez expressed his viewpoint that no promoter be employed who ridiculed Negro baseball by booking the Clowns. Rather than voting in opposition, Effa Manley and Ed Gottlieb did not vote, and Saperstein was retained.[199]

But the trouble did not end there—it rarely did when it came to the magnates of the Negro Leagues as they endlessly hashed out their differences and then oftentimes rehashed them; like many academics, they had titanic, bloody battles over their places in the hierarchy and over what appeared to be rather insignificant amounts of money.

Saperstein Accused of Monopoly by Posey

— *Cleveland Call and Post*, August 16, 1941

In this case, Cum Posey felt the need to continue the battle with Saperstein and the NAL owners even after the June joint meetings had resolved the issue. Posey wrote an open letter on August 8, 1941, to the "Sports Editor" in which he critiqued Saperstein's self-serving and self-aggrandizing practices in earning himself over $2,000 booking NAL games and additional money publicizing the upcoming East-West Game: "There should be no place in Negro or any other kind of baseball for a man like this."[200] Despite all this six clubs of Negro baseball (all from the West) voted to have Saperstein publicize the East-West game on the radio and in the White dailies. His cut of this game was over $1500.00. What Posey wanted was to eliminate outside White operators from making profits on Negro League operations: "we are irrevocably committed to the total obliteration of all opportunitists (sic) out of organized Negro baseball."[201]

Following Posey's broadside attack on Saperstein and the NAL owners, the NNL held its final meeting in New York City on September 13, 1941. In the main, the NNL meeting was about passing five resolutions affecting the NNL/NAL relationship. The resolutions concerned monetary issues regarding East-West games and a possible Negro World Series and proscriptions against playing any Cuban team other than the New York Cubans and playing league or postseason games against the Ethiopian Clowns. As Cum Posey recorded it and reinforced in his "Posey's Points" column, the NNL planned to dissolve the joint agreement with the NAL if it did not accept these resolutions.[202]

The key question was whether the NAL would indeed agree to these NNL positions, as columnist Fay Young opined that "for the time being, the West is just about tired of being dictated to by the East."[203] And recall that the Negro League commissioner debate itself remained unresolved—as Major Jackson had a figurehead position as the NAL-only commissioner: "he has sort of an honorary position—and the East ignores him because they have never voted for any commissioner."[204]

Despite the continuing disputes, the leagues had seen dramatic increases in attendance in several league cities in 1941.[205] And in a letter from Effa Manley to Cum Posey dated October 13, 1941, she declared that the Newark Eagles had "a gross business of $61,000.00. That is a lot of money anywhere. If we did that much, I am sure the Grays and some others did even more. All this to say the baseball is a really large business and growing all the time. It is really high time we started to handle it like a big business."[206]

In 1941 the business of Negro League baseball did not end up including a Negro World Series, as the NAL champion Monarchs, with help from peripatetic Satchel Paige, won both halves of the 1941 NAL season, while first-half NNL pennant winner Homestead defeated the second-half winner Cubans in a playoff series, three games to one.[207] As 1941 ended and 1942 dawned, the U.S. weathered a surprise attack on Pearl Harbor and entered World War II—but would the NAL agree to make peace with the NNL at home while war was waged abroad?

1942

The NAL and NNL prepared for year-end meetings as an uncertain landscape for America—and baseball—unfolded. No one really knew what lay ahead as America mobilized for war on two fronts. Before there were any indications from President Roosevelt as to whether professional baseball could operate during wartime, the NAL went ahead as planned with its usual year-end meeting, this time on December 27 and 28, 1941, in Chicago. While Cum Posey was given a special invitation to attend the NAL meeting by NAL prexy J.B. Martin, he declined to attend, as he knew that Tom Wilson would be representing the NNL—and Wilson would be pressing the resolutions passed at the September 1941 NNL meeting to a vote of the NAL clubs, with the joint agreement between the two leagues ostensibly at stake.[208]

The NAL blinked—and adopted the NNL resolution to ban teams from both leagues playing the Ethiopian Clowns, albeit after much discussion including Wilson presenting the NNL view that "the painting of faces by the Clowns players, their antics on the diamond and their style of play was a detriment to Negro League baseball." They also agreed not to play any assemblage of Cuban players other than the Harlem-based NNL Cuban Stars.[209] The NAL admitted Cincinnati to its league while deferring any decision on the St. Louis Stars. The league also considered a plan put forward by William G. Nunn, the managing editor of the *Pittsburgh Courier*, who had previously been an officer of the NNL. Nunn wanted to start an annual memorial game, to be called the Rube Foster-C.I. Taylor memorial game, the proceeds to be used to establish a home for disabled former Negro League players. The NAL deferred action on Nunn's idea, with J.B. Martin indicating that he thought it worthwhile while Commissioner-without-portfolio Major Jackson expressed his opposition.[210]

The NNL initially planned to meet in Baltimore on January 3, 1942, but the meeting was postponed several times until it was finally held on February 14 and 15. In a series of letters written by Effa Manley, she expressed the view that there was a need for an earlier meeting due to uncertainties caused by the war but several owners kept delaying the meeting to stop her from persuading the majority to drop Tom Wilson in favor of Judge Joseph Rainey as 1942 NNL president.[211] Effa Manley expressed the belief that the NNL was poorly run by Wilson, needing an "efficient Chairman" because "we have never played the same number of games, our admission prices are all different, our umpire situation is pitiful, our contracts are not anything."[212]

The mid-February kickoff meeting of the NNL's 1942 season was held in Baltimore. In Black America, the backdrop to this meeting was the newly instituted Double Victory campaign run by the *Pittsburgh Courier* based upon a letter the *Courier* received and published in its January 31, 1942, edition. The letter suggested that Black America should respond to the war by seeking a "Double Victory"—simultaneously battling, and ultimately vanquishing, fascism abroad and racism at home. Beginning with the February 7, 1942, edition of the *Courier*, a Double Victory logo appeared on the masthead, leading to 970 Double Victory items published in the *Courier* by year-end 1942, as Double Victory clubs, hairdos, pin-up girls of the week, parades, and baseball games all emanated from the *Courier*'s crusade.[213]

Manleys Bolt NNL Meeting in a Huff

— *New York Amsterdam News*, February 21, 1942

Cumberland Posey expected that the meeting would be "a lengthy session with everybody raising a rumpus at times"—and he would not be disappointed.[214] The meeting was noteworthy in that 1) The 1941 slate of NNL officers—President Wilson, VP Bolden, and Secretary-Treasurer Posey—were re-elected with but one dissenting vote, that of the Newark Eagles; 2) after Effa Manley could not even get her nomination of Judge Rainey for NNL president seconded, she and husband Abe departed the meeting, an action headlined by the *New York Amsterdam News* thusly: "Manleys Bolt NNL Meeting In a Huff"[215]; 3) according to Art Carter, upon leaving Effa declared that "we are through. We cannot operate under the present setup and so the league will have to go on without Newark."[216]; 4) the NNL agreed to put 5 percent of the receipts of the upcoming 10th annual East-West Game in its treasury; 5) The NNL formalized an agreement with the NAL to resume playing a Negro World Series, last played in 1927 when the combatants were representing the first incarnation of the NNL and the Eastern Colored League; 6) NAL cooperation was not without misgivings, with J.B. Martin expressing his league's dissatisfaction with being strong-armed by the NNL: "We are willing to cooperate with you in all matters to the fullest … but we just don't like the way you say things."[217]; 7) the league formally acknowledged the "colored press" and voted to endorse a publicity plan to be presented at the next NNL meeting in response to speeches by sportswriters Joe Bostic of the *New York Amsterdam News* and Art Carter of the *Baltimore Afro-American* complaining of the league failing to acknowledge the role of the Black press in supporting organized Negro baseball[218]; 8) a renewed application by Gus Greenlee to bring a new Pittsburgh Crawfords franchise into the NNL was tabled; and 9) St. Louis Stars owner Allen Johnson stated that he would merge his NAL club with the New York Black Yankees, with J.B. Martin suggesting that fireworks would occur at an upcoming NAL meeting regarding the disposition of St. Louis players who were, in his judgment, still NAL property regardless of Johnson's actions to become a part of an NNL franchise.[219]

With all that activity, some of it unresolved, the NNL decided to hold a follow-up meeting in Philadelphia on February 28. At the meeting, the Newark Eagles, who had flirted with the possibility of operating independently with the aid and support of Abe Saperstein, declared that they would rejoin the NNL despite losing out on reforming it administratively.[220] Effa Manley was nowhere near done decrying the inefficiency of league operations while Gus Greenlee suggested that Abe Manley would have been the best candidate to oppose Tom Wilson, but the status quo would nevertheless be continued and Newark would participate.[221]

Greenlee would not be allowed to rejoin the league. Not only did he fail to show up at the February 28 meeting, but the players he intended to reclaim now belonged to other clubs.[222] At this meeting, there were indications that the Foster-Taylor Memorial Home for indigent players would be supported by the league; however, this researcher could find no other future references to this initiative in the Black press. Perhaps the developing war and efforts to support the military with benefit games took the attention of Negro League ownership away from the dire straits of former players.

The NAL had a final meeting before the beginning of its season on May 10; other than setting its season's schedule, the league declared that it would not allow its teams to play the Black Yankees as long as new co-owner Allen Johnson took former St. Louis Stars players for the Yanks and away from the NAL.[223] That ban was lifted during the season, but the acrimony surrounding this conflict showed that all was not harmonious between the two circuits.

With President Roosevelt having given the "green light" for professional baseball to be played during wartime, all expectations were of a prosperous one for Black baseball: "the league should break all attendance records as every city in which the regular league games are played is booming with war workers anxious to find some form of pleasurable relaxation."[224] In fact, many games involving Black teams and players drew large crowds, including an attendance of approximately 45,000 fans for the August East-West Game. Other heavily attended games included exhibitions pitting Satchel Paige against military teams, a Yankee Stadium doubleheader involving the Monarchs and three NNL teams, and regular interleague games at Washington's Griffith Stadium between the now Homestead-Washington Grays and the Monarchs.[225]

Midseason saw June NAL and joint NNL-NAL meetings, where routine scheduling of second-half games and the planning of the East-West Game to be held on August 16 and an Army benefit game two days later were discussed. One significant move made at the joint meeting was the removal of Abe Saperstein from the role of publicity director of the upcoming East-West Game.[226] Perhaps this action was in retaliation for Saperstein's decision to form a rival league, the Negro Major League, with mostly Midwestern teams including Syd Pollock's now-Cincinnati Clowns. The new league disbanded in midseason, and the Clowns then played NAL stalwarts Memphis, Birmingham, and Kansas City in August but Saperstein paid the price for the anger of the established leagues at the various actions of "clowning," his attempted takeover of lucrative bookings, as well as creating a rival league—or did he? Even a contemptuous critic like Posey "acknowledged that Saperstein had done a good job booking teams, and pointed out that most of the league owners 'were glad to be booked by Saperstein.'"[227]

Ultimately, NAL President J.B. Martin felt "elated over the success made by the league" in 1942.[228] There were challenges aplenty as gas and rubber rationing made league transportation an issue, and players such as Monte Irvin and Willie Wells abandoned Negro League teams for the more lucrative and relatively less prejudiced Latin American venues. The NAL pennant winner Kansas City Monarchs won the first Negro World Series in 15 years by 4-0 over the perennial champion Grays, the postseason meeting of the two leagues signifying at least somewhat more cooperation between them.[229] Yet lurking in the wake of increasing fan attention to Negro League operations was the start of efforts to integrate White baseball, efforts fostered by the war shining a beacon of light on American hypocrisy as evidenced by fighting a war for freedom abroad while oppression of its Black citizens continued at home.

1943

As it prepared hopefully for the 1943 season, the Negro American League held its annual winter meeting on December 27, 1942, a two-day meeting for the six teams expected to play in 1943—the Chicago American Giants, Kansas City Monarchs, Memphis Red Sox, Birmingham Black Barons, Cincinnati-Cleveland Buckeyes, and Jacksonville Red Caps—in which the knotty problem of tire and gasoline rationing would be preeminent in their discussions.[230] NAL President Martin, as noted above, was quite sanguine about his now six-year-old league, as he claimed that "while interest in Negro baseball has increased at least 50 per cent, a greater interest is expected in 1943."[231] Martin stated confidently that the information from the Office of Defense Transportation (ODT) was propitious for planning their operations for the next year.[232] According to author Paul DeBono, that confidence did not extend to the future success of the Negro Leagues if the color line in White baseball fell.[233] As 1943 unfolded, however, the NAL, and especially the NNL, would contend with shifting stances by the ODT that first severely restricted public-transit options for both leagues and later, after extensive lobbying efforts by the leagues and other sympathetic entities, partially relaxed these restrictions.

Members of the Black press remained extremely critical of league operations despite the recent financial successes. Fay Young likened Black baseball to a "rudderless boat" which, he believed, dismayed its fan base by 1) its practice of picking club owners as league presidents, 2) its players capriciously moving between uniforms, and 3) its failure to create one league with East and West divisions.[234] If Young was correct about such fan sentiments, the leagues in 1943 were not responsive to these concerns. The first NNL meeting of 1943, held on January 23 in Philadelphia, reaffirmed the status quo as Tom Wilson, Ed Bolden, Cum Posey, and Abe Manley were re-elected as president, vice president, secretary, and treasurer, respectively. The NNL discussed potential player shortages, with one suggested strategy being the use of weekend players working in war production industries. The league picked Effa Manley to direct NNL war relief efforts, intending that each club hold at least one benefit game and jointly, an all-star benefit contest.[235]

Everything seemingly was in order for a prosperous season, albeit one where war priorities would take precedence. The January 23, 1943, edition of the *Pittsburgh Courier* reported prematurely that unlimited gas rations for bus travel had been approved for both the Negro and major leagues.[236] Surprisingly, ODT's director Joseph Eastman ordered a ban on the use of private buses by baseball teams and other entities effective March 15.[237] Both Negro leagues now had a problem on their hands, as the alternative of train transportation with a limited supplemental automobile travel allowance of 360-470 miles per month for athletes was deemed unfeasible by J.B. Martin and the NAL.[238]

Immediate efforts at negotiating a solution included a meeting arranged by Washington Senators owner Clark Griffith between the ODT and Posey and Martin, attempts by the leagues to operate and acquire limited travel rights, and even a petition drive launched by Kansas City Monarchs owners Tom Baird and J.L. Wilkinson that was supported by then-Senator from Missouri Harry S. Truman. With none of those measures succeeding to persuade ODT to revise its draconian travel order, both leagues had to adapt to the circumstances. The NAL especially had a big problem as "the more compact NNL was capable of functioning within these limitations."[239] Each held a meeting in late March which in significant part discussed methods of addressing the travel restrictions. Surprisingly, the NNL chose to postpone the drawing up of their schedule until a subsequent meeting, to be held in Philadelphia on April 10, whereas the more seriously affected NAL nonetheless announced its season's schedule at this meeting, which was held in Chicago, the venue for most of the NAL meetings.[240]

The NNL's March meeting was held in Washington, D.C., which had become the primary home of the Homestead Grays. The league decided on seven NNL teams competing in 1943, with one team to be owned by former

Black Yankees co-owner George Mitchell and whose location had yet to be determined. The NNL's scheduling plans involved sticking to the bigger cities, as well as holding games "in easily accessible places to Virginia and nearby Maryland where defense workers are congregated, in response to the planned travel restrictions."[241] Fay Young, in reporting on the NAL meeting, provided the contradictory inputs of an announced schedule and quoted J.B. Martin saying that "the Negro American League will not be able to operate this season."[242] Dan Burley, writing for the *New York Amsterdam News*, weighed in with the pronouncement that "Negro Baseball this summer seems doomed," blaming the "dilly-dallying practices of Negro League owners" who were "sitting back smoking big black cigars" while their major-league counterparts wrung concessions from ODT director Eastman.[243]

What was really going on in early 1943? Despite the dark pronouncements of Black baseball's viability, both leagues were scrambling in their own ways to put together an operating plan dealing with the significant travel restrictions imposed upon them by ODT, while they hoped to get some relief that would enable them to operate substantially as they did in 1942. Some suggested options were 1) they could sell their buses and travel by rail; 2) they could simply "carry on" while attempting to get "special considerations" from Eastman; or 3) they could use trains and commercial buses.[244]

The NNL held its follow-up meeting and planned to operate within the travel restrictions, even as it joined the NAL in applying for relief. It focused its meeting instead upon its new franchise location and other operating issues. It was decided that the new team, owned by George Mitchell and Allen Johnson, would play its home games in Harrisburg and be called the Harrisburg-St. Louis Stars, succeeding 1942's New Orleans-St. Louis Stars. Still to be figured out was who would control players from last year's Black Yankees since George Mitchell had previously co-owned the Yankees with James Semler—a battle between the Harrisburg-St. Louis and New York contingents was sure to follow.[245] Meanwhile, the NNL decided on its first-half schedule, while choosing their umpires (and raising their pay) and passing provisions protecting players who did not receive timely contract payments by declaring them free agents and penalizing the teams that failed to pay players in a timely fashion.[246]

Despite the challenging conditions, both leagues carried on. According to Neil Lanctot, the NAL succeeded in gaining an allowance of 2,000 miles per month per team by late June because of its acknowledged difficulties in traveling publicly in the South; the NNL was excluded from this arrangement because it did not have significant Southern travel.[247] And, as they often did, the two leagues accused each other of stealing players and battled over the entry of the Ethiopian Clowns into the 1943 NAL. Cum Posey was notified by J.B. Martin on May 1 that Posey was in violation of the joint league agreement as his team fielded players under contract to the Memphis Red Sox and Kansas City Monarchs. He responded with a letter released to the Black press countercharging that the NAL had repeatedly broken the joint agreement by stealing NNL players, by playing the Clowns, and by not giving to the NNL East-West Game receipts it had earned.[248]

What ensued was a "five-hour hectic meeting" on June 1 in Philadelphia.[249] In the minutes of the meeting, President Wilson opened up the discussion by trying to operate as a peacemaker between the two leagues. He said, "Tampering with players was bad, and would result in tearing down what it took years to build up. ... It was [therefore] necessary under existing conditions for everybody to do some sacrificing to help keep baseball going and avoid fights between the two leagues."[250] But fight they did, as charges and countercharges flew back and forth between clubs of both leagues. Both NNL President Wilson and NAL President Martin signed an order finding four NNL clubs, the Harrisburg Stars, New York Black Yankees, Washington Homestead Grays, and Philadelphia Stars; and the Cleveland Buckeyes of the NAL—were in violation of the joint agreement and ordering a total of 10 players either returned to their original clubs or exchanged for other players.[251] An uneasy peace or at least a truce followed, as the order was largely obeyed and even misgivings by NNL clubs over the presence of the Clowns in the NAL gradually faded.[252]

As the war's tide began to turn toward the Allied forces, so too did the Negro Leagues prosper. The August 1 East-West Game drew 51,723 fans, the most of any East-West contest.[253] On August 2, right after the East-West contest, the two leagues reconvened in Chicago for a joint meeting, rare this late in the season. There were discussions of how to handle the problem of approaching the Mexican government to get cooperation in bringing Negro League players back from Mexico, and NNL President Wilson, at the behest of NAL President Martin, ruled that a Negro League team could not go to another Negro League city to play a game against a different opponent than that city's team without the local team's approval.[254] There was also interleague conflict, as third baseman Marvin Carter was playing alternately for the Harrisburg-St. Louis Stars of the NNL and the NAL's Memphis Red Sox. The issue was settled by Stars owner Mitchell saying "he would not play Carter any longer" after Mitchell stated that he had "intended on using Carter in two important games that he had booked."[255] It was not in dispute that Carter belonged to the Memphis Red Sox all along.

Negro League baseball had its best year ever from a financial standpoint in 1943.[256] The NAL's Birmingham Black Barons won the league's first half and proceeded to win a five-game playoff against the second-half winner Chicago American Giants before losing a seven-game Negro World Series to the Homestead Grays, a series replete with "irregularities and disputes."[257] Despite all the squabbles and strife between and within the two leagues, the year 1943 ended at a high point for the institution of Black baseball. But a December 3 meeting—not including Negro League owners, but between a Black delegation largely composed of newspaper figures and a delegation of major-league owners and officials—foreshadowed a challenge to Negro League magnates greater than the intense conflicts they had between owners and leagues—the eventual opening of major-league baseball to Black ballplayers.

1944

As usual, the NAL planned its winter meeting for a date prior to that of the NNL. The NAL owners and officers were mostly interested in 1) reaping favorable publicity for the success of the prior season, which would hopefully carry over into 1944, 2) planning for the coming season, including working out some of the problems that marred last year's Negro World Series, and 3) settling some of its conflicts with its rival and sometimes partner NNL.[258] Before the December 19 meeting, however, *Pittsburgh Courier* sportswriter and trailblazer for baseball integration Wendell Smith weighed in about the larger issue that the Negro League baseball magnates needed to contend with—preparing for the inevitable day when White baseball would come calling for their best ballplayers.

In his December 18, 1943, column entitled "Smitty's Sports Spurts," Smith both lauded the Negro League owners for having "attained 'big business' classification" by having their best financial year ever in 1943 and

(Courtesy of Memphis Public Library)

Birmingham Black Barons owner Tom Hayes shows off his team's bus at the entrance to Birmingham's Rickwood Field, where his franchise played its home games

warned them that such success necessitated "sound business tactics" and "a long range program designed to bring them even larger profits in the future." What Smith (and others) saw coming was a time when the major leagues would come calling—and he believed that currently, "the Negro owners are in no position to bargain with major league teams for their players. The Negro owners will have to accept what they are offered." In essence, he foresaw the refusal of Branch Rickey to pay any money for signing the first Black player based on Rickey's claim that the Negro Leagues were disorganized and therefore whatever contracts existed need not be recognized. In Smith's judgment, "the business methods of the Negro American and National leagues are not up to par and it wouldn't take much arguing on the part of a major league owner to prove that the two Negro leagues are not organized. And, if the Negro leagues aren't organized, then a major league owner is in no way compelled to recognize the contracts and agreements which ordinarily apply to trades and sales of ball players."[259]

Smith therefore suggested that the Negro American League would be wise to begin planning for the future at its midwinter meeting, because the current prosperity would not last. He expressed the belief that NAL President J.B. Martin was a good businessman, who would have help from other capable NAL owners, naming Cleveland's Ernest Wright, Birmingham's Abe Saperstein and Tom Hayes, Dr. B.B Martin of Memphis, and Tom Baird of Kansas City as partners in developing a sustainable business model, in today's parlance.[260]

In this author's estimation, the appearance of Smith's blueprint for Negro baseball's future success and suggestions for preparing a plan for baseball integration was at least partly occasioned by the unprecedented meeting between the Black press and major-league baseball on December 3, 1943. Smith believed that the timing of future actions by the major leagues to integrate was as yet uncertain. Nevertheless, it was significant that 44 major-league owners and baseball officials, including Commissioner Kenesaw M. Landis, saw fit to meet with publishers Ira Lewis of the *Pittsburgh Courier* and John Sengstacke of the *Chicago Defender*, along with leading sportswriters including Wendell Smith, and even former athlete and current singer/performer Paul Robeson. The meeting suggested that White baseball realized that it could no longer ignore the presence of a Black baseball world and the potential future interrelationship with its own baseball operations.[261]

The meeting, held at the Roosevelt Hotel in New York, included passionate speeches by publishers Lewis and Sengstacke plus Paul Robeson decrying the color line and pointing to changing attitudes of the American public on integrated performances in sports and in the entertainment world. Judge Landis repeated his claim that there "has never been, formal or informal, or any understanding, written or unwritten, subterranean or sub-anything, against the hiring of Negroes in the major leagues." Ira Lewis pushed back, insisting that an unwritten understanding among the White baseball establishment to bar Black players indeed existed.[262]

What did this meeting signify, if anything? According to Brian Carroll, whose book on baseball integration traced the process through the actions of the Black press, "[T]hough the meeting failed to produce tangible results, it marked the first time integration was included on big league baseball's formal agenda, and Landis's invitations were major league baseball's first issued to men of color."[263] Similarly, the *New York Amsterdam News*, in its January 1, 1944, edition, provided a summary of major 1943 developments that included the following assessment of the meeting: "Nothing definite was accomplished, but it did mark a step forward.[264]

But how would the Negro League magnates and league officials deal with the potential future implications of this unprecedented contact between representatives of the Black press and the White baseball establishment? On the eve of the December 19 NAL meeting, President J.B. Martin provided the NAL response to talk of future integration, stating that "we are not opposed to any movement which would advance Negro players to the major leagues." He went on to say that "we should not be expected to solve this problem. It is solely a major league issue. We cannot force them to admit Negro players, nor will we assume that responsibility."[265] Neil Lanctot characterized Martin's response to the issue as "dodging responsibility." Lanctot went on to describe as "evasive" Martin's reaction to suggestions like that of Rollo Wilson that the two league presidents should seek an affiliation with major-league baseball as a precursor to integration."[266] What Martin did address was the issue of contractual rights as he made it known that any NAL players desired by major-league owners would only be "released with our permission"—but he added that he did not expect this to happen in 1944.[267]

Meanwhile, the NNL was doing even less than the NAL in acknowledging any role in promoting the integration of White baseball. The *New York Amsterdam News* reported that NNL President Thomas Wilson informed the newspapers that Black players entering the major leagues was "none of its concern" as the NNL could not compromise its access to major-league ballparks by raising the issue. Just like Martin, Wilson announced his league's position in advance of the NNL's winter meeting, which was held in New York on January 5 at the Hotel Theresa.[268]

What, then, did transpire at the first 1944 winter meetings of the NAL and NNL? The NAL reelected President Martin, Vice President Ernest Wright, owner of the Cleveland Buckeyes, Secretary Robert Simmons, traveling secretary of the Chicago American Giants, and Treasurer Wilkinson, owner of the Kansas City Monarchs.[269] The NAL clubs also decided to count all games between league clubs in the league standings and to require each team to play at least 30 games in each half of the coming season to be eligible for the league pennant. They also ruled that any player must be on his team 30 days prior to the season's end to be eligible for any postseason play.[270] As to postseason play, the NAL decided unilaterally that the Negro World Series would now be seven games and would be played solely in the home cities of the competing teams.[271]

From its own vantage point, the NNL apparently was planning to reexamine its joint agreement with the NAL at its 11th annual meeting.[272] Since NAL President Martin, along with his brother B.B. of the Memphis Red Sox, Syd Pollock of the Cincinnati (a.k.a. Ethiopian) Clowns, and Winfield Welch of the Birmingham Black Barons were all in attendance, it was open season for revisiting old grievances, as a heated discussion between NNL owners and their NAL counterparts ensued regarding the Memphis Red Sox having played the St. Louis Stars in September 1943 when the NNL had suspended the Stars. Eddie Gottlieb brought up the 1942 issue of Syd Pollock's Ethiopian Clowns (at that time based in Cincinnati) playing against NAL clubs in accusing the NAL of again breaking their joint agreement.[273] Would the two leagues ever get along?

George Mitchell, manager of St. Louis, attended the NNL meeting, but was "barred from the closed meeting." Not only Mitchell, but the members of the press were also barred from the meeting as "the assembled magnates took all their squabbles behind closed doors" and had a five-hour meeting, after which they took the newspaper reporters out to dinner and announced that they would send out a release to those same papers.[274] Why did the magnates yet again keep their best sources for league publicity out of their meeting? Maybe they were tired of having their dirty laundry aired by the league, but leaving them out in the cold would not stop the negative reportage from coming out. The press speculated that Mitchell would come up with the money to pay off St. Louis's 1943 obligations to the NNL and then join the NAL in 1944, otherwise why would he be "walking the Theresa corridors, his hands locked behind him?"—certainly he was not there to accompany the equally locked out press![275]

In more mundane business matters, the NNL re-elected the prior year's league officers, and newly renamed President Wilson formed a committee to contact ODT and attempt to arrange to use their own buses in 1944, a plan that came to fruition sometime before the season opened when ODT offered the same 2,000 miles per month per team travel allowance to the NNL that it gave only to the NAL in 1943.[276]

When the NAL reconvened in Chicago on March 5 and 6 for its last preseason meeting, media reportage was scarce, as the decisions of NAL owners were mostly routine in nature. The *Chicago Defender* reported that the Ethiopian Clowns were allowed to shift their home base to Indianapolis from Cincinnati because of a conflict in bookings in Cincinnati—owner Syd Pollock had wanted to play games at the home of the Cincinnati Reds, Crosley Field, but decided not to because they were not allowed by the Reds to use the clubhouse. According to Rebecca Alpert, Pollock instead arranged to play home games at American Association Park in Indianapolis even though the Clowns still played a few games in Cincinnati.[277] Otherwise, the NAL finalized its league schedule but did not finalize the naming of a league statistician.[278]

In contrast, the NNL's final preseason meeting in New York on March 2 and 3 contained "much debate and discussion"—with an undercurrent of contention between, yet again, different factions of NNL owners. Although most of the meeting was taken up with scheduling, a significant decision was made regarding the hiring of a statistician, as the league rejected Wendell Smith's offer to be its statistical agent and hired the Al Munro Elias agency instead.[279] By virtue of this choice, the NNL rejected the recommendation of Effa Manley, who had encouraged Smith to present his offer to the NNL owners, and simultaneously angered vocal elements of the Black press. Back in December, Smith had offered to compile statistics for both leagues for $5,000 or one league for $3,000.[280] Effa Manley believed that getting the fans superior information would mean a great deal to Black baseball, but acknowledged resistance to hiring Smith.[281] Smith had made enemies among NNL league owners, Cum Posey in particular, resulting in the choice of Elias, which had substantial experience but also was offering a lower price of $425 for the season.[282]

In particular, Dan Burley, employing the nom de plume of Don Deleighbur, contended that the hiring of White agency Elias and snubbing of Black reporter Smith was another example of "complete anti-Negroism" by the NNL, along with its "favoring of the Jim Crow Policy of the major leagues" by refusing to push for baseball integration. Burley/Deleighbur went on to suggest that the hiring of Elias instead of Smith constituted an "affront to Smith's ability" but also a rejection of the Negro press overall, who had given Black baseball "thousands of dollars in free space on sports pages throughout the land."[283] Supporting Burley, Bob Williams, sports editor of the *Cleveland Call and Post*, said that the rejection of Smith was a reflection of the "'selfish interests' in Negro baseball in 1944,'" a failure to acknowledge that "the Negro Press has stuck its neck out for Negro baseball" by choosing not to reciprocate for the valuable space given to it in the Black newspapers and instead "pass up the opportunity in order to save a few paltry dollars." For Williams, the decision on Smith, along with inaction on supporting integration of Black players into major-league baseball, led to "Negro Sports writers raising a question this year: HAVE THE NEGRO LEAGUES BROKEN FAITH WITH THE NEGRO PRESS?"[284]

In his *Cleveland Call and Post* column dated March 25, Williams did acknowledge that "INTEGRATION WOULD DISINTEGRATE THE NEGRO baseball leagues."[285] In reply to Dan Burley's broadside, Posey picked up on Williams's concession, stating that the desire of the Black press to foster integration led to its essentially "offering a whole Negro enterprise to White business men" which "would automatically put organized Negro baseball out of business." In Posey's view, he and the other NNL owners were facing "racial antagonism" from members of the Black press in part because they were not enthusiastically participating in the push toward integration of baseball championed especially by Wendell Smith and also by many other Black sportswriters. The end of Posey's letter to the press, which appeared side-by-side with Williams's "Sport Rambler" column of March 25 in the *Cleveland Call and Post*, stated thusly: "There is enough race antagonism rampant without members of our race constantly seeking self angrandisement (sic). In sports through race pressure."[286]

Despite the underlying and ever-present tensions between owners, between leagues, and between the leagues and the Black press, the March 11, 1944, *Pittsburgh Courier*'s headline for its column on the final NNL preseason meeting was "National League Set for Season." Trades were discussed, and one was completed: Pitcher Percy "Pete" Forrest was traded by the New York Black Yankees to Newark for pitcher Freddie Hopgood and outfielder Ed Stone.[287] According to gadfly Dan Burley, the NNL had one final meeting just prior to the start of the NNL season on May 21, a Philadelphia confab in which the clubs voted unanimously to take over all St. Louis Stars players as Stars owner George Mitchell had not paid off his debt to the league. NNL President Wilson reportedly wired NAL President Martin asking him to require NAL clubs to release Stars players so they could report to the NNL clubs claiming them.[288] Of course, the two leagues continued to battle over these players.

As the war in Europe reached its "D-Day," the two leagues operated quite successfully in 1944. Attendance was brisk for the fourth straight year and at year's end, sportswriter Alvin Moses characterized the 1944 Negro League season as a "banner year financially."[289] The NNL held a scheduling meeting on June 19 in Philadelphia, where it was decided not to offer Gus Greenlee an associate membership for his revived Pittsburgh Crawfords. Since the Homestead Grays were now playing mostly in Washington, Greenlee requested to play at Forbes Field in Pittsburgh when the Grays were not there. Greenlee's intent was to "build Sunday baseball" and he felt that he was owed an opportunity to rejoin the league because of "my record of past contributions to Negro baseball."[290] While the *Afro-American* reported simply that Greenlee was denied an associate membership, Cum Posey later stated that Greenlee was offered an associate membership, but not in Pittsburgh. Posey insisted that league precedent supported President Wilson's ruling that a team could not play home games in a city where another team (his Homestead Grays) had their home grounds unless that team consented. [291]

Rebuffed, Greenlee would not go away quietly. He announced the signing of several players from each league during the weekend of the annual East-West Game, and met secretly with the All-Stars of both leagues, encouraging them to strike for a larger profit share. And Greenlee announced his plans to form a rival league in 1945.[292] Clearly, Gus Greenlee would be a force to be reckoned with in 1945—and nobody yet knew that Branch Rickey would be a partner in Greenlee's new league, mostly as a subterfuge for approaching Negro League players to sign with the Brooklyn Dodgers.

At the June 19 meeting, the NNL also decided to refuse to allow Abe Saperstein, now part owner of the NAL's Birmingham Black Barons, to promote its games, which included the upcoming East-West contest. According to Neil Lanctot, the NNL and NAL had drafted a new joint agreement in early 1944 limiting a promoter to 10 percent of the net receipts for a game he promoted; Cum Posey charged that Saperstein had taken more than 40 percent in some instances.[293] Finally, Posey reported that he surveyed all the NNL owners at this meeting and they unanimously agreed that Negro League baseball needed a "commissioner to straighten out matters between the two leagues and rule organized Negro baseball."[294] Posey stated that the NNL was in accord with the Black press on the need for a commissioner; he was in this instance agreeing with Wendell Smith, who had written to Effa Manley earlier in 1944 that the only way to get the owners to follow rules and regulations was to elect a commissioner. Would the leagues finally listen to Smith, who had "constantly pleaded for a Commissioner"?[295] If all the discord between the Black press and Black baseball since the December 3, 1943, meeting between the major leagues and the delegation of Black publishers was a guide, the answer was a likely "no"—unless ownership and current leadership in both leagues had finally come to their senses.

The NAL also had one more league meeting during the 1944 season. As was often the case, the NAL's June 13 Chicago meeting had little notable news, if the *Chicago Defender*'s brief reportage was to be believed. In addition to setting second-half schedules, the NAL announced the release of catcher Bruce Petway and the purchase of right fielder Jimmie Crutchfield by Cleveland.[296]

Ultimately, the 1944 season ended with the NNL pennant-winning Homestead Grays besting the NAL pennant-winning Birmingham Black Barons 4 games to 1. The Negro World Series had now been played for three straight years after a 14-year hiatus—and even though Wendell Smith had been rejected as statistician for the leagues, he had been appointed to a three-man commission with noted sportswriters Fay Young of the *Chicago Defender* and Sam Lacy of the *Baltimore Afro-American* to rule on any disputes arising from a now officially-designated championship series.[297] J.B. Martin was so pleased with the lack of controversy over the World Series that he called it "the finest thing that has happened in Negro baseball. … It is the first time we've had a Series in which the fans, leagues, and clubs could look toward it with confidence and pride."[298]

The 1944 season should have given both the NNL and NAL reasons for optimism for a successful and prosperous future. But there had been a Thanksgiving surprise—Commissioner Kenesaw Mountain Landis suddenly died on November 25, 1944. The baseball world was turned on its ear—and change, in an America poised to imminently defeat the forces of evil abroad and confront those same forces at home, was in the offing.

1945

For the first time in the eight years of a two-league structure in Black baseball, the NNL and NAL scheduled their annual first winter meetings as preludes to a subsequent joint meeting the following day. Ordinarily, the leagues met jointly in midseason (although in 1944 there was no reported joint meeting of the two leagues at any time of the season), to work out in-season disputes as well as iron out plans for the annual East-West Game and, more recently, plan a postseason World Series. In 1940, there was a joint session on February 24, though this meeting followed earlier NNL and NAL meetings, the NAL back in December and the NNL in early February. Why was there a need for a two-league gathering at the beginning of the winter offseason?

Clues can be found in a December 6, 1944, letter reading like a press release found in Effa Manley's files. This letter, which lists league Presidents Wilson and Martin and NNL Secretary Posey at bottom, announces the calling of a joint meeting in New York on Friday, December 15, in New York at the Theresa Hotel. The letter mentioned the airing of grievances of two or three teams, clearing up the still ongoing battle between the leagues over the "St. Louis situation which caused a rift between the two leagues," discussing the potential blacklisting of players who jumped their teams and "outlaw clubs" they jumped to, as well as issues involving the East-West Game, in which the players' 1944 strike threat had earned them a substantial raise to $200 from $25 that they had gotten previously.[299]

The final paragraph of the December 6 meeting announcement, however, may have been the most critical. It mentioned "rumors of a third league of Negro Baseball" which NNL and NAL franchise holders were determined not to allow.[300] The specter of Gus Greenlee and other independent clubs organizing a rival league still existed, and the NNL and NAL would be prepared.

Related to the concern over Greenlee, however, was the reality of major-league Commissioner Landis's recent death. In describing the agenda for this early joint meeting, the *New York Amsterdam News* suggested that among matters to be discussed was "the effect the death of baseball czar Judge Kenesaw Mountain Landis will have on park owners and what will be the attitude of Landis' successor as high commissioner of baseball."[301] The immediate concern was threats to the NNL and NAL on getting playing dates at major-league ballparks; but lurking in the background, at least implicitly, were the rumblings of movement on ending the color line by signing Negro League players. Would Landis's successor have a different attitude about allowing Black players into the major leagues? Negro League owners saw threats to their viability everywhere—but the operations of the major leagues were arguably the biggest threat to their existence both in the short term and in the long run.

The press also found itself cooling its heels outside of the two league meetings on December 15. According to Wendell Smith, after the Black sportswriters threatened to "give the moguls some 'very bad press' the media was "welcomed with open arms" at the joint meeting on Saturday, December 16.[302] What the "assembled scribes" missed witnessing at the league meetings was tension and disputes in the hitherto cooperative NAL environment and smooth and untroubled proceedings in the usually raucous NNL atmosphere.[303] The NAL meeting included a split vote on the re-election of J.B. Martin, as owners Thomas Hayes of Birmingham and Syd Pollock of Cincinnati/Indianapolis voted for attorney and former Negro League player James Shackleford to replace Martin.[304] In addition, the brothers Martin, president J.B. and owner B.B. of the Memphis Red Sox, voted to retain Robert Simmons as secretary, but the other four teams prevailed in replacing him with Fay Young, sportswriter for the *Chicago Defender*. According to the *Defender*, the voting process was animated, with objections given to Martin calling for a vote to succeed himself as NAL president, while his brother B.B. "strenuously objected" to an alternative suggestion of Hayes (a friend of B.B. Martin's) as president, and a "lengthy speech" made by J.B. Martin in favor of retaining Simmons as secretary which was ultimately voted down.[305]

In contrast, the NNL again re-elected its entire slate of officers, although the *New York Amsterdam News* relied on "reports that sifted in from the smoke-filled room where the boys talked over secret league maneuvers."[306] Wendell Smith, in his column entitled "Caught on the Fly at the Baseball Meeting," quoted Syd Pollock and his secretary Bunny Downs as saying that "bad publicity is better than no publicity."[307] One can only speculate whether the periodic keeping of the news hounds out of meetings generated controversy and thereby publicity, or whether it ultimately discouraged the media from giving full support to promoting Black baseball.

Otherwise, though, the big news from these winter meetings was the forming of two committees. At the Saturday afternoon joint session, the leagues chose Cum Posey and Ed Bolden to represent the NNL and B.B. Martin and Tom Hayes to represent the NAL to form a group deputized to present a list of candidates to be commissioner overseeing the two leagues. They also chose Abe Manley and Alex Pompez as NNL representatives, and Tom Baird of the Kansas City Monarchs and Ernest Wright of the Cleveland Buckeyes as NAL representatives on a committee tasked with detailed planning for the annual East-West Game, with special attention to avoiding a repeat of the labor dispute that marred the 1944 contest.

The previous afternoon, both leagues also met jointly and listened to William Nunn, managing editor of the *Courier* (and former NNL secretary) declare that Negro League baseball had grown into a big business, necessitating ownership action in "building your fences" and specifically, choosing a baseball czar to oversee the game and a planning committee for a successful East-West affair.[308] Apparently, ownership responded with alacrity to Nunn, as they had not done to the suggestions of Wendell Smith and others over the years. But nothing was simply executed when it came to the operations of the Negro Leagues.

Finally, trades and trade rumors filled the air. James "Soldier Boy" Semler, owner of the Black Yankees, purchased Ted "Double Duty" Radcliffe from the Birmingham Black Barons. Kansas City sent catcher Quincy Trouppe to Cleveland for pitcher Theolic "Fireball" Smith. And Memphis hoping to make James "Cool Papa" Bell their manager, offered outfielder Cowan "Bubba" Hyde to the Homestead Grays in return for Bell, but Posey turned that deal down. Cleveland owner Ernie Wright also rejected what he characterized as "a bad deal" that would have sent outfielder Buddy Armour to Kansas City for pitcher Jack Matchett.[309]

Before any more NNL or NAL meetings were held, one more "Black baseball" league meeting was held—one that was not at all welcomed by the existing leagues. On December 27, 1944, in Pittsburgh, the formative meeting of the "United States Negro Baseball League" (usually referred to as the United States League or USL) was held. The league, which included six formerly independent teams, chose Gus Greenlee as its vice president and Wendell Smith as secretary, but left the president slot open for a "nationally known lawyer and athlete "who they wished to convince to accept."[310] That individual turned out to be James Shackleford, the losing candidate at the recent NAL meeting for the NAL presidency.

The new league included the controversial St. Louis Stars, the Philadelphia/Hilldale Daisies (to be moved to Brooklyn in May and renamed the Brooklyn Brown Dodgers), the Chicago Brown Bombers, the Detroit City Motor Giants, the Atlanta Black Crackers, and Greenlee's Pittsburgh Crawfords.[311] According to Greenlee, once he had been rejected by the NNL for an associate membership in 1944, he was also rejected by the NAL as "the American league owners were afraid of creating trouble by taking me after the National has rejected my bids."[312] Though Greenlee claimed that he was not competing with the two existing Negro Leagues, the *Courier* believed otherwise, suggesting that his entry would be problematic for the NNL and NAL, who would need to "launch a new and vigorous program" to compete with Greenlee's league.[313] Both leagues, therefore, should have had plenty of incentive to straighten out some of their more dysfunctional elements within their own structures and between the NNL and NAL.

When the NNL reconvened in New York late February or early March for their second and last preseason meeting, however, it primarily focused on undermining the fledgling structure of Greenlee's new circuit. As reported by the *New York Amsterdam News*, the "biggest bombshell of mid-winter baseball palavering" was the announcement by Birmingham manager Winfield Welch that Abe Saperstein would not book games nor would he be "connected with the newly-formed (Gus Greenlee & Co.) U.S. League," even though it mentioned that Saperstein was part of the financing of the St. Louis Stars, one of the six teams in the new league.[314] In other activities, NNL owners turned down an application for associate membership from an Indianapolis contingent, saying that the presence of an Indianapolis team in the NAL in essence meant that the NAL had authority over any Black baseball to be played in that city. And the newly-reorganized Negro Southern League's President R.R. Jackson declared his league to a be a minor-league circuit, offering to develop players for the NNL and NAL in return for their protection of his operations.[315]

The NAL followed suit, holding its final preseason meeting on March 5 and 6 in Chicago. One notable difference in this year's proceedings was the degree to which each league participated in each other's meetings, as it was NAL team manager Welch of Birmingham who, accompanied by NAL President J.B. Martin, prominently participated in the prior NNL discussion by declaring Saperstein's independence from the new USL, while NNL league owners Pompez, Abe Manley, Ed Gottlieb, and NNL President and Baltimore owner Wilson all attended the NAL conference. It certainly seemed that the threat of a new operation (one that would soon be joined by Branch Rickey) in Black baseball was effectively bringing the rival NNL and NAL together in protection of their legitimacy in the eyes of Black fans as well as the Black press.[316] In fact, at this meeting the NAL "fell in line with the Negro National League's action" in rejecting a franchise bid of the same Indianapolis interests who had applied for an associate membership at the recent NNL confab, even though this could mean that the NAL Clowns would not have access to the American Association park in Indianapolis that it had previously used, as the failed bidders were now expected to join the USL and had "'tied' the ball park up. …"[317]

Dizzy Dismukes, now the business manager of the Kansas City Monarchs, announced at this meeting that the Monarchs had signed Jackie Robinson to play the infield, noting that he had been a "top-notch baseball player before joining the Army." In reality, Robinson had batted .097 for the 1940 varsity UCLA baseball team, and shared the team lead in errors committed; his prowess as an all-around athlete, starring in football, basketball, and track, had more to do with his reputation as a quality baseball player invoked by Dismukes.[318] Finally, the NAL declared at this meeting that it would adhere to a 25 percent mileage reduction in scheduling the 1945 season in accordance with the request of the ODT.[319]

That mileage reduction also applied to the major leagues and resulted in the cancellation of the 1945 major-league All-Star Game, according to Neil Lanctot.[320] So what would be the fate of the East-West contest in 1945? The East-West contest could have been canceled, but it was apparently saved by J.B. Martin claiming that it was "ninety-eight percent a Chicago affair" and would therefore not involve heavy travel.[321] According to correspondence between William Nunn of the *Pittsburgh Courier* and Abe Manley, however, a significant discrepancy existed between Martin's view of the East-West Game committee's authority and that of the committee members. Nunn proposed that the committee decide upon allocation of the game's receipts, perform a thorough study of the game's promotion, consider ncreasing pricing, stage a banquet on the night prior to the game, and underwrite the sportswriter's expenses.[322] Manley responded by agreeing with all of Nunn's proposals, but informing him that the East-West committee was told by J.B. Martin at the NAL meeting that their sole responsibility for the East-West Game was to solve any problems associated with players striking as they did in 1944.[323] More correspondence ensued, with Nunn making clear that he wanted no part in chairing the East-West committee if it was limited to dealing with player compensation,[324] and Posey weighed in by declaring in a May 5, 1945, *Norfolk Journal and Guide* column that "there is too much control over this game in the hands of one man, Dr. J.B. Martin."[325]

While this conflict played out, the major leagues held an April 24 meeting in which they announced that they had elected Albert B. "Happy" Chandler the new commissioner of baseball, and also that the American and National Leagues had agreed to a request by Sam Lacy of the *Baltimore Afro-American* to set up a committee to study "colored baseball" with an intention of exploring how to incorporate it into "the organized game" and eventually, bring Black ballplayers to the major leagues.[326] And on May 7, Branch Rickey held a press conference in which he announced his involvement with the USL through the Brooklyn Brown Dodgers, and simultaneously blasted the Negro Leagues for being "leagues in name only and not in practice" due to their need for booking agents and their shaky player contracts.[327] When you add in tryouts at Dodgers training camp for pitchers Terris McDuffie and first baseman Dave "Showboat" Thomas, as well as the infamous Red Sox tryout of Jackie Robinson, outfielder Sam Jethroe, and infielder Marvin Williams, one could easily conclude that there was more going on that affected the status of Negro League baseball than ever before—and on June 12, the leagues would be deciding how to proceed on the choice of a Black baseball commissioner.

Negro League historian Neil Lanctot considered the June 12, 1945, joint meeting of the NNL and NAL to be one of critical importance in the history of the Negro Leagues.[328] In addition to the vote on commissioner of the two leagues, the response of the leagues to Sam Lacy's committee and the handling of preparations for the East-West Game would be decided. Effa Manley reported as the lone NNL or NAL club owner to have attended Branch Rickey's May 7 USL press conference, and representatives of the Mexican League were "lurking in Chicago" with their assumed intent being "taking star players from both Leagues to play in Mexico."[329]

If this meeting was a test of the strength of conviction of both Negro Leagues to work together and address their myriad challenges and organize systems to handle internal conflicts and outside threats, the leagues would get a failing grade. Although NNL President Wilson "spoke for three minutes asking for a harmonious meeting," what he got was no agreement on a new commissioner and inaction on most of the other burning issues.[330]

Two candidates ran for commissioner: Bob Church, a Black millionaire and Tennessee political figure with no previous baseball experience, and Judge William Hueston, a former federal official and also president of the first Negro National League from 1927 through 1931.[331] Predictably, Church was nominated by Memphis Red Sox officer (and third Martin brother) W.S. Martin while Hueston was proposed by Posey as "the East's candidate for baseball commissioner." As described by Posey in his "Posey's Points" column of June 23, 1945, Effa Manley defected from the Eastern bloc in supporting Church, so that it was "only an aggressive fight by the remaining Negro National League members ... that kept Memphis, Tenn.—the weakest baseball city in organized Negro baseball—from becoming the capital of Negro baseball."

Not only was it decided to require a three-fourths majority, but also to have a written ballot—and once the 7-to-5 vote for Church failed to achieve the necessary approval, a motion for a second ballot failed.[332] In describing the ultimate inaction by the leagues, Rollo Wilson, who had been observing league proceedings since the second NNL began, commented as follows: "The National and American League clubmen showed that they want no commissioner. ... No second vote was taken which would seem to evidence that nobody except the fans, the newsmen and possibly a minority of the owners want a check-rein on Negro baseball."[333]

Other non-responses from this crucial joint meeting included: 1) In response to Effa Manley's report on the USL/Branch Rickey press conference, a suggestion, but no subsequent vote, on a proposed committee of two players and two club representatives to question Rickey and the two major-league presidents, Ford Frick and William Harridge, about what they expected from the two Negro Leagues, 2) an instruction to NAL Chairman Martin to let Sam Lacy know that his letter forming the committee to study Black baseball that included major-league officials and known Black figures and asking for a Negro League representative "had been received and read" as the joint membership took no position on it, 3) a motion "putting the East-West [Game] up to Dr. J.B. Martin" was made by Kansas City owner Tom Baird and seconded by Cleveland owner Wilbur Hayes but no vote was recorded. The only mention of the East-West Game committee was that it had previously allocated $100 compensation for each player chosen; a motion carried to allow each team $300 to split among players who were not chosen for the contest.[334]

Only one other in-season meeting was covered by the Black press in 1945. The NNL held a special meeting in early July in New York, one characterized by the *Baltimore Afro-American* as "one of the most progressive in the history of the organization," in which the league imposed a $500 penalty on the New York Black Yankees for causing two forfeits of games in the past month along with $50 fines on manager George Scales and infielder Buddy Barker for refusing to leave the field after being thrown out of the game. In addition, the league decided to impose a five-year suspension on players who either had already jumped to the Mexican League or planned to do so in the future.[335] That the league announced a punitive action against the Black Yankees clearly surprised Sam Lacy, who predicted that "the NNL officials ain't a going to do nothing to the Black Yankees" because Bill Leuschner, booking agent owner of the Black Yankees and the Bushwicks, had power over them.[336]

Despite the organizational paralysis and contention that continued to beset the two leagues, they continued to be prosperous in 1945. Attendance around the league continued to be solid; particularly noteworthy was the attendance of 101,818 fans to nine weeknight Negro League games at Philadelphia's Shibe Park, when its two major-league tenants, the A's and the Phillies, only drew 773,020 fans combined for their entire home seasons.[337] The Cleveland Buckeyes swept the Homestead Grays, four games to none, in the 1945 Negro World Series, played in the immediate aftermath of V-J Day.[338] Cleveland Buckeyes general manager Wilbur Hayes had predicted correctly that his team would win the 1945 NAL pennant back in December 1944 at the NAL's winter meeting; but who could predict the firestorm of excitement, condemnation, and pressure (the last on Negro League owners and officials) that would be unleashed with the October 23, 1945, announcement of the signing of Jackie Robinson by Branch Rickey and the Brooklyn Dodgers?[339]

PART 3: INTEGRATION AND STORM CLOUDS —AND THE DEMISE OF THE NNL (1945–1948)

ROBINSON SIGNS

Although Jackie Robinson signed an agreement with the Brooklyn Dodgers organization on August 28, 1945, the actual signing of a contract to play with the Montreal Royals in the International League for the 1946 season occurred and was announced on October 23, 1945.[340] The signing was hailed in most public pronouncements, including the initial response of NAL President J.B. Martin, whose league had employed Robinson in 1945. The October 27, 1945, *New York Times* published a letter that Martin sent to Branch Rickey in which he wrote: "I take great pleasure on congratulating you for your moral courage in making the initial step which will give the Negro ball players a chance to participate in the major leagues."[341]

The early comments by the Kansas City Monarchs owners were mixed. Both J.L. Wilkinson and Tom Baird indicated that they were "happy to see any Negro player make the major league grade.[342] Wilkinson, though, also noted that "we have been out some expense in training players such as Robinson" and that "something should be done to prevent White organized baseball from just stepping in and taking our players."[343] According to the November 3, 1945 *Baltimore Afro-American*, "Baird was reported to have protested the signing of Jackie and threatened an appeal to Baseball Commissioner A.B. (Happy) Chandler."[344] The *Afro-American* went on to say that Baird had wired them to say that he had been "misquoted and misinterpreted. We would not do anything to hamper or impede the advancement of any colored player, nor would we do anything to keep any colored player out of the White major leagues."[345]

Behind the scenes, Effa Manley and J.B. Martin exchanged letters discussing how to handle this monumental turn of events. Manley suggested to Martin that John Johnson, chair of New York Mayor Fiorello LaGuardia's Committee on Unity, which had a baseball subcommittee that had been part of the impetus toward baseball integration, could arrange a meeting with National League President Ford Frick and Branch Rickey to see what could be done about getting compensation for any of their ballplayers signed by the major leagues. Effa Manley realized that "the future of Negro Baseball was in question" as Jackie's signing threatened the livelihood of Negro League ers, yet she also seemed to get that diplomatic efforts must be made to work with White baseball to set precedents for future such signings.[346] In return, Martin agreed that Frick and not Chandler should be approached and that some compensation should be received for Robinson "to set up a principle for the ones to follow. There will be no price named, for we are not going to jeopardize Robinson's chance."[347]

Martin also realized that he needed to say more publicly about the signing and its ramifications. Accordingly, he put out a statement in early November denying that the NAL objected to Robinson's signing and once again lauding Rickey for the stand he took which would provide opportunity for Black players to advance to the majors, while expressing the belief that Rickey "must have a big heart" and "is too big not to compensate the Kansas City Monarchs for Jackie Robinson." At the same time, he acknowledged that Rickey had called the Negro Leagues "a racket" and felt the need to mention various business procedures of the Negro Leagues that indicated that "we have an organization" with "By-Laws and Constitution, contracts and Gentlemen's Agreements which have always been carried out by the two leagues" although "we will admit that we do not have a commissioner."[348] In reporting on Chandler's statement, the *Cleveland Call and Post* editorialized that Martin's statement "indicates the usual slipshod technique of the Negro leagues"—and there is no doubt that Branch Rickey would have agreed with the Call and Post.[349]

Further steps were needed, in the eyes of the Black press as well as the Negro League owners and operators. In the November 10 *Call and Post*, sports editor Bob Williams had a lot to say about Martin, Monarchs ownership, and the two leagues—and none of it was pretty. He characterized the initial NAL statements on the signing as "confusing, asinine, or at best, irrational" and added that "Dr. J.B. Martin, league prexy, hemmed, hawed and beat around the bush in typical presidential style, while, on a tangent of his own, T.Y. Baird injected the first sour note of the development" by questioning the signing without compensation. Williams acknowledged that both Baird and Martin found "safer ground" but indicated that they were in danger of permanently damaging Negro baseball unless they gave unqualified support to the Robinson deal. And what about the NNL? When Williams wrote his commentary, the NNL apparently had released no public statements—Williams ironically stating that "they have never been quite so silent on matters heretofore which were definitely none of their business."[350]

Cum Posey was indeed busy behind the scenes. He sent a letter to Commissioner Chandler dated November 1, 1945, along lines similar to that of Martin's public statement, but going a bit further. Posey not only enumerated factors that indicated organized business practices on the part of the NNL (and said that he assumed the NAL "operates in the same manner" given their joint agreement) but mentioned that other NNL players had been recently approached by the Dodgers. He made it clear that "we are not protesting the signing of Jackie Robinson or any other player of organized Negro baseball. We are protesting the manner in which he was signed. We feel that the clubs or Organized Negro Baseball … should be approached, and deals made between clubs involved. … That is the only way in which we can be assured that Negro baseball can continue to operate."[351]

Posey sent a copy of his letter to Chandler to Washington Senators owner Clark Griffith, who responded to Posey by saying that "Organized baseball has no moral right to take anything away from [your two leagues] without their consent" while calling Rickey's characterization of Negro League baseball as a racket an "assertion you can prove not to be true."[352] Griffith expressed a hope that Commissioner Chandler would protect the rights of the Negro League clubs to their players and suggested to Posey that "you folks should leave no stone unturned to protect the existence of your two established Negro Leagues."[353] It is important to remember that Posey's Grays were tenants of Griffith's Senators and lucrative ones at that—so Griffith had a vested interest in the viability of the Negro Leagues, and a desire to keep mining cheap talent from Joe Cambria's scouting of Latin countries without competition from this new resource. Griffith had not shown any interest in signing Negro Leaguers, nor would the Senators bring their first Black player Carlos Paula, to the majors until September 1954, almost nine years after Branch Rickey signed Jackie Robinson.[354] No, Clark Griffith was not going to make it any easier for Branch Rickey to pave the way for the signing of more Negro Leaguers—and, therefore, he was sympathetic to the arguments of Posey and the other Negro League owners.

Clearly, a special meeting was in order—and so the leagues held a joint meeting on November 9 at their usual ew York venue, the Hotel Theresa in Harlem. And not just the NNL and the NAL were meeting. The USL was originally scheduled to meet in Chicago on the same day, then shifted to New York to accommodate Branch Rickey. The USL was also going to meet at the Hotel Theresa on the 9th, and ultimately moved their gathering to the YMCA to avoid confusion over "rooms 102-3 at the Hotel Theresa where such meetings were held."[355] USL President Shackleford attempted to get NNL and NAL members to come to his meeting, but got little response to his invitations. According to Dan Burley's account in the *New York Amsterdam News*, "Negro League Baseball's troublesome course seemed heading for a violent explosion" as the three leagues (and also the minor-league NSL) strategized about how to deal with the major leagues and each other. At the joint NNL/NAL meeting, the announced intent was to strategize about how to stop "Organized White Baseball from raiding Organized Negro Baseball."[356]

Negro Baseball Plots All-Out War On Rickey, Others Seeking Players

— *New York Amsterdam News*, November 17, 1945

Apparently, those terms were used advisedly, as Burley noted the sending of a letter to Chandler at this meeting in which the league magnates described Black baseball as having been organized for 15 years and having followed White organized baseball's rules, and suggesting that Branch Rickey was now violating those rules by not dealing directly with the Black owners.[357] While Burley also expressed the belief that all three leagues were attempting to become a part of organized White baseball, the November 17 *Chicago Defender* made no mention of this goal, saying that the NNL and NAL "sought to have White organized baseball owners deal with Negro organized baseball owners in a businesslike manner and to halt the tampering with their players."[358] At the end of 1945, organized Negro baseball was in quite a pickle.

The result was that Chandler offered hope that, once the Negro Leagues were better organized, they could apply to be a part of a system of White baseball that would put all—White major and minor leagues, Black major and minor leagues, and even amateur baseball—under Commissioner Chandler's jurisdiction.[363]

President Martin, however, put out a press release after this conference because he wanted to underscore the desire of the Negro Leagues for being a part of one system of White baseball but make clear that they had no desire to segregate their ballplayers within the Negro Leagues, thereby impeding their advancement into major-league baseball. Chandler had also said that "The Negro Leagues favor keeping their own boys and with their leagues on a sound basis. … [T]hey expect those boys to want to stay in their class."[364] Black baseball was trying to walk a tightrope, ensuring its future by gaining legitimacy from White baseball but also appearing to support opportunities of Black players to leave the Negro Leagues and play integrated baseball, as long as appropriate compensation was arranged for releasing the players from their Negro League contracts. Martin needed to make clear that he did not support the expressed views of Chandler which made it appear that Chandler "viewed a strong Black organization as a substitute for integration" or Martin would be lambasted by the Black press for obstructing the advancement of Black civil rights in favor of the selfish business interests of the two Negro Leagues.[365]

One thing Martin and Wilson did not support was the recommendation by Chandler that the leagues would be better off with presidents who were not also club owners.[366] Wilson had been ill until recently, but he still ran for another term as NNL president at the February 20-21 meeting of NNL owners in New York. This time, Cum Posey and Effa Manley together backed an opposition candidate, Samuel Battle, a parole board commissioner who had been a New York City patrolman as far back as 1911 and was one of the first Black appointees to that post.[367] Posey had been critical of the two league presidents looking to reinforce their power through their dealings with Chandler.[368] Unfortunately, Posey was seriously ill, so it was his co-owner Rufus Jackson who nominated Battle; Posey would die in March of 1946. The other four NNL teams still backed Wilson, and even Rufus Jackson, after the 4-to-2 vote for Wilson, did not want it recorded that he supported Battle. The league also replaced Ed Bolden, voting in Alex Pompez as the new vice president, and chose Curtis Leak as acting secretary given Cum Posey's declining health.[369]

Both Wilson and J.B. Martin, who attended the meeting, discussed their January 17 session with Chandler. Wilson reported that Chandler approved the new contracts modeled after those of the major leagues but said that the old contracts were not acceptable.[370] Chandler offered consideration of a petition for the Negro Leagues to be recognized by White baseball as a minor league;

(National Baseball Hall of Fame Library)

Negro League baseball magnates meet at the Hotel Teresa on June 20, 1946, in New York City. The owners had all attended the Joe Louis boxing bout the night before. The meeting was to plan the second-half schedule for the 1946 season. Left to right: Syd Pollock (Indianapolis Clowns), Tom Wilson (Baltimore Elite Giants), Tom Baird (Kansas City Monarchs), W.S. Martin (Memphis Red Sox), J.B. Martin (NAL President and Chicago American Giants), Ernest Wright (Cleveland Buckeyes), Fay Young (Chicago Defender writer), Wilbur Hayes (Buckeyes), and Tom Hayes Jr. (Birmingham Black Barons).

Wilson indicated that he considered Black baseball to be below major league but above the International League in caliber.[371] Martin added that Chandler's public statements were "contrary to the ones he had made in his meeting with Mr. Wilson and myself."[372] It was reported in the *Courier* that J.B. Martin said that NAL owners would wait for the Joe Louis fight with Billy Conn in June to come back to New York for their next joint meeting—giving an indication of the priorities of the NAL magnates.[373]

During the second day of the meeting, the league voted to limit fees for renting ballparks to 25 percent of receipts, to play 40 games in each half of the 1946 schedule, to petition White baseball for recognition, to approve a working agreement with the NSL, to invite sportswriter Art Carter to their next meeting to "discuss the possibility of a public relations set up," and to postpone deciding on applications for two new franchises in the NNL from Gus Greenlee and USL President John Shackleford. In the minutes, a "long drawn out discussion" of applications by Greenlee for a team in Montreal and possibly Rickey for a Brooklyn team led to a conclusion (without Greenlee and Shackleford present) to ask for a $2,500 franchise fee for either team and judgment that the owners "morally wanted to do something for Gus Greenlee."[374]

The NAL held its next meeting on February 24 and 25 in Chicago. In this meeting, whose primary purpose was to set the 1946 NAL schedule, the league turned down an application from Greenlee and Shackleford for an NAL team in Detroit because they could not provide assurance that Briggs Stadium, home of the Detroit Tigers, was available. There was discussion of granting an associate membership to W.S. Welch for a team in either Detroit or Cincinnati—the league was apparently willing, but Welch could not decide whether to accept it or have an independent club.[375]

Before holding its June joint meeting with the NAL, the NNL had two more special meetings in 1946. The first, on March 12, was held in Baltimore. The NNL decided at this meeting to turn down Gus Greenlee's request to rejoin the NNL with two franchises, one in either Boston or Brooklyn and the other in Montreal, as it saw "no benefit to the league members" by adding any franchises, although it went on record as giving Greenlee first preference in the future "if he obtained a city that would be beneficial to league members."[376]

Both the decision and the process through which the NNL made this decision to exclude Greenlee were heavily criticized by William Nunn. In his *Courier* column of March 23, Nunn called the decision a breach of ethics. He charged that the NNL knew it would turn Greenlee down when it deferred its decision on Greenlee's application in February and delayed it to do damage to the USL, which was trying to set up operations for 1946 even though it had "limped through its first season" in 1945.[377] Nunn expressed the belief that Greenlee was an innovative owner who would have contributed a great deal to the Negro Leagues going forward; rejecting him indicated that the all the Negro League owners "won't see the light. Some just can't keep pace with the changing trends. Others continue stubbornly in the same old pattern because they're sore with those who so correctly advocated for a change."[378]

As the managing editor of the *Pittsburgh Courier* and a man who had been chairman of the ill-fated East-West Committee, which had "never been permitted to function and the details were handled by the President of the [Negro] American League," Nunn may have had an axe to grind but he also had a respected voice among the press.[379]

Another respected voice of the press, Art Carter, was hired for $1,000 for the season by the NNL at the March 12 special meeting. Carter was asked to do public relations for the league, which included tracking of the club standings and creating good will for the league with the press, something sorely needed.[380] The league did get some positive press immediately for this hiring and for moving "towards other reforms to make the league a more practicable working organization" including a players pool with compensation for third- and second-place clubs, cash prizes to the league's leading pitcher, hitter and "home run clouter," and the forming of a constitution committee to revise the NNL constitution along the lines of the National League constitution, preliminary to applying for recognition from Commissioner Chandler.[381]

The second NNL special meeting was held in Philadelphia on May 6, 1946, right at the start of the NNL season. The primary focus of this meeting was cracking down on players who had been thrown out of a game by an umpire or had struck an umpire as well as players who had abandoned the Negro Leagues for Mexico. The league ruled that players would be fined $100 and suspended 10 days for striking an umpire, and fined escalating amounts of $10, $25, and $50 for first, second, and third ejections from games. The league banned eight players, including future Hall of Famers Ray Dandridge and Raymond Brown, for jumping to Mexico.[382]

The meetings were coming fast and furious this year, so that six weeks after its second special meeting, the NNL met jointly with the NAL on June 19 and then followed with its own meeting on June 20. The NAL had its own league meeting on June 20 as it set its second-half schedule and "were in New York in time to witness the Louis knockout of Billy Conn" the previous night.[383] In the joint meeting, the two leagues not only decided on August 18 as the date for the annual East-West Game in Chicago, but they also agreed on a second East-West Game (sometimes referred to as the Dream Game) to be played in Washington on August 15. There was also discussion of the lack of coverage the two leagues were getting from the *Pittsburgh Courier*. When William Nunn acknowledged the validity of the complaint and promised that the *Courier* would give the NNL more publicity, an order to have Art Carter investigate was dropped.[384] The need to pressure the *Courier* to increase its coverage of Negro League baseball was an ominous sign for the future of the Negro Leagues, as there was an obvious shift toward covering Jackie Robinson, and also John Wright, Roy Partlow, Don Newcombe, and Roy Campanella, all of whom were playing in the minor leagues of White baseball in 1946.

The NNL had still one more special meeting in 1946, this one held in Philadelphia on July 15, in order to organize the second East-West Game in Washington (which had been decided on at the joint meeting). The July 27, 1946, edition of the *Norfolk Journal and Guide* listed players from the six NNL teams that were being considered for selection for the game, including Josh Gibson, Buck Leonard, and Sam Bankhead of the Homestead Grays, Monte Irvin, Leon Day, and Larry Doby of the Newark Eagles, Orestes "Minnie" Miñoso and Silvio Garcia of the New York Cubans, Bill Byrd of the Baltimore Elite Giants, and Gene Benson of the Philadelphia Stars.[385]

This illustrious group of players, including several future Hall of Famers, was an indication of the continuing vitality of the NNL in 1946. Another indication of the quality of the league was the quality of the seven-game Negro World Series won by the NNL pennant winner Newark Eagles over the NAL pennant winner Kansas City Monarchs. That World Series was later characterized by longtime New Jersey sportswriter Jerry Izenberg as "the greatest World Series ever played between the Negro National and American Leagues."[386] The Series was a back and forth struggle, with Kansas City winning games 1, 3, and 5 to take a 3-2 series lead, and the Eagles winning games 6 and 7, the latter a 3-2 win in front of "more than 13,000 vociferous fanatics" at Newark's Ruppert Stadium.[387] The series featured pitchers Satchel Paige and Hilton Smith for the Monarchs and Leon Day for the Eagles (all future Hall of Famers) as well as 1946 NAL batting leader Buck O'Neil and Hall of Famer Monte Irvin in a starring role. Monte swatted three home runs, two of them in the crucial Game 6, and drove in the first run and scored the winning run in Game 7.[388] Author Brian Carroll described the 1946 Negro League as having had a "banner season" but also reported his own content analysis that showed that the *Pittsburgh Courier* and *Chicago Defender*'s coverage of the Negro Leagues "sharply declined in 1946 as Robinson's major league debut approached."[389]

Negro League owners realized that their window of opportunity was closing—and without any concrete encouraging news from Chandler, they arranged a September 26, 1946, meeting between Effa Manley, Alex Pompez, and Curtis Leak and National League attorney Louis Carroll. In the meeting, they asked Carroll about their prospects for recognition by the major leagues. As reported in a document found in Effa Manley's files, Carroll said it was premature to assess, but that the NNL "needed a concrete program and proof that [we] were operating our business along the lines of established business principles." Carroll said that Commissioner Chandler would want to see the new Negro League constitution and Carroll would keep them informed of developments.[390] But 1947 would bring Jackie Robinson to the major leagues—and Wendell Smith, so instrumental in Jackie's signing, opined that although recent seasons had been profitable ones for the Negro Leagues, "the lush days haven't been here long and they won't be here much longer" as he expressed sympathy even for those owners who "aren't wholly in support of this campaign to bring more Negro players into the majors. But we'll forgive them and go along with them because they can't do anything about it anyway."[391]

1947

"As 1947 dawned, most owners, players, fans, and sportswriters had little reason to recognize that an era in Black baseball had ended and the future of the once prosperous institution would soon be in doubt."[392] So said Neil Lanctot in his coverage of the period of baseball integration, combined with the changing postwar world that faced the institution of Black baseball. Lanctot was pointing out that 1946 was also, for the sixth straight year, one of strong attendance figures for the Negro Leagues, so that when the owners of the NAL and NNL convened for their late 1946/early 1947 league meetings, they were not inclined to fully grasp how perilous their future path would be. [393] Nor would Negro League players, who had yet to appear in the White major leagues, or even Black sportswriters, who had long warned the Negro League owners to get their house in order when postwar prosperity and the beginnings of baseball integration converged, be likely to fully realize just how fast the future prospects of the Negro Leagues would decline in 1947.

As was generally the case, the NAL held the first winter meeting on December 26 and 27 in Chicago. In reporting on the meeting, the January 4, 1947, *Chicago Defender* focused on the mundane details of a meeting in which the previous slate of NAL officers was re-elected, the league decided to defer any decision on Abe Saperstein's application to enter the Cincinnati Crescents as a 1947 NAL franchise, W.S. Martin announced that his newly built $250,000 ballpark in Memphis would be ready for the new season, and R.S. Simmons resigned his position as the traveling secretary of the Chicago American Giants. The NAL owners wanted six or eight clubs in the league for 1947 and were also waiting to hear whether teams in Detroit and St. Louis would apply.[394]

The NNL held its first winter meeting on January 5, 1947, in the Hotel Theresa in New York, as it usually did. The major piece of news of this meeting was a change in leadership—the league elected John H. Johnson, a pastor and police chaplain, to succeed Tom Wilson, who was co-president of the Negro League in 1938 and thereafter, had been president for the past eight years, despite numerous attempts, usually involving the Manleys, to unseat him. This time around, the Manleys were again involved in finding an alternative to Wilson—and their efforts to elect someone different were enhanced by Wilson being advised to give up the job by his personal physician for reasons of poor health.[395]

Several challengers to Wilson's presidency were discussed. In addition to Johnson, they included Judge William C. Hueston, who had been president of the first NNL from 1927 through 1931 and had been a candidate for Negro Leagues commissioner in 1945; sportswriter and 1946 NNL publicity agent Art Carter; Frank Forbes, formerly business manager of the 1935 New York Cubans among other positions in Black baseball and currently a judge on the New York State Athletic Commission; Samuel Battle, last year's challenger to Wilson's throne; and a Harlem lawyer named John Doles. That Johnson was the "handpicked candidate" of the Manleys influenced his being chosen to successfully run against Wilson.[396]

Johnson's victory was generally welcomed by the press, not only because it meant that the NNL had finally picked a non-owner to head their operations, but also for the actions he promised to work for that would ostensibly strengthen the league. In his "The Sports Beat" column of January 11, 1947, Wendell Smith welcomed the new president, seeing him as a "righteous man … a non-owner … who will not be vulnerable to charges of favoritism and gerrymandering. … [H]is hands are clean and he will make decisions as he sees fit."[397] Johnson addressed the need for the league to "get its house in order," for quite some time a favorite exhortation to the league from various members of the Black press, and specifically develop a balanced schedule of league games, and redraw the league's constitution with an eye toward gaining recognition from White baseball.[398] Although Dan Burley saw Johnson as a "conservative choice" with limited prior connections to baseball, Effa Manley believed that Johnson's election "will also give the lie to hints that we don't want Negroes to go to the major leagues because our new commissioner was one of the most forceful fighters on former Mayor LaGuardia's committee [on baseball]. … [W]e want them to go in an organized fashion and not be virtually "kidnaped" (sic)."[399]

In his 'Confidentially Yours' column of January 11, 1947, Burley did cynically suggest that the NNL owners hiring Pastor Johnson was "a long step forward in eliminating the practice of cussing out loud at their powwows, especially when splitting up the money is the main agenda at such gatherings." More seriously, Burley asked a crucial question: "Will the hard-headed club owners give Johnson all the authority he demands, and will they abide by his decisions?" Burley was doubtful that the owners would cede control to Johnson, given their failure to follow the rulings of Commissioner Ferdinand Morton, the last independent ruler of Black baseball back in the early years of the second NNL.[400]

There was no doubt that Johnson, as pastor of St. Thomas Episcopal Church in Harlem, a chaplain of the New York City Police Department as well as a former member of Mayor LaGuardia's well-respected Committee on Unity (which has since been credited by many researchers as being influential in the process of baseball integration) had the potential to earn respect while introducing needed reforms. The real question was whether Johnson could create sufficient change in league practices to fully replace what the *Pittsburgh Courier* once called "the loose-leaf organizational structure of the two leagues" which enabled Branch Rickey to sign Jackie Robinson and eschew compensation to the NAL's Monarchs because he deemed the two leagues as "in effect … not actually organized."[401] The jury was out, and it was worth noting that the NAL still had J.B. Martin, owner of the Chicago American Giants, as its president, and the two leagues still had not chosen an independent commissioner to oversee their joint operations.

In 1947 the two leagues chose to have their first joint meeting on February 24 and 25, this time in Chicago, NAL territory, at the Appomattox Hotel on the 24th and the Hotel Grand on the 25th.[402] The realities facing the two leagues seemed to be leading them to more and earlier joint sessions in which a mutual decision process was vital. Each league was also holding its own session in Chicago, although these were to be primarily for arranging their first-half schedules.[403]

In the joint sessions, returning NAL President Martin acted as chairman, which was not surprising given that the NNL had a new leader in Johnson. The leagues decided to more closely coordinate their respective schedules, starting their season on the first Sunday in May and ending it on September 15, and playing the same number of games in each circuit.[404] The March 1, 1947, *New York Times*, reporting on this joint meeting, added that the two leagues were planning on adopting the major-league model of playing all World Series games in the two home cities of the competing teams, departing from their typical practice of playing in several league cities. They also mentioned the banning for five years of several players who had jumped to the Mexican League including the Philadelphia Stars' star second baseman Marvin "Tex" Williams and the infamous Ted "Double Duty" Radcliffe.[405] The *Atlanta Daily World*'s reporting of the same meeting was especially focused on Radcliffe, who was "seen in the lobby of the hotel" with his younger brother and fellow Negro Leaguer Alex. "Double Duty" was described as being known by the owners as the "Peck's bad boy" of Negro League baseball, and he "felt the wrath" of the NNL and NAL owners as they banned him from playing any league or nonleague club in league games or in exhibitions.[406]

In the individual league meetings, the NAL admitted two new franchises, the Detroit Senators and the perennially-wandering St. Louis Stars, while denying Abe Saperstein a franchise for his Cincinnati Crescents. Employing a bit of hyperbole, the *Cleveland Call and Post* described the NAL meeting as "a sensational history making session" with the adding of two teams along with upholding the 1946 ban on ballplayers who jumped to Latin American countries, demonstrating that the NAL "has a planned program for maintaining its high standards among the nation's top-notch baseball leagues." The *Call and Post* also described an "elegant plea" by Saperstein for a Cincinnati franchise that would play at the Cincinnati Reds ballpark, Crosley Field. Despite the "impressive style" of Saperstein's presentation, the NAL decided that St. Louis had more advantages.[407] In contrast, the *Atlanta Daily World* must have been singularly unimpressed with Saperstein's pitch or have missed it entirely, as it reported that Saperstein missed the meeting.[408]

The NNL meeting, naturally presided over by new President Johnson, centered upon the adoption of a new constitution and bylaws using those of the International League as a model.[409] The NNL also declared that the Black Yankees would play at Yankee Stadium when at home, that the Cubans would play at the Polo Grounds, and that the Newark Eagles would play some games at Ebbets Field.[410]

One could conclude that, as the 1947 season commenced, both the NNL and the NAL were in their own way attempting to legitimize their operations, the NNL with more formalized methods of operations and tighter bonds with major-league owners through their park operations, the NAL with an expanded league and the enforcement of discipline on jumping players that may have been modeled after the five-year ban instituted by Chandler against major-league players who had jumped to Mexico. They were also continuing to work together to mimic major-league operations with an eye toward getting formal recognition by Chandler, as Effa Manley believed they would get more money from major-league owners for their Black players if they were recognized as part of major-league operations, and without such significant compensation, they would have a very bleak future.[411]

The 1947 Negro League season was played against the backdrop of Jackie Robinson debuting as the first African American major leaguer of the twentieth century, with Larry Doby soon following as the first American League player of color. Staying in the limelight, even in the eyes of Black America, would prove to be quite a challenge. In his "The Sports Beat" column of June 14, 1947, Wendell Smith reported that the Negro Leagues were experiencing "a definite decline in interest and probably at the turnstiles, too." He blamed the "moguls of the Negro American and Negro National League" for not sending their standings to the Black press with regularity and generally not keeping the Black public informed of their doings, claiming that the owners were "dodging the issue" by saying that Jackie Robinson's advance to the majors had destroyed their former prosperity.[412] But Smith was also dodging the issue as he failed to acknowledge that the *Courier* and other Black newspapers were no longer giving comprehensive coverage to the Negro Leagues.[413]

There was at least some recognition by Negro League owners that they needed to curry favor with the Black press, as the second joint NNL/NAL meeting of 1947, which was held June 10 and 11 in New York, included a banquet at Small's Paradise, a venerable New York Black nightclub, with the Black sportswriters as guests of honor. Although J.D. Martin ended up being the keynote speaker, the two leagues attempted to get Branch Rickey to attend and accept an award for breaking the color barrier with the signing of Jackie Robinson. That Martin's speech spoke of Black baseball's full support for integration did not negate the missed opportunity to "score a public relations coup" that Rickey's presence and participation would have engendered.[414]

The joint meeting included the usual determination of the date of the East-West All-Star Game, which would be held on July 27, and the planning of each league's second-half schedule. In addition, the leagues announced that Ray Brown of the Homestead Grays and Gready McKinnis of the Chicago American Giants were being reinstated after previously being banned for not returning from Mexico before a set deadline date. Earlier, NNL President Johnson had temporarily banned Claro Duany, a Cuban who had played in Mexico in 1946, but Cubans owner Pompez protested that ban, saying Duany had been released by the Cubans and had not jumped to Mexico. Banning Duany was an indication that Johnson was meting out appropriate discipline, thereby keeping them in line with major-league rulings by Chandler. But at the joint meeting, Duany was also reinstated. Whatever the merits of each case, rescinding the bans indicated that the leagues needed returning players desperately, as owners like Pompez pressured the leagues to reinstate their players so they could compete successfully for postseason berths and draw fans who came out to see the star players on Negro League rosters.[415]

Two other issues raised at the June 10 and 11 joint meetings showed the spreading cracks in the façade of the Negro League operations. Manager Homer Curry of the Philadelphia Stars appeared as a spokesperson for a player committee to create a pension plan for retired Negro League players. According to the *Norfolk Journal and Guide*, the owners first expressed interest but then determined that the financial outlay of $75,000 to $100,000 made it too expensive for them. Also, the two leagues decided to eliminate free passes for visiting players because it reduced the owners' profit margin.[416]

The season concluded with a bang—and several whimpers. The New York Cubans won their first league pennant, and dispatched the 1945 World Series winner the Cleveland Buckeyes in five games. An exciting series saw the Cubans lose the first game at home in New York and then win four straight games on the road—but those road games were played in Philadelphia and Chicago before the series finale in Cleveland, contrary to the declaration at the February joint meetings that all World Series games would be played in the home cities of the competing teams, as the Negro

Leagues reverted to the traveling cities model they had previously used to reach enough fans. The first two games drew decent crowds of 5,500 for a rained-out game at the Polo Grounds and 9,000 for a game at Yankee Stadium, but the rest were sparsely attended.[417]

Financially, the solid gains that the Negro Leagues had made in solvency over the past six years were largely wiped away in one year. According to Lanctot, "the overall attendance decline in Black baseball during 1947 was startling" even though the leagues still drew from a core of loyal fans despite competition from the major leagues.[418] While author Carroll, in his exposition focused on the role of the Black press in baseball integration, stated that only two teams, the World Series contestants Cleveland Buckeyes and New York Cubans, made money in 1947, evidence suggests that the Cubans actually lost money, with Pompez claiming to have lost $20,000.[419]

Before beginning what would turn out to be the final season of the Negro National League in 1948, the Negro Leagues were beset with two essential truths. The first, as expressed by Joseph Pierce in his 1947 tome *Negro Business and Business Education*, was what he described as a Negro businessman's dilemma—"he disapproves of racial segregation but as a business man has a vested interest in segregation because it creates a convenient market for his goods and services."[420] This dilemma captures the essence of the apparent unwillingness of Negro League owners to prepare for the eventuality of integration as well as their slow and inconsistent response to its early stages—they did not want to give up the captive audience they had as a result of White baseball's institutional racism.

The second truth, which was devastating to their future prospects, was expressed by Neil Lanctot as a summary of 1947: "[T]he year also exposed the essential weaknesses of Black business when subjected to outside competition."[421] The competition from the major leagues was not going to recede, and even though the rest of the teams (besides the three who brought Black players to the major leagues in 1947) would do so with "deliberate speed," the audience for Negro League baseball would, for the most part, never return.

1948

The Negro Leagues did indeed survive 1947 intact. The year had been wildly successful for Jackie Robinson in the major leagues, as he won the Rookie of the Year Award and competed—and starred—in a losing World Series effort, but the other four Black players who made their major-league debuts in 1947—Dan Bankhead for the Dodgers, Larry Doby for the Indians, and Willard Brown and Hank Thompson for the St. Louis Browns—had very little success. There was every reason to expect more debuts of Black major leaguers in 1948—at least, for the Dodgers and the Indians (the Browns could easily describe their first integration efforts as a fiasco)—but the other major-league organizations were still rather hesitant to move forward and sign Black players. Horace Stoneham, for one, had told *The Sporting News* in early 1948 that he had yet to find a Black player to "fit in our plans."[422] At the end of the 1947 season, the Negro League owners and officials still had high hopes that they would be incorporated into the system of White baseball, and that they would become a well-paid conduit for Black talent to the major leagues. They could also anticipate that the process of baseball integration would be slow to develop, meaning that the Negro Leagues would not lose their most talented players precipitously, and they would have time to develop more young, outstanding Black players to first star on their teams before they were sold to White organizations.

Before the Negro Leagues held their annual year-end winter meetings, the National Association of Professional Baseball Leagues, the organization that governed minor-league baseball, held its three-day convention from December 3 through 5 in Miami. On the eve of the three-day meeting, George Trautman, entering his second year as president of the minor leagues after succeeding William Bramham at the end of 1946, announced that he saw no need for further expansion of the minor leagues, saying that "our main job is not to seek additional leagues but to strengthen all our existing leagues."[423] During the three days, the minor leagues dealt with business items such as guaranteeing a minimum salary for umpires and also discussed a resolution by the Pacific Coast League to become a third major league.[424] What the various newspapers reporting on the National Association convention did not report for some time was the decision by an executive committee of the National Association made during the Miami convention to turn down a written application of the two Negro Leagues to join White baseball. A letter written on December 17,

1947, to NNL President Johnson and NAL President Martin said that "the committee was of the opinion that it would be impossible to do anything with these applications at this time."[425] The main obstacle was territorial rights in that Negro League clubs played in major- and minor-league parks in the same territories played in by those major- and minor-league teams.[426]

In examining the actions taken by both Negro Leagues in their initial winter meetings prior to the 1948 season, knowing that the leagues now knew that their hopes of affiliating with White baseball had been dashed informs the actions that they took to desperately shore up the foundation of their now sinking ship, though they were not yet ready to publicly acknowledge the devastating news.

As always, the NAL held the first winter meeting, on December 29 in Chicago. Unlike the meetings of previous years, which were usually held at hotels, this one was held at 910 Michigan Avenue, Room 612. The January 3, 1948, *Chicago Defender* reported that, along with re-electing 1947's NAL officers, there was discussion about possible player trades, Chicago city tax increases, and rises in hotel and restaurant prices.[427] Were rising costs, 1947 financial losses, and most recently the National Association's denial of affiliation for the Negro Leagues with White baseball leading league magnates to economize on their meeting space?

What was not speculative was that an uncertain economic future led to a decision to turn down applications for new franchises in New Orleans and Nashville in favor of staying with six clubs, as the owners were "not caring to venture out too far in 1948 as the season looked uncertain for such a move."[428] Economics were also responsible for the NAL passing a $6,000 club salary cap for the 1948 season.

The NAL announced several managerial changes for the new season, including Buck O'Neil replacing Frank Duncan as manager of the Kansas City Monarchs, Lorenzo "Piper" Davis taking over the managerial duties of the Birmingham Black Barons from Tommy Sampson, and Quincy Trouppe, after being sold by the Cleveland Buckeyes to the Chicago American Giants, leaving Cleveland's manager post to Alonzo Boone and taking over the position in Chicago.[429] And President J.B. Martin announced that the team he owned, the Chicago American Giants, was accusing the San Diego Padres of the Pacific Coast League of tampering with the 1947 NAL batting leader—catcher John Ritchey—by signing him to a 1948 contract, while simultaneously owner J.L. Wilkinson repeated his now more than two-year-old accusation regarding Rickey violating the Monarchs' contractual rights to Jackie Robinson. Unfortunately, Martin's charge was investigated and quickly found to be invalid by Commissioner Chandler, because Chicago could not produce a 1947 contract for Ritchey, further underscoring the similar circumstance of Robinson not having a written contract.

Martin was clearly embarrassed, claiming that all the other American Giants were signed, and it was simply a "costly oversight" that defeated his claim.[430] Luckily for Martin, the Padres decided to honor the nonexistent contract and pay a "satisfactory sum" to the Giants for Ritchey, but Wendell Smith commented that the dubious claim of tampering underscored that Negro League operations were still "slipshod" long after Robinson was signed without compensation.[431]

The NNL held its first winter meeting on January 19, 1948, in New York at its usual haunt, the Hotel Theresa. The league joined the NAL in creating a $6,000 per team salary limit, as it was responding to its own economic straits along with the problems it shared with the NAL.[432] In particular, Dan Topping, who succeeded Larry MacPhail as owner and front man of the New York Yankees, had recently released attendance figures showing that attendance at Negro National League games at Yankee Stadium had dropped to over 63,000 patrons in 1947 from in excess of 155,000 in 1946—and Dan Burley estimated that such Yankee Stadium contests in 1945 drew over 200,000 fans. Burley's conclusion—"when Robinson went into big league baseball he took the Negro attendance at all-Negro contests with him."[433]

In addition to saving money through team salary limits, the NNL saw the potential of economic gain in selling younger players that they developed to the major and minor leagues, mentioning as an example the $15,000 that Bill Veeck paid the Newark Eagles for Larry Doby.[434] One could argue, however, that the recent failed attempt to gain recognition from the National Association, combined with the disastrous attempt by the NAL to challenge the major leagues on the Ritchey and Robinson signings, cast doubt that the Veeck signing of Doby would be a successful model for future sales of Black players to White baseball. In addition, Effa Manley's success in selling Doby to Veeck in 1947 was a marked contrast to her failure to get Rickey to pay her for the Dodgers signing Newark Eagles pitcher Don Newcombe in 1946, and their failed attempt to sign star infielder-outfielder Monte Irvin without compensating the Eagles in 1948—and the Newark Eagles did have all of their players signed to written contracts at least since the early 1940s.[435]

Otherwise, the NNL decided to continue to ban players who had jumped to Mexico (despite the exceptions it made for Brown, McKinnis, and Duany in 1947) as the Homestead Grays failed to persuade the other owners to overturn it. The league re-elected its 1947 officers, which meant that the owners were reasonably satisfied with the efforts made by Johnson in his first term as NNL president. The league also entertained the possibility of expanding to eight teams, but for the time being it passed on the application of the Richmond Giants, as it could not convince the Asheville, North Carolina, Blues to apply and was not interested in having seven teams.[436]

In his commentary on the January 19 meeting, Dan Burley revealed the previously unreported failure of the two leagues to affiliate with White baseball. Burley published two columns in the January 24, 1948, *New York Amsterdam News*. His "Confidentially Yours" column, which was more of a notes column, expressed his opinions of the important decisions the league had made and added that "the meeting featured little else but re-electing all officials and some discussions they didn't want made public," while his news column was the first published account to report the rejection of the affiliation application, which could well have been one discussion the NNL was trying to keep private for the time being.[437]

It was not until February 23, 1948, that NNL President John Johnson expressed the anguish of his league over its rejection by the National Association. That day, he released a statement outlining the tangled history of two years of failed promises and dashed hopes for the Negro Leagues. Johnson had been a member of the subcommittee on baseball integration that was part of New York Mayor Fiorello LaGuardia's Committee on Unity, when in mid-September 1945, fellow committee member and Yankees owner Larry MacPhail submitted his own written statement regarding "The Negro in Baseball." MacPhail's statement that he would support admitting the Negro Leagues to White baseball "IF and when the Negro leagues put their house in order—establish themselves on a sound and ethical operations basis—and conform to the standards of White baseball" was now cited in Johnson's statement of February 23 as the basis for a two-year process of attempting to conform to MacPhail's—and later Commissioner Chandler's—requirements.

Johnson stated that the Negro leagues had taken the active steps of formulating a new constitution and adopting uniform contracts, yet "in spite of improved organization, when these two Negro leagues made formal application for admission to organized baseball. … They were turned down cold. … Two years after MacPhail's recommendations were made, the Negro leagues still possess no status, no voice, no rights, no relationship at all to the major or minor leagues."[438] Johnson praised Rickey's signing of Robinson as a contribution to solving the "question of the Negro in baseball," in sharp contrast to the inaction of White baseball to the fulfillment of MacPhail's recommendations. The result, according to Johnson, was that the Negro Leagues were currently in a "precarious situation" after the "well-nigh disastrous season" of 1947.[439]

At this point, it hardly mattered who the real villain was—MacPhail for suggesting a false pathway to major-league recognition in September 1945; Chandler for reinforcing that possibility in a meeting with the NNL and NAL presidents on January 17, 1946; National League attorney Louis Carroll for suggesting that there was still some purpose to continuing to apply for recognition when he met with NNL officials on September 26, 1946; or Branch Rickey for setting the precedent for denying that the Negro Leagues were sufficiently organized to deserve compensation when he signed Jackie Robinson on October 23, 1945.[440] The two Negro Leagues now knew that they had no future as a part of the White baseball establishment—they would have to find their own way to survive.

The NAL and the NNL continued to meet and (later on) compete—separately and jointly—throughout 1948. The NAL quietly held its schedule meeting in Chicago back at the Hotel Grand on February 21 and 22. The most important news had already been announced prior to the meeting—that J.L. Wilkinson had sold his half-interest in the Kansas

City Monarchs to co-owner Tom Baird due to his failing eyesight.[441]

The NNL had its next meeting at the end of February or the beginning of March. There was inconclusive discussion of adding two more teams, now including a possible Brooklyn franchise along with earlier applicant Richmond, and temporary approval of Jim Semler's proposal to move his New York Black Yankees to Rochester, New York, leaving New York City venues to Alex Pompez's New York Cubans. In addition, the league promised to consider a proposal to create an interlocking schedule with the Negro American League, which would mean that interleague games would be formally included in each other's league schedules and count in their respective league standings.[442] As was frequently the case when new league proposals were considered, neither proposal ever materialized.[443] The NNL reconvened in New York on March 14 and 15 to finalize its first-half schedule.

The two leagues had their annual midseason joint meeting on June 23 and 24 in New York, preceded by an NNL gathering on the morning of the 23rd. They announced their annual East-West all-star contest would be held in Chicago on August 22, followed by the third (and last) Eastern All-Star Dream Game in Yankee Stadium on August 24. Other declared actions prior to the meeting were the lifting of a ban against the Negro American Association because they stopped exploring the possibility of a franchise in Baltimore, which would infringe on the territorial rights of the NNL's Baltimore Elite Giants, and retaining a 10-day suspension against Thomas Butts, shortstop for those same Giants, for striking an umpire.

The leagues now rejected the interlocking schedule, the possibility of including interleague contests within each league's standings, because they could not work out the extensive bus travel required to include such contests in a regular slate of games. They also met with a representative of the Caribbean Federation of Leagues, who wanted an accord with the Negro Leagues on banning ineligible players as an adjunct to their being given "special classification by the National Association"—since the Negro Leagues had a "tacit understanding with organized baseball to conform with its law and regulations and therefore wanted to be in harmony with them."[444] It certainly seemed that everyone—the Mexican League, the Caribbean Federation, even the Pacific Coast League—had a better chance of getting what they wanted from White baseball than did the Negro Leagues.[445]

The 1948 season culminated in a five-game triumph by the Homestead Grays, still featuring first baseman Buck Leonard, in his 16th of 18 successive seasons playing for Homestead, over the Birmingham Black Barons, for whom 17-year-old Willie Mays drove in the winning run in their only triumph. Two of the all-time great Negro League teams contesting the Negro League Fall Classic with an all-time-great ballplayer and several other top-notch talents still drew limited attention from the Black press. Though newspapers including the *Baltimore Afro-American*, *Pittsburgh Courier*, and *Chicago Defender* did run some stories on the Grays-Black Barons series, they did not run box scores and paid a great deal more attention to the Cleveland Indians, featuring Larry Doby and Satchel Paige, triumphing over the Boston Braves in the 1948 major-league World Series.[446]

The season was not without its highlights, but it was also replete with failures and indignities. Starting with the February 1948 announcement by NNL President Johnson of the denial of major-league affiliation, the Negro Leagues were simultaneously dealing with Jackie Robinson telling a reporter that "Negro baseball needs a housecleaning from bottom to top," followed by an article written by Robinson appearing in the June 1948 issue of Ebony magazine entitled "What's Wrong with Negro Baseball?" in which Robinson "outlined the unpleasant lifestyle in Black baseball" along with the questionable business dealings of Negro Leagues owners. Newark Eagles owner Effa Manley pushed back very forcefully against Robinson's charges, suggesting that he was "ungrateful" and did not comprehend how much had been sacrificed by the operators of Black baseball. But the damage had been done—arguably, Manley only succeeded in widening the distance between those who were working toward integration and the owners of a declining Black baseball institution just trying to survive.[447]

Attendance continued to drop significantly in 1948, limited only by how far it had previously fallen in 1947 from its peak years from 1941 through 1946. The 1948 East-West Game held on August 22 still drew more than 42,000 fans, but the Dream Game at Yankee Stadium held two days later drew fewer than 18,000 fans, far fewer than the expected crowd of 40,000 reported in the August 21, 1948, *New York Amsterdam News*.[448]

By September 1948 the shoes were beginning to drop. First, the New York Black Yankees "discontinued league activities in late August."[449] Next, Homestead Grays owner Rufus Jackson lamented that "something must be done. We are experiencing our worst season in years and I don't know what the solution is."[450] On September 9, five days before the opening game of the Negro World Series, Effa Manley held a press conference at which she announced that the Newark Eagles were for sale. While she negotiated with various buyers, the future of the Grays also appeared in doubt, even as they were winning the Negro World Series.[451] Effa Manley "said that more than $100,000 had gone through her fingers the past three years" while Jackson's books had recorded losses of $35,000 in 1947 and another $10,000 in 1948, for a total of $45,000.[452]

While Rome was burning, NAL President J.B. Martin declared that Negro baseball had not been hurt by the advancement of Black players to the major leagues, and that the "million-dollar business" of "our baseball" was "here to stay." While he acknowledged vaguely that "Negro baseball has become a paramount issue," he evinced the belief that "since we can now furnish players for the majors, we are now stronger, especially financially. Martin's pronouncements were reported in the November 24, 1948, *Atlanta Daily World* and it is important to note that he did not mention the NNL in his reassurances of the future viability of "our baseball."[453]

The final disposition of the Negro National League was determined in a special two-day joint meeting held in Chicago on November 29 and 30, 1948. The facts were that at the meeting, the New York Black Yankees, the now-Washington Homestead Grays, and the Newark Eagles formally dropped out of the Negro National League, while the other three 1948 NNL clubs, the Philadelphia Stars, the Baltimore Elite Giants, and the New York Cubans, along with the new Houston club, purchased from the Manleys and transplanted from Newark, were added to the NAL to form one 10-team circuit.[454]

A survey of the headlines of some of the leading Black newspapers revealed somewhat different perspectives on the ending of a 16-year run by the second Negro National League and the early prospects for a successful 1949. The *Cleveland Call and Post* headline was the most positive: "Negro Baseball Leagues Merge Into Ten-Team Circuit."[455] There was no mention of disbanding teams, rather a merger of forces. The *Chicago Defender* and the *Baltimore Afro-American* were balanced, each including a reference to one or more teams quitting but also indicating a future entity: "2 More Teams Quit Baseball, Keep Single Loop" headlined the *Defender* piece, while "Grays Quit League; New Circuit Formed" was the headline in the Afro-American.[456]

The *Pittsburgh Courier* headline only spoke of failure—"National Circuit Folds Up." In evocative and telling language, the *Courier* article describing the demise of the longest-lasting league in Negro League history started as follows:

"Like a ship without a rudder, Negro baseball was drifting wildly in a deep sea of utter confusion this week as owners of teams in the Negro National and American Leagues met here in a joint meeting designed to save the battered hull of what was once a profitable financial vessel."[457]

According to Negro League historian John Holway, the great Rube Foster, having brought together owners of top Black clubs of the Midwest on Friday, February 13, 1920, and convinced them of the need to organize into a Negro National League, told them "We are the ship … all else the sea."[458] Twenty-eight years later, the leading Black newspaper in America described a now leaky vessel with one of its two engines no longer working. But the surviving Negro American League would not breathe its last breath until 1962.

PART 4: THE SURVIVING NAL —THE END OF THE NEGRO LEAGUES (1949–1962)

THE LAST YEARS OF THE NEGRO AMERICAN LEAGUE

"Some one (sic) … has to make the public realize that Negro baseball must go on. It is horrible to think that just because four Negroes are accepted into the major leagues, Negro baseball is doomed. If that happens, no less than 400 young men will lose their jobs as players in our league. We can't let that happen."[459]

So stated Effa Manley, the "One-Woman Riot" of Negro baseball, in her newly self-defined role as the unofficial ambassador of Black baseball, now that she was no longer a Negro League owner.[460] Outspoken to the end, Effa Manley would now operate from the sidelines as the Negro American League operated in an environment of declining interest from the Black press and the Black fan base as they attempted to put a competitive product on the field and remain financially viable. Manley was not wrong that abandoning Black baseball was premature given the preliminary steps that major-league baseball had taken to incorporate Black athletes into their system. Only Jackie Robinson, Roy Campanella, the ageless Satchel Paige, and Larry Doby, the four Black players she referenced, had established themselves in the major leagues by the end of 1948. In its new one-league format with 10 teams competing, it was an exaggeration to claim that 400 players still would make their livelihood from Negro American League baseball in 1949, but about half of that—200 or more—was certainly accurate.[461] The Negro American League owners therefore trudged onward, fulfilling the obligation Effa Manley outlined and continuing to provide a showcase for the skills of many Black ballplayers as the development of an operating pipeline to the major leagues for the best of these individuals continued.

This article's final part will provide a brief summary of the basic operations and the slow yet relatively steady decline of the NAL, the final remaining Negro major league. The league continued to exist in some form through the 1962 season—starting with 10 teams in 1949 and ending up with but three in 1962. The NAL continued to have one or two winter meetings every year until the 1962 season, and usually had a midseason meeting to schedule games for the season's second half. These meetings tended to be limited to basic operations such as working out the schedule, planning for the annual East-West Game, and especially trying to maintain the number of teams in the league from season to season. On August 26, 1962, when the last of 30 East-West All-Star Games was played, not in Chicago, but in Kansas City, the Negro Leagues had essentially staged their last contest.[462]

1949

As noted earlier, the first winter meeting of 1949 was on November 29 and 30, 1948, an earlier date than usual, occasioned by the NNL's dissolution. When the NAL reconvened on February 7 and 8, 1949, at 910 Michigan Avenue, Room 612, the same location as its December 29, 1947, meeting, the league was primarily concerned with establishing the framework for its new operations.[463] The recorded minutes of this meeting noted that "by common consent, it was agreed that there be an East and West Division and the standing be carried separately" but did not actually specify the teams that would play in each division.[464] Since the league approved the moving of owner Ernest Wright's Cleveland Buckeyes to Louisville and was also adding the Houston Eagles to replace the Newark Eagles while dropping the Homestead Grays and the New York Black Yankees from the former NNL, the Indianapolis Clowns were now placed in the East so that each division would have five teams.[465] The East Division included the Baltimore Elite Giants, New York Cubans, Philadelphia Stars, Indianapolis Clowns, and the Louisville Buckeyes, while the West Division had the Chicago American Giants, Memphis Red Sox, Kansas City Monarchs, Birmingham Black Barons, and Houston Eagles.[466]

Naturally, the one-league, two-division setup did not eliminate ownership battles. The February meeting discussed but did not resolve an ownership dispute among the three Martin brothers, NAL President J.B., who in addition to owning the Chicago American Giants had a partial ownership stake in the Memphis Red Sox and his brothers W.S. and B.B. Martin. J.B. wanted to relinquish his rights in the Memphis club equally to his brothers, who were arguing over their resulting share percentages of the team.[467]

At the midseason scheduling meeting, held at the same location as the February meeting on June 22 and 23, 1949, the discussed ownership battle was between new Houston owner Doctor Young and New York Cubans owner Alex Pompez over the rights to Negro League star Ray Dandridge. In this instance, the dispute was resolved with Pompez giving Young $750 for Dandridge.[468] Otherwise, the NAL discussed the process of player selection for the 1949 East-West contest, to be held on August 14, 1949 at the usual venue, Chicago's Comiskey Park, while deciding not to continue the Eastern Dream Game, which had been held for the past three years.[469]

At year's end, the Kansas City Monarchs swept a four-game Negro World Series from the Baltimore Elite Giants. The Giants won both halves of the East Division's split season; the Monarchs won the West Division's first half, but the second-half-winning Chicago American Giants forfeited a playoff series, leaving Kansas City as the West's contestant in this last Negro League fall classic.[470] Not only did Chicago and Kansas City not play each other for the West Division pennant in 1949, but the West Division did not publish their standings.[471] It was not an especially good harbinger for 1950 and beyond.

1950–1955

The first half of the 1950s saw the Negro American League start with its full 1949 complement of 10 teams in two divisions, East and West, at the beginning of 1950. By the end of 1950, the East Division had one team, the Cleveland Buckeyes, drop out after playing only two games and two others, the New York Cubans and the Philadelphia Stars, play shortened schedules.[472] The 1951 season saw the league deciding to form four-team East and West divisions, with Cleveland not returning and the New York Cubans also being dropped from the league.[473] It was not surprising that by 1952, the league had further consolidated into one six-team division; by 1953 it was down to four teams. In 1954, the league added two teams, Detroit and Louisville, but by 1955 the NAL was again a four-team outfit, where it would essentially remain through the end of the decade.[474]

Prior to the first scheduled meeting on January 14 and 15, 1950, owner Tom Hayes of the Birmingham Black Barons suggested that the NAL "confine its operations to the Deep South," primarily playing in cities like Atlanta, Memphis, New Orleans, and Birmingham, and thereby "seek refuge and security behind the jim crow curtain of the Deep South."[475] As the January 5, 1950, *Atlanta Daily World* put it, the "owners will grapple with the problem of completely surrendering the Eastern section of the United States to major league baseball or finding a way to lure customers through the turnstiles to see their teams play."[476]

The league ended up postponing this meeting to February 7 and 8, by which time the "Southern strategy" was no longer being considered, other than continuing to play in Memphis, Birmingham, and Houston, as the other Northern teams were still a part of the league. Wendell Smith, in his "Sports Beat" column of February 18, 1950, described the NAL as "on the ropes and ready for the killing," while in contrast, the owners at the meeting were expressing optimism that their "roughest days" were in the past, and, as the headline to the *Pittsburgh Courier*'s February 18 piece suggested, 1950 would be their best season since 1945.[477] By the time of the NAL's midseason schedule meeting, it was clear that the league still had a "serious problem of making the turnstiles click more often," and according to the June 24, 1950, *Norfolk Journal and Guide*, "the league was ready to call it quits but J.B. Martin … persuaded the owners to carry on."[478]

It never really got any better after that. As year by year the number of teams declined, ownership of the remaining teams continually changed hands. For example, in 1951 J.B. Martin, while continuing on as NAL president, announced at the January 3 and 4 winter meeting held in Chicago (where almost all NAL meetings were now held) that he had sold the Chicago American Giants to former Giants manager Winfield Welch for $50,000.[479] Then, at the midseason meeting held on June 14 and 15, the league announced (but ultimately did not succeed in) the selling of the Baltimore Elite Giants to William S. Bridgforth of Nashville from Henryene Green, the widow of Bill Green, who in turn had acquired the team after longtime NNL President Tom Wilson died in 1947.[480] According to Cal Jacox's column in the May 17, 1951, *Norfolk Journal and Guide*, "Today, the Negro American League is concentrated solely on developing future talent for the majors and the minors."[481] And, it would seem, trying to avoid a total failure of the institution.

At the first meeting of 1952, the Eagles, who had shifted operations to New Orleans from Houston in 1951, withdrew from the NAL.[482] With only six teams remaining and down to one division, Birmingham Black Barons owner Tom Hayes, one of those promoting a Southern-based NAL in 1950, said at the league meeting that things were "up in the air" as he expressed doubts about the league's future.[483] Hayes had tried to sell the franchise at the end of 1951, and though he continued to own the team in 1952, he brought in William Bridgforth, who had supposedly bought the now-disbanded Baltimore team to move it to Nashville but would instead be "affiliated" with the Barons.[484]

Tom Hayes, Black Barons' Owner Sees Dim Future For Negro Loop

— *Atlanta Daily World,* January 10, 1952

By 1953, the league was down to four teams—longtime members the Kansas City Monarchs, Birmingham

Black Barons, and Memphis Red Sox, and the Indianapolis Clowns, who became NAL members in 1944 for the first time after overcoming the opposition of primarily NNL owners to their extensive clowning and presenting of racial stereotypes. The league postponed its first meeting in December, with several owners unable to attend, but President J.B. Martin, in announcing that the meeting would be held in February, proclaimed, "I do believe that 1953 will be the best year the Negro American League has had in many years."[485] While Martin maintained a show of optimism, the Black press covered the NAL less and less. This researcher could not find any reports of a midseason meeting, and although press coverage continued, many of the articles were shorter and less detailed about league operations.

In 1954, hope sprang anew as the NAL, "anticipating a boom in Negro baseball interest this year," admitted Detroit and Louisville as the fifth and sixth league members at its February meeting.[486] Rumors were afoot, however, that the Kansas City Monarchs, a member of the original Negro National League of 1920 and thereafter a steady presence in the successor leagues, would leave the NAL and go independent.[487] Though sources conflict about whether Kansas City stayed in the league, merely considering leaving it was an ominous sign for the future.

Whether or not Louisville and Kansas City participated in the 1954 NAL, the Indianapolis Clowns and the Louisville club (called the Buckeyes back in 1949 but later referenced in the media without a club name) dropped out of the NAL at the 1955 winter meeting.[488] The big announcement of this meeting was the relocation of the annual East-West Game to Kansas City after 22 successive—and generally successful—years at Chicago's Comiskey Park. Monarchs owner Tom Baird had been reportedly seeking the transfer of venue for the past four years, as attendance at the annual classic had dropped from above 50,000 at its peak during World War II to around 10,000 in 1954.[489] In a rare Milwaukee midseason meeting, the league reversed its earlier vote at the behest of NAL President Martin and decided to keep the game in Chicago.[490]

According to Neil Lanctot, by the end of the 1955 season the league was truly in trouble. The Monarchs suffered their worst season now that they were competing with the newly relocated Kansas City Athletics for fans, as owner Tom Baird stated that the Athletics had "cut our … crowd over 2/3."[491] By the beginning of 1956, Baird sold off most of his players to major- and minor-league teams, and the remainder of his team to Ted Rasberry, a man who became heavily involved in the very final years of NAL operations. As Rasberry would primarily operate out of Michigan with rare dates in Kansas City, the cornerstone franchise of the NAL was largely gone.[492] But the league would go on.

1956–1959

"Negro baseball, a sport that appears to be wobbling on its last legs, will hold a league meeting in Memphis, Tenn., Feb. 18. The Negro American League confab will be chaired by Dr. J. V. (sic). Martin, president of the four-team loop.

"The NAL was handed a severe jolt recently when it was announced that Tom Baird, owner of the Kansas City Monarchs, had decided not to field a team during the coming season. The departure of the Monarchs leaves only three teams in the loop. Unless a fourth team can be added it appears as if the NAL will have died."[493]

The above constituted the entire column of the February 18, 1956, *Pittsburgh Courier*, reporting that the NAL was just about dead. But it was wrong. With the selling of three teams, the league reconstituted as a four-team loop and limped onward. At the meeting, Detroit Stars owner Ted Rasberry purchased the Kansas City Monarchs while he attempted to sell his Detroit team. The Birmingham Black Barons were sold to Dr. Anderson Ross, road secretary of the Memphis Red Sox in the 1920s.[494] The league now consisted of Detroit, Kansas City (but in name only), Memphis, and Birmingham, which would soon be renamed the Birmingham Giants.[495]

Although by now there was very little reportage in the Black press on the operations of the league, the February 23, 1957, *Chicago Defender*, reporting on an upcoming March 15 meeting of the NAL in Memphis at the offices of Dr. B.B. Martin, quoted NAL President J.B. Martin as saying, "I believe it will be a better year than we've had for a long time" as he said that some independent clubs had expressed interest in joining the league.[496] Martin lacked credibility in his assessment, as he had been saying for years that the league was in good shape, and now was indirectly acknowledging that prior years had not been successful. Nevertheless, at a meeting in April, the league announced that teams in Mobile and New Orleans would join Memphis, Birmingham,

Kansas City, and Detroit in a six-team circuit.[497] It seemed that the attempt in 1950 to make a league concentrated in the South might become reality—but Mobile and New Orleans did not finish the second half of the season.[498]

In 1958, the NAL held a spring meeting in which Arthur Dove, a potential team owner from Raleigh, was turned down in his attempt to get a franchise as the league had no interest in an odd number of teams and would continue with the same four clubs—Birmingham, Memphis, Detroit, and Kansas City, the last two represented by Ted Rasberry, who operated primarily out of Michigan and would represent both Detroit and Kansas City at meetings.[499] On May 7, 1958, *New York Times* reporter Roscoe McGowen reported that two NAL doubleheaders were planned for June 1, when the Memphis Red Sox would take on the Detroit Clowns and June 29, when the Memphis Red Sox would play the Kansas City Monarchs.

McGowen also said that the four NAL teams were planning a 140-game season.[500] Although it is very unlikely that such a long season, at least in league play, was completed by any NAL team, the two doubleheaders at Yankee Stadium were played, with the Detroit Clowns splitting their June doubleheader with Memphis in front of 15,000 spectators, and the Kansas City Monarchs sweeping the Memphis Red Sox with an attendance of 7,500.[501]

So there was still a bit of life in the NAL at the end of 1958. And 1959 brought the possibility of new franchises, with five applications reportedly being considered at the upcoming February 10 NAL meeting in Memphis as possible new league members.[502] Unfortunately, by season's end, of the six teams that opened the campaign, the two new teams in Raleigh, North Carolina, and Newark, New Jersey, "threw in the towel" while only the stalwart Memphis Red Sox, Kansas City Monarchs, Detroit Stars, and Birmingham Black Barons "managed to keep swinging until the last ball was pitched."[503] As 1959 ended, the NAL was still alive—but not for very long.

1960–1962

The Negro American League's remaining four franchises—the Raleigh Tigers, who were apparently revived for the 1960 season, the Detroit-New Orleans Stars, the Kansas City Monarchs, and the Birmingham Black Barons—met again sometime in early April to plan for the 1960 season.[504] Not only had the Newark Indians, who made a brief appearance in the 1959 NAL, dropped out of the league, but the Memphis Red Sox also ceased operations, a "crushing blow" for the league.[505] At this juncture, J.B. Martin was still the titular head of the NAL, but he reportedly had "limited his duties mainly to presiding over league meetings, keeping an eye on team personnel, and sponsoring the East-West All-Star Baseball Game. …"[506] The real power behind the throne was Ted Rasberry, the NAL vice president, who "has virtually taken over the field operations of the circuit and controls many of the administrative functions."[507] In his May 27, 1960, column in the *Atlanta Daily World*, sportswriter Marion Jackson expressed the view that Rasberry had new ideas of how to make the league profitable. These included limiting travel, finding useful old ballparks to play in, creating new associate memberships, and finding new talent by playing in areas like Atlanta and Philadelphia.[508]

Unfortunately, most of the ideas suggested by Jackson were not new—and by now, with all 16 major-league teams finally integrated, the sources for Black talent were being mostly tapped into by White baseball. The league played on and held its final Chicago East-West Game on August 21, 1960. The West defeated the East by a score of 8-4 in front of approximately 5,000 fans.[509] In the August 23, 1960, *Defender* there was a picture of J.B. Martin shaking hands with longtime Chicago Mayor Richard Daley, but there was no article on the game, just a few lines under the photograph reporting the score and mentioning the deciding four-run rally.[510]

At the beginning of 1961, representatives of the four surviving teams—the Raleigh Tigers, Detroit Stars, Kansas City Monarchs, and Birmingham Black Barons—met in Chicago in late February or early March to go over league plans.[511] The league decided to switch its East-West Game for the first time to a place outside Chicago—to Yankee Stadium, a locale with a rich history of well-attended Negro League doubleheaders and years of league contests.[512]

Cal Jacox's August 12, 1961, column in the *Norfolk Journal and Guide* began as follows: "Though there are many fans who are unaware of its present existence, the Negro American League is still active on the baseball front."[513] Jacox talked about Satchel Paige pitching for the Monarchs that year, but noted that publicity was virtually nonexistent for the league, a seeming contradiction given that Satchel was always a one-man publicity machine![514]

No doubt the highlight of the penultimate season of the NAL was Paige pitching three scoreless innings to start the August 20, 1961, East-West contest, getting the win in a 7-1 triumph for the West.[515] J.B. Martin estimated that more than 20,000 people would show up, much more than in recent years of East-West Games, given a large advance sale.[516] Once again President Martin was unrealistic, just like his yearly expressed expectations of another outstanding NAL season, as attending the contest were a mere 7,245 fans—a pale shadow of the throngs that used to attend this yearly highlight of the Negro League season.[517]

In 1962 the league had only three teams—the Birmingham Black Barons, Kansas City Monarchs, and Raleigh Tigers—though the Philadelphia Stars were an associate member. J.D. Martin stepped down as league president, and reportedly Ted Rasberry became president.[518] There is no record of league meetings, league officials other than Rasberry, or a regular season slate of games, as the teams apparently operated by barnstorming.[519] The league held a 30th—and final—East-West All-Star Game, this time in Kansas City. On August 26, 1962, the West All-Stars defeated the East by a score of 5-2. Jackie Robinson was given two plaques and a key to the city, and local resident Satchel Paige, who had won last year's East-West Game at the age of 55 but did not pitch in this one, was honored as well.[520] Although the NAL never declared that it had disbanded, the Center for Negro League Research has found no evidence to suggest that there was any operating NAL in 1963.[521] The era of Black baseball had ended.

CONCLUSION

The January 27, 1961 Memphis-based *Tri-State Defender* published an article entitled "Dark Shadows." The article described the demolition of Martin Stadium on Crump Boulevard in Memphis.[522] Martin Stadium was built in 1947 with an estimated $250,000 spent by the Martin brothers, owners of the Memphis Red Sox, to create one of the two most significant ballparks built for Negro League play, the other being Greenlee Field, built for the powerhouse NNL Pittsburgh Crawfords back in 1932, the year prior to the start of the second NNL.[523] The stadium had an 8,000 seating capacity but attendance had typically been only a few hundred people at Memphis Red Sox games in their last three years of play until they closed operations at the end of the 1959 season.[524]

"The dream that was Martin stadium was predicted (sic) on the belief that there would always be a place in the American scheme of things for organized Negro baseball."[525] A poetic statement, but one that flies in the face of the hopes and aspirations of a subjugated race of people. The *Tri-State Defender* was expressing nostalgia for bygone days of great performances, great performers, and stadiums filled with people, mostly Black people, who celebrated the outstanding stars of their race who were denied the privilege of playing in White baseball.

Negro League Baseball was a contentious, in some instances disorganized, immensely important institution, run by owners who made it possible for those great contests to happen. The story of this era is still being studied and must continue to be told.

Notes

1 Leslie Heaphy, *The Negro Leagues 1869–1960* (Jefferson, North Carolina: McFarland, 2003), 98,103,106.

2 William Leuchtenberg, *Franklin Roosevelt and the New Deal* (New York: Harper and Row, 1963) as quoted in Neil Lanctot, *Negro League Baseball: The Rise and Ruin of a Black Institution* (Philadelphia: University of Pennsylvania Press, 2004),18.

3 David Kennedy, *Freedom From Fear: The American People in Depression and War, 1929–1945* (New York: Oxford University Press, 1999).

4 See https://www.nlbm.com/s/current.htm; *Thomas Aiello, The Kings of Casino Park: Black Baseball in the Lost Season of 1932* (Tuscaloosa, Alabama: University of Alabama Press, 2011), 3.

5 See Heaphy, *The Negro Leagues*, 133-34.

6 Ibid., 54; Neil Lanctot, *Negro League Baseball*, 9; https://www.nlbm.com/s/team.htm

7 *Pittsburgh Courier*, January 16, 1932; see also Alan J. Pollock, *Barnstorming to Heaven: Syd Pollock and His Great Black Teams* (Tuscaloosa, Alabama: University of Alabama Press 2006),77-78. Syd Pollock, later the owner of teams in various cities that were called the Clowns, was at that time proprietor of a team called the Cuban House of David or the Cuban Stars. Pollock's Cuban Stars were entered in the 1932 East-West League; Alejandro "Alex" Pompez launched an earlier team called the Cuban Stars which was a member of the ECL. Adrian Burgos, Jr., *Cuban Star: How One Negro-League Owner Changed The Face of Baseball* (New York: Hill and Wang, 2011), 45-67.

8 Heaphy, *The Negro Leagues*, 42.

9 *Pittsburgh Courier*, December 31, 1932; *Chicago Defender* December 24, 1932; Aiello, *The Kings of Casino Park*, 5.

10 *Chicago Defender*, December 24, 1932.

11 *Chicago Defender*, December 24, 1932.12 *Pittsburgh Courier*, December 31, 1932.

13 *Pittsburgh Courier*, January 7, 1933.

14 *Chicago Defender*, February 25, 1933.

15 *Pittsburgh Courier*, March 4, 1933.

16 Lanctot, *Negro League Baseball*, 10.

17 Rob Ruck, *Sandlot Seasons: Sport in Black Pittsburgh* (Urbana, Illinois: University of Illinois Press, 1987), 149-51.

18 Email, Jim Overmyer to Bill Nowlin, October 2, 2017.

19 *Pittsburgh Courier*, August 15, 1942.

20 Email, Jim Overmyer to Bill Nowlin, October 2, 2017.

21 *Pittsburgh Courier*, February 11, 1933; In Wilson's March 4, 1933 *Courier* column, he reported that "reports from the West last week" indicated that Greenlee had been elected permanent chairman of the NNL—he was clearly referring to the February 15 meeting in Indianapolis. *Pittsburgh Courier*, March 4, 1933.

22 Lanctot, *Negro League Baseball*, 23-24.

23 *Pittsburgh Courier*, March 4, 1933.

24 "Speaking of Sports," *Chicago Defender*, February 25, 1933.

25 "Speaking of Sports," *Chicago Defender*, February 25, 1933.26 *Chicago Defender*, February 5, 1933.

27 *Chicago Defender*, February 5, 1933.28 *Chicago Defender*, February 5, 1933.29 *Pittsburgh Courier*, March 11, 1933. The NNL in 1933 was sometimes referred to as the Negro National Association.

30 *Pittsburgh Courier*, March 11, 1933. 31 *Chicago Defender*, March 18, 1933.

32 Lanctot, *Negro League Baseball*, 20.

33 Paul DeBono, *The Chicago American Giants* (Jefferson, North Carolina: McFarland, 2007),133.

34 *Norfolk Journal and Guide*, July 8, 1933. This was the first reference found to a league constitution.

35 *Norfolk Journal and Guide*, July 8, 1933. 36 Lanctot, *Negro League Baseball*, 22; "Posey's Points," *Pittsburgh Courier*, August 15, 1942.

37 "Posey's Points," *Pittsburgh Courier*, August 15, 1942.

38 Lanctot, *Negro League Baseball*, 22.

39 "Posey's Points," *Pittsburgh Courier*, August 15, 1942.

40 *Pittsburgh Courier*, July 8, 1933.

41 *Pittsburgh Courier*, August 12, 1933.

42 *Pittsburgh Courier*, August 12, 1933.

43 *Pittsburgh Courier*, July 22, 1933.

44 *Pittsburgh Courier*, July 22, 1933.45 *Pittsburgh Courier*, January 29, 1938. The *Courier* column discusses how divisive and disordered the 1937 NNL was and says that the league needs a "'dictator'... a man who will set a course and follow it...regardless!" and ends with the statement that what Negro baseball" needs most at PRESENT is a revival of the Rube Foster method!" See also *Chicago Defender*, February 15, 1936. The *Defender* column, written by Candy Jim Taylor, indicates that the owners are at fault for various problems in the NNL and says that the greatest success and best men in baseball were in the original NNL in the 1920's.

46 Larry Lester, *Black Baseball's National Showcase* (Lincoln: University of Nebraska Press, 2001), 37 citing *Kansas City Call*, September 14, 1933 (19,568); Lanctot, *Negro League Baseball*, 23 (12,000).

47 Heaphy, *The Negro Leagues*, 108.

48 *New York Amsterdam News*, September 27, 1933.

49 *Pittsburgh Courier*, August 12, 1933.

50 *Pittsburgh Courier*, September 16, 1933.

51 *Pittsburgh Courier*, January 6, 1934.

52 *Pittsburgh Courier*, January 6, 1934.53 *Pittsburgh Courier*, January 5, 1935. John Clark, the secretary of the NNL, stated that notices were sent to "all prospective club owners, Cum Posey and Prentice Byrd were the only men to respond" in his comprehensive description of 1934 meetings published at the beginning of 1935. In contrast, Cum Posey's version was that he attended along with representatives of Pittsburgh and Nashville. *Pittsburgh Courier*, January 20, 1934.

54 *Pittsburgh Courier*, January 5, 1935.

55 *Pittsburgh Courier*, January 6, 1934.

56 *Pittsburgh Courier*, February 17, 1934; January 5, 1935.

57 *Pittsburgh Courier*, January 5, 1935.

58 *New York Amsterdam News*, March 17, 1934.

59 Lanctot, *Negro League Baseball*, 33-34.

60 *Pittsburgh Courier*, January 5, 1935.

61 Rebecca Alpert, *Out of Left Field: Jews And Black Baseball* (New York: Oxford University Press, 2011), 51-52.

62 *Pittsburgh Courier*, June 2, 1934.

63 *Pittsburgh Courier*, June 2, 1934.64 *Atlanta Daily World*, July 9, 1934.

65 *Pittsburgh Courier*, June 16, 1934.

66 *Pittsburgh Courier*, June 30, 1934.

67 *Pittsburgh Courier*, July 14, 1934.

68 *Atlanta Daily World*, July 9, 1934.

69 *Chicago Defender*, July 14, 1934.

70 Once again, different sources provide different attendance figures. Lester reports an attendance of 30,000, while Lanctot has it as above 25,000. Lester, *Black Baseball's National Showcase*, 61; Lanctot, *Negro League Baseball*. 38.

71 DeBono, *The Chicago American Giants*, 137.

72 Lanctot, *Negro League Baseball*, 37.

73 *Philadelphia Tribune*, September 13, 1934.

74 *New York Amsterdam News*, October 20, 1934.

75 *New York Amsterdam News*, November 10, 1934; DeBono, *The Chicago American Giants*, 137.

76 *Pittsburgh Courier*, September 15, 1934 as quoted in Lanctot, *Negro League Baseball*,38; *Baltimore Afro-American*, January 19, 1935 as quoted in Lanctot, *Negro League Baseball*, 39.

77 In his history of the Chicago American Giants, Paul DeBono pointed out that "the supposed World Series between the Chicago American Giants and Philadelphia Stars would not generate anything near the amount of fan interest, so it made sense from a business standpoint to schedule the games at Yankee stadium" even though they disrupted the league championship playoff. DeBono, *The Chicago American Giants*, 137.

78 Lanctot, *Negro League Baseball*, 40.

79 *Atlanta Daily World*, January 4, 1935.

80 Burgos, *Cuban Star*, 84; Lanctot, *Negro League Baseball*, 24.

81 Lanctot, *Negro League Baseball*, 41.

82 The Bacharach Giants also sent a representative to the conference but were refused admission to the league, as was a team from Boston. *Atlanta Daily World*, January 23, 1935; see also *Chicago Defender*, January 19, 1935.

83 *Chicago Defender*, January 19, 1935.

84 *Atlanta Daily World*, January 23, 1935; *Chicago Defender*, January 19, 1935.

85 *Pittsburgh Courier*, March 16, 1935.

86 *Pittsburgh Courier*, March 16, 1935; *New York Amsterdam News*, March 16, 1935.

87 Lanctot, *Negro League Baseball*, 44.

88 *New York Amsterdam News*, March 16, 1935.

89 Lanctot, *Negro League Baseball*, 46.

90 *New York Amsterdam News*, August 31, 1935.

91 *Pittsburgh Courier*, November 16, 1935.

92 Lanctot, *Negro League Baseball*, 48-50.

93 Heaphy, *The Negro Leagues*, Appendix D, 241.

94 Courtney Smith, "A Fine Line Between Admiration and Animosity: Ed Bolden's Philadelphia Stars, the Negro National League, and the *Philadelphia Tribune*, 1933–1938," *Black Ball* Vol.6 (Fall 2013), 45-46 citing *Philadelphia Tribune*, January 16, 30 1936

95 *Chicago Defender*, January 18, 1936.

96 *Chicago Defender*, February 15, 1936.

97 *Chicago Defender*, February 15, 1936.98 *Chicago Defender*, February 29,1936.

99 *New York Amsterdam News*, March 14, 1936.

100 *Chicago Defender*, June 27, 1936.

101 Heaphy, *The Negro Leagues*, 110.

102 Lanctot, *Negro League Baseball*, 53.

103 *Chicago Defender*, October 24, 1936; see also Lanctot, *Negro League Baseball*, 54-55.

104 *Chicago Defender*, October 24,1936.

105 *Philadelphia Tribune*, July 30, 1936 as quoted in Lanctot, *Negro League Baseball*, 55.

106 *Pittsburgh Courier*, August 29,1936 as quoted in Lanctot, *Negro League Baseball*, 55.

107 *Chicago Defender*, October 17, 1936.

108 *Chicago Defender*, December 19, 1936.

109 *New York Amsterdam News*, January 2, 1937.

110 *New York Amsterdam News*, January 16, 1937.

111 *New York Amsterdam News*, January 16, 1937.112 *Pittsburgh Courier*, January 30,1937.

113 *Pittsburgh Courier*, March 27, 1937.

114 Lanctot, *Negro League Baseball*, 58.

115 Burgos, *Cuban Star,* 101.

116 Burgos, *Cuban Star*, 100; Lanctot, *Negro League Baseball*, 59-62.

117 *New York Amsterdam News*, June 19, 1937.

118 Lanctot, *Negro League Baseball*, 65-66.

119 *Chicago Defender*, February 27, 1937.

120 *Chicago Defender*, February 27, 1937.

121 DeBono, *The Chicago American Giants*, 144-45.

122 Lanctot, *Negro League Baseball*, 59.

123 Heaphy, *The Negro Leagues*, 111.

124 *Chicago Defender*, September 25, 1937 as quoted in DeBono, *The Chicago American Giants*, 144.

125 *Pittsburgh Courier*, September 18, 1937.

126 *Chicago Defender*, October 9, 1937.

127 Lanctot, *Negro League Baseball*, 67.

128 *Pittsburgh Courier*, January 29,1938.

129 Document titled "League Meeting," 1938 Newark Eagles Records, Newark Public Library. Documents from this set of files will be referred to as "Manley Files" hereinafter.

130 Manley Files.131 *Chicago Defender*, February 26, 1938.

132 *Pittsburgh Courier*, January 29, 1938.

133 *Pittsburgh Courier*, February 5, 1938.

134 Lanctot, *Negro League Baseball*, 75.

135 *Pittsburgh Courier*, February 5, 1938 (states upcoming meeting will be on February 19); *Pittsburgh Courier*, March 19, 1938.

136 *Pittsburgh Courier*, March 12, 1938.

137 *Chicago Defender*, March 19, 1938.

138 Lanctot, *Negro League Baseball*, 74.

139 Lanctot, *Negro League Baseball*, 76.140 Heaphy, *The Negro Leagues*, 112.

141 *Chicago Defender*, December 18, 1937.

142 *Pittsburgh Courier*, February 26, 1938; *Chicago Defender*, February 26, 1938.

143 *Chicago Defender*, February 26, 1938.

144 Heaphy, *The Negro Leagues*, Appendix D, 241.

145 *Chicago Defender*, July 2, 1938.

146 *Pittsburgh Courier*, December 17, 1938.

147 *Pittsburgh Courier*, December 17, 1938.148 *Chicago Defender*, January 14, 1939.

149 Lanctot, *Negro League Baseball*, 78-79.

150 *Pittsburgh Courier*, February 25, 1939.

151 Summary of 1939 NNL meeting by Cum Posey, Manley Files. Although this meeting description does not specify the meeting date, the matters covered accord with the description of the February NNL meeting discussed in the February 25, 1939 edition of the *Pittsburgh Courier*.

152 *Pittsburgh Courier*, February 25, 1939.

153 Document titled "Notes/Memo by Cum Posey," which describes spring 1939 NNL business, Manley Files.

154 *Chicago Defender*, February 18, 1939.

155 Letter, Cum Posey to Effa Manley, April 14, 1939, Manley Files.

156 Lanctot, *Negro League Baseball*, 83; Minutes, Meeting of Negro National League, June 20, 1939, Manley Papers.

157 *Atlanta Daily World*, July 1, 1939

158 Agreement Between The Negro National League and the Negro American League, Joint Meeting June 20, 1939, Manley Papers.

159 Minutes, Combined Meeting of the Negro National League and the Negro American League, June 20, 1939, Manley Papers.

160 Minutes, Joint Meeting of Negro National and Negro American League, August 27, 1939, Manley Papers.

161 Lanctot, *Negro League Baseball*, 84.

162 Minutes, Meeting of Negro National League, August 28, 1939, Manley Papers.

163 Heaphy, *The Negro Leagues*, Appendix D, 241.

164 Letter, Cum Posey to Abe Manley, October 17, 1939, Manley Papers; Lanctot, *Negro League Baseball*, 84-85.

165 Draft of Statement of Abe Manley to NAL Owners, December 9, 1939, Manley Papers. The statement, which has handwritten notations, does not explicitly state who it is intended for but its date and subject matter clearly reference an NAL meeting on December 9 at which Abe's wife Effa would attend and present his thoughts.

166 Lanctot, *Negro League Baseball*, 86.

167 Lanctot, *Negro League Baseball*, 87.168 Report on annual meeting of Negro American League, December 9 and 10, 1939, Manley Papers. After Effa Manley's failed attempt to nominate Judge Hastie, the Judge wrote to tell her that he would not be able to handle the "larger job of guidance, direction and publicity" because of his current commitments, which included being Chairman of the National Legal Committee of the NAACP. Letter, William Hastie to Effa Manley, February 1, 1940, Manley Papers.

169 Letter, William Hastie to Effa Manley, February 1, 1940, Manley Papers; *Chicago Defender*, December 16, 1939 as quoted in Lanctot, *Negro League Baseball*, 87.

170 *Chicago Defender*, February 10, 1940.

171 *Pittsburgh Courier*, February 3, 1940

172 See, e.g. *Pittsburgh Courier*, May 11, 1940

173 *Baltimore Afro-American*, February 10, 1940; Letter, Effa Manley to Art Carter, February 7, 1940, Manley Papers. Since the Black press published on a weekly basis, one would presume that the Feb. 10 edition came out several days earlier, otherwise Effa would not have been able to date her letter February 7 and criticize Carter for his "column of Feb. 10 in the Afro" unless she was either clairvoyant or she erroneously dated the letter!

174 Letter, Effa Manley to Art Carter, February 7, 1940, Manley Papers.

175 *Baltimore Afro-American*, February 10, 1940; *Chicago Defender*, February 10, 24,1940; *Pittsburgh Courier*, February 10, 1940. Both the *Afro-American* and *Defender* accounts contain vivid accounts of the Posey/Manley confrontation. The *Courier* account described the deadlock in more neutral terms. On February 24, two weeks after the original reportage of this meeting, the *Defender* quoted Effa as saying that "the league ought to be run for colored by colored." Recent evidence suggesting that Effa could have been White places statements like these and others by Effa Manley in a different light.

176 *Baltimore Afro-American*, March 2, 1940; Adrian Burgos, *Cuban Star*, 152 citing *New York Age*, March 9, 1940.

177 Minutes, Joint Meeting Negro National and Negro American Leagues, February 24, 1940, Manley Papers.

178 *Chicago Defender*, June 29, 1940.

179 Letter, Effa Manley to B.B. Martin and Thomas Wilson, June 2, 1940, Manley Papers; Lanctot, *Negro League Baseball*, 91.

180 *Chicago Defender*, June 29, 1940.

181 Heaphy, *Negro League Baseball*, 116; *Chicago Defender*, June 29, 1940.

182 *Pittsburgh Courier*, November 9, 1940.

183 *Pittsburgh Courier*, May 11, 1940.

184 *Chicago Defender*, January 4, 1941.

185 *Chicago Defender*, January 4, 1941.186 *Baltimore Afro-American*, January 11, 1941.

187 *Baltimore Afro-American*, January 11, 1941; *Pittsburgh Courier*, January 11, 1941.

188 *Baltimore Afro-American*, January 11, 1941; *Pittsburgh Courier*, January 11, 1941.189 *Baltimore Afro-American*, January 11, 1941; *Pittsburgh Courier*, January 11, 1941.

190 *New York Amsterdam News*, January 11, 1941; see also Burgos, *Cuban Star*, 152.

191 *Baltimore Afro-American*, January 11, 1941.

192 *Chicago Defender*, January 18, 1941.

193 *Chicago Defender*, March 1, 1941.

194 *New York Amsterdam News*, March 8, 1941.

195 *Pittsburgh Courier*, March 29, 1941; Alpert, *Out of Left Field*, 72-74.

196 *Chicago Defender*, May 24, 1941.

197 Lanctot, *Negro League Baseball*, 105.

198 *Pittsburgh Courier*, June 28, 1941.

199 *Pittsburgh Courier*, June 28, 1941.200 *Cleveland Call and Post*, August 13, 1941.

201 *Cleveland Call and Post*, August 13, 1941.

202 Resolutions passed at NNL Fall Meeting, September 15, 1941, Manley Papers; *Pittsburgh Courier*, December 27, 1941.

203 *Chicago Defender*, October 25, 1941.

204 *Chicago Defender*, October 25, 1941.205 Lanctot, *Negro League Baseball*, 110.

206 Letter, Effa Manley to Cum Posey, October 13, 1941, Manley Papers.

207 Heaphy, *The Negro Leagues*, Appendix D., 241.

208 *Pittsburgh Courier*, December 27, 1941.

209 *Pittsburgh Courier*, January 3, 1942.

210 *Atlanta Daily World*, December 31, 1941.

211 Letter, Effa Manley to Rufus "Sonnyman" Jackson, January 2, 1942, Manley Papers; Letter, Effa Manley to Joseph Rainey, January 26, 1942, Manley Papers.

212 Letter, Effa Manley to Joseph Rainey, January 26, 1942, Manley Papers.

213 Duke Goldman, "The Double Victory Campaign and the Campaign to Integrate Baseball," *Who's on First: Replacement Players in World War II* (Phoenix, Arizona: Society for American Baseball Research, 2015), 405-06; Patrick Washburn, "The *Pittsburgh Courier*'s Double V Campaign in 1942," *American Journalism* (Vol. 74, No. 2 1986), 73-74.

214 *Pittsburgh Courier*, February 14, 1942.

215 *New York Amsterdam News*, February 21, 1942.

216 *Baltimore Afro-American*, February 21, 1942.

217 *New York Amsterdam News*, February 21, 1942.

218 *Baltimore Afro-American*, February 21, 1942; *New York Amsterdam News*, February 21, 1942.

219 *New York Amsterdam News*, February 21, 1942.

220 Alpert, *Out of Left Field*, 78; *Pittsburgh Courier*, March 7, 1942.

221 Letter, Gus Greenlee to Abe Manley, February 21, 1942, Manley Papers.

222 *New York Amsterdam News*, March 7, 1942.

223 *Atlanta Daily World*, March 11, 1942.

224 *Baltimore Afro-American*, May 9, 1942 as quoted in Lanctot, *Negro League Baseball*, 119.

225 Lanctot, *Negro League Baseball*, 127-28.

226 Minutes, Joint Meeting Negro American and Negro National Leagues, June 10, 1942, Manley Papers; *Pittsburgh Courier*, June 20, 1942.

227 *Pittsburgh Courier*, October 31, 1942 as quoted in Alpert, *Out of Left Field*, 81.

228 *Chicago Defender*, December 12, 1942.

229 Heaphy, *Negro League Baseball*, Appendix D., 241.

230 *Chicago Defender*, December 27, 1942.

231 *Chicago Defender*, December 12, 1942.

232 *Chicago Defender*, December 12, 1942.233 DeBono, The Chicago American Giants, 160.

234 *Chicago Defender*, December 19, 1942.

235 *New York Amsterdam News*, January 30, 1943. Although the *Amsterdam News* stated that Wilson's "entire cabinet was reelected for another term," in actuality Abe Manley was restored to the treasurer post after two years of Posey serving as both secretary and treasurer of the NNL. In light of the ongoing power plays and the reality of shifting alliances between owners, Abe Manley's being voted back into his previous league office is worth nothing.

236 *Pittsburgh Courier*, January 23, 1943.

237 Lanctot, *Negro League Baseball*, 129.

238 Lanctot, *Negro League Baseball*, 132.239 .Lanctot, *Negro League Baseball*, 131-32.

240 *Baltimore Afro-American*, April 3, 1943; *Chicago Defender*, April 3, 1943.

241 *Baltimore Afro-American*, April 3, 1943.

242 *Chicago Defender*, April 3, 1943.

243 *New York Amsterdam News*, April 3, 1943.

244 *Pittsburgh Courier*, April 10, 1943 (sell buses and train travel); *Baltimore Afro-American*, April 17, 1943 (carry on and try for special considerations); *Chicago Defender*, April 17, 1943 (trains and commercial buses).

245 *Chicago Defender*, April 17, 1943.

246 *Baltimore Afro-American*, April 17, 1943.

247 Lanctot, *Negro League Baseball*, 133-134.

248 Press Release, May 2, 1943, Manley Papers.

249 *Chicago Defender*, June 12, 1943.

250 Minutes, Meeting of Negro National League, June 1, 1943, Manley Papers.

251 Minutes, Meeting of Negro National League, June 1, 1943, Manley Papers. The original vote on the resolution to return the 10 players had Newark not voting and Homestead and Cleveland voting no. But Homestead and Cleveland objected to any ruling on the vote, which led to extensive rearguing of the issue. After another vote with the same result, Presidents and Martin and Wilson signed the order.

252 Lanctot, *Negro League Baseball*, 138.

253 Brian Carroll, *When to Stop the Cheering? The Black Press, the Black Community, and the Integration of Professional Baseball* (New York: Routledge, 2007), 129.

254 Minutes, Joint Meeting of the Negro American and Negro National Leagues, August 2, 1943, Manley Papers.

255 Minutes, Joint Meeting of the Negro American and Negro National Leagues, August 2, 1943, Manley Papers.

256 Alpert, *Out of Left Field*, 84.

257 Carroll, *When to Stop the Cheering?*, 129.

258 J.B. Martin was reported as saying that 1943 had been the most profitable year in league history and that he expected an even better year in 1944. *Pittsburgh Courier*, December 18, 1943. The *Courier* also reported that the NAL would resist efforts by some NNL owners to form a one-league structure. In addition, there was to be discussion of disputes over NAL players being used without permission by NNL teams, in one instance by the Homestead Grays during the Negro World Series. *Chicago Defender*, December 18, 1943.

259 *Pittsburgh Courier*, December 18, 1943.

260 *Pittsburgh Courier*, December 18, 1943. See also Carroll, *When to Stop the Cheering?*, 131-132. According to Carroll, Smith's column, however inadvertently, provided cover for major-league owners to question Negro League legitimacy. Carroll goes on to characterize Smith's columns on Negro League operations as "patronizing" and delivering "unvarnished criticism" of Negro League owners, likely leading to both leagues rejecting his offer to compile statistics for league games for a fee.

261 *Pittsburgh Courier*, December 18, 1943. See also, Lester, *Black Baseball's National Showcase*, 208-210; Lanctot, *Negro League Baseball*, 245.

262 Lanctot, *Negro League Baseball*, 245; *Pittsburgh Courier*, December 11, 1943 as quoted in Lester, *Black Baseball's National Showcase*, 209.

263 Carroll, *When to Stop the Cheering?*, 129.

264 *New York Amsterdam News*, January 1, 1944.

265 *Atlanta Daily World*, December 29, 1943.

266 Lanctot, *Negro League Baseball*, 247 citing *Philadelphia Independent*, January 2, 1944.

267 *Atlanta Daily World*, December 29, 1943.

268 *New York Amsterdam News*, January 15, 1944; *Pittsburgh Courier*, January 1, 1944. Wilson's statement on baseball integration appeared in a printed brochure whereas Martin's was an oral response.

269 *Chicago Defender*, December 25, 1943. Traveling secretary Simmons was reelected even though some NAL owners had concerns about a team's road secretary doubling as the league's secretary. *Chicago Defender*, December 18, 1943.

270 *Chicago Defender*, December 25, 1943.

271 *Norfolk Journal and Guide*, January 1, 1944.

272 *Pittsburgh Courier*, January 1, 1944.

273 *Chicago Defender*, January 15, 1944.

274 *New York Amsterdam News*, January 15, 1944.

275 *New York Amsterdam News*, January 15, 1944.276 *New York Amsterdam News*, January 15, 1944. Lanctot, *Negro League Baseball*, 134; *Pittsburgh Courier*, March 11, 1944. Although Lanctot states that the NNL "would not receive relief until February 1944 when the ODT accepted the league's somewhat dubious claim that it also operated in the south," the March 11 edition of the *Courier* states that no definitive word from ODT had yet to be received although it was assumed that approval of the 2,000 mile allowance was imminent. This author has found no evidence that the NNL did not end up receiving the allowance.

277 *Chicago Defender*, March 11, 1944; Alpert, *Out of Left Field*, 86.

278 *Baltimore Afro-American*, March 18, 1944.

279 *Pittsburgh Courier*, March 11, 1944.

280 Lanctot, *Negro League Baseball*, 141.

281 Letter, Effa Manley to Wendell Smith, February 7, 1944, Manley Papers.

282 Lanctot, *Negro League Baseball*, 141-42.

283 *Atlanta Daily World*, March 14, 1944.

284 *Cleveland Call and Post*, March 25, 1944. The "all in caps" is reproduced here as it appears in the column by Bob Williams.

285 *Cleveland Call and Post*, March 25, 1944. 286 *Cleveland Call and Post*, March 25, 1944. 287 *Pittsburgh Courier*, March 11, 1944. The *Courier* column mentioned "a rumor circling the lobby" that owner Semler of the Black Yankees would trade Hopgood and Stone to the Philadelphia Stars for pitcher Terris McDuffie. Hopgood and Stone did end up on the Stars, but McDuffie would pitch for Newark in 1944.

288 *New York Amsterdam News*, May 20, 1944.

289 Lanctot, *Negro League Baseball*, 147; *Philadelphia Tribune*, January 6, 1945 as quoted in Lanctot, 147.

290 *Baltimore Afro-American*, June 24, 1944; *Pittsburgh Courier*, June 17, 1944. The Afro-American reported that the meeting's big news was that the press was admitted to the sessions, with the "bigwigs of the NNL finally agreeing to call off their series of 'executive sessions…'" Unfortunately, deciding to finally provide full access to the press in 1944 turned out to be too late given

the soon-to-be integration of major league baseball and attendant dramatic shift in the coverage of the Black press away from the Negro Leagues.

291 *Baltimore Afro-American*, June 24, 1944; *Philadelphia Tribune*, July 1, 1944.

292 Lanctot, *Negro League Baseball*, 147.

293 Lanctot, *Negro League Baseball*, 145; *Baltimore Afro-American*, July 1, 1944.

294 *Norfolk Journal and Guide*, July 29, 1944.

295 Letter, Wendell Smith to Effa Manley, May 19, 1944, Manley Papers.

296 *Chicago Defender*, June 24, 1944.

297 Heaphy, *The Negro Leagues*, Appendix D, 241; Lanctot, *Negro League Baseball*, 143.

298 *Philadelphia Tribune*, September 16, 1944 as quoted in Lanctot, *Negro League Baseball*, 143.

299 Letter reading as a press release, December 6, 1944, probably written by Cum Posey for league presidents Tom Wilson and J.B. Martin, Manley Papers; *New York Amsterdam News*, December 16, 1944.

300 Letter reading as a press release, December 6, 1944, Manley Papers.

301 *New York Amsterdam News*, December 16, 1944. The article criticized Landis for failing to encourage steps towards integration but noted that he did not interfere in rental arrangements between major-league clubs and Negro League owners.

302 *Pittsburgh Courier*, December 23, 1944. According to the *Amsterdam News*, after the media was barred from Friday's league meetings, some "went home in a huff. Others got some minor details from the joint session…," *New York Amsterdam News*, December 23, 1944.

303 *Pittsburgh Courier*, December 23, 1944; *Chicago Defender*, December 23, 1944.

304 *Pittsburgh Courier*, December 23, 1944.

305 *Chicago Defender*, December 23, 1944.

306 *New York Amsterdam News*, December 23, 1944.

307 *Pittsburgh Courier*, December 23, 1944.

308 *Pittsburgh Courier*, December 23, 1944.309 *Pittsburgh Courier*, December 23, 1944.

310 *Chicago Defender*, January 6, 1945.

311 See, e.g., Lanctot, *Negro League Baseball*, 263-271; Heaphy, *The Negro Leagues*, 198-200. There were several apparent shifts in ownership and location of United States League (USL) franchises in 1945, along with the sudden involvement of Branch Rickey in May of 1945. This article will only cover the USL as it pertains to the ongoing issues of the NNL and NAL.

312 *Pittsburgh Courier*, January 6, 1945.

313 *Pittsburgh Courier*, January 6, 1945.314 *New York Amsterdam News*, March 3, 1945. The article mentioned that Saperstein was involved in the operations of the Indianapolis-Cincinnati Clowns and the Birmingham Black Barons of the NAL, along with his financial interest in the USL St Louis franchise. Clearly, Saperstein was all over the map—given his role in booking Negro League games, promoting the East-West Game, and owning basketball's Harlem Globetrotters.

315 *New York Amsterdam News*, March 3, 1945. 316 *Pittsburgh Courier*, March 17, 1945. NNL and NAL owners had attended each other's meetings in the past, but the cooperative involvement in each other's affairs represented by a) supporting each other in the rejection of a new Indianapolis franchise and b) essentially keeping Saperstein "off limits" to USL operations seems to this author a departure from largely acrimonious dealings between the two leagues in the past.

317 *Pittsburgh Courier*, March 17, 1945. 318 Ibid; Arnold Rampersad, *Jackie Robinson* (New York: Alfred A. Knopf, 1997), 74.

319 *Pittsburgh Courier*, March 17, 1945.

320 Lanctot, *Negro League Baseball*, 252.

321 Letter, J.B. Martin to V.T. Corbett, April 5, 1945, Records of the Office of Defense Transportation, National Archives at College Park, College Park, Maryland as quoted in Lanctot, *Negro League Baseball*, 253. It is interesting to note that the final line of "Posey's Points" in the June 23, 1945 *Pittsburgh Courier* stated that East-West Game attendance in 1945 would be "limited almost entirely to Chicago fans," thereby bolstering J.B. Martin's claim. *Pittsburgh Courier*, June 23, 1945.

322 Letter, William Nunn to Abe Manley, March 22, 1945, Manley Papers.

323 Letter, Abe Manley to William Nunn, April 7, 1945, Manley Papers.

324 Letter, William Nunn to Tom Baird, May 9, 1945, Manley Papers.

325 *Norfolk Journal and Guide*, May 5, 1945.

326 Lanctot, *Negro League Baseball*, 259-262; *Baltimore Afro-American*, July 14, 1945.

327 *Baltimore Afro-American*, May 19, 1945 as quoted in Lanctot, *Negro League Baseball*, 266.

328 Lanctot, *Negro League Baseball*, 272.

329 Minutes of Joint Session, June 12, 1945, Manley Papers.

330 Minutes of Joint Session, June 12, 1945, Manley Papers.331 Lanctot, *Negro League Baseball*, 273.

332 Minutes of Joint Session, June 12, 1945, Manley Papers.

333 *Philadelphia Tribune*, June 23, 1945.

334 Minutes of Joint Session, June 12, 1945, Manley Papers.

335 *Baltimore Afro-American*, July 14, 1945.

336 *Baltimore Afro-American*, July 14, 1945. Lacy's column appeared on July 14, the same date the *Afro-American* published a separate piece reporting the fine on the Black Yankees and a week after the *Norfolk Journal and Guide* published their article reporting the fine. One can only speculate that Lacy's piece was written before the announced punishment or that he did not believe it would be enforced. *Norfolk Journal and Guide*, July 7, 1945.

337 Lanctot, *Negro League Baseball*, 274.

338 Heaphy, *The Negro Leagues*, Appendix D, 241. After V-J day, the *Pittsburgh Courier* stopped putting a "V V" between printed articles as a symbol of 1942's Double Victory campaign, presumably because victory in the war had been achieved. There is no evidence that the *Courier* knew that victory in the campaign for baseball integration had also been achieved, as Jackie Robinson's August 28, 1945 agreement with the Dodgers was a secret, not being announced until October 23. Duke Goldman, *The Double Victory Campaign*, 407.

339 *Pittsburgh Courier*, December 23, 1944.

340 Rampersad, *Jackie Robinson*, 129.

341 *New York Times*, October 27, 1945.

342 *Chicago Defender*, November 3, 1945.

343 *Kansas City Call*, October 26, 1945 as quoted in Lanctot, *Negro League Baseball*, 280 ("we have been out"); *Pittsburgh Courier*, November 3, 1945 as quoted in Lanctot, *Negro League Baseball*, 280 ("something should be done").

344 *Baltimore Afro-American*, November 3, 1945.

345 *Baltimore Afro-American*, November 3, 1945.346 Letter, Effa Manley to J.B. Martin, October 26, 1945, Manley Papers. Johnson would be elected NNL president in 1947.

347 Letter, J.B. Martin to Effa Manley, October 29, 1945, Manley Papers.

348 Statement of J.B. Martin from the Office of the Negro American League, November 1945 (undated specifically but referred to in early November newspaper articles), Manley Papers.

349 *Cleveland Call and Post*, November 3, 1945.

350 *Cleveland Call and Post*, November 3, 1945.

351 Letter, Cum Posey to Albert B. Chandler, November 1, 1945, Manley Papers.

352 Letter, Cum Posey to Albert B. Chandler, November 1, 1945, Manley Papers.353 Letter, Clark Griffith to Cum Posey, November 5, 1945, Manley Papers.

354 Robert McGregor, *A Calculus of Color: The Integration of Baseball's American League* (Jefferson, North Carolina: McFarland, 2015), 149.

355 *New York Amsterdam News*, November 17, 1945.

356 *New York Amsterdam News*, November 17, 1945.357 *New York Amsterdam News*, November 17, 1945.

358 *New York Amsterdam News*, November 17, 1945; *Chicago Defender*, November 17, 1945.

359 *Pittsburgh Courier*, December 22, 1945.

360 *Pittsburgh Courier*, December 22, 1945; *Chicago Defender*, December 22, 1945.

361 *Atlanta Daily World*, December 22, 1945.

362 Undated resolution, likely in late 1945 or early 1946, Manley Papers.

363 *New York Times*, January 21, 1946.

364 *Hartford Courant*, January 22, 1946.

365 Lanctot, *Negro League Baseball*, 285.

366 *Pittsburgh Courier*, February 16, 1946.

367 Lanctot, *Negro League Baseball*, 284-85.

368 *Pittsburgh Courier*, January 5, 1946.

369 Minutes of regular meeting, Negro National League, February 20, 1946, Manley Papers.

370 Minutes of regular meeting, Negro National League, February 20, 1946, Manley Papers.371 Minutes of regular meeting, Negro National League, February 20, 1946, Manley Papers. Wilson also claimed that Chandler "said nothing against owners being officers of the league." While Chandler may not have specifically raised such an objection when meeting Wilson, his objection to club owners holding the office of President had been reported in the media, as previously noted. *Pittsburgh Courier*, February 16, 1946

372 Minutes of regular meeting, Negro National League, second day, February 21, 1946, Manley Papers.

373 *Pittsburgh Courier*, February 16, 1946.

374 Ibid. Crossed out was a statement that "legally they were not obligated to him or anyone else."

375 *Philadelphia Tribune*, March 9, 1946.

376 Minutes of special meeting, Negro National League, March 12, 1946, Manley Papers.

377 Heaphy, *The Negro Leagues*, 200.

378 *Pittsburgh Courier*, March 23, 1946.

379 *Pittsburgh Courier*, December 22, 1945.

380 Minutes of special meeting, Negro National League, March 12, 1946, Manley Papers.

381 *Pittsburgh Courier*, March 23, 1946.

382 *Philadelphia Tribune*, May 11, 1946.

383 *Chicago Defender*, June 29, 1946.

384 Minutes of Joint meeting, Negro American League and Negro National League, June 19, 1946, Manley Papers.

385 *Norfolk Journal and Guide*, July 27, 1946.

386 *Newark Star-Ledger*, May 19, 1996

387 Effa Manley and Leon Hardwick, *Negro Baseball Before Integration* (Chicago: Adams Press, 1976),96.

388 Doron "Duke" Goldman, "Monte's Missions: Mastering Mexico, Military Service, Defeating Monarchs and Minor League Magic," *Black Ball* Vol 9 (2017), 54-55.

389 Brian Carroll, "The Black Press and the Integration of Baseball: A content analysis of changes in coverage," *Cooperstown Symposium on Baseball and American Culture* (Jefferson, North Carolina: McFarland, 2003), 216-231 as quoted in Carroll, *When to Stop the Cheering*, 150,152.

390 Report of Meeting With Louis Carroll, Lawyer For The National League, September 26, 1946, Manley Papers.

391 *Pittsburgh Courier*, May 3, 1947.

392 Lanctot, *The Negro Leagues*, 306.

393 Lanctot, *The Negro Leagues*, 306.394 *Chicago Defender*, January 4, 1947; *Chicago Defender*, December 21, 1946.

395 *Chicago Defender*, January 11, 1947. The *Defender* claimed that in 1946 Wilson had tried to "relinquish the office but the owners insisted that he serve another year."

396 Lanctot, *Negro League Baseball*, 307-309. Lanctot's sources indicate that despite Wilson's ill health, he was still supported by Baltimore and Philadelphia for another term. Manley championed Johnson and was supported by the Grays and Cubans owner Alex Pompez. A deadlock was averted when Black Yankees owner Semler voted for Johnson despite having supported Wilson in previous years. Lanctot speculates that Semler's support was won over by an offer to be the exclusive promoter at Yankee stadium as Cum Posey had once suggested that "Semler will do anything if money is shoved at him." Letter, Cum Posey to Abe Manley, October 25, 1942, Manley Papers, as quoted in Lanctot, *Negro League Baseball*, 301 n.13. See also James A. Riley, *The Biographical Encyclopedia of The Negro Leagues* (New York: Carroll & Graf, paperback edition, 2002), 287,400 (biographical information on Forbes and Hueston).

397 *Pittsburgh Courier*, January 11, 1947.

398 *New York Amsterdam News*, January 11, 1947.

399 *New York Amsterdam News*, January 11, 1947; *People's Voice*, February 1, 1947 as quoted in Lanctot, *Negro League Baseball*, 309.

400 *New York Amsterdam News*, January 11, 1947.

401 *Pittsburgh Courier*, December 22, 1945.

402 *Atlanta Daily World*, March 5, 1947.

403 *Chicago Defender*, February 22, 1947.

404 *Atlanta Daily World*, March 5, 1947.

405 *New York Times*, March 1, 1947.

406 *Atlanta Daily World*, March 5, 1947.

407 *Cleveland Call and Post*, March 1, 1947.

408 *Atlanta Daily World*, March 1, 1947.

409 *New York Times*, March 1, 1947.

410 *Atlanta Daily World*, March 1, 1947. The *Daily World* also reported that Ed Gottlieb would no longer have to be involved in booking Yankee Stadium games. This decision gives credence to the conjecture by Lanctot mentioned in footnote 396 above that Semler may have been "bought off" by opportunities to promote his own games at Yankee Stadium.

411 See Adrian Burgos, *Cuban Star*, 179, citing *Baltimore Afro-American*, April 20, 1946.

412 *Pittsburgh Courier*, June 14, 1947.

413 Carroll, *When to Stop the Cheering?*, 156-57. Carroll gives the example of the *Chicago Defender* giving extensive coverage to Jackie Robinson's game-winning home run in the 1947 major-league World Series and minor coverage of the New York Cubans winning the 1947 Negro World Series.

414 Lanctot, *Negro League Baseball*, 312-13.

415 *Baltimore Afro-American*, June 21, 1947. For a discussion of the Duany case, see Burgos, *Cuban Star*, 171-72.

416 *Norfolk Journal and Guide*, June 21, 1947. Note that other sources say that the league was willing to consider playing yearly benefit games to raise money for a pension fund. See *Baltimore Afro-American*, June 21, 1947; Heaphy, *The Negro Leagues*, 215 citing Joint Meeting minutes, June 10, 1947, Tom Baird Papers, University of Kansas Libraries, Lawrence Kansas (rescinding visiting passes).

417 Burgos, *Cuban Star*, 175-76; *Cleveland Call and Post*, October 11, 1947.

418 Lanctot, *Negro League Baseball*, 317.

419 Carroll, *When to Stop the Cheering?*, 156; *Cleveland Call and Post*, October 11, 1946. Columnist and noted early Black baseball historian A.S. "Doc" Young, who reported the $20,000 loss figure in the *Call and Post*, stated that he considered Pompez's claim to be exaggerated, but author Roberto Echevarria also reported that Pompez claimed to have lost money in 1947. Roberto Echevarria, *The Pride of Havana: A History of Cuban Baseball* (New York: Oxford Press, 1999), 207.

420 Joseph A. Pierce, *Negro Business and Business Education* (Boston: Springer Science + Business Media, 1995 reprint), 219.

421 Lanctot, *Negro League Baseball*, 318.

422 *The Sporting News*, March 17, 1948 as quoted in Lanctot, *Negro League Baseball*, 336.

423 *Hartford Courant*, December 3, 1947.

424 *Hartford Courant*, December 3, 1947; *New York Times*, December 6, 1947.

425 *Washington Post*, February 6, 1948.

426 *Washington Post*, February 6, 1948.427 *Chicago Defender*, January 3, 1948.

428 *Philadelphia Tribune*, January 3, 1948.

429 *Philadelphia Tribune*, January 3, 1948.

430 *Atlanta Daily World*, January 13, 1948.

431 *Pittsburgh Courier*, January 24, 1948 as quoted in Lanctot, *Negro League Baseball*, 325.

432 *Atlanta Daily World*, January 24, 1948.

433 *New York Amsterdam News*, January 3, 1948.

434 *Atlanta Daily World*, January 24, 1948.

435 See, e.g., 1941 contract of Monte Irvin, Manley Papers. The Eagles ultimately received $5,000 for Monte Irvin's contract in 1948 after successfully fighting off the Dodgers' overtures. The level of compensation for Irvin may have been a more realistic standard for future signings than that for Doby.

436 *New York Amsterdam News*, January 24, 1948. Richmond and Asheville joined another new Negro League, the Negro American Association.

437 Dan Burley, "Confidentially Yours," *New York Amsterdam News*, January 24, 1948, 13; *New York Amsterdam News*, January 24, 1948, 12.

438 *New York Amsterdam News*, September 22, 1945 (MacPhail statement); *Boston Globe*, February 24, 1948 (Johnson statement).

439 *Boston Globe*, February 24, 1948.

440 It deserves mention that at about the same time Johnson announced his bitter disappointment at being betrayed by organized baseball, Commissioner Chandler was reportedly having an official meeting with representatives of the Mexican league. It was to be the first official meeting between the organizations since the Mexican leagues raided the major leagues in 1946 and signed several of their players, and Chandler suspended those players for five years in response. The meeting was to include a discussion of a future affiliation of the Mexican league with organized baseball. *New York Times*, February 21, 22, 1948.

441 *Chicago Defender*, February 21, 1948.

442 *Baltimore Afro-American*, March 6, 1948; *New York Amsterdam News*, March 6, 1948; *Atlanta Daily World*, March 11, 1948.

443 Lanctot, *Negro League Baseball*, 328; *Atlanta Daily World*, June 29, 1948.

444 *Atlanta Daily World*, June 29, 1948.

445 *Atlanta Daily World*, June 29, 1948. Although the Pacific Coast League never succeeded in their attempt to become the third major league, they successfully petitioned to become an "open" classification, which exempted their players from the annual draft of minor-league players under certain conditions, and gave the Pacific Coast League a status between Triple A and major league. *New York Times*, January 1, 1952. Such a status may well have been appropriate for the Negro Leagues given the level of talent they featured during the two-year period between Jackie Robinson's signing and the rejection of their application to affiliate with organized baseball. As previously mentioned, at the February 20 and 21, 1946 NNL meetings, NNL President Wilson had assessed Black major-league baseball as being below White major league but above the Triple-A International League in caliber.

446 Richard Puerzer, "The 1948 Negro League World Series," *Bittersweet Goodbye: The Black Barons, The Grays, And The 1948 Negro League World Series* (Phoenix, Arizona: Society for American Baseball Research 2017), Frederick Bush and Bill Nowlin, eds., 386, 388.

447 *Philadelphia Tribune*, February 14, 1948 as quoted in Lanctot, *Negro League Baseball*, 332 (outlined); Jackie Robinson, "What's Wrong with Negro Baseball?" *Ebony*, June 1948 as quoted in Lanctot, *Negro League Baseball*, 332; Effa Manley, "Negro Baseball Isn't Dead," *Our World*, August 1948, as quoted in Lanctot, *Negro League Baseball*, 334.

448 Thomas Kern, "The 1948 East-West All-Star Games." *Bittersweet Goodbye*, Frederick Bush and Bill Nowlin, eds., 369, 371; *New York Amsterdam News*, August 21, 1948.

449 *Baltimore Afro-American*, December 11, 1948.

450 *Baltimore Afro-American*, September 4, 11, 1948, as quoted in Lanctot, *Negro League Baseball*, 337.

451 Lanctot, *Negro League Baseball*,

452 *Pittsburgh Courier*, December 11, 1948. Whether or not Effa Manley meant that her team lost $100,000 from 1946 through 1948, it is worth noting that 1946 was the year that her Newark Eagles won their only Negro League World Series.

453 *Atlanta Daily World*, November 24, 1948.

454 *Chicago Defender*, December 11, 1948.

455 *Cleveland Call and Post*, December 4, 1948.

456 *Chicago Defender*, December 11, 1948; *Baltimore Afro-American*, December 11, 1948.

457 *Pittsburgh Courier*, December 11, 1948.

458 John Holway, *Blackball Stars* (Westport, Connecticut: Meckler Books 1988), 21.

459 *Pittsburgh Courier*, December 11, 1948.

460 *Pittsburgh Courier*, December 11, 1948.461 It is possible that Effa Manley was including other leagues like the Negro American Association and the Negro Southern League (NSL) when she came

up with the figure of 400 remaining Black ballplayers. As of 1950, those two leagues still existed, and they apparently reformulated into one Negro Southern Association in 1951. See *Atlanta Daily World*, June 15, 1950 and *Atlanta Daily World*, March 27, 1951.

462 *Pittsburgh Courier*, August 25, 1962.

463 Minutes, Schedule Meeting of the Negro American League, February 7 and 8, 1949. Minutes provided by SABR's Negro Leagues Committee Chair Larry Lester, August 2017.

464 Minutes, Schedule Meeting of the Negro American League, February 7 and 8, 1949. 465 Minutes, Schedule Meeting of the Negro American League, February 7 and 8, 1949. The offered justification for approving the move of the Buckeyes to Louisville was that "the appearance of Larry Doby and Satchel Paige with the major league Cleveland Indians had attracted most of the Buckeye fans." *Atlanta Daily World*, February 15, 1949. The team was sold by Wright to former Cleveland Buckeyes business manager Wilbur Hayes, who brought the team back to Cleveland for the 1950 NAL season. See *Pittsburgh Courier*, February 18, 1950.

466 *Atlanta Daily World*, February 15, 1949.

467 Minutes, Schedule Meeting of the Negro American League, February 7 and 8, 1949.

468 Schedule Meeting of the Negro American League, June 22 and 23, 1949. Minutes provided by Larry Lester, August 2017.

469 Schedule Meeting of the Negro American League, June 22 and 23, 1949. 470 Heaphy, *The Negro Leagues*, Appendix D, 241.

471 Dick Clark and Larry Lester, editors, *The Negro Leagues Book* (Cleveland, Ohio: Society for American Baseball Research, 1994), 163.

472 Clark and Lester, 163.473 Clark and Lester, 163; *Norfolk Journal and Guide*, January 20, 1951.

474 Clark and Lester, 163; *Norfolk Journal and Guide*, January 20, 1951. This researcher found conflicting information on the number of teams who played in the 1954 NAL. In *The Negro Leagues Book*, only four teams—the Indianapolis Stars, Memphis Red Sox, Birmingham Black Barons, and Detroit Stars—appear in the standings. But the March 27, 1954 *Baltimore Afro-American* stated that six teams, including the perennial NAL entry the Kansas City Monarchs, who were not in the 1954 standings in *The Negro Leagues Book*, and two new teams, in Louisville and Detroit, would play the 1954 season. The February 5, 1955 *Chicago Defender* stated that two teams—the Indianapolis Clowns and Louisville—were dropped from the league to again make it a four-team circuit. *Baltimore Afro-American*, March 27, 1954; *Chicago Defender*, February 5, 1955. Additional research or perhaps other existing resources may resolve this difference.

475 *Atlanta Daily World*, January 4, 1950.

476 *Atlanta Daily World*, January 5, 1950.

477 Wendell Smith, *Pittsburgh Courier*, January 18, 1950; *Pittsburgh Courier*, January 18, 1950 (roughest days).

478 *Chicago Defender*, June 17, 1950; *Norfolk Journal and Guide*, June 24, 1950.

479 *Baltimore Afro-American*, January 13, 1951.

480 *Pittsburgh Courier*, June 23, 1951. Apparently, the sale did not go through, and Baltimore operated as a traveling team through much of 1951, and was dropped from the league at the January 1952 meeting. *Chicago Defender*, January 5, 1952.

481 *Norfolk Journal and Guide*, May 17, 1951.

482 *Chicago Defender*, January 5, 1952.

483 *Atlanta Daily World*, January 10, 1952.

484 *Chicago Defender*, January 5, 1952; *Pittsburgh Courier*, February 23, 1952.

485 *Pittsburgh Courier*, February 7, 1953.

486 *Pittsburgh Courier*, February 13, 1954; *Baltimore Afro-American*, March 27, 1954.

487 *Chicago Defender*, February 6, 1954.

488 *Chicago Defender*, February 5, 1955.

489 Ibid. One can speculate that moving the game to Kansas City may have been related to keeping Tom Baird happy and his Kansas City Monarchs in the rapidly shrinking NAL, after his dalliance with independent play in 1954.

490 *Pittsburgh Courier*, June 11, 1955.

491 Letter, Tom Baird to Oscar Rico, May 21, 1955, Tom Baird Collection, box 3, correspondence about Cuban Giants, 1954 as quoted in Lanctot, *Negro League Baseball*, 385.

492 Lanctot, *Negro League Baseball*, 385-386.

493 *Pittsburgh Courier*, February 18, 1956.

494 *Chicago Defender*, March 3, 1956.

495 The *Pittsburgh Courier* reported that new owner Ross changed the name because previous owner Floyd Meshack had the "Black Barons" name copyrighted, but also noted that the "old name of the club had long been offensive to a large segment of the baseball fans." *Pittsburgh Courier*, March 24, 1956.

496 *Chicago Defender*, February 23, 1957.

497 *Norfolk Journal and Guide*, May 4, 1957.

498 *Chicago Defender*, March 29, 1958.

499 *Chicago Defender*, April 12, 1958.

500 *New York Times*, May 7, 1958. This author does not know anything about the Detroit Clowns.

501 *Pittsburgh Courier*, June 7, 1958 (Clowns vs. Red Sox); *New York Times*, June 30, 1958 (Monarchs vs. Red Sox).

502 *Atlanta Daily World*, January 6, 1959.

503 *Atlanta Daily World*, December 11, 1959.

504 www.cnlbr.org/Portals/0/RL/Demise%20of%20the%20Negro%20Leagues.pdf, accessed March 15, 2017. Some of the facts from the 1960–1962 period are drawn from this website. Here, the Birmingham team is called the "Black Barons" and is now owned by Arthur Dove. Perhaps Dove changed the name back to its original when he acquired the club. This source and others continues to include the Kansas City Monarchs as a league team although Neil Lanctot has indicated that the team rarely played in Kansas City.

505 www.cnlbr.org/Portals/0/RL/Demise%20of%20the%20Negro%20Leagues.pdf, accessed March 15, 2017.

506 *Atlanta Daily World*, May 27, 1960.

507 *Atlanta Daily World*, May 27, 1960.

508 *Atlanta Daily World*, May 27, 1960.

509 *Chicago Defender*, August 23, 1960.

510 *Chicago Defender*, August 23, 1960.

511 *Cleveland Call and Post*, March 11, 1961.

512 *Atlanta Daily World*, April 18, 1961.

513 *Norfolk Journal and Guide*, August 12, 1961.

514 *Norfolk Journal and Guide*, August 12, 1961.515 *Philadelphia Tribune*, August 22, 1961.

516 *Chicago Defender*, August 20, 1961.

517 www.cnlbr.org/Portals/0/RL/Demise%20of%20the%20Negro%20Leagues.pdf

518 www.cnlbr.org/Portals/0/RL/Demise%20of%20the%20Negro%20Leagues.pdf The report was a self-report.

519 www.cnlbr.org/Portals/0/RL/Demise%20of%20the%20Negro%20 Leagues.pdf520 *Chicago Defender*, August 28, 1962.

521 www.cnlbr.org/Portals/0/RL/Demise%20of%20 the%20Negro%20Leagues.pdf

522 *Tri-State Defender*, January 27, 1961.

523 *Chicago Defender*, January 4, 1947; Riley, *Biographical Encyclopedia*, 339 (Greenlee Field).

524 *Tri-State Defender*, January 27, 1961.

525 *Tri-State Defender*, January 27, 1961.

Closer

OSCAR CHARLESTON

David J. Malarcher

This poem was published in the Baseball Research Journal*, 1978.*

Sleep, Charlie! thou, the great, the strong!
Within the depths of mud and mire!
While high above the diamond throng
Thy sterling statue in retire
Proclaims the splendor of thy game,
Thy paramount, unequaled fame!

Thou wert the best who roamed the field!
Thy stalwart fingers never failed
The batters' erring fate to seal,
The pitchers' powers wrought to frail!
Oh! would thy skill could live always
To stir the sportsman happy praise!

Sleep, Charlie! I, who knew thee well,
Do here declare to Earth and time
In Heaven's language, thus, to tell,
In poignant poetry divine,
The glory of thy destiny
Thus this undying rhyme to thee!

Sleep, Charlie! now in holy dust!
(As mighty Cobb and Petway rest)
Bearing the praise of all of us,
The diamond's greatest and the less
Here honor we on thee bestow,
That ages will thy greatness know.

CONTRIBUTORS

JEREMY BEER is a founding partner at American Philanthropic in Phoenix, Arizona. He is the author of *The Philanthropic Revolution: An Alternative History of American Charity* and the editor of *America Moved: Booth Tarkington's Memoirs of Time and Place, 1869–1928*. Beer's writing on sports, society and culture has appeared in the *Washington Post, National Review*, and the *First Things*. More recently, his book *Oscar Charleston: The Life and Legend of Baseball's Greatest Forgotten Player* was awarded the Society for American Baseball Research (SABR) 2020 Seymour Medal for the best book of baseball history or biography.

JAMES E. BRUNSON III is an art historian who specializes in American modernism. He is the author of *The Early Image of Black Baseball* (2013) and the three-volume *Black Baseball, 1858–1900: A Comprehensive Record of the Teams, Players, Managers, Owners and Umpires* (2019). His articles have been published in *NINE: A Journal of Baseball History and Culture* and *Base Ball: A Journal of the Early Game*. A practicing artist who specializes in watercolor painting, Brunson taught visual culture at Northern Illinois University.

BRIAN CARROLL is an assistant professor of journalism in the department of communication at Berry College. His first book, *When to Stop the Cheering? The Black Press, the Black Community and the Integration of Professional Baseball*, was named a finalist for SABR's Seymour Medal. It was also named Book-of-the-Year by the organization's Negro Leagues Committee. Carroll's second title is *Writing for Digital Media*, a book revised and expanded into *Writing & Editing for Digital Media* in 2014. In 2015, *The Black Press and Black Baseball: A Devil's Bargain* was published , and winner of the 2016 Robert Peterson Recognition Award for the best book. The author is grateful to Misty Watson and Lindsay Beute for their research assistance, and the late Margaret A. Blanchard for guidance on an earlier version of the article included here.

RICHARD "Dick" CLARK (1946-2014) was co-editor of *The Negro Leagues Book*, published in 1994, often called the bible of Black baseball. The eminent historian and bibliophile contributed to more than 100 books about Negro Leagues history. For more than three decades, Clark served as chairman of SABR's Negro Leagues Research Committee and editor of the *Courier*, its quarterly newsletter. Clark also co-chaired the Negro Leagues Researchers & Authors Group (NLRAG), from 2000 to 2004, a comprehensive study of African American baseball from the Civil War up through the min-1950s, appropriately called "Out of the Shadows." In 2006, he served on the *Special Negro Leagues Committee* for the National Baseball Hall of Fame & Museum, selecting a record 17 Negro League players, executives, and managers.

DUKE GOLDMAN is a longtime SABR member specializing in the Negro Leagues, Monte Irvin, and the process of baseball integration. Duke is a recipient of the 2017 Robert Peterson Recognition Award for his *Black Ball Journal* articles and other SABR publications, as well as two SABR-McFarland Research Awards, one of them for this article on Negro League business meetings. Goldman roots for the Mets, Red Sox, and every New York Yankees opponent.

PETER GORTON is the Presentation Services Coordinator for Faegre, Baker & Daniels, an international law firm based in Minneapolis. He is a former broadcast journalist who has written dozens of articles about John Donaldson, including a chapter in *Swinging for the Fences: Black Baseball in Minnesota* (Minnesota Historical Society Press, 2005). He is the founder of "The Donaldson Network," a group of over 450 researchers, authors, and historians dedicated to the rediscovery of Donaldson's baseball career. Gorton is the co-founder of johndonaldson.bravehost.com, a website detailing the career of "The Greatest Colored Pitcher in the World." His efforts on behalf of Donaldson have been honored by SABR's Negro Leagues Committee with the 2011 Tweed Webb Lifetime Achievement Award, recognizing long-term contributions to the field of Negro League and Black baseball research. Gorton resides in Northeast Minneapolis with his wife and two children.

JOHN GRAF is a member of SABR's Negro Leagues Research Committee who works for the Wisconsin State Assembly as an assistant clerk. He is a past winner of the Jerry Malloy Negro League Conference's "Significa" (trivia) contest and has been a newspaper sportswriter and radio news reporter/announcer. Graf lives in Janesville, Wisconsin.

STEVEN R. HOFFBECK is a Professor of History at Minnesota State University Moorhead and general editor/ author of "Swinging for the Fences: Black Baseball in Minnesota," which won a *Sporting News*-SABR Baseball Research Award in 2005. Hoffbeck, his wife, and family reside in Barnesville, Minnesota.

JOHN HOLWAY, born in 1929, has been writing books about baseball since 1944. His works have often been heavily reliant on anecdotes and have been in the forefront of compiling Negro League statistics while debunking myths about the leagues. The prolific writer has authored several books about the Negro Leagues, most notably *The Complete Book of Baseball's Negro Leagues* and *Voices from the Great Black Baseball Leagues*. He also wrote a 1955 book on Japanese baseball (*Japan is Big League in Thrills*), one of the first English-language books on the subject. In 1988 he won the Casey Award for Best Baseball Book of the year with *Blackball Stars: Negro Leagues Pioneers*. In 2011, he was among the second class of inductees to receive SABR's 2011 Henry Chadwick Award.

JAY HURD, a longtime member of SABR, is a librarian and museum educator. He studies and presents on the Negro Leagues and is a regular attendee of the annual Jerry Malloy Negro League Conference. Jay has contributed articles to the SABR Biography Project and other publications. A fan of the Boston Red Sox, he recently relocated from Medford, Massachusetts to Bristol, Rhode Island and enjoys meetings of the Lajoie-Chapter of SABR.

JAPHETH KNOPP received a B.S. degree in Religious Studies and M.A. in American History from Missouri State University. He received his Ph.D. in History at the University of Missouri. He lives with his wife, Rebecca Wilkinson, and their son Ryphath. He can be contacted at Japheth.knopp@gmail.com.

LARRY LESTER is co-founder of the Negro Leagues Baseball Museum and serves as chairman of SABR's Negro League Research Committee. Since 1998, he has organized the annual Jerry Malloy Negro League Conference, the only scholarly symposium devoted exclusively to Black Baseball. He is the author of *Rube Foster in His Time*, *Black Baseball's National Showcase: The East-West All-Star Game 1933–1953*, *Baseball's First Colored World Series: The 1924 Meeting of the Hilldale Giants and Kansas City Monarchs*, and *The Negro Leagues Book* (with Dick Clark), which has been updated in a second volume (with Wayne Stivers) available on Kindle. Lester lives in Raytown, Missouri. Lester is winner of the 2016 Henry Chadwick and 2017 Bob Davids awards.

DAVE "Gentleman Dave" MALARCHER (1894–1982), a former SABR member who lived in Chicago, was a Negro League teammate of Hall of Famer Oscar Charleston and, obviously, a great admirer. He was, according to historian James A. Riley, "a smooth fielding third baseman who did his best hitting in the clutch…a speedy switch-hitter who could bunt and run the bases in the Rube Foster style of baseball." Malarcher was born in Whitehall, Louisiana to a former slave mother and farm laborer father. He played under C.I. Taylor with the Indianapolis ABCs and succeeded Foster as manager of the Chicago American Giants in a Black baseball career that spanned from 1916–1934**.** A college man who attended the Dillard University, the poet and lifelong learner was highly-respected for his intellectual prowess and gentlemanly demeanor. In retirement in Chicago, Malarcher joined SABR and ran an insurance and real estate business.

JERRY MALLOY (1946-2000) was a pioneer researcher who has been honored by the creation of an annual Negro League Conference named for him, as well as a book prize. His first great contribution to baseball history was *Out at Home: Baseball Draws the Color Line, 1887*. This monumentally important essay, published in *The National Pastime* in 1983, transformed our understanding of Black baseball and won commendation from C. Vann Woodward, the preeminent historian of American race relations. Malloy's subsequent work included a contextual republication of *Sol White's History of Colored Baseball with Other Documents on the Early Black Game, 1886–1936*. The late Jules Tygiel, also a 2015 Chadwick Award recipient, said of him, "His articles for SABR were pathbreaking and exceptional and rank among the very best this organization has ever published. Even more so, I doubt that the best among us have ever been as generous with their research and support as was Jerry."

JAMES OVERMYER writes and lectures on baseball history, primarily African American. He is author of *Queen of the Negro Leagues: Effa Manley and the Newark Eagles*, *Black Ball and the Boardwalk: The Bacharach Giants of Atlantic City, 1916–1929*, and more recently *Cum Posey of the Homestead Grays: A Biography of the Negro Leagues Owner and Hall of Famer*.

TODD PETERSON is a Kansas City-based visual artist, educator, and historian. He received Yoseloff-SABR Baseball Research Grants in 2006 and 2010; and was a winner of the Norman "Tweed" Webb Lifetime Achievement Award in 2009 and 2013. Peterson has written and edited several articles and books about the Negro Leagues, including *Early Black Baseball in Minnesota* (2010), and *The Negro Leagues Were Major Leagues* (2019).

GERI DRISCOLL STRECKER is a professor at Ball State University, were she teaches English and Sport Studies. As a 2011 fellow at the Virginia B. Ball Center for Creative Inquiry, she led a 15-credit seminar exploring Black Baseball in Indiana. That same season at the Jerry Malloy Negro League Conference in Indianapolis, she gave an impactful and powerful presentation entitled, *Black Baseball in Indianapolis during the Rise of the KKK*. Strecker has won three McFarland-SABR Research Awards, including one for her fall 2009 *Black Ball: A Negro Leagues Journal* article printed here, *The Rise and Fall of Greenlee Field: Biography of a Ballpark*.

JOHN THORN is the author and editor of numerous books, including *Total Baseball: The Official Encyclopedia of Major League Baseball*, *Total Football: The Official Encyclopedia of Major League Football*, *Treasures of the Baseball Hall of Fame*, *The Hidden Game of Baseball*, *The Glory Days: New York Baseball 1947–1957*, and *The Armchair Book of Baseball*. His 2011 book, *Baseball in the Garden of Eden: The Secret History of the Early Game*, published by Simon & Schuster, was an in-depth chronicle of the seminal development and pioneers of the sport. A *New York Times* review of the latter book referred to Thorn as "a researcher of colossal diligence." Thorn served as the senior creative consultant for the 1994 Ken Burns documentary *Baseball*. On March 1, 2011, he was named Official Baseball Historian for Major League Baseball. Thorn is the recipient of the 2006 Bob Davids award and the 2013 Henry Chadwick award.

JULES TYGIEL (1949-2008) made his most lasting research contribution for his classic 1983 book, *Baseball's Great Experiment: Jackie Robinson and His Legacy*. A sweeping history of the integration of the game focusing on Robinson through the 1950s, with a firm grasp of the American narrative as well as a central baseball personality, the book is often cited as one of the best in sports literature. A professor of history at San Francisco State University, Tygiel wrote in the introduction to *Great Experiment*, "Writing this book has allowed me to combine my vocation as a historian and my avocation as a baseball fanatic." Tygiel wrote books and articles on many subjects, but often returned to his favorite sport. His book *Past Time: Baseball as History* (2001) won SABR's Seymour Medal as the best book of baseball writing that year. Tygiel is winner of the 2010 Henry Chadwick award.

SABR Books on the Negro Leagues and Black Baseball

From Rube to Robinson: SABR's Best Articles on Black Baseball

From Rube to Robinson brings together the best Negro League baseball scholarship that the Society of American Baseball Research (SABR) has ever produced, culled from its journals, Biography Project, and award-winning essays. The book includes a star-studded list of scholars and historians, from the late Jerry Malloy and Jules Tygiel, to award winners Larry Lester, Geri Strecker, and Jeremy Beer, and a host of other talented writers. The essays cover topics ranging over nearly a century, from 1866 and the earliest known Black baseball championship, to 1962 and the end of the Negro American League.

Edited by John Graf; Associate Editors Duke Goldman and Larry Lester
$24.95 paperback (ISBN 978-1-970159-41-7)
$9.99 ebook (ISBN 978-1-970159-40-0)
8.5"X11", 220 pages

Pride of Smoketown: The 1935 Pittsburgh Crawfords

The 1935 Pittsburgh Crawfords team, one of the dominant teams in Negro League history, is often compared to the legendary 1927 "Murderer's Row" New York Yankees. The squad from "Smoketown"—a nickname that the *Pittsburgh Courier* often applied to the metropolis better-known as "Steel City"—boasted four Hall-of-Fame players in outfielder James "Cool Papa" Bell, first baseman/manager Oscar Charleston, catcher Josh Gibson, and third baseman William "Judy" Johnson. This volume contains exhaustively-researched articles about the players, front office personnel, Greenlee Field, and the exciting games and history of the team that were written and edited by 25 SABR members. The inclusion of historical photos about every subject in the book helps to shine a spotlight on the 1935 Pittsburgh Crawfords, who truly were the Pride of Smoketown.

Edited by Frederick C. Bush and Bill Nowlin
$29.95 paperback (ISBN 978-1-970159-25-7)
$9.99 ebook (ISBN 978-1-970159-24-0)
8.5"X11", 340 pages, over 60 photos

The Newark Eagles Take Flight: The Story of the 1946 Negro League Champions

The Newark Eagles won only one Negro National League pennant during the franchise's 15-year tenure in the Garden State, but the 1946 squad that ran away with the NNL and then triumphed over the Kansas City Monarchs in a seven-game World Series was a team for the ages. The returning WWII veterans composed a veritable "Who's Who in the Negro Leagues" and included Leon Day, Larry Doby, Monte Irvin, and Max Manning, as well as numerous role players. Four of the Eagles' stars—Day, Doby, Irvin, and player/manager Raleigh "Biz" Mackey, as well as co-owner Effa Manley—have been enshrined in the National Baseball Hall of Fame in Cooperstown. In addition to biographies of the players, co-owners, and P.A. announcer, there are also articles about Newark's Ruppert Stadium, Leon Day's Opening Day no-hitter, a sensational midseason game, the season's two East-West All-Star Games, and the 1946 Negro League World Series between the Eagles and the renowned Kansas City Monarchs.

Edited by Frederick C. Bush and Bill Nowlin
$24.95 paperback (ISBN 978-1-970159-07-3)
$9.99 ebook (ISBN 978-1-970159-06-6)
8.5"X11", 228 pages, over 60 photos

Bittersweet Goodbye: The Black Barons, The Grays, and the 1948 Negro League World Series

This book was inspired by the last Negro League World Series ever played and presents biographies of the players on the two contending teams in 1948—the Birmingham Black Barons and the Homestead Grays—as well as the managers, the owners, and articles on the ballparks the teams called home. Also included are articles that recap the season's two East-West All-Star Games, the Negro National League and Negro American League playoff series, and the World Series itself. Additional context is provided in essays about the effects of baseball's integration on the Negro Leagues, the exodus of Negro League players to Canada, and the signing away of top Negro League players, specifically Willie Mays. Many of the players' lives and careers have been presented to a much greater extent than previously possible.

Edited by Frederick C. Bush and Bill Nowlin
$21.95 paperback (ISBN 978-1-943816-55-2)
$9.99 ebook (ISBN 978-1-943816-54-5)
8.5"X11", 442 pages, over 100 photos and images

"This compilation, a distillation of all that is important to the society's members . . . showcases the SABRite at his or her baseball-loving, stat-obsessed best."
—Paul Dickson, *Wall Street Journal*

nebraskapress.unl.edu

The SABR Digital Library

The Society for American Baseball Research, the top baseball research organization in the world, disseminates some of the best in baseball history, analysis, and biography through our publishing programs. The SABR Digital Library contains a mix of books old and new, and focuses on a tandem program of paperback and ebook publication, making these materials widely available for both on digital devices and as traditional printed books.

Greatest Games Books

TIGERS BY THE TALE:
GREAT GAMES AT MICHIGAN AND TRUMBULL
For over 100 years, Michigan and Trumbull was the scene of some of the most exciting baseball ever. This book portrays 50 classic games at the corner, spanning the earliest days of Bennett Park until Tiger Stadium's final closing act. From Ty Cobb to Mickey Cochrane, Hank Greenberg to Al Kaline, and Willie Horton to Alan Trammell.
Edited by Scott Ferkovich
$12.95 paperback (ISBN 978-1-943816-21-7)
$6.99 ebook (ISBN 978-1-943816-20-0)
8.5"x11", 160 pages, 22 photos

FROM THE BRAVES TO THE BREWERS: GREAT GAMES AND HISTORY AT MILWAUKEE'S COUNTY STADIUM
The National Pastime provides in-depth articles focused on the geographic region where the national SABR convention is taking place annually. The SABR 45 convention took place in Chicago, and here are 45 articles on baseball in and around the bat-and-ball crazed Windy City: 25 that appeared in the souvenir book of the convention plus another 20 articles available in ebook only.
Edited by Gregory H. Wolf
$19.95 paperback (ISBN 978-1-943816-23-1)
$9.99 ebook (ISBN 978-1-943816-22-4)
8.5"X11", 290 pages, 58 photos

BRAVES FIELD:
MEMORABLE MOMENTS AT BOSTON'S LOST DIAMOND
From its opening on August 18, 1915, to the sudden departure of the Boston Braves to Milwaukee before the 1953 baseball season, Braves Field was home to Boston's National League baseball club and also hosted many other events: from NFL football to championship boxing. The most memorable moments to occur in Braves Field history are portrayed here.
Edited by Bill Nowlin and Bob Brady
$19.95 paperback (ISBN 978-1-933599-93-9)
$9.99 ebook (ISBN 978-1-933599-92-2)
8.5"X11", 282 pages, 182 photos

AU JEU/PLAY BALL: THE 50 GREATEST GAMES IN THE HISTORY OF THE MONTREAL EXPOS
The 50 greatest games in Montreal Expos history. The games described here recount the exploits of the many great players who wore Expos uniforms over the years—Bill Stoneman, Gary Carter, Andre Dawson, Steve Rogers, Pedro Martinez, from the earliest days of the franchise, to the glory years of 1979-1981, the what-might-have-been years of the early 1990s, and the sad, final days.and others.
Edited by Norm King
$12.95 paperback (ISBN 978-1-943816-15-6)
$5.99 ebook (ISBN978-1-943816-14-9)
8.5"x11", 162 pages, 50 photos

Original SABR Research

CALLING THE GAME:
BASEBALL BROADCASTING FROM 1920 TO THE PRESENT
An exhaustive, meticulously researched history of bringing the national pastime out of the ballparks and into living rooms via the airwaves. Every play-by-play announcer, color commentator, and ex-ballplayer, every broadcast deal, radio station, and TV network. Plus a foreword by "Voice of the Chicago Cubs" Pat Hughes, and an afterword by Jacques Doucet, the "Voice of the Montreal Expos" 1972-2004.
by Stuart Shea
$24.95 paperback (ISBN 978-1-933599-40-3)
$9.99 ebook (ISBN 978-1-933599-41-0)
7"X10", 712 pages, 40 photos

BioProject Books

WHO'S ON FIRST:
REPLACEMENT PLAYERS IN WORLD WAR II
During World War II, 533 players made the major league debuts. More than 60% of the players in the 1941 Opening Day lineups departed for the service and were replaced by first-times and oldsters. Hod Lisenbee was 46. POW Bert Shepard had an artificial leg, and Pete Gray had only one arm. The 1944 St. Louis Browns had 13 players classified 4-F. These are their stories.
Edited by Marc Z Aaron and Bill Nowlin
$19.95 paperback (ISBN 978-1-933599-91-5)
$9.99 ebook (ISBN 978-1-933599-90-8)
8.5"X11", 422 pages, 67 photos

VAN LINGLE MUNGO:
THE MAN, THE SONG, THE PLAYERS
40 baseball players with intriguing names have been named in renditions of Dave Frishberg's classic 1969 song, Van Lingle Mungo. This book presents biographies of all 40 players and additional information about one of the greatest baseball novelty songs of all time.
Edited by Bill Nowlin
$19.95 paperback (ISBN 978-1-933599-76-2)
$9.99 ebook (ISBN 978-1-933599-77-9)
8.5"X11", 278 pages, 46 photos

NUCLEAR POWERED BASEBALL
Nuclear Powered Baseball tells the stories of each player—past and present—featured in the classic Simpsons episode "Homer at the Bat." Wade Boggs, Ken Griffey Jr., Ozzie Smith, Nap Lajoie, Don Mattingly, and many more. We've also included a few very entertaining takes on the now-famous episode from prominent baseball writers Jonah Keri, Joe Posnanski, Erik Malinowski, and Bradley Woodrum
Edited by Emily Hawks and Bill Nowlin
$19.95 paperback (ISBN 978-1-943816-11-8)
$9.99 ebook (ISBN 978-1-943816-10-1)
8.5"X11", 250 pages

SABR Members can purchase each book at a significant discount (often 50% off) and receive the ebook edtions free as a member benefit. Each book is available in a trade paperback edition as well as ebooks suitable for reading on a home computer or Nook, Kindle, or iPad/tablet.
To learn more about becoming a member of SABR, visit the website: sabr.org/join

Friends of SABR

You can become a Friend of SABR by giving as little as $10 per month or by making a one-time gift of $1,000 or more. When you do so, you will be inducted into a community of passionate baseball fans dedicated to supporting SABR's work.

Friends of SABR receive the following benefits:

- ✓ Annual Friends of SABR Commemorative Lapel Pin
- ✓ Recognition in This Week in SABR, SABR.org, and the SABR Annual Report
- ✓ Access to the SABR Annual Convention VIP donor event
- ✓ Invitations to exclusive Friends of SABR events

SABR On-Deck Circle - $10/month, $30/month, $50/month

Get in the SABR On-Deck Circle, and help SABR become the essential community for the world of baseball. Your support will build capacity around all things SABR, including publications, website content, podcast development, and community growth.

A monthly gift is deducted from your bank account or charged to a credit card until you tell us to stop. No more email, mail, or phone reminders.

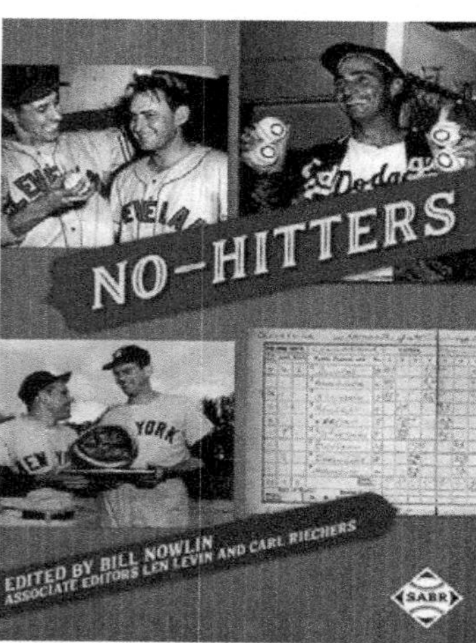

Join the SABR On-Deck Circle

Payment Info: ________Visa ________Mastercard

Name on Card: ______________________________

Card #: ______________________________

Exp. Date: __________ Security Code: __________

Signature: ______________________________

- o $10/month
- o $30/month
- o $50/month
- o Other amount ______________

Go to sabr.org/donate to make your gift online

Society for American Baseball Research

Cronkite School at ASU
555 N. Central Ave. #416, Phoenix, AZ 85004
602.496.1460 (phone)
SABR.org

Become a SABR member today!

If you're interested in baseball — writing about it, reading about it, talking about it — there's a place for you in the Society for American Baseball Research.

SABR memberships are available on annual, multi-year, or monthly subscription basis. Annual and monthly subscription memberships auto-renew for your convenience. Young Professional memberships are for ages 30 and under. Senior memberships are for ages 65 and older. Student memberships are available to currently enrolled middle/high school or full-time college/university students. Monthly subscription members receive SABR publications electronically and are eligible for SABR event discounts after 12 months.

Here's a list of some of the key benefits you'll receive as a SABR member:

- Receive two editions (spring and fall) of the *Baseball Research Journal*, our flagship publication
- Receive expanded e-book edition of *The National Pastime*, our annual convention journal
- 8-10 new e-books published by the SABR Digital Library, all FREE to members
- "This Week in SABR" e-newsletter, sent to members every Friday
- Join dozens of research committees, from Statistical Analysis to Women in Baseball.
- Join one of 70+ regional chapters in the U.S., Canada, Latin America, and abroad
- Participate in online discussion groups
- Ask and answer baseball research questions on the SABR-L e-mail listserv
- Complete archives of *The Sporting News* dating back to 1886 and other research resources
- Promote your research in "This Week in SABR"
- Diamond Dollars Case Competition
- Yoseloff Scholarships
- Discounts on SABR national conferences, including the SABR National Convention, the SABR Analytics Conference, Jerry Malloy Negro League Conference, Frederick Ivor-Campbell 19th Century Conference, and the Arizona Fall League Experience
- Publish your research in peer-reviewed SABR journals
- Collaborate with SABR researchers and experts
- Contribute to Baseball Biography Project or the SABR Games Project
- List your new book in the SABR Bookshelf
- Lead a SABR research committee or chapter
- Networking opportunities at SABR Analytics Conference
- Meet baseball authors and historians at SABR events and chapter meetings
- 50% discounts on paperback versions of SABR e-books
- Discounts with other partners in the baseball community
- SABR research awards

We hope you'll join the most passionate international community of baseball fans at SABR! Check us out online at SABR.org/join.

SABR MEMBERSHIP FORM

	Standard	Senior	Young Pro.	Student
Annual:	❑ $65	❑ $45	❑ $45	❑ $25
3 Year:	❑ $175	❑ $129	❑ $129	
5 Year:	❑ $249			
Monthly:	❑ $6.95	❑ $4.95	❑ $4.95	

(International members wishing to be mailed the Baseball Research Journal should add $10/yr for Canada/Mexico or $19/yr for overseas locations.)

Participate in Our Donor Program!

Support the preservation of baseball research. Designate your gift toward:

❑ General Fund ❑ Endowment Fund ❑ Research Resources ❑ ____________

❑ I want to maximize the impact of my gift; do not send any donor premiums

❑ I would like this gift to remain anonymous.

Note: Any donation not designated will be placed in the General Fund.
SABR is a 501 (c) (3) not-for-profit organization & donations are tax-deductible to the extent allowed by law.

Name ______________________________

E-mail* ______________________________

Address ______________________________

City ____________________ **ST**________ **ZIP**__________

Phone ____________________ **Birthday** ____________

*** Your e-mail address on file ensures you will receive the most recent SABR news.**

Dues $____________

Donation $____________

Amount Enclosed $____________

Do you work for a matching grant corporation? Call (602) 496-1460 for details.

If you wish to pay by credit card, please contact the SABR office at (602) 496-1460 or sign up securely online at SABR.org/join. We accept Visa, Mastercard & Discover.

Do you wish to receive the *Baseball Research Journal* electronically? ❑ Yes ❑ No

Our e-books are available in PDF, Kindle, or EPUB (iBooks, iPad, Nook) formats.

Mail to: SABR, Cronkite School at ASU, 555 N. Central Ave. #416, Phoenix, AZ 85004

10/19

Made in the USA
Columbia, SC
14 February 2021

32289119R00122